ICT Based
Information Management
in Indian Libraries

Prof. (Dr.) Kailash C. Sahoo

ICT Based
Information Management in Indian Libraries

Festschrift
in honour of
Prof. (Dr.) K.C. Sahoo

Prof. (Dr.) R.G. Prasher
Former Dean, Dr. Harisingh Gour University, Sagar

Dr. R.K. Sharma
Librarian, United Nations Information Centre for India and Bhutan
New Delhi

BOOKWELL
New Delhi

ISBN: 978-93-80574-33-2

First Published in 2012 by:

BOOKWELL

3/79, Nirankari Colony, Delhi 110009, India
Ph: 91-11-27601283, 27604536
E-mail: bkwell@nde.vsnl.net.in
bookwelldelhi@tmail.com
Website: www.bookwellindia.com

Typeset by:
Shubham Typeset Processing
Delhi

Printed at:
D.K. Fine Art Press (P) Ltd., Delhi

Contents

Preface

Development of all types is dependent on right decision. Right decision in turn depends on right information at right time. Information remains an essential input for research and development of all types. The progress of society is dependent on the level of information its people have. Information, therefore, needs to be communicated freely, with unrestricted flow. Information communication involves the determination of the information needs of the users, their information-gathering habits, the available sources of information and what do these yield, and the dissemination and communication of information through various means.

There is information explosion now. To the existing huge mass of knowledge and information is added a vast amount of information generated by the central and state governments all over the world. The problem today is how to cope with this huge and difficult–to-control mass of information. The qualitative aspect also cannot be ignored. How to provide a right user his right information by sorting out the core-information from ever-expanding mass of chaff is another problem. The processing, retrieving, evaluating, and packaging of generated information is one aspect, communication of 'pin-pointed, exhaustive, and expeditious' information to the scholars, scientists, specialists, decision-makers and other consumers is another, and more important one.

In this process of managing and communication of information, the present day technological advances are playing a vital role. Information and Communication Technologies (ICT) in fact have brought about a revolution in it. Computers are now being used for the processing, consolidating, and repackaging of information in a big way. Information is transmitted from one point to another by electronic media through telecommunication. Telecommunication networks are there to handle digital machine readable data and to use telephone lines, micro-waves and communication satellites to transfer such data. ICT advances have made it possible to provide library services and access to information even outside the library. A *library without walls* or a *virtual library* is now becoming a reality.

The LIS scene is changing fast in the face of new challenges and in response to new demands. The advent of new technologies and their application to LIS work and services is further accelerating the pace of this change. Library professionals are experiencing a transition from stand alone libraries to library and information networks; from printed publications to digital documents; from ownership of graphic records to access to information. They have taken cognizance of this transition and are redefining their roles. Today total knowledge and information, which is presently available in the libraries in the form of books and other documents, can be put on the World Wide Web, making the libraries totally web-based. Knowledge and information of all types can be accessed, desired information can be seen or read, as also printed, if so required.

Peers in the field of library profession have come together and joined hands to present the *ICT Based Information Management in Indian Libraries*. This Volume contains in all 34 papers by as many as 44 authors and joint authors. Briefly, there are two papers on Sahoo, five on Knowledge Management, 17 on ICT Application, two on HRD, two on Reading Habits and Accessing Information, two on Information Seeking Behaviour, two on Research Productivity and of the last two, one is on Text-book archive at NCERT and another is on Plagiarism.

And all this as a tribute to and in honour of Professor (Dr.) K.C. Sahoo, Dean, Dr. Harisingh Gour University, Sagar who has served the library profession with zeal and dedication. Here is an opportunity for us to propose our personal thanks to all the contributors for their learned papers.

55-B, Udham S. Nagar,
Civil Lines, Ludhiana-141001
26 January 2012

Dr. R.G. Prasher
Dr. R.K. Sharma
Editors

List of Contributors

Agarwal, Umesh Kumar, Deputy Librarian, Mohanlal Sukhadia University, Udaipur-313001

Agrawal, Anil, Assistant Librarian, Central Library, BHU, Varanasi-221005

Babbar, Parveen, Assistant Librarian, IGNOU, New Delhi-110068

Bajpai, R.P., Associate Professor, DLIS, MGCGV, Chitrakoot Email: rpbajpai@gmail.com

Bharat Kumar, Assistant Librarian, Management Development Institute, Gurgaon–122 007, Haryana Email: Bharat.Kumar@hotmail.com

Borse, T.R., Librarian & HOD LIS, North Maharashtra University, Jalgaon-425001

Chakraborty, Hirak Kanti, Head, DLIS, Sampurnanand Sanskrit University, Varanasi, Lucknow-226025

Choukhande, Vaishali, Associate Professor & Head, DLIS, Sant Gadge Baba Amravati University, Amravati Email: vchoukhande@ rediffmail.com

Chaurasia, Neeraj Kumar, Assistant Librarian, Central Library, Indian Institute of Technology (IIT), New Delhi

Chaurasia, Pankaj, Assistant Librarian, National Institute of Public Cooperation and Child Development, New Delhi

Das, K.C., Head, PG DLIS, Utkal University, Bhubaneswar-751004

Garg, R.G., Head, SOS Library & Information Science, Jiwaji University, Gwalior

Jadia, Manish Kumar, UGC-JRF, New Delhi E-mail: sagar143soni@gmail.com

Jain, Vivekanand, Deputy Librarian, Central Library, BHU, Varanasi Email: vivek_digora@rediffmail.com

Jena, Kamal Lochan, Librarian, College of Engineering & Technology, Bhubaneswar – 751 003 E-mail: kljena@rediffmail.com

Jena, Puspanjali, Reader, PG DLIS, Utkal University, Bhubaneswar Email: pjutkal1987@yahoo.co.in

Joshi, Manoj K., Associate Professor, D.L.I.Sc.,Kurukshetra University Kurukshetra-136 119

Majumdar, Kamalendu, Indian Institute of Technology, Kharagpur E-mail : kamal@library.iitkgp.ernet.in

Mal, Bidyut Kumar, Librarian-in-charge, Puravanchal University, Jaunpur (U.P.)

Malyacharya,Vijeta, School of Telemedicine & Biomedical Informatics, SGPGIMS, Lucknow

Mukherjee, Bhaskar, Assistant Professor, Department of Library & Information Science, Banaras Hindu University. Email: mukherjee. bhaskaar@gmail.com

Naidu, G.H.S., Librarian, Devi Ahilya Universityu, Indore Email:ghsnaidu@gmail.com

Panda, Krushna C., Head, PG DLIS, Sambalpur University, Jyoti Vihar-768 019 Email: krushna52@yahoo.co.in

Pandey, Madhav, University Librarian, IG Agricultural University, Raipur-492006

Pant, Prem Prakash, Faculty, SOS Library & Information Science, Jiwaji University, Gwalior

Prasher, R.G., 55-B,Udham Singh Nagar, Civil Lines, Ludhiana-141001 Email: principalprasher@rediffmail.com

Rajput, P.S., UGC-JRF, SOS Library & Information Science, Jiwaji University, Gwalior (M.P.) E-mail: prabhat.t82@gmail.com

Ratha, Bhupindra, Lecturer in School of LIS, DA University, Indore Email:bhu26@gmail.com

Rawtani, M.R., Head, DLIS, University of Rajasthan, Jaipur

Samantaray, Moorttimatee, Deputy Librarian-in-charge and Head, DLDI, NCERT, Sri Aurobindo Marg, New Delhi-110016 E-mail: murtimati.rath@gmail.com

Saraf, Sanjiv, Deputy Librarian, BHU, Varanasi E-mail: gyanshrisanjiv@ rediffmail.com

Sharma, Ashish Kumar, Assistant Librarian, Central Library, Gurukul Kangri University, Haridwar (U.K.) Email: Ashish1077@ yahoo.co.in

Sharma, Hemant, Associate Professor, SOS in Library & Information Science, Jiwaji University, Gwalior

Sharma, Pawan, Librarian, ITM University, Gwalior

Sharma, R.K., Librarian, United Nations Information Centre for India & Bhutan, 55 Lodi Estate, New Delhi-110003 Email: sharma@unicindia.org

Sharma, Sanjeev, Assistant Professor, Kurukshetra University, Kurukshetra E-mail: Sanju_sharma2004@rediffmail.com

Silawat, Ravi, M. Phil Student, School of LIS, Devi Ahilya University, Indore Email: rsilawat99266@gmail.com

Singh, Rajesh Kumar, Assistant Librarian, Central Library, BHU, Varanasi E-mail:rksb17@yahoo.com

Singh, U. N., Librarian, Guru Gashidas Vishwavidyalaya, Bilaspur (CG) E-mail: unsggu@yahoo.in

Singhai, Monika, Research Scholar (JRF), SOS in Library and Information Science, Jiwaji University, Gwalior E-mail : monikasinghai@gmail.com

Suman Lata, Central State Library, Chandigarh (U.T)

Tailang, Mukta, Librarian, CIC, Chitrakoot Email: omsainathmukta@ gmail.com

Thapa, Neelam, Dept. of Library & Information Science, Dr. Harisingh Gour University, Sagar

Tripathi, Harish Kumar, Librarian, ICAR, Anusandhan Bhawan, New Delhi

Upadhyay, M.P., SPA, Ramanujan College, University of Delhi, Delhi

Verma, Jyoti, School of Telemedicine & Biomedical Informatics, SGPGIMS, Lucknow Email: jyotiverma341@gmail.com

Vijayavargia, Prakash Chandra, Ph.D. Scholar, DLIS, Mohanlal Sukhadia University, Udaipur-313001

1

My Student Days at Sambalpur
Remembering the Kindness of Dr. K.C. Sahoo

Dr. R.K. Sharma
Librarian, United Nations Information Centre for India & Bhutan
55-Lodi Estate, New Delhi-110003
E-mail: sharma@unicindia.org

I can vividly recall that day in April 1980, when I hesitantly, first wrote to Prof. Sahoo, with only a reference of a colleague of mine, for seeking information on BLISc course at Sambalpur University and the possibility of my admission in the said course. To my surprise, he not only sent me the application form but also informed me of the historic change in the admission rules at the Department of Library & Information Science, Sambalpur University, which permitted students from outside Odisha to be admitted to the BLISc course, a policy change in which Prof. Sahoo was as instrumental as the then Head of Department Prof. R.K. Rout. With his guidance and support, I was one of the four lucky students from outside Odisha to be admitted to the BLISc Course.

I was so determined to get the BLISc degree, that I took two important decisions early in my life: (1) I opted out of my well- paid service at the Delhi University Library System, in the Department of Library & Information Science, on leave without pay basis, as the Department refused to grant me leave on full pay for my studies; and (2) To leave my newly wedded wife alone back home, after only three months of our marriage. My challenges did not end just there. I was away from a very homely environment for the first time. The most difficult task was to adjust to a totally different culture and society. To top it up, I was a pure vegetarian, which was unheard of in that society. Thus, in these difficult times, the decision to undertake the course often weighed quite heavily on my mind.

The serene and natural beauty of Sambalpur University Campus was a contrast from the dusty and noisy atmosphere of Delhi. It was an eco-friendly environment surrounded by hilly landscape, a river and India's longest dam, the Hirakud. DLIS—Sambalpur, however, was less attractive being accommodated in the building of the Department of Physics then. Only BLISc programme was being run with two regular teachers—R.K.Rout and K.C.Sahoo. Two part-time teachers, from the University Library, were B.P.Mahapatra and Prahlad Panda. Prof. K.C.Sahoo used to teach us Library Classification (Theory and Practice). He was polite and soft-spoken teacher, quite knowledgeable in his subject. His teaching style was student-friendly. He explained to the students complex problems of Library Classifications with ease, giving suitable examples. Among the visiting faculty, the DLIS used to invite, I still remember of Prof. Karisadappa, from Karnataka University, who gave us daily 3-hour lecture for ten days on Information and Documentation. It was at that time an enormous amount of information to be understood and absorbed. I also remember our study tour to Bhubaneswar and Puri which was quite useful and I learnt the working of a reprographic unit first time at the Orissa University of Agriculture & Technology.

First time in my life I was staying in a hostel along with about 20 fellow students. There I hit off a friendship in a true sense with my class-mate, Bhaskar Ganti. He not only helped me in settling down in many ways at the campus but he also proved to be a source of inspiration throughout my stay at the Sambalpur University. Postponement of examinations was a regular feature at the University as the local students could pressurize the HOD, Registrar, and even the Vice-Chancellor so easily to have their way in getting the duration of the Course extended. Ganti and myself raised our joint voice against this malpractice and wrote about it to all the authorities. Though both of us were labeled as 'rebels' but we were able to get our one-year Course completed in one and a half year against the usual two years!

During my student days the Sambalpur University faced one of the worst strikes by its students. Not only the teaching programme of the University came to a halt, even the dining arrangement at the hostel was paralysed. Per force the local students left the hostel and went to their respective homes, leaving us, the students from outside the State, to suffer. With hostel facilities crippled, we were surviving on snacks only. When Dr. Sahoo came to know this sorry state of affairs, he immediately summoned me to his place and ordered me to have meals with him everyday, till the strike ends. Mrs. Sahoo took extra pains in cooking vegetarian food for me. During those difficult days, Mr. & Mrs. Sahoo made me comfortable, giving me the feelings as if I was a member of their family. I cannot forget their love and affection they bestowed upon me then, as also later on.

Prof. Sahoo's and my relationship goes back 30 years. I have had the unique privilege of being his student and also his class- mate at various stages of my education. Later on, coincidentally, we both were Ph.D. students of Prof. R.G. Prasher, the then Head, Department of Library & Information Science and Dean, Faculty of Arts, Dr. Harisingh Gour University, Sagar. Thus I had the rare opportunity of doing Ph.D. alongside another Ph.D. Scholar, who has been my teacher. Although, earlier Prof. Sahoo was my teacher, during our research at Sagar University, he always treated me like a colleague and never showed any sign of superiority. It was indeed a moral boost for me. On a lighter note, on a rare occasion as it would be, I truly enjoyed him getting stern strictures on his research work from Prof. Prashar who was a demanding teacher and a hard taskmaster. I feel extremely fortunate and lucky to have had the pleasure of training under two stalwarts of the library profession and who also happened to be perfectionists. But I guess that it brought out the best in every student who has trained under them, including me.

Prof. Sahoo received his Masters in Library and Information Science from Delhi University and his Doctorate in LIS from Dr. Harisingh Gour University, Sagar. He has published two books and contributed a number of research papers in professional journals. He has also guided a number of scholars for their Ph.D. degree. He started his professional career as an Assistant Librarian at Utkal University way back in 1968 and later joined Sambalpur University as a Lecturer. In due course of time he became an Associate Professor and headed the DLIS, Sambalpur University for two terms. Presently, he is serving as the Head of Department of Library and Information Science and Dean of Faculty of Arts, Dr. Harisingh Gour University, Sagar (M.P.).

The idea of this festschrift volume first occurred to Prof. Prasher. Since then he has been a moving spirit in completing this project.

Bringing out a festschrift volume for a student is a rare of rarest example and speaks volumes for the student and the teacher alike. Perhaps, this act is very special, whereby a teacher bestows upon his student an immemorial gift. This clearly shows Prof. Prasher's unique approach that has made him a role model of fine human virtues. One lesson that I learn from this gesture of Prof. Prasher is that happiness comes from giving and not acquiring and from caring and not from exploitation. This attitude maintains two-track relationship between a teacher and his student that remains intact for ever.

We must not forget that we are not only the inheritors but also the custodians of a great legacy. May God bless us all to carry forward Prof. Sahoo's brilliant ideas and leadership for the development of future libraries? I firmly believe that his life and work will be of great inspiration to the LIS professionals of India, especially to today's young library professionals. May I conclude quoting a saying: '... tears will not come when you miss a person. It comes when you do not want to miss person.... Just feel it!

2

DLIS, Sagar University
in Sahoo's context

Prof. (Dr.) R.G. Prasher
55-B, Udham Singh Nagar, Civil Lines,
Ludhiana-141 001
E-mail: principalprasher@rediffmail.com

KC Sahoo as a PhD Scholar

After day's hard work when I reached my house late in the evening, my otherwise docile wife pounced upon me."You have no business to be that harsh to Sahoo" she told me sternly, adding further, "he is doing his work all right." That day as usual I had lost my temper at Kailash, asking him to put in more in his research work to improve its quality and to accelerate its progress. My rough behaviour, lack of due appreciation of the quality of his research work, and indictment of the speed at which it was progressing brought tears in his eyes. Another point of my irritation was his top priority to attend to the sick and ill persons who came to him for treatment; and this at the cost of his research work. My priority was that he should complete his research work early, his priority, on the other hand, was to serve the needy even if it delayed his research work. The clash of our priorities had made me a bit harsh towards him. Better, still better and faster, still faster was my motto. I was quite intolerant of the slow speed. Both of these, however, had no norms or benchmarks and, therefore, unjustified.

I was really sorry for what I did or said but I lacked moral courage to express it to the aggrieved. Arrogance or keeping up a false prestige was the reason. I therefore did not protest when my wife rebuked me for the incident of the day. Kailash had taken study leave for two or three years to do his Ph.D. a few years back, but joined back his duties without completing his research work. His research guide must be a great person who permitted it to happen. Had I been in his place, I would not have allowed it. My extra harshness towards this scholar was due to this fact also. And I had accepted the challenge to see that Kailash gets his Ph.D. degree and with credit. I thank God Almighty that the battle was won. His research work was adjudged as very good and pioneering also. It has been published and is available to the larger audience in India and abroad. His capability stands testified.

Kailash's Long Association with DLIS of Sambalpur University

Sagar University and Sambalpur University were quite warm in their academic relationship. Teachers from both the Universities frequently participated in teaching and examination work of each other. I have been visiting the Department of Library & Information Science of Sambalpur University (DLIS-Samb) as and when invited. Kailash, who was my counterpart at Sambalpur University, also used to visit the Sagar University in connection with teaching, research or examination work from time to time.

Kailash was a teacher of Library and Information Science to earn his livelihood. He was a homeopath to administer medicines to sick and needy. My impression during my visits to Sambalpur was that he taught his students sincerely as a matter of his duty but treated his patients with passion as a social responsibility. No money was charged from the patients, he treated them free of cost, paying for their medicines from his meager salary. Staff members, teachers, officers and vice-chancellors of the Sambalpur University were among his patients. This added to his popularity on the campus. Among the students of DLIS he was quite popular, more so because of his helping nature, simplicity, and tremendous patience. He was maintaining cordial relations with his colleagues in DLIS-Samb, faculty members and administrative staff of the University. Perhaps, Professor Raut, his senior, was the only exception in this

I was always in a hurry to finish my assignment at Sambalpur and return to Sagar to be at my desk. As such there was no opportunity or inclination to study or to understand the power politics of DLIS-Samb or of University there. The impression I carried was that Kailash was an honest, sincere, hardworking and non-controversial person. I befriended him because of these qualities. Though there were still many years to go, my impression about him led me to think that he could be a possible candidate to step into my position after my retirement. Because of this I did play some role to get him in Sagar as my successor, purely in the interest of our DLIS-Sag. My good wishes for him anyway were always there.

Because of not so pleasant relations that Kailash had with Raut, I did not have much contact with him, though to be fair to him, he was always courteous and kind to me. Parida and Chaudhary were other two sincere and dedicated teachers at DLIS-Samb. We had mutual regard for each other and I always enjoyed their company and learnt a lot from their long teaching experiences which they freely shared with me.

During my occasional visits to Sambalpur, as I stated above, I was more concerned with the assignment for which I was invited. There was no time to look deep into the working of the Department there. My general impression was that the DILS-Samb was functioning alright, with dedicated faculty and satisfied students.

Kailash's University Quarter at Sambalpur—an Ashram

I used to stay in the University Guest-House, but was invariably fed at the Kailash Babu's. His wife, Sanyasini, was a very good cook and an excellent host. I always enjoyed the best hospitality during my one-day visit once or twice a year.

Kailash Babu had transformed his University quarter into an *Ashram*. Every thing was at peace and general atmosphere was of a perfect tranquility. The performance of *puja* in the morning as also in the evening with religious fervor was a regular feature. Kailash's father was always on the move, attending to this or that small work in the house. He did not talk much, and liked silence. The house had an extensive and well kept kitchen garden, yielding fresh vegetables for meals, flowers for *puja,* trees bearing variety of fruits—coconut, mango, kaju, banana, etc. to eat. They had one or two cows to yield them fresh and pure milk. I always found some needy relatives of Kailash staying with them to complete their education.

Sagar University's DLS at AEC Centre Pachmarhi, 1963—

I had a long association with this DLIS Sagar. A Department of Library Science was started by the Indian Army at their AEC Training College and Centre at Pachmari in 1963, the year I joined the Indian Military Academy at Dehradun for my Pre-Commission training. Two former studants of DLIS Delhi University—Sachdeva and Malhan—were temporarily appointed to teach in this new Department under the charge of Sub. Wazir Singh. Lt S.D. Sehgal was one of the students of the first batch and a student of Sub Wazir Singh. After the completion of the Course and declaration of results, Lt Sehgal took over the Department, being an Officer. In the changed circumstances, the student was the head and the teacher was his subordinate. There could have been mutual respect but it was not there. Some sort of bickering was going on. The Commandant, Lt Col Gogte did not like it and was keen to put an end to this indiscipline. Consequently, in March 1964, even during my Young Officers' course, I was called upon to look after this Department. Sehgal was shifted to the Department of Mathematics. After I completed my YOs' Course I was posted at Pachmarhi to head the Department of Library Science there. This Department was affiliated with the Sagar University and as such a part of it. There was no DLIS at the University Headquarters then. As a young army officer, I was the Chairman of Board of Studies of Library Science and a member of the Academic Council of the University, being the head of DLS at Pachmarhi

I ran the DLS at Pachmarhi till March 1968 when I sought premature release from the Indian Army to join Punjab Agricultural University at Ludhiana (PAU). From PAU, where I was a Deputy Librarian till 1977, I moved to Rajendra Agricultural University, Pusa, Bihar as its University Librarian. Though this position was quite important, University Librarian being a statutory officer of the University like any other Dean or Director, still my love for teaching persisted. As an Army Officer, I have been teaching B.Lib.Sc. course; as a Deputy University Librarian at PAU, I have been teaching Technical Writing course to the M Sc and PhD students. As such I was always keen to seek a change and join teaching profession.

DLS at University HQ at Sagar

H.S.Sengar, my friend and classmate, joined Sagar University as Librarian in 1967. He was an Asst. Librarian at the Jabalpur University till then. Librarian's position at Sagar was in the Reader's pay scale then. Sagar DLS was established by Sengar much afterward perhaps in the late 1970s to run B.Lib.Sc programme. Sengar as the Librarian looked after this Department as its Head and ran it ably and successfully with the help of his such colleagues as S. Sundreswarn, Chaturvedi, Ragho, and B.P. Shrivastava. Dr. G.D. Bhargava from Vikram University, Ujjain also extended good help in teaching and examination work when called upon. The University created the position of a Reader to appoint one to look after this Dept. I was one of the members on the selection committee to recommend Sengar for this position. Sengar wanted to continue both as a Librarian and Reader-Head of DLIS and to this University was not agreeable. Ultimately he chose Librarianship in preference to Headship in Reader's grade, the pay scale in which he was already serving. I have been responding to Sagar University's invitations for extension lectures and tried to give my best to the students there. The Department was to remain without a separate Head for some time more

UGC Visiting Professorship at Sagar University

Sagar University was in the grip of lawlessness during 1982 and the M.P. Government had to enforce emergency there. M.B. Malhotra, the former Secretary to the Governor of Madhya Pradesh was appointed as the Vice-Chancellor with all the powers of the Academic Council and Executive Council of the University. Malhotra, being an experienced and competent IAS officer, restored the normalcy in the University within a short time. Since he meant business and was positive in his approach, faculty as also students willingly cooperated with him. Sagar University saw accelerated development during the tenure of Malhotra. It was during his tenure that two post-graduate programmes—MJMC and MLibISc—were planned and started in 1983-84 academic session. Credit must go to Sengar for starting MLibISc programme. It was because Sengar had a good rapport with the Vice-Chancellor, Rector and the Registrar of the University. And they all helped him to start this programme. During the time this programme was being planned, I had a chance to come to Sagar for lectures in DLIS for about a week. Sengar has been extra kind to me throughout. On my last day at Sagar he took me to the Vice-Chancellor so that I may pay regards to him. There he mentioned to the VC in very glowing terms about my qualifications, experience, publications, present status, etc. My teaching work at Sagar during that visit as excellent was also stated. He summed up that the University needs such a person for the Department of Library Science. VC was hearing attentively all what Sengar said. He remarked: "You say he is your class-mate and friend, and he is already a Professor in a University. But we have a position of a Reader only. Will it be fair to bring a Professor as a Reader here? It would not be like a friend." Both of us left the room of VC. Desire makes a man fool. I must admit that I was ready to join Sagar University as a Reader also. And most probably I had told this to Sengar. God's grace was that he did not tell the VC that Prasher was willing to join the University as a Reader.

An opportunity came when Sagar University decided to introduce Master's course in Library Science. Solely because of the efforts of Sengar, I was invited to DLIS Sagar as a UGC Visiting Professor for one academic year to teach MLibISc students. The inside story—true or false— was that two candidates —Kaula and Prasher— were short-listed. Professor P.B. Mangla was requested by the University, as an expert, to recommend one of these two on the basis of better suitability. Mangla recommended my name. This offer was mainly because of the efforts of Sengar and less because of my standing as a teacher of LIS. Since I was already in the cadre of a University Professor, there was no problem for the UGC to agree to the proposal of the University.

I left my family at Pusa and joined Sagar University as a Visiting Professor in November 1983. Dr Kasliwal, the former Principal of Indore Law College was another Visiting Professor in the Law Department of the University. He was staying with us in the University Guest House along with his Doctor wife. Another Visiting Professor in the Department of Sociology was also there. I was working very hard both in the Department, and in the Guest House supervising students' dissertation work and getting these typed after due corrections. The academic community of the University was keenly observing my work and might be comparing it with that of other

Visiting Professors. Guest House in charge, Major Aahi, and Registrar(Exams) B.P.Dixit, who was also staying in the Guest House, were all praise for my work and , I suppose, must be conveying their impression about me to the VC. Both of them, as everybody knew, were very sincere, dedicated and competent officers, and were not involved in the petty politics of the University. VC would come almost every evening to the Guest House and would sit for a few minutes in its then well-kept garden and listen the sacred *bhajans* which he had got arranged for the students. Sometimes VC would invite one of the Visiting Professors for a cup of tea at the lawns of University Guest House. But such meeting would last for 10 to 15 minutes only. During the whole period of about 11 months I might have met the VC twice or thrice, that too in the Guest House on such informal invitation for a cup of tea.

University Professorship at Sagar University, December 1984

After about 11 months the interview for the post of Professor in DLIS was held, with three or four top external experts on the selection committee. I was selected as a Professor. Though this committee was for the selection of a professor, Sengar's case was also placed before it to be promoted and placed in the pay-scale of a professor. Without such a selection committee this promotion for him was not possible. Sengar amply deserved this promotion, though it was managed with the help of his friends. Assistant Librarian's case was not taken up and he remained where he had been for years because he had no influential friend to support him. After the notification of our selection I asked to be relieved as Visiting Professor. It was done and I rushed to Pusa to get myself relieved from RAU. At Katni railway station I learnt about the assassination of Prime Minister Indira Gandhi. What followed was an abnormal situation, trains were empty and the atmosphere really tense. I decided to travel to Pusa via Dhanabad. Though I was holding a ticket for first class, I preferred to travel by sleeper class out of fear as the whole first class compartment was empty. On reaching Dhanbad I found that all the roads were deserted and there were news of riots in the city. Somehow, I reached my brother's place safely. Then I learnt that train services have been disrupted. I had to wait for two days at Dhanbad for situation becoming normal. Against the advice of our friends, I traveled to

Pusa by a night train and reached there safely. Vice-Chancellor at RAU Pusa was kind and without much delay, I was given a lien of three years and was relieved to join my new assignment at the Sagar University. In December1984 I joined as a regular University Professor in the DLIS of the University. I had left as Head, DLIS Sagar University in 1968, I joined back as HOD again after 16 years.

Sengar Wanted Headship of DLIS – Sag

Sengar wanted to continue as the Head of Department of Library & Information Science. But the University Administration in its wisdom did not agree to this arrangement, the official and personal help of Rector V.C. Mishra and Registrar Dhawan notwithstanding. I was not aware of this development, neither VC sought my views about it. Establishing an independent DLIS was perhaps already decided. A University is always a great organization. Conflicting and opposing forces continue to operate endlessly. I am sure the Vice-Chancellor must have been briefed against the arrangement which Sengar and his friends were contemplating. Otherwise also Malhotra knew his job well and was in complete control of the University. He was a mature administrator and a sharp person, and it was difficult for anybody to befool him or to influence his actions. With the University not agreeing to his continuation as Head DLIS, Senger felt upset. This was a normal behaviour and anybody in his place would have reacted the same way. The Department he was losing was perhaps his first love. And he had done a lot to establish and develop it without much help from the University. So long as Malhotra remained as VC, Sengar maintained a low profile and *status quo* but after his departure he started withdrawing himself along with his resources from DLIS-Sag on this or that pretext.

Towards Reorganisation of DLIS Sagar University

Sengar's changed attitude notwithstanding, about 10 months' period gave me enough time to establish myself as a teacher. Also I developed a very good rapport with my students and staff. A teacher is strong if his own students respect him or at least do not go against him; and an HOD is strong if his staff members respect him and support him. Luckily, I had both with the grace of God.

I had no role in snatching from Sengar his DLIS. Separating the teaching department from the Library was as per the policy of the University. I was only a cause for it. As such I was silently watching the development, and was concentrating on my teaching and research work with vigour and devotion. Except for library classification at MLibSc level, I had no difficulty in teaching various papers. Since the payment of remuneration was involved, the services of Library staff such as Sundareswrn, Chaturvedi, and Ragho were available. The University also permitted us to invite teachers from outside under UGC Fellowship programme. Though such *adhoc* arrangement was not proper, somehow we carried out the teaching work of BLibISc and MLibISc programmes satisfactorily. In view of the stories(true or false) doing the rounds that there were malpractices going on in the Library Classification and Cataloguing practical papers, we changed them into written papers, as is in other Universities, to be set and evaluated by examiners appointed by the University and the answer-books duly preserved as per rules. We wanted to maintain the credibility of the examination and to eliminate the scope of any malpractice. We also introduced the admission test for both the courses for ensuring better intake and also for eliminating the discretion at any level in giving admission without consideration of merit. M.P. Satija from GNDU was a great help in teaching library classification during 1985-86 and 1986-87 sessions, when Sengar gave up taking classes in DLIS.

Jagtar and Gupta Join DLIS—Sag

Jagtar Singh and R.K. Gupta joined DLIS as Lecturer and Reader respectively in early 1987. With three regular teachers and two or three part-time teachers the Department started functioning in a normal way. Jagtar was a product of DLIS-Panjab University, and knew his subject well. Sharp and witty, he was a never-tiring teacher. The contribution of Jagtar in the growth and development of DLIS was really significant. He gave the best he could to the students during his stay in DLIS during 1987-88 and 1988-89 sessions.

DLIS-Sag Shifted to its Own Building

A separate small building for DLIS was ready by the end of 1988 and we shifted from the Library to this building. Professor Yash Pal, the then Chairman of UGC, inaugurated DLIS-Sag building in February 1989. With our shifting to new building another link with the University Library was snapped.

Many Aspirants for Admission in DLIS-Sag—Tough Time for Us

Two University Departments were such where it was difficult for the aspirants to get admission easily because of tough competition. These were Pharmacy and Library and Information Science. Pharmacy Department was well-organised and had its own importance and reputation in India. DLIS, however, was being reorganized. It was coming up as an apolitical, work-oriented, and disciplined one. The intake in the courses there was merit-based through a university admission test with no internal or external interference. Faculty was dedicated to achieve the set goals and the students were serious, sincere, motivated and hardworking. The result was that most of our students got selected for various positions either through the State Public Service Commission or otherwise. This gave rise to a general impression among the student community and their parents that if one is to have a sure employment; one should go in for BLibISc and MLibISc courses in DLIS. This impression was not a false one but was based on the ground reality. Depending on our resources we had a fixed number of seats for both the Courses, decided by the Academic Council of the University. As such we could accommodate only a limited number of students that too as per merit, not everybody.

A Transparent Admission Process

We had kept the admission process independent and transparent. The papers were set by the external examiners and submitted to the Registrar under sealed covers. The Registrar got them printed and kept them in his custody till handed over to the Superintendent of Examination half an hour before the commencement of the test. The examiners received the answer-books in sealed covers. The examiners after evaluation sent their marks-sheets in sealed covers to the Head who would pass these on to the University appointed Result Compiling Committee as these were. The sealed covers were opened by the Committee, tabulation was done, and merit lists for both the Courses were finalized. These merit lists were made public after these were approved by the Vice-Chancellor.

Our Patience Helped Us

Admission time was a tough time for the HOD in particular. He was to face the influential *netas* and *goonda* elements from the city who were supporting their respective candidates not in the merit list. These *netas* and *goondas* in Sagar University were so strong as had no fear of the University Administration. The latter was in fact helpless before them. Since we could not deviate from the pre-decided rules and were not willing to compromise on principles, our attitude was interpreted as rigid and unhelpful by the seekers of unlawful admission and their friends. The unwarranted and baseless criticism of such seekers of admission and their powerful friends notwithstanding, the good thing was that no Vice-Chancellor interfered with our affairs, and in fact each one stood like a rock behind us, pressure of *netas* on him was also there.

HOD's best friend by then had turned the latent enemy of DLIS-Sag. He with the help of his friends was doing his utmost to fish in the troubled water. He would instigate those aspirants who unfortunately could not make grade in the merit list to pressurize the DLIS Head for their admission. But whenever this gentleman met the Head he would show utmost regards and professed the best of friendship with him. But for us it was a business as usual and we never bothered or cared about his activities and intrigues. One of his colleagues would often tell the HOD that the person had been a successful trouble-maker all through, but was helpless in our case. We had faith in God Almighty and He never let us down. A vast majority of the University faculty and its administrative staff appreciated our efforts and gave us a solid support.

There are people in India who think that the rules or laws do not exist for them or can be bent or moulded to accommodate their unlawful demands. With their money or muscle power they think that they can get anything done. Most of the people in authority instead of asserting even when they are right, bow before these *goonda* elements and oblige them as per their wishes against the rules. Even law enforcing authorities are awfully afraid of these *goondas*. As these *goondas* are not challenged but are obliged, they have grown bold and fearless. The general belief is that not obeying such element meant trouble. The HOD was an ordinary and simple human being with no friends to support him, but he faced this rough weather boldly and with patience and stood his grounds for three successive years. No Vice-Chancellor, none from the university or district administration came to his rescue. If the Head had not been physically assaulted, it was because of God's grace. HOD's office staff and faculty members would slip away as soon as these elements entered the Department, leaving him alone to face these goons. The lesson learnt was that if truth is on your side, you would not only sustain but win also. Some faculty members would often tell HOD that his own 'best friend' was behind all that HOD also knew it but would feign ignorance about his friend's role. The friend was also happy, believing that his activities were not known to the Head. His intrigues, instigations, and activities to disrupt the working of our Department notwithstanding, moral strength of the Head remained un-demolished. This seasonal rough weather also did not affect our teaching and research programme. Our students also showed greater keenness to learn and worked whole heartedly and vigorously, bringing in popularity and credit to the Department. Their placement after the completion of the Course was also encouraging. After three academic years from 1986-87 to 1988-89, there were no man-made problems, and we were in a happy state. The goonda element learnt that things are done as per the rules in DLIS-Sag, and the Head cannot be terrified by empty threats and compelled to do what is not right. Also our students spread a positive message about us among their fellow friends and people of Sagar city. Of course the saner element among the university community and city population had always been appreciative of our good work and supported us.

JK Mishra Joins after Jagtar's Departure

In early 1989 Jagtar was offered Lecturership by the Punjabi University, Patiala. Since it was nearer his home, he accepted the offer and shifted to the Punjabi University. DLIS-Sag lost a capable and dedicated teacher and HOD his affectionate colleague.

Shortly after Jagtar left, J.K. Mishra joined the DLIS-Sag as a Lecturer on a regular basis. He was a product of DLIS Delhi. An honest, sincere and hardworking young man, he knew his subject well. To an extent he was a good replacement of Jagtar. JK discharged his teaching responsibilities to the satisfaction of the students, always bringing in changes and innovations. The students were exposed to computers and IT application to the work and services of the libraries.

Research Work and Research Products

DLIS, during this phase along with teaching work, started giving special attention to research work which had already been initiated. The result was that the HOD brought out a number of publications, important among them were: *Index and Indexing Systems; Information and its Communication; Managing University Libraries; India's University Libraries: Organization, Operation and Services.* The research work of Ravinder, Roshan, Kailash, and JK -all PhD scholars—was at different stages and was progressing well. They submitted their respective theses after the completion of their research work one after another and were awarded PhD degrees. The quality of the research work was acknowledged by the peers in profession. Four among the research scholars of that time are already in Professor's cadre. Three scholars have got their theses published commercially. The research work of Borse was also progressing well. It was completed in due time and he too was awarded PhD degree. Soon after, he also became a University Librarian in professor' grade. The quality of MLibISc dissertations, completed under the supervision of different faculty members, was also very good and a matter of satisfaction for the faculty of DLIS-Sag.

Mishra held the Fort—1997 to 1999

Reader and Professor left DLIS on their respective superannuation in the first half of 1997, leaving JK Mishra, a Lecturer then, alone among regular staff to hold the fort. RK Gupta, Reader moved to Lucknow. Professor Prasher left Sagar in July 1997 to take up another assignment as the University Librarian at the Guru Nanak Dev University, Amritsar. J.K. Mishra looked after the Department for two sessions—1997-98 and 1998-99 successfully, many problems notwithstanding. Mishra, as I knew him, was a bold and very self- respecting person. He would solve his problems himself rather than involving others. I too was very busy at my new desk at Amritsar. As such I was not aware of what was happening at Sagar. Anyway, he ran the Department successfully as per established norms with the help of ad-hoc teachers provided by the University. One thing which stood out was that he did not compromise on principles, followed the rules and kept those who were out to play with the established norms of DLIS-Sag at arms length. Even the VC and a State Minister failed to compel him to do something not permissible under the rules, I was told.

Mishra had his own moral character. Being a law graduate also he knew well what was legal and what was illegal. He would not do what he considered not correct even under duress. He, therefore, had difficulties with the VC who was a politician and had been an MLA. But Mishra stood his grounds

Kailash as Professor at Sagar University

When the position of Professor was advertised in 1997, Kailash along with others applied for it. After the interview he was placed at no. 2 after Dr M.P. Satija, then a Reader at Guru Nanak Dev University. Satija received the offer in due course of time. It was a difficult decision for Satija to leave Amritsar. GNDU has its own reputation because of very rich infrastructural and intellectual resources. Then Amritsar was Amritsar, an important city of his home State Also he had growing children attending first rate academic institutions, and disturbing this arrangement would not have been proper. The UGC promotion policy was also there and, therefore, Professorship at GNDU itself was not a distant dream for Satija. He, after due consideration, declined the offer when the University was really fed up with his false excuses. Thus he took a considerable long time to arrive at this decision. This delayed the filling up of position with the candidate at no 2. Dr Kailash C. Sahoo joined as a Professor at Harisingh Gour Vishwavidyalya, Sagar in August 1999, after completing all the necessary formalities at the Sambalpur University.

MP Satija and JK Mishra were selected for the post of Professor and Reader respectively. Mishra joined as a Reader, vacating the post of the Lecturer which he was holding. Satija, as already mentioned , was indecisive and ultimately declined the offer. This delayed the appointment of Professor in DLIS-Sag.

Floodgate for PhDs

During 1998-1999 the University, bypassing DLIS-Sag and Mishra, opened a floodgate for PhD under the guidance of a retired Librarian and a College Librarian. The former was neither a Ph.D. in Library & Information Science nor a regular teacher of LIS. The latter too was never a teacher of LIS on a regular basis. A large number of persons got themselves registered for PhD and were awarded the degree. Since the matter is sensitive, it shall not be proper to comment on it. In the State Universities, I understand, if a vice-chancellor wishes to do a thing, he can manage to get it done. Some members on Board of Studies and Academic Council shall see that the wishes of the vice-chancellor are carried out. All the legal formalities are duly completed to cover illegality and academic dishonesty.

On joining the University, Sahoo could not or did not check the tide. And it is still continuing. The retired College Librarian who has never been a regular teacher in any DLIS has been given the freedom to help many persons in getting Ph.D.degrees under his supervision. Except the Sagar University, perhaps such things are not happening in other Universities of India. Sahoo is a gentleman and a peace loving person. He tries not to commit any irregularity, but is not in the habit of going out of his way to pickup a quarrel to stop irregularities of others, even when it concerns the Department under his charge.

Relations of Mishra and Sahoo

Kailash was new to Sagar as also DLIS there, and he did not know much about the master players and intriguers who had been inimical to the DLIS-Sag and the norms it was following throughout. He also did not take his colleague JKM into confidence while establishing relationships with such persons, perhaps, he though, it was not necessary also. The 'best friend', who had managed to come back a few years after his retirement would flatter Sahoo, tried to befriend him and cultivate relations with him at the cost of Mishra. His immediate purpose was to wean Sahoo away from Mishra and to make him dependent on him. Sahoo did not see through this game and in the initial stages danced to his tunes. It resulted into a misunderstanding between the two colleagues—Sahoo and Mishra—which persisted for years. Sahoo and Mishra had different norms, ways and styles of functioning and, therefore, what was the misunderstanding first aggravated into a rift later. Mishra did his duties in DLIS but had no relations with his Head, or respect for him, or involvement with the Department. It was a sort of withdrawal and leaving Sahoo to do whatever he liked or wished. Though later on Sahoo maintained a distance with the master intriguer, but the damage had already been done. After the master intriguer was sent away his deputy, however, kept Sahoo in good humour throughout, and used him and his Department to his advantage even against the rules or norms.

Sahoo and Mishra were both my students and I was attached with both of them. The relations between the two made me sad. Because I knew the nature of Mishra, I therefore did not talk about it with him, but would always advise Sahoo to improve the relationship with his colleague for the betterment of the Department. My understanding was that Sahoo was flexible and would not stand on prestige to accept a good or well-meaning advice. Mishra was not like that. Once he decided he would not change. Out of respect for me he might not have argued with me on this matter, but nevertheless he would not change the course he had chosen. So in spite of my wishes and requests, there had been no rapprochement between the two. This rift naturally affected the working of the Department and its discipline because there were only two regular teachers in a post-graduate department and they too were at logger head. Due to the estrangement of the two, even the regular office assistant was indifferent and did not bother much for the HOD.

Sahoo ran DLIS with ad hoc Teachers

Sahoo was to exist and had to run the Department under his charge, the prevailing situation notwithstanding. His patience and tenacity stood him well. The only way out for him was to seek the help of outside professionals and persons. Two, who had acquired MLIS degrees through distance mode of education, came handy to him. At different points of time Sahoo got these two to register for their PhD degree under his supervision and availed of their services for class-room teaching and office-work respectively. Some ad hoc teachers were also engaged to run the teaching programme properly. The very fact that a number of students of DLIS-Sag cleared UGC-NET almost every year and were getting good placements goes to prove that the Department was being run successfully. The credit should go to the dedicated teachers and sincere students.

Every vice-chancellor has the commitment to provide quality education through the university he presides. With the exception of a few Indian universities, this commitment remains as an unfulfilled sacred promise only. With the pulls and pushes of the politicians for getting their illegal and unlawful work done; as also in the perverted power politics of the university and students'indiscipline, the question before the worthy VC is his own survival. He has neither time nor energy nor will to see what is happening in various teaching departments or to find out if these have necessary resources or congenial environment to carry out their normal functions. Some VCs, instead of facing the uncomfortable situation at the campus boldly, chose to remain away from university headquarters on this or that pretext for most of the times.

Indifferent Administraion and Distance Education

Quality education needs quality intake, need-based scholarly faculty, and adequate physical facilities. In the DLIS-Sag it is not the same as it was in the past, though there were quite a few deficiencies then also. Two reasons contributed to it. One was the apathy of the university administration which did not provide the needed resources to the DLIS-Sag. For instance, it could not fill the position of Professor in time, and that of a Lecturer in 12 years. The position is still vacant. Adhoc or part-time or guest faculty cannot be a replacement of regular and committed faculty. Then there is not enough money for the purchase of books and equipment. Computer Lab today is an essential part of a DLIS. A really good computer lab is nowhere visible in the Department. The second reason is the introduction of LIS education through distance mode. It is only to make money without imparting worthwhile education. In some of the Universities it is a fraud as the quality of intake as also of the education imparted is a suspect.These problems are known to all, including Sahoo. Pestering the university administration or quarrelling with it or criticizing it proves costly to an individual. Passing the days and having a peaceful life is a rule today. It ensures regular salary month after month. Hell with the DLIS and its proficiency! *Om, shaanti shaanti*!

Expressing our Sense of Gratitude

DLIS-Sag, like the sacred Ganges, continues its eternal journey. Faculty and students came and went away after playing their due roles. History shall tell whose role was positive and whose was negative. I have been a lucky witness of as also a participant in this journey of DLIS-Sag.All said and done, I bow my head to Dr H S Sengar who established this Department and guided its destiny in its formative stage. I pay my respectful regards to such part-time teachers as Sundereswaran, Chaturvedi, Ragho, Shrivastavsa, Neelam and others who toiled to give this Department a solid foundation. I express my sense of gratitude to R K Gupta, Jagtar Singh, J K Mishra who have been my affectionate colleagues and who worked with dedication and commitment to strengthen this Department and to take it to new heights. There were many others like G D Bhargava, Krishan Kumar, S S Murthy, M P Satija, H R Chopra who came and shared their expertise with our students. I gratefully acknowledge their help. The role of Biswas and his successor Shukla, our office assistants as also of Babba Ganesh and Dashrath has also been significant.But if this Department is known all over the country it is because of our students who are serving as successful professionals throughout India. Many among them are occupying important positions as rectors, deans, university professors, university librarians and so on. In totality they truly represent the Department—DLIS-Sag. We all are proud of them and sincerely wish them all success and happiness.

Sahoo has Won

All this, true or false, a positive attitude of Dr. K.C. Sahoo towards life, his general contentment, and happy disposition are worth noting. He helps anybody and everybody who comes to him, provided the rules permit that. None has seen him to use his high position to harass anybody. Even when he favoures somebody, he does it gracefully without claiming a credit for it. Even in the days of moral degradation. Prof. Sahoo remains a benchmark of what a perfect gentleman. One may not be an excellent teacher, or an able and effective administrator, but if one is a good human being he wins. Sahoo has won.

3

Information Literacy: Need of the Hour

Dr. Neelam Thapa
Department of Library & Information Science
Dr. Harisingh Gour University, Sagar

Abstract

The information literacy programmes at global and national level are studied. The study shows that that information literacy programme in India is still in a very preliminary state as compared to developed countries. We are still far from realizing the need and potential of information literacy. It is suggested that concrete measures like establishing a National Forum on information literacy, drafting national level policies for the implementation of information literacy programmes and adoption of international standards for information literacy should be taken up immediately by the Government of India.

Introduction

Literacy or ability of communication consisting of reading, listening, speaking and writing is essential for all. Since the emergence of the information society, with its rapidly evolving information technologies, and ever increasing quantities of information, the term literacy is related to and merged with other terms such as computer literacy, digital literacy, hyper-literacy, information technology literacy, interactive literacy, internet literacy, library literacy, media literacy, multiple literacy, network literacy, oral literacy and visual literacy. Therefore, in today's digital era, the adequacy of literacy skills, previously recognized as the instrument for life-long learning, should be re-evaluated and developed. The term information literacy has been used as a collective term concerning all or several of literacies mentioned above. Information literacy needs to be developed and maintained throughout life, not only by information users, but also by librarians and other information workers[1].

Information literacy is a set of abilities requiring individuals to "recognize when information is needed and have the ability to locate, evaluate, and use effectively the needed information"[2]. Information literacy programmes help develop these information abilities in an individual.

The need for information literacy is even more in higher education because higher education institutions are asked to provide students with both problem-solving and decision-making skills that will enable them to compete in today's changing workplaces. To meet this objective, it is required to prepare students to be information literate individuals who have ability to locate, process and use information effectively. Higher education should help students to become lifelong, self-directed and independent learners, the requirement being that the students need to become excellent producers and consumers of informaton[3].

Objectives of the Study

The objectives of the study are:

- (i) To get an insight on information literacy programmes at the global level;
- (ii) To study the status of information literacy in India;
- (iii) To highlight the need and prospects of conducting information literacy programmes in India; and
- (iv) To suggest measures for implementing information literacy programmes in India.

Methodology

An extensive search for information relevant to the study was conducted by going through primary and secondary sources of information both in print and electronic format. Internet resources were also searched using various search terms and also links were followed to make the search more comprehensive. The data thus collected was analyzed, filtered and summarized.

Information Literacy: Definition and Concept

Information literacy has been defined both as a skill and as a process. Some scientists opine that it is related to computer use and digital data but many believe that its scope is much broader. It has also been defined as an amalgamation of many different literacies.

According to the US National Commission on Library and Information Science, 2003 information literacy "encompasses knowledge of one's information concerns and needs, and the ability to identify, locate, evaluate, organize and effectively create, use and communicate information to address issues or problems at hand; it is a pre-requisite for participating effectively in the information society, and is part of the basic human right of life-long learning"[4].

Chauhan, Prem Chand and Murthy[5] define information literacy as "the ability in an individual to recognize, when information is needed, what information is needed, how information is located or retrieved, how to evaluate it and how to use it effectively. Here, the information should be in online form only". They have stressed on information being digital and online.

But, Baradol and Gopakumar[6] define information literacy as "the process of knowing when and why information is required, where to find it, and how to evaluate, use and communicate it in an ethical way. It is the combination of all the skills (competencies) that are required for the effective and maximum use of information".

ACRL Standards Committee, 2000[7] opine that information literacy is related to information technology skills, but has broader implications for the individual, the educational system, and for the society. Information technology skills enable an individual to use computers, software applications, databases, and other technologies to achieve a wide variety of academic, work-related, and personal goals. Information literate individuals necessarily develop some technology skills. Information literacy, while showing significant overlap with information technology skills, is a distinct and broader area of competence. Increasingly, information technology skills are interwoven with and support information literacy.

According to Lau[8], the Chairman of the Information Literacy Section of IFLA information literacy comprises of many information competencies and development of all these competencies can only help a student to become effective learner.

Information literacy has many times been also defined by characterizing an information literate person. In 1992, Doyle[9] described an information literate person as one who:

(i) Recognizes that accurate and complete information is the basis for intelligent decision making;

(ii) Recognizes the need for information;

(iii) Formulates questions based on information needs;

(iv) Identifies potential sources of information;

(v) Develops useful search strategies;

(vi) Accesses source of information including computer based and other technologies;

(vii) Evaluates information;

(viii) Organizes information for potential applications;

(ix) Integrates new information into an existing body of knowledge; and

(x) Uses information in critical thinking and problem solving"

The Council of Australian University Librarians (www.caul.edu.au/caul-programs/information-literacy/publications) has mentioned about the qualities of an information literate person. According to this, the qualities of an information literate person are:

(i) Recognize a need for information

(ii) Determine the extent of information needed

(iii) Evaluate the information and its sources

(iv) Incorporate selected information into their knowledge base

(v) Use information effectively to accomplish a purpose

(vi) Understand economic, legal, social and cultural issues in the use of information

(vii) Access and use information ethically and legally

(viii) Classify, store, manipulate and redraft information collected or generated.

Information Literacy: The Global Scenario

The idea of information literacy was conceptualized long back in European countries during 1970's and now recognized as critical literacy for the 21st century[10].

Literature survey shows that developed countries realized the importance of building information power through information literacy in 1980's and by the 1990's they took concrete steps in that direction. In USA, the National Forum on Information Literacy (NFIL) was established in 1989 and the Institute of Information Literacy (IIL) in 1998. The US Department of Education included Information Literacy in National Education Technology Plan as one of the five goals in December 2000[11].

There are many other information literacy organizations in USA which impart training in information literacy and also develop standards for the same. Some of these are:

(i) ACRL's Instruction Section (Association of College and Research Libraries)

(ii) ALA's Library Instruction Round Table (LIRT)

(iii) Library Orientation Exchange (LOEX)

(iv) California Clearinghouse on Library Instruction (CCLI)

(v) Southern California Instruction Librarians (SCIL)

(vi) National Forum on Information Literacy (NFIL)

(vii) The TLT Group: Teaching, Learning and Technology

(viii) IFLA Information Literacy Section

Many information literacy, research, or information problem solving models have been developed for teachers to use with pupils. Some of them are listed below:

(i) The Big 6 (http://big6.com/)

(ii) Research Cycle (http://www.fno.org/dec99/rcycle.html)

(iii) The Seven Pillars Model (SCONUL, U.K. Standing Conference of National and Univ. Libraries, 1999 http://

www.sconul.ac.uk/groups/information literacy/sp/sp/model.html)

(iv) SAUCE (http://ictnz.com/SAUCE.htm)

(v) Lane Clarke's Model (http://www.laneclark-ideasys.com/seminar_inquiry.htm)

(vi) The Research Cycle (http://www.questioning.org/recycle.html)

(vii) Doug Johnsons Info Literacy Model (http://www.doug-johnson.com/survival-skills-for-the-information-jungle / html)

(viii) Information Literacy Scope and Sequence (http://encompass.cerfinfo.com/RSModel.htm)

(ix) Applying the 4 Steps of Problem Solving to Information Literacy (http://tinyurl.com/gvmkh)

The American Association of School Libraries (AASL) and Association of Education and Communication Technology (AECT) have also provided standards to foster information literacy skills in students[12].

Information Literacy Competency Standards for Higher Education were reviewed by the ACRL Standards Committee and approved by the Board of Directors of the Association of College and Research Libraries (ACRL) on January 18, 2000 at the Midwinter Meeting of the American Library Association in San Antonio, Texas. These standards were also endorsed by the American Association for Higher Education (October 1999) and the Council of Independent Colleges (February 2004).

Three standardized information literacy survey techniques have been developed for use in higher education. In the United States, a consortium of library scientists developed a test of IL knowledge based on the Association of College and Research Libraries (ACRL) standards called Standardized Assessment of Information Literacy Skills (SAILS). More recently, the Education Testing Service (ETS) has also published a computer based survey that they term iSkills Test, formerly known as ICT skills[13]. In Australia, a report on Information Skills Survey (ISS) has been published[14].

In Australia, the Australian and New Zealand Institute for Information Literacy strives to help the students select information from credible sources. When students believe everything they research on the internet must be true, they are not able to conduct valid research. Because, doing research involves analyzing information i.e., students must be able to know when information comes from a reputable source. The Australian and New Zealand Institute for Information Literacy (ANZIIL) believes that those students who understand how to process information will be productive throughout their lives. These students will know how to decide whether something is true. The students should be able to tell when information sources are biased (www.anziil.org).

Information literacy program team of National Library Board (NLB), Singapore, established in September 1995, is engaged in developing and delivery of information literacy.

The necessity of a person's special training to life in the information society is underlined in the main documents of the World Summit on the Information Society, two stages of which took place in Geneva in 2003 and in Tunis in 2005.

The leading international organizations, initiating discussion and studying the problems of a person's training to Life in the Information Society are: UNESCO and the International Federation of Library Associations and Institutions (IFLA). Due to the efforts of these organizations, the concept of information literacy has been formed at present. IFLA has an Information Literacy section whose primary objective is to foster international cooperation and to promote information literacy in all types of libraries. IFLA-ALP (Action for Development through Libraries) and UNESCO-IFAP (Information For All Programs) are ambitious programmes in this direction. IFLA organized a workshop on information literacy in 2005 in Buenos Aires, Argentina. The problems of information literacy were the subject of discussion at the 75th IFLA General Conference "Libraries create future based on cultural heritage" (Milan, 21-28 August 2009), where there was a mutual sitting of "Literacy and Reading" sector and "Information Literacy" sector. It was united by the theme "Libraries are engines of various kinds of literacy of the 21st century"[15].

As part of their work to advocate information literacy and support information professionals, IFLA Literacy Section conducted two joint programmes for the IFLA conference 2010. The first programme, *Making It Count: Social Science Data Literacy as an Information Fluency,* explored the availability of Social Science data and the skills needed to access, understand and use it for sustainable economic and social development. The topic of this programme linked up with the concept of transliteracy and multiple literacies. The Information Literacy Section aims to increase partnership and for this reason, this was a joint programme with the Social Science Libraries Section. It was a success with 190 participants. The second conference programme was also a joint venture, combined with the Reference and Information Services Section. The programme, entitled *Don't Wait to be Asked: Towards Next Generation Reference Services and Information Literacy,* aimed at identifying what kind of reference services meet the needs of the 21st century users, while enhancing their information literacy for lifelong learning. Another goal in the strategic plan of the Section was to develop the concept of information literacy as a multi-cultural, multifaceted concept of relevance to the global society. To reflect on the different meanings of information literacy, the section arranged a pre-conference satellite in Gothenburg entitled information literacy: context, community, culture[16]. This programme was also a big success with 470 attendants. It was also podcasted.

Information literacy, as described in the Alexandria Proclamation of 2005, is essential for individuals to achieve personal, social, occupational and educational goals. Information literacy skills are necessary for people to be effective lifelong learners and to contribute in knowledge societies. This is why information literacy was endorsed by UNESCO's Information for All Programme (IFAP) as a basic human right[17].

In Germany, the enhancement of information literacy skills has become one of the core activities of German librarians and information professionals working in higher education environments. The first information literacy enhancement activities date from the late nineties of the 20th century when more and more electronic media were licensed by university libraries. In 2001, the Institute of Social Studies (Sozialforschungsstelle) in Dortmund published the alarming results of an official investigation into students' abilities to deal with electronic sources, stating that these abilities were insufficient and deserving further advancement. In defining the enhancement of information literacy as a core activity, university libraries were asked to participate in university teaching in general and to contribute substantially to students' information skills. A large number of university libraries now offer information literacy training programs for students of these colleges. University librarians offer information literacy products to students both outside and within the core curriculum, but as a general rule, information literacy products are compulsory within the core curriculum. It makes sense that the training of the teaching librarians is based upon the standards of education theory incorporated by universities in Germany.

Most of the information literacy librarians of Germany have linked their job with those of their partners, creating bottom-up networks, working committees, and communication tools. Due to the federal nature of education in Germany, there is a variety of regional information literacy Working Committees (Arbeitsgemeinschaften) established in a German Federal State or a region. Corresponding to the federal understanding of all educational matters there are also diverse settings of Information Literacy Standards, a phenomenon, foreigners find difficult to understand and digest. The German Information Literacy community may be well diversified, but it nevertheless has managed to create a major communication tool for the whole community: the gateway http://www.informationskompetenz.de/ hosted by the library of Ludwig Maximili[18].

In Russia, during 1970's in information training programmes, the emphasis was on training to use library, library catalogues and card files and development of reading culture. In 1980's, considerable attention was given on training skills of orientation in information resources, instructions for using information retrieval systems and assimilation of information search algorithm. Decade 1990's was characterized by inclusion into information training, how to use a personal computer and liquidation of computer illiteracy, training skills of databases use, electronic sources and the Internet. The first decade of the 21st century was marked by special interest to information communication technologies (ICT) and e-learning.

Research and Development Institute of Information Technologies in Social Sphere (further the Institute) of Kemerovo State University of Culture and Arts (KemUCA) has been working within the UNESCO's 'Information for All Programme' since 2000. Researchers of the Institute decided to purposefully and systematically carry out information training programme for the younger generation in Kuzbass. The idea behind this programme was to integrate or bring together different organizations and people from various professions. The research scientists of the Institute believe: the key figures in promoting the ideas of information literacy and Information Culture are the teachers and the librarians. Teachers of "Principles of Information Culture" have been graduating from Belovo Pedagogical College since 2002. The Institute has strong long-standing contacts with the two centres of advanced qualification of Kemerovo region namely: (i) Kuzbass Region Institute of Training and Retraining of Educators which works with teachers and school librarians (KRIT & RE) and, (ii) Kuzbass Region Institute of Professional Education (KRIPE) which works with teachers and librarians of professional colleges. In these centres, staff at the Institute conducts lectures and workshops on "Principles of Personal Information Culture". Professional advancement programmes for teachers and librarians is not just stationary in these two regional centres. The Institute staff travel to hinterland to conduct training seminars and lectures to master classes on new forms and methods of information for training children and youth in libraries and schools in remote areas of Kuzbass. In conclusion, it should be noted that, at present, the information training of citizens is of particular relevance and social significance in relation to the development and growth of Information Society, the global nature of ICT, the strategic direction of Russia on the path of innovative development of key sectors of economy and public life. Analysis and interpretation of experiences with the information training suggest that the solution to this problem is not possible through ad hoc, non-system libraries, carried out solely on the basis of the initiative. The state approach is required to organize information training programmes of citizens. One solution is to introduce the "Principles of a Person's Information Culture" as a compulsory course into the educational process of educational institutions at all levels of education. The real help in its practical implementation could be made by the libraries. Implementation of the course "Principles of a Person's Information Culture" in a library is the best way to demonstrate the educational function of this social institution[19].

Many more research studies have been conducted in developed countries since the beginning of 2000 to assess the importance of information literacy and suggest means for its effective implementation.

Pawinun, Nyamboga and Kemparaju[20] have studied the issues of information technology and higher educational development and the advances of the digital library in Thailand and Kenya. They stress on the need for information literacy and opine that the context of information literacy is of a wide range consisting of the traditional library literacy, the basic computer and telecommunication literacy, etc. and so information literacy programme should have different sections and should be provided through different methods.

Studies show that information literacy training greatly enhances the output of the students. A quasi-experimental study was conducted with two clusters of 13 year old students who did a project based assignment. One cluster received personalized coaching on information literacy and other did not receive such coaching. The study shows that the students who received personalized coaching obtained better scores for their project and showed better mastery in the learning and research process through the ability to use various information resources, presented more reliable and authentic information and included proper citations and a complete bibliography in their project report[21].

Vezzosi[22] has presented a project on information literacy carried out at the University of Parma, Italy. A multi-year information literacy programme was offered to a group of students attending the Environmental Science degree course. Students' learning was measured and assessed all along the development of the programme. The study shows that the students improve, along their study path, in terms of knowledge and skill. Also, their aptitude towards information develops in the direction of increasing awareness and independence.

Stanger[23] has given his views on the implementation of information literacy in Higher Education. He opines that libraries should play a supporting role and the information literacy programme should be implemented by the faculty of the concerned discipline. His opinion is contrary to the widely shared belief that the library, particularly those funded by educational institutions, should be the lead agency in articulating, promoting, and developing the community's information literacy.

Perez and Murray[24] argue that better understanding and more effective measurement of ICT literacy are needed to gauge readiness for pursuing higher education and entering the workforce. A model is proposed that points out that skill and knowledge, along with attitudes towards IT, coalesce in the context of reflective self awareness and purposeful intent to allow a computer user to achieve generativity - the ability to generate new skills and knowledge - that form the basis for creativity. They also emphasize that, in the absence of strong theoretical foundations and effective standardized assessments, ICT literacy will continue to play a fourth, barely audible fiddle to its three more established counterparts.

Indian Scenario

The above study shows that information literacy is globally recognized as the need of the hour and various information literacy programmes are being conducted throughout the world. John[25] in his paper has listed several attempts at international level, viz.,

(i) The National Forum on Information Literacy, USA, 1990.

(ii) EDUCATE Project, Europe, 1993-94.

(iii) National Informalization Programme, Ukaraine and Russia, 1986.

(iv) Japans National Council on Education Reform, Japan, 1989.

(v) Learning for Future, Australia, 1993.

He adds that there are other several programmes and policies of information literacy in the world, but the name of India is not in the list.

The Society for Information Science (SIS), in its 23rd Annual Convention had a sub theme on information literacy. Authors from the different parts of the country presented papers related to the topic. Need for information literacy in digital environment was recognized and some authors advocated for integrating information literacy in the curriculum.

The theme of the 51st all India library conference of Indian Library Association held at Kurukshetra University, Haryana was "Information literacy and lifelong learning".

Joshi and Sharma[26] conducted a questionnaire-based survey of first year PG students in Departments of Library and Information Science, Hotel and Tourism Management, Physics and English of Kurukshetra University, to know their need for information literacy education. The study shows that students have low awareness of their information needs and that they need help in Library and Internet use. They suggest for implementation of systematically planned information literacy programme through both instructor and self-learning mode.

Baradol and Gopakumar[27] have discussed the information literacy models prescribed by US National Commission on Library and Information Science, American Library Association, U.K. Standing Conference of National and University Libraries. They have highlighted the lack of information literacy in India and suggested a phase-wise approach to develop information literacy in the country.

Rao and Nagar[28] have recognized the need for information literacy for both teachers and learners. They have stressed on the need for integrating information literacy at various levels of academic activities to improve the quality of education.

Higher education scenario in India is fast growing and increased use of IT has helped in promoting higher education. But there is a need for information literacy activities to enhance the better exploitation of information for various creative activities. India needs to establish a National Information Literacy Forum to develop information literacy awareness in the country[29].

Mandal and Panda[30] have suggested that SCROM (Sharable Content Object Reference Model), which is a widely emerging e-learning standard, developed by the US Department of Defence to address training, development and delivery inefficiencies across its service branches, can be used in India for providing e-literacy.

Information and Library Network (INFLIBNET), Ahmedabad has conducted information literacy programmes to promote information literacy in higher academia and research community and to ensure proper utilization of e-resources by the users. Their information literacy activities include in-house training programmes, user awareness programmes, special training programmes to access Chemical Abstracts database and Jstor e-journals and national level seminars on e-resources[31].

Choudhary and Sethi[32] have attempted to identify the level of skill and efficacy in the library professionals of the university libraries of Orissa, India. The study shows that though the library professionals have basic computer knowledge they should be provided with training on use of IT tools for information searching and using e-resources. Library professionals should also be aware of IPR. They have suggested for providing requisite financial benefits to library professionals for rendering highly technical and modern library services which can be a great motivating factor towards promoting information literacy.

Gedan and Agashe[33] have discussed about the information literacy programmes in India. Their study shows that programmes conducted by the government are literacy programmes and not information literacy programmes. However, IITs, IIMs and Universities do conduct information literacy programmes. But these are mainly conducted by the publishers/aggregators and limited to training in use of their e-journals and databases. They suggest that information literacy should be introduced within the national curricula at all levels including lifelong learning programmes.

Delhi University launched an e-platform to integrate IT with education. IITs have also launched their e-portal to provide students with study material and lecture programmes. IGNOU has developed a database (e-gyankosh) of reading material for different courses being offered by it, for its distance learners. But not much stress is there on providing training for information literacy by these organizations and also no significant steps have been taken by the national and state governments in this direction.

Need for Information Literacy

The ability of a nation to use and create knowledge as capital determines its capacity to empower and enable its citizens by increasing human capabilities. India today stands poised to reap the benefits of a rapidly growing economy and a major demographic advantage that will see the country having the largest resource of young people in the world in the next few decades. The challenge and the opportunity is to galvanize our national potential into a dynamic resource: an informed, enlightened and capable young Indian citizenry which would not only enhance and enrich the processes of national development, but could be a positive force in the world. To make the best of these opportunities to underpin national progress, and to respond to global challenges more strongly than ever before, India needs a knowledge-oriented paradigm of development to give its people and institutions a competitive advantage in all fields of knowledge (The Knowledge Commission Report, 2007).

Information literacy is increasingly important in the contemporary environment of rapid technological change and proliferating information resources. Because of the escalating complexity of this environment, individuals are faced with diverse, abundant information choices-in their academic studies, in the workplace, and in their personal lives. Information is available through libraries, community resources, special interest organizations, media, and the Internet, and increasingly, information comes to individuals in unfiltered formats, raising questions about its authenticity, validity, and reliability. In addition, information is available through multiple media, including graphical, aural, and textual, and these pose new challenges for individuals in evaluating and understanding it. The uncertain quality and expanding quantity of information pose large challenges for the society. The sheer abundance of information will not in itself create a more informed citizenry without a complementary cluster of abilities necessary to use information effectively[34].

According to Breivik, "In this Information Age, it does not matter how well people can analyze or synthesize; if they do not start with an adequate, accurate and up-to-date body of information they will not come up with a good answer"[35].

The need for information literacy is as follows[36]:

(i) Rapid increase in the stream of information due to information revolution.

(ii) Advent of information and communication technologies.

(iii) Vast variety of information sources.

(iv) Changing shape of libraries.

(v) Wide dispersal of information.

(vi) Increase in number of users.

(vii) Research on complex and inter-disciplinary topics.

It is a fact that in today's society only an info-literate can be a fountain-head. Developing countries like India, Pakistan, etc. are not making use of various information resources. The gap between the info-rich and info-poor is widening day by day. There is an urgent need to reduce this gap in order to have social harmony. One of the practical solution is to make people information literate. A massive and action oriented information literacy programme at various levels in various sectors is needed. Unfortunately, India has lagged behind in taking initiative to implement information literacy programmes. Successful information literacy programmes will make people self-motivated learners and thinkers, who are creative, analytical and effective, thereby creating a society that is info-literate[37].

The importance of information literacy has been recognized in developed countries. Enormous research has been carried out in USA, UK, New Zealand, Australia and Mexico. In the higher education sector, library and information professional bodies like Association of College and Research Libraries (USA), Council of Australian University Librarians (Australia) and Society of College, National and University Libraries (UK) have produced standards for information literacy. It has been widely discussed and implemented in national curricula as well as in tertiary non-formal and life-long learning in developed countries. But in India, there is no awareness of the term information literacy and its application in higher education and life-long learning[38].

Information Literacy and Life-long Learning

Information literacy also forms the basis for life-long learning. It is common to all disciplines, to all environments and to all levels of education, while recognizing the disparities in learning styles and in the nature and development of literacy in different countries. It enables the learners to master content and extend their aims to develop both critical understanding and active participation. It enables students to interpret and make informed judgments as users of information sources; but it also enables them to become producers of information in their own right, and thereby to become more powerful participants in the society[39].

One of the goals of bibliographic instruction and information literacy programmes is to help the library users obtain the skills they need to pursue knowledge at any age, independent of a formal educational institution. Public libraries play an important role in meeting this need because they provide access to materials in a wide range of subjects at various reading levels, not only for students enrolled in a formal curriculum but for anyone interested in reading and learning (ODLIS – Online Dictionary for Library and Information Science).

According to IFLA's "Guidelines on Information Literacy and Lifelong Learning", Information Literacy and Lifelong Learning have a strategic, mutually reinforcing relationship with each other that is critical to the success of every individual, organization, institution, and nation-state in the global information society. These two modern paradigms should ideally be harnessed to work symbiotically and synergistically with one another if people and institutions are to successfully survive and compete in the 21st century and beyond.

Both of these concepts are:

- largely self-motivated and self-directed.
- self-empowering.
- self-actuating.

Theoretically, one could pursue the goal of becoming more information literate but not continuously over one's lifetime. Conversely, one could pursue the goal of lifelong learning but not without having first become information literate. Taken alone, neither path maximizes the potentiality of the individual to "learn to learn."

Harnessed together, information literacy and Lifelong Learning could substantially improve:

- Set of personal choices and options opened up for, and offered to, an individual in the context of personal, family and societal matters.
- Quality and utility of education and training in both formal school settings preceding entry into the workforce, and later in informal vocational or on-the-job training settings.
- Prospects of finding and keeping a satisfying job and moving up the career ladder rapidly and with appropriate rewards, and making cost-effective and wise economic and business decisions.

Information literacy is a "set of skills" that can be learned. That set of skills includes a certain attitude toward learning itself, the use of tools, such as online tutorials, the use of techniques, such as working with groups, and the use of methods, such as a reliance on mentors, coaches and ombudspersons.

In contrast, lifelong learning is a good habit that must be acquired and accompanied by the adoption of a positive frame of mind. The willingness to change and a curiosity or thirst for knowledge are very helpful pre-conditions to Lifelong Learning.

An information literate individual is able to[40]:

- Determine the extent of information needed.
- Access the needed information effectively and efficiently.
- Evaluate information and its sources critically.
- Incorporate selected information into one's knowledge base.
- Use information effectively to accomplish a specific purpose.
- Understand the economic, legal, and social issues surrounding the use of information, and access and use information ethically and legally.

Information Literacy and Higher Education

Developing lifelong learners is central to the mission of higher education institutions. By ensuring that individuals have the intellectual abilities of reasoning and critical thinking, and by helping them construct a framework for learning how to learn, colleges and universities provide the foundation for continued growth throughout their careers, as well as in their roles as informed citizens and members of communities. Information literacy is a key component of, and contributor to lifelong learning. Information literacy competency extends learning beyond formal classroom settings and provides practice with self-directed investigations as individuals move into internships, first professional positions, and increasing responsibilities in all arenas of life. Because information literacy augments students' competency with evaluating, managing, and using information, it is now considered by several regional and discipline-based accreditation associations as a key outcome for college students.

For students not on traditional campuses, information resources are often available through networks and other channels, and distributed learning technologies permit teaching and learning when the teacher and the student are not in the same place at the same time. The challenge for those promoting information literacy in distance education courses is to develop a comparable range of experiences in learning about information resources as are offered on traditional campuses. Information literacy competencies for distance learning students should be comparable to those for "on campus" students[41].

Internet, the Information Superhighway, has brought everything within the reach of an individual but it is also wrought with many problems. Brevik[42] has highlighted these problems,

(i) The reliability, currency and relevance of information gathered from Internet sources are difficult to determine.

(ii) Text, images and graphic designs can be manipulated.

(iii) Hypertext may illustrate how ideas connect but they can also lead to false connections and disguise agendas.

(iv) Only 6% of the total information on Internet is scientific or academic, rest is of commercial nature.

(v) Due to the fast rate of obsolescence, even the 6% of information may be outdated.

(vi) On the Internet, only half of the information required to complete a job can be found and 30% of an individual's search time is spent looking for the other half.

The California State University information literacy assessment studies conducted in 2000 and 2001 show an over reliance on Web based information resources. It also shows that students generally search using keywords rather than controlled vocabulary terms which may many times lead to irrelevant retrievals[43].

Higher education, today, has made available a variety of new information resources and evolving array of information technology and access structure. Students have also picked up the skills to send electronic mail, chat and download music but many have not learnt how to effectively locate information; evaluate, synthesize and integrate ideas; use information or give proper credit for information used[44].

Brevik[45] emphasizes on implementation of information literacy to teach students critical thinking skills that will help them determine when and where to find information and how to identify, access, evaluate and effectively use that information.

She also opines that to be successful in preparing today's students for Lifelong Learning in the 21st century, there must be an unprecedented cooperative effort between higher education and the schools to incorporate information literacy skills into the basic curriculum - starting in kindergarten.

Suggestions

It is evident from the extensive literature survey that developed countries woke-up to the need for information literacy way back in 1990s and since then they have made tremendous efforts towards its implementation. But, in India, information literacy has not been discussed seriously and so little has been done to implement it. It is suggested that:

(i) India should develop a National Forum on information literacy.

(ii) Concrete policies should be made for implementation of information literacy.

(iii) Information literacy should be implemented in phased but fast-track manner at all levels.

(iv) India should adopt International Information Literacy Standards and should also develop its own standards to meet the local variations/demands.

(v) Information literacy should be incorporated in the curricula at all levels of education.

(vi) India has realized the potential of distance education, it has to now develop an information literacy programme to specially meet the requirements of distance learners.

(vii) The training of library professionals and academicians as information literacy instructors should be taken up on war footing.

Conclusion

Our country is a fast growing economy with a large percentage of youth. We are also steadily moving towards a complete technology based Information Society. But, we are not taking the right measures to harness, access, classify or analyse all the information being generated and stored. Kehoe[46] has rightly said, access to vast amount of information is not the whole answer. The power to discover the right information quickly and easily, to separate nice to know from need to know information is essential, if superhighway users do not drown in electronic junk information. An information flood does not necessarily mean that people become informed.

Developed countries have realized the potential of information literacy and taken concrete steps for its implementation by creating National Forums and Institutes on information literacy. They have also developed standards for information literacy. They have incorporated information literacy in their development plan and education curricula. Unfortunately, in our country, information literacy has not even been conceptualized. Some small scattered efforts have been made in the form of seminars/conferences and workshops to use specific kind of databases. But, we are yet to take our first big step towards information literacy.

We will have to move fast to implement information literacy at all level, otherwise our efforts towards education reforms, technological developments and research will be diminished. Not recognizing information literacy as the need of the hour today will affect not only efficiency but also the quality of education and research tomorrow.

References

1 IFLA. Guidelines for Information Literacy for Lifelong Learning, IL Section,2006, p.7-8. Available at: http://www.ifla.org (Accessed on 28 August 2011)

2 ALA (American Library Association), http://www.ala.org/ala/acrl/acrlpubs/white papers/presedential.htm (Accessed on 28 August 2011)

3 Pawinun P, Nyamboga C M and Kemaraju T D, *Information Literate Users and the Digital Society*, Proceedings of 4th International Conference of Asian Digital Libraries, Bangalore, 10-12 December 2001, 231-246.

4 Webb Jo and Powis C, *Teaching Information Skills*, (Facet Publishing, London), 2004, p.7-8.

5 Chauhan S K, Prem Chand and Murthy T A V, Information Literacy for Indian Academicians: INFLIBNET Initiatives, *Journal of Library and Information Science*, 31(1) (2006) 45-52.

6 Baradol A K and Gopakumar V. *Role of librarians as presented in the Information Literacy Models*. Proceedings of 51st All India Conference of ILA on Libraries, Information Literacy and Lifelong Learning, Kurukshetra University, Kurukshetra, Haryana, 16-18 December 2005, 198-208.

7 ACRL (Association of College and Research Libraries) Standards Committee, 2000. http://www.acrl.org (Accessed on 28 August 2011)

8 Lau J, *Guidelines on Information Literacy for Lifelong Learning*, (Information Literacy Section, IFLA), 2006, p.1-10.

9 Doyle C S, *Outcome measures for Information Literacy within the National Education Goals of 1990*, Final Report to National Forum on Information Literacy, 1992.

10 Bruce C S, *Information Literacy as a catalyst for education change: A background paper*. White Paper prepared for UNESCO, 2002. <http://eprints.qut.edu.au/4977/1/4977-1.pdf> (Accessed on 28 August 2011)

11 Virkus S, Information Literacy in Europe: A literature review, *Information Research*, 8(4) (2003). http://informationr.net/ir/8-4/infres84.html (Accessed on 28 August 2011)

12 AASL/AECT (American Association of School Libraries and Association of Education and Communication Technology), *Information Power: Building partnership of learning*, (AASL/AECT, Chicago), 1998. http://www.ala.org/ala/mgrps/divs/aasl/aaslarchieve/pubsarchieve/informationpower/Information LiteracyStandards_final.pdf (Accessed on 28 August 2011)

13 ETS (Education Testing Service), *iSkills Assessment*, 2008. < http://www.ets.org/iskills> (Accessed on 28 August 2011)

14 Catts R, *Information Literacies and Lifelong Learning: Keynote Address*, Annual Conference, Swedish Library Association, Boras, Sweden, 2005.

15 Gendina N, *Information Literacy in Russia*, (Information Literacy Publications, IFLA), 2009. <http://www.ifla.org/ files/information-literacy/publications/il-report/russia-2010.pdf> (Accessed on 28 August 2011)

16 IFLA Information Literacy Section, Newsletter, 8(1) (2010). http://ifla.org/ file/ information-literacy/ newsletters/ february-2010.pdf (Accessed on 28 August 2011)

17 Catts R and Lau J, *Towards Information Literacy Indicators*, (UNESCO, Paris), 2008.

18 Orde vom Heike and Wein F, Erfurt, *Information Literacy: An International State-of-the-Art Report*, (Information Literacy Publications, IFLA), 2009. http://www.ifla.org/files/information-literacy/publications/il-report/germany-2009.pdf (Accessed on 28 August 2011)

19 Gendina N, (2009), op.cit 15.

20 Pawinun P, Nyamboga C M and Kemaraju T D, (2001), op.cit. N.3.

21 Mokhtar I A, Schubert F and Shaheen M. Guide Me, Show Me: Personalized Coaching as a means of instilling Information Literacy competencies in students, *LIBRES (Library and Information Science Research Electronic Journal)*, 17 (2) (2007) . http://libres/curtin.edu.au/libres17n2/ contents.htm (Accessed on 28 August 2011)

22 Vezzosi M, Linking teaching and learning: A longitudianal approach to the assessment of Information Literacy, Italy, 2008. <http://edoc.hu-berlin.de/ conferences/ bobcastsss2008/vezzosi-monica-202/PDF/ vezzosi.pdf> (Accessed on 28 August 2011)

23 Stanger K, Information Literacy in Higher Education: A perspective on the roles of librarians and disciplinary faculty, *LIBRES (Library and Information Science Research Electronic Journal)*, 19 (1) (2009) . http://libres.curtin.edu.au/libres19n1/ (Accessed on 28 August 2011)

24 Perez J and Murray M C, Generativity: The new frontier for information and communication, *Technology Literacy, Interdisciplinary Journal of Information, Knowledge and Management*, V. 5, 2010, p.127-137.

25 John K, *National Information Literacy Programmes: Need for enriched approach*, Proceedings of 51st All India Conference of ILA on Libraries, Information Literacy and Lifelong Learning, Kurukshetra University, Kurukshetra, Haryana, 16-18 December 2005, 283-291.

26 Joshi M K and Sharma S, *Need for Information Literacy education in Kurukshetra University*, Proceedings of 51st All India Conference of ILA on Libraries, Information Literacy and Lifelong Learning, Kurukshetra University, Kurukshetra, Haryana, 16-18 December 2005, 249-258.

27 Baradol A K and Gopakumar V, (2005), op.cit. N.6.

28 Rao A S and Nagar B R, *Information Literacy: It's impact on teaching and learning in 21st century*, Proceedings of 51st All India Conference of ILA

on Libraries, Information Literacy and Lifelong Learning, Kurukshetra University, Kurukshetra, Haryana, 16-18 December 2005, 237-248.

29 Karisiddappa C R and Rajgoli I U, *Need for Information Literacy activities in the changimg higher education environment in India,* Proceedings of 51st All India Conference of ILA on Libraries, Information Literacy and Lifelong Learning, Kurukshetra University, Kurukshetra, Haryana, 16-18 December 2005, 209-220.

30 Mandal M and Panda K C, E-learning: A new challenge to engineering education, *IASLIC Bulletin,* 51(4) (2006), 234-241.

31 Chauhan Suresh K, Prem Chand and Murthy T A V, (2006), op.cit. N.5

32 Choudhary B K and Sethi B B, Computer literacy of library professionals in the university libraries of Orrisa: An analytical study, *IASLIC Bulletin,* 54(1) (2009) 15-30.

33 Gedam P B and Agashe A T, *Information Literacy competencies and programmes in India,* Proceedings of International Conference on Academic libraries, Delhi, Oct. 5-8, 2009, p. 520-528.

34 ACRL (Association of College and Research Libraries) Standards Committee, 2000. Op.cit. N.7.

35 Doyle C S, Information Literacy in an Information Society a Concept for Information Age, (ERIC Clearing House on IT, New York), 1994.

36 Jayprakash A and Gupta Yogender V, *Information Literacy: Need to promote the use of digital information services in modern era,* Proceedings of 51st All India Conference of ILA on Libraries, Information Literacy and Lifelong Learning, Kurukshetra University, Kurukshetra, Haryana, 16-18 December 2005, 292-301.

37 Shah P C, Information Literacy to strengthen the democracy and national development, *DLIBCOM,* 4(9) (2009) 1-2.

38 Karisiddappa C R and Rajgoli Iqbalahmad U, (2005), op.cit. N.29.

39 Pejova Zdravska, *Information Literacy: An issue which requests urgent action in developing countries and countries in transition,* White Paper prepared for UNESCO, the US National Commission on Libraries and Information Science and the National Forum on Information Literacy, for use at the Information Literacy meeting of experts, Prague, The Czech Republic, 2002.

40 ACRL (Association of College and Research Libraries) Standards Committee, (2000). Op.cit. N.7.

41 ibid.

42 Breivik P S, 21st Century learning and information literacy, *Change*, 37(2) (2005) 21-27.

43 California State University, *Information Competence Assessment Phase Two, Summary Report*, 2002. <http://www.csupomona.edu./~library/reference/phase2summary.htm> (Accessed on 28 August 2011)

44 Kumar S and Kumar S, *Promoting Information Literacy in Higher Education*, Proceedings of 51st All India Conference of ILA on Libraries, Information Literacy and Lifelong Learning, Kurukshetra University, Kurukshetra, Haryana, 16-18 December 2005, 221-228.

45 Breivik P S, (2005), op.cit. N.42.

46 Kehoe L, Casting the net worldwide, *Financial Times*, 30 (1993) 11.

4

Information Journey through Knowledge Desegregations in Digital Environment

Dr. U. N. Singh
Librarian, Guru Gashidas Vishwavidyalaya, Bilaspur (CG)
E-mail: unsggu@yahoo.in
Dr. Kamalendu Majumdar
Indian Institute of Technology Kharagpur
E-mail: kamal@ library.iitkgp.ernet.in

Abstract

This paper evaluates the changing information requirements of users through their "information journey" in domains of academia through in-depth analysis of findings from interviews. Focus on groups and observations of users have identified three stages to this journey—information initiation, facilitation (or gathering) and interpretation. The study shows that though digital libraries are supporting aspects of users' information facilitation but there are still requirements for them to better support users' information work in context. Users are poorly supported in the initiation phase, as they recognize their information needs, especially with regard to resource awareness. The users are satisfying themselves through the information trustworthy and understanding what it means for a particular individual. Desegregation is the breakdown of observation, usually a common branch of a hierarchy. A scientific journal article is comprised of standard components, such as author names, an abstract, figures, a bibliography, and sections describing methods and results. While creating of digital documents and new tools for manipulating them it comes the ability to facilitate the desegregation of journal articles into separate components.

Introduction

To keep digital library information requirements simple and alive by now, the designers have not only to deal with increasingly complex data sources but are continually confronted by the complexity of different user needs and abilities. The focus of this paper is on the way that users' information requirements change over time. We do this by reference to the users' 'information journey', which has been found to consist of three important stages — information initiation, facilitation (or gathering) and interpretation by focusing on what we are calling here facilitation, within the broader context of information use and in particular, considers how an information need may arise and how existing tools support that early phase of information work and subsequently how user make sense of (or interpret) information in the light of their own needs. For example, interpreting the significance of mathematical findings in context of Database Design.

Changing Needs of Users

Within the academic domains, time-based aspects of social and contextual issues are key elements of information usage (e.g. who's responsible for providing or interpreting the next bit of information, how important the information is at this stage, etc.). As digital libraries can change the context of work practices of people and restructure their relationships with each other and the task at hand, that's why these elements need to be studied. Research reveals that temporal elements of information seeking behaviors in the academic domains report that faculties/ guides are the most important drivers for the information journey.

1. Faculties/ guides are the first information reference point for academic (for initiation and facilitation).
2. Library staff provides the contextual information and interpretation that cannot usually be provided in hardcopy format (interpretation).

In these domains contextualization of information is also important, and that contextualized understanding is often achieved through negotiation with library staff. However, the crucial difference between the domains is that the collaboration highlighted in the academic domain is that between librarians and the users. Although digital library research has concentrated on the facilitation of information, there have been a growing number of studies analyzing the interpretation and use of information. Breqer argues that digital libraries should be more pro-active, and notes the importance of interpretation and application of information for digital libraries. He argues that value can be added during the mediation process through information translating (e.g. language services) and publication. Recent applications demonstrate how digital library information can be integrated within the authoring and publishing process and support the interpretation of information. Integrated environments for both seeking and organizing information are utilized to support the sequential activities of the writing process.

Digital Library Application Used

A pre-defined concept of a 'Digital Library' was not employed, so that users could explore what they perceived as comprising a digital library. However, the resources referred to most frequently by the user as digital library (such as the ACM Digital Library and the Cochrane Library) [fig-1] with both domain.

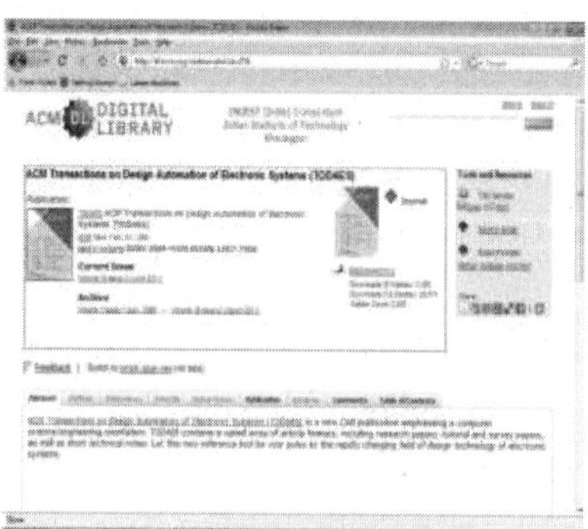

a. ACM Digital library

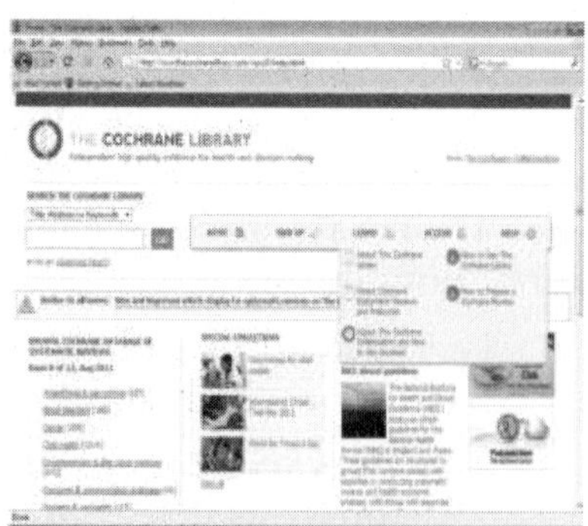

b. Cochrane Library

Figure 1. Academic Library

Academics and Academic Librarians

The findings writing the academic domains are based on data gathered from a university that is split over several geographically distributed campuses. Focus groups and in-depth interviews were used to gather data from 25 academics and librarians from 4 different campuses within the university. All of the respondents had a high degree of computer literacy and had used digital libraries at some point.

Data Collection and Analysis

Three issues guided the focus of questions within all the studies:

- Perceptions of individual's roles within the organization and their information requirements (both changing and constant).
- Perceptions of information practices, social structures and organizational norms (again both changing and constant).
- The evolution of practices, structures and norms, and their impact on information resource awareness, acceptance and use.

Table 1: Participant Descriptive Data

Group	Job	Status & Role	No	Major DLs used
Academic	Lectures (CS, Business, Humanities)	Research & Teaching roles (Lecture to Professor	12	ACM Dl & LEXIS
Library	Librarians (Business, Engineering, Humanities)	Subject Librarian through Senior Library Management)	13	Several DL like Cochorane, ACM Digital library

Result

The data analysis from all settings have shown that users interact with information temporally, traveling through a personal or a team-based information journey. The journey has three stages:

- Information initiation: Someone, something or some event initiates information requirements.

- Information facilitations: Someone or some system facilitates required information retrieval.
- Information interpretations: Someone or some system supports contextual information interpretation and /or modification.

The results are reviewed in two sections: an overview of the resources for user ethnic information journey and a detailed analysis of the sub-issues relating to each stage of the information journey (i.e. initiation, facilitation, interpretations) , specifically in relation to digital libraries.

Users' Information Journey Resources Use

People are supported on their information journey by both online and offline resources, and also by their social interactions. The findings from our studies reveal the role of different resources in the users' transitions through the stages of their information journey [Table2]

Digital libraries were identified as mainly supporting the facilitation of information (rather than initiation or interpretation) in the users' information journey. Academic librarians were found, however, to utilize digital libraries. Typically, specialized offline resources also support their need for serendipitous interactions with articles indirectly related to their area of expertise.

Table 2: Pattern of resources usage

	Initiation		Facilitations	
Academic / Librarian	Colleague , DL email alert & bulletin	Coursework/ Personal query	Digital Library, Book, Web	Colleague
Lectures	Colleague	Course Development, Research	Book, colleague, Web, Some Digital Libraries.	As above

Conclusion

This paper identifies users changing information needs over time via an 'information journey' that involves the use of online and offline resources. In the first stage of the information journey, information requirements are initiated by either an active specific task or condition, or passively (e.g. by friends and family, information intermediaries or the press). After initial information requirements have been established, most users require support in facilitating its retrieval and then its interpretation and application.

Digital library designers will learn from these findings that there are many additional ways that users within the academic and other domain require information resources to support their journeys.

Recent digital library advances have facilitated access to different types of temporal data. However, digital libraries have further to go in supporting temporal users changing needs for all type of information (both theoretical and practical) according to varying contextual requirements. One major problems identified was that of resource awareness. Unlike academicians, librarians were aware of a wide variety of digital library resources and utilized them to their full potential. They also utilized alerts to keep them abreast of frequent changes and to initiate further searches. Few other users were aware of these tools. Ultimately, digital library application should seek to support users' changing needs in the type of information required and what they wish to do with that information with RSS Feed.

References

1. Adams A and Blandford A. The unseen and unacceptable face of digital libraries. Journal of Digital Libraries, 12(2) 2011: 71-81.
2. Albers M.J, Multidimensional analysis for custom content for multiple audiences, In Proceeedings of ACM SIGDOC '11 pp.12-15
3. Allen R B, A query interface for an event gazetteer. In proceding of the 9th ACM/IEEE-CS Joint Conf. On Digital Libraries (2010), pp. 72-73..
4. Majumdar K, Socialcare information systems (SOCIS) for information age, FID '98 Article No – 0202119 pp- II-1-5.

5

Knowledge Management in Digital Era

Anil Agrawal
Assistant Librarian
Central Library, Banaras Hindu University
Varanasi - 221005

1. Introduction

Communication technology has brought about some fundamental changes during the past few years and has influenced both teaching and knowledge management. Digital networks are transforming the way we work and are reshaping our personal communication and entertainment. The application of Information and Communication Technology in the performance of the library activities has facilitated the organisers to manage knowledge better and promote its use among the seekers of information. The librarians today are to ensure that the right information is delivered to the right person at the right time so as to help them to take the most appropriate decision. This also complies with S.R.Ranganathan's Fourth Law of Library Science. Knowledge Management as a system is developing rapidly in the present era in the form of computer-based collection and organisation of knowledge (data or information) and its dissemination. In that the digitization process helps towards knowledge or information to be shared with others through Internet/ Intranet.

2. Knowledge Management

Knowledge management is a set of processes that govern the creation, distribution and use of knowledge. It is also described as a collaborative process through which organizations generate value for their intellectual assets. T.Beckman states about knowledge management: "Knowledge is reasoning about information and data to actively enable performance, problem solving, decision making, learning and teaching." The process includes formal procedures to collect such information as the lessons learned during project executions and the best practices occurring throughout the organization, and a well-established infrastructure, network for transferring knowledge between employees are tools to facilitate process. Once the process captures the organization's knowledge, the real power occurs when the users while utilizing the information, use it by putting the shared information into action. It protects intellectual decay, seeks opportunities to enhance decisions, services and products through adding intelligence, increasing value and providing flexibility. Exchange of knowledge is more likely to happen in a network environment, particularly when there is commonality of interests and shared problems to solve.

2.1 *Knowledge Management in Libraries*

Knowledge Management in the libraries is getting more and more important along with the development of knowledge economy. Human Resource Management is the core of knowledge management in libraries. The most important resource in the knowledge economy system is the talents who grasp knowledge. In the knowledge economy era, the libraries will give importance to training and education of the library staffs to raise their knowledge level and ability of acquiring and innovating knowledge.

2.2 *Knowledge Management Technologies*

The technologies of knowledge management, in brief, are:

a) *Web Technologies*: It includes metadata tagging, intelligent search, e-commerce, content management, record management, archiving and backup.

b) *Training*: It includes e-learning, distance training, multimedia, and intelligent littering systems.

c) *Artificial Intelligence*: This includes expert systems, machine learning, text generation, and natural language.

d) *Communication*: This includes documents management collaboration, groupware, and direct creativity technologies.

e) *Knowledge Discerning*: This includes data warehousing, data mining, text mining, knowledge visualization, and knowledge repository.

3. Role of Library Professionals in Knowledge Management

In recent years technologies are changing very fast. Library professionals are searching for the new roles in order to fit themselves into space that is referred to as digital world librarians. So, there should be improved processes and additional technological tools that will help to manage information. The most important one is to preserve the documents through digitization and making them accessible on demand or when needed.

3.1 Digitization and its purpose

Digitization is the process of converting analog information into digital format. The materials to be converted could be letters, manuscripts, books, photographs, maps, audio recordings, microforms, motion pictures, ephemera, etc. Three-dimensional objects can also be digitized. The goal of digitization is to improve access to the materials. To that end, most digitized materials become searchable via databases on the Internet.

Libraries collect and preserve sources of information in order to serve the relevant among them to information seekers. The most obvious benefit of digitization is to preserve and provide the aggregation of various resources, in digital form, using digital technology. Resources are preserved for future generation and simultaneously these are made accessible for the current use also.

In order that the materials to be digitized, they must be converted using a method to capture the material digitally (e.g., scanning, digital photography, digital recording) without altering the information that the material contains. That means that the digital representation contains the same information/data as the analog representation.

A wide variety of equipment is available to assist in this process. Standards and guidelines exist in order to ensure that the conversion processes used are consistent and correct so that the results are of a high-quality.

3.1.1 Steps for Digitization

Phase I

The following points need be considered in this phase:

- Selection of samples and producing test images.
- Preservation-quality images: types and resolution , enhancement, grayscale and colour
- Image compression
- Defining and deriving access-quality images
- Hardware for scanning

Phase II

In this phase, actual work starts for the digitisation of the document. The document is scanned with the suggested type and resolution and then the images are compressed and stored in the archival storage. To link the images from point to point, programmes are prepared by using HTML and Microsoft FrontPage packages. The access is given by the WWW browser to the end users.

3.1.2 Tools Required for Digitization

Primary tools required for digitization of documents can be categorized into :

- Hardware
- Software

3.1.2.1 Hardware

(a) Computer

Since the power of digital image creation lies in computer, speed of computer is of vital concern.

- **CPU :** It is the computer's brain. Primary task of CPU is to receive programme instructions, process and send them. CPU's speed and sophistication in managing information is crucial to the efficient use of programmes like Adobe Photoshop.

- **PCI Bus** : Computer does not work alone. It processes the information flowing to and from it over a data highway called BUS. Now-a-days BUS speed is increasing fast.
- **Ethernet**: It is a network protocol. It allows data to be transferred to printers and other computers faster than data sent over standard serial port. It speeds up the process several times faster.
- **Silicon Graphics:** It is being used to have high quality output. It is used for effects. It can transform a wire-framed model into photo realistic 3D object.
- **RAM:** Digital images and digital imaging software can quickly gobble up the entire RAM in the system. It must be realized that without enough RAM, it is not possible to load or create digital image of the size and number of colors we wish.

(b) Storage Devices

Digital images are voracious. In no time they eat up all the space on the system disk. For working in digital imaging field, one has to have enough capacity for storage, editing, backup, archive, etc.

- **Hard drives:** Graphic professionals recommend a minimum of oneTB storage space for graphic system depending on the type of work. Speed of hard drive is measured by seek time and by transfer rate. Faster the hard drive lower the seek time.
- **Removable hard drive:** It can be used for backing up digital images and storing files.
- **Optical drive:** It can hold data upto 25GB
- **DAT drive (Digital Audio Tape):** It is one of the most economical media to store data. The latest models can store more than 300 GB data. With DAT, the archiving and retrieving of data is not fast because information is recorded and accessed sequentially.

- **DVD ROM drive:** It is an essential peripheral for digitisation. To use a DVD ROM, to view photo images, XA (extended architecture) is needed, which enables to add new photo DVD images on DVD RW until its storage capacity is full. While purchasing DVD ROM drive, speed needs to be considered. Presently various speed models are available.
- **Flash memory:** It is primarily used in memory cards, USB flash drives, solid state drives. Its memory varies from one Gigabyte to several Gigabyte.

(c) Monitors

Monitor's sharpness, size and clarity of colours is crucial to create professional looking digital images. It is suggested to have an 18" monitor with 24 bit colour card.

(d) Digitizing Devices

Digitizing devices convert photos, artwork and raw materials of the real world into digital data that can be edited by graphics programmes. The most common digitizing devices are:

- ➢ Scanners
- ➢ Digital Cameras

- **Scanners :** Scanners are primarily used to digitise photographs, artwork and slides. They come in all shapes and sizes. Some produce sharp, high quality images while others produce only acceptable images for positioning purposes. There are many types of scanners, such as, Flat bed scanner, Slide scanner, Rotary drum, Quick document scanner, etc.
- **Digital Camera:** Digital camera digitizes image on the click of a button, often storing image to a tiny hard disk or battery powered memory chips. The images are then downloaded to a computer through a cable connected to its SCSI or serial port.

(e) Out Put Devices

Printers, Modem and CD/DVD Writer are some of the output devices.

3.1.2.2 *Software*

There are a number of softwares, which can be used for different functions:

- For editing images.
- For page layout programmes, to integrate text and graphics.
- File transferring utilities, to share files between computer platforms.
- File translation programmes, to convert files from graphics.
- File compression software.

The recommended softwares are Adobe Photoshop, Paintshop Pro, Frontpage. Professional software, etc. along with some of the open source software like dspace and greenstone.

4. Digital Library

Digital library is an electronic collection of real or virtual resources. A digital library may allow either online or offline access to the elements it organizes and houses, and may include multimedia as well as multilingual data. Digital libraries attach content specific and highly descriptive metadata such as, descriptors or keywords to describe each item in the collection. There are several advantages of a digital library over a conventional library. These include minimizing storage space and cutting down costs of library maintenance and resource distribution

Although conventional libraries do preserve socio-cultural ambiences within their spaces, a digital library can provide more equitable and widely distributed access at lower costs. Moreover, it may be most appropriate means of organizing intellectual artifacts that cannot be represented or distributed in printed formats, such as audio/video multimedia contents. According to the National Science Foundation, a digital library ought to serve as an intellectual commons, where diverse members of the community may share their knowledge and practices. The Association for Research Libraries (ARL) points out that the digital libraries can serve as a network of links to other digital libraries.

5. Challenge to Library Professionals in Digital Era

Due to emergence of a digital library, the role of library professionals has changed from traditional to digital environment. Now-a-days users face an information landscape that is totally different form the sheltered heavens. Today, the library without walls has become a reality. While the delivery of services and resources has changed formats, the basic values and norms of profession have remained constant. The production, diffusion and transfer of knowledge are the major tasks which the librarians are to perform.

Realizing the significant changes in information seeking behaviour of the users through the use of the internet, libraries have responded by making their catalogues and collections available online, and also making changes in their infrastructure towards adopting new services as per the needs of the user community.

6. The Indian Scenario

India is faced with severe challenges including the need for better educational resources as well as appropriate technology infrastructure. Early research suggests that the process of making resources available through digital libraries in India may suffer a great deal due to:

(i) Lack of relevant content;

(ii) Poor connectivity in rural and urban areas; and

(iii) Dearth of meta-data standards capabilities.

Digital libraries in India would afford greater access to resource material, outweigh operational costs of setting up conventional libraries, and create better opportunities for knowledge management. Through internet it has now become possible to be a part of the'Global Village' and exchange information rapidly. With all these facilities it is possible to access hundreds of databases and make the information available to the user community in the country. The tools and technologies are there, so there is no excuse for us in India, not to start planning digital libraries. Some of the institutions in the country have already started this work and some others are planning to start. The notable among these are: National Informatics Centre (New Delhi), Banaras Hindu University (Varanasi), University of Madras (Chennai), Survey of India Library (Dehradun), and many more.

The digitized media is a very important tool for searching and locating the information faster to the targeted user. In order to achieve that goal a national network and expertise is essential, which the National Informatics Centre is providing to the libraries in India. It is now up to the libraries to utilise these facilities so as to provide pin-pointed, better and quick services to the users.

References

1. Beckman, T. (1997), A Methodology For Knowledge Management, International Association of Science and Technology for Development AI and Soft Computing Conference: Banff, Alberta, Canada.
2. Jeevan, V. K. A (2000). Flow, availability and accessibility of Information to Science, Engineering and Technology, 19th National Seminar paper IASLIC, p.41-48.
3. Kalyani Krishnan. Knowledge Management : The Role of Digitized Libraries. Paper presented in ICAL 2009, held at University of Delhi, New Delhi, 5th to 8th October, 2009.
4. Mahapatra, Piyush Kanti and Chakrabarti, Bhubaneswar (2002). Knowledge management in libraries. New Delhi, Ess Ess Publications
5. Nattar, S and Selvakumar, M (2009). Knowledge management in Libraries. ILA Bulletin, 45(1-2), p. 14-17.
6. Sharma, Shobha, Arya Sukriti and Gopal Krisan (2006). Knowledge management in digital library : A challenge to library professionals. ILA Bulletin, 42(2), p.10-13.
7. Sheng Xiaoping (1999). Knowledge management of libraries in 21st century. Library Magazine, Vol.8, p. 29-32.
8. Singha, Krishnamati, Shrivastava, V D and Singha, Gouri. Essence of Knowledge management on libraries in modern era. Paper presented in 3rd Convention PLANNER, held at Assam University, Silchar, 10-11 Nov., 2005.
9. Sood, Aditya Dev & Chandrasekharan, Uma. Digital Libraries in India : A baseline study. CKS Working paper, A report commissioned by EDC.

6

Role of Librarian in Knowledge Management

Dr. Vaishali Choukhande (Gudadhe)
Associate Professor & Head, DLIS
Sant Gadge Baba Amravati University, Amravati
E-mail : vchoukhande@rediffmail.com

Abstract

The author focuses the role of librarian in Knowledge Management. The issues and challenges are discussed. Advance services need be provided by using ICT tools and techniques, knowledge management systems, internet, web resources, digital library, virtual library, etc. The libraries seek to share information and knowledge among the academic community within the institution. Knowledge management has become a key issue in universities due to changes in knowledge cultures.

Keywords: Knowledge Management; ICT; Information Management; Digital Library; Virtual Library; Library and Information Centre

Introduction

The challenge of Knowledge Management is to determine what information within an organization qualifies as "valuable." All information is not knowledge, and all knowledge is not valuable. The key is to find the worthwhile knowledge within a vast sea of information. The term Knowledge Management (KM) has become a key issue for government, industry and certainly Information

Technology (IT) executives. Organizations are becoming increasingly aware of the importance of managing knowledge, like any other asset, to improve their competitive advantage. Knowledge Management is only a perspective for implementing organizational change, which it gets people to record knowledge and then share it.

One of the aims of Knowledge Management in libraries is to promote the knowledge exchange among library staffs, strengthen innovation consciousness and abilities, and enhance the library staff's enthusiasm and abilities for learning, making the knowledge most efficiently applied to the library activities and rebuilding the library into a learning organization. A library, as it is well-known, plays a vital role in organizing, managing and disseminating knowledge among the users.

A set of knowledge management processes as proposed by P. Galagan are:

- Generating new knowledge.
- Accessing knowledge from external sources.
- Representing knowledge in documents, databases, software and so forth.
- Embedding knowledge in processes, products, or services.
- Transferring existing knowledge around an organization.
- Using accessible knowledge in decision-making.
- Facilitating knowledge growth through culture and incentives.
- Measuring the value of knowledge assets and the impact of knowledge management.

Characteristics of Knowledge Management in Libraries

The role of KM in libraries has become more and more important along with the development of knowledge economy. It is a new management mode. The following characteristics are comparable with conventional management.

1. Information Technology is a Tool for KM

Knowledge acquisition is the starting point of knowledge management in libraries. The application of information technologies enlarges the scope of knowledge acquisition, raises knowledge acquisition speed and reduces knowledge acquisition cost. It is impossible to accomplish such important tasks by using man's brains only in the modern society in which the knowledge changes with each passing day. It will be possible to link closely knowledge sources and knowledge workers by computer networks, thus constructing knowledge networks in libraries based on realization of single-point information. (Wang,1999)

2. Human Resource Management in KM

An initiative of MHRD "AAKASH" (Sakshat Tablet) has been launched by the Ministry of HRD on 5th October, 2011 to provide the distance education to the end users through E-Learning support. A-VIEW class room is simple, user friendly video conferencing software. It provides wide opportunity to an experienced faculty to teach his/her expertise in a live interactive mode to various geographical places around the world. It also provides an environment where students can continue learning on their own. Document sharing, Whiteboard, Audio-Video and Chat are the major functionalities of A-VIEW. A-VIEW Meeting, a conference center where meeting halls have no walls. Colleagues from across the globe will be brought together face-to-face electronically to share the information. (www.aview.in). Library as a resources centre should provide all types of material, which is required in teaching-learning process.

3. User Services in KM

There are various services to be provided in the library through Intranet i.e. Directory service, staff news, budget information, Reports, Agreements, policies, Management information, E-Journals, Forms, Training material, Question banks, Discussion groups, Archive, OPAC, Repositories, etc.

Knowledge Management Benefits:

The Knowledge management benefits can be categorized as follows:

- Knowledge benefits.
- Intermediate benefits.
- Organizational benefits.

A typical example would be of an organization or an academic institution or a government agency which has numerous physical files. Categorization and segregation into working databases allows the users who need specific information to access the databases more efficiently through word or category searches instead of having to sift through so many folders. Updating of these databases will also result in having the most recent and relevant information and knowledge stored and easily accessible by any staff and users who may need any specific information. The category of organizational benefits includes better/faster innovation, improved user service, reduced knowledge loss, and increased productivity for better performance.

Library as a Knowledge Management Centre

Library and information centres should develop and renovate its infrastructural design, library sources and advanced services by using ICT tools and techniques, Knowledge management systems, Internet, Web resources, Digital libraries, Virtual libraries, etc.

Following is the data wise technologies to be developed for the knowledge management.

- Intranet within an organization
- Document management systems
- Information retrieval systems
- Relational and object databases
- Electronic publishing
- Groupware and work flow systems
- Push technologies
- Help desk applications
- Brain storming applications
- Data warehousing and data mining

The Knowledge can be created, stored and disseminate through the following resources:

- Research publications of the teachers
- Research publications of the students

- Recorded invited lectures of the stalwarts
- Recorded experiments in the practical laboratory
- Demos, tutorials, assignments, etc.
- Web Portal of the library
- Web OPAC of the library
- Subject Experts panel
- Customers service
- Reports
- Products
- Markets
- Video conferencing among the librarians and users.
- Virtual library tours
- Photo gallery of the events
- Publications of the institution

In short libraries can create knowledge repositories to serve the users in the Knowledge Management Centre.

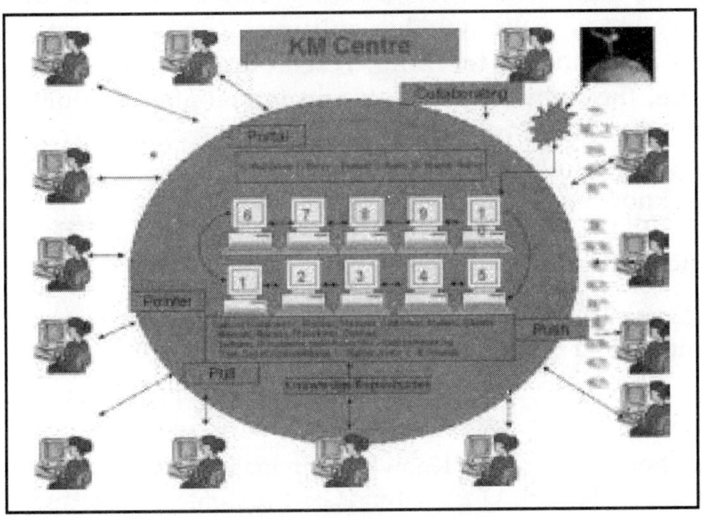

Role of Librarian in Knowledge Management

Role of Librarian has changed in the Knowledge Management era. The library should be well equipped with the computers, Internet, and networking facility. Information technology and systems can provide effective support in implementing knowledge management. There are various issues of library to be handled jointly by the librarian and IT professionals. Librarians should work together with IT professionals and others to develop an appropriate knowledge management systems. The traditional library should be appended with the digital and virtual environment to provide the service effectively and efficiently.

Conclusion

Knowledge management as it evolved in the business sector is slowly gaining acceptance in the academic sector. Libraries face a challenge to better create and disseminate knowledge to society and also they have traditional focus on the acquisition of knowledge and learning. Among these challenges are financial pressures, increasing public scrutiny and accountability, rapidly evolving technologies, changing staff roles, diverse staff and student demographics, competing values and a rapidly changing world. A university seeks to share information and knowledge among the academic community within the institution. Knowledge management has become a key issue in the universities due to changes in knowledge cultures. They are part of society through engaging in teaching, research and community service. Therefore, the knowledge created in universities through research and teaching should be relevant to the end users. Government is also focusing on higher education to provide quality education and to manage knowledge effectively.

References

1. Galagan, P. (1997). "Smart Companies (Knowledge Management," Training and Development Vol.51(12). p.20-25.
2. Wang, Delu. (1999). The collection and processing of knowledge. http://www.bsti.ac.cn/bsti_kmchina/gei/048_001.htm
3. Shanhong, Tang (2009) Knowledge management in libraries in the 21st century. *In* 66th IFLA Council and General Conference. Jerusalem, Israel, 13-18th August.
4. Aswath, Lalitha and Gupta, Sangita (2006) Knowledge management tools and academic library services *In* ICAL 2006 – Vision and roles of the future academic libraries. Educational Roles of Academic Libraries

5. Sharma, Ajay Kumar. (2010) Knowledge management and new generation of libraries information services: A concepts. *International Journal of Library and Information Science* Vol. 1(2) p. 024-030, March, 2010. (http://www.academicjournals.org/ijlis)

7

Knowledge Management
Some Obstacles

Dr.(Mrs.) Puspanjali Jena
Reader, P.G. Dept. of Library and Information Science
Utkal University,Vanivihar,Bhubaneswar, ODISHA
E-mail : Pjutkal1987@yahoo.co.in

Abstract

In knowledge management environment creating knowledge is based on experience; the other way is through teamwork. Either way, the outcome is the same, because the focus is knowledge sharing. Team formation and teamwork begin with experienced individuals working jointly on a project. Knowledge sharing is influenced by personality, attitude, vocational reinforces, and work norms. The concept also considers organizational culture, company strategies, and organization policies. It is not so straightforward, because people are more used to knowledge hoarding than knowledge sharing. Knowledge architecture is a combination of people, content, and knowledge sharing. They are interdependent and inseparable. People with knowledge provide content, relying on technology to transfer and share knowledge. Thus the present paper focuses on the different hindrances in the case of knowledge sharing in any type of organization.

Introduction

Knowledge management (KM) is a newly emerging, interdisciplinary business model knowledge within the framework of an organization as its focus. It is rooted in disciplines, including business, economics, psychology, and information management. Knowledge management involves people, technology, and processes in overlapping parts. KM contains several integral parts:

- Using accessible knowledge from outside sources.
- Embedding and storing knowledge in business processes, products, and services.
- Representing knowledge in databases and documents.
- Promoting knowledge growth through the organization's culture and incentives.
- Transferring and sharing knowledge throughout the organization.
- Assessing the value of knowledge assets and impact on a regular basis.

Basic needs of knowledge management

Based on the author's years of experience and existing literature, several trends are worth noting: Knowledge is productive only when it is captured in people's minds. Because most knowledge is acquired on the job, through training and in interaction with people, it behoves every organization to nurture and invest in the skill level of employees so that they become more productive in present and future jobs. With proper incentives and benefits, this is the kind of investment that promotes loyalty and discourages defection.

- *Knowledge*: More and more companies are discovering that leveraging knowledge is best served through decentralized intelligence. This means empowerment of leverging knowledge workers and funneling tacit and explicit knowledge to the level where the actual work is performed. This type of decentralization is expected to make organizations more responsive to a changing environment, where the time for decision making is measured in seconds, not in hours. Companies that have human knowledge updated regularly will find greater opportunities for creativity and innovation through the unique ideas that inevitably result.
- C*reativity:* It is worth repeating that the driving force of knowledge work is creativity—an essential driver for

innovation. The key is not so much the amount of knowledge available, but how knowledge is used. This is a major parting point from knowledge automation systems. Creativity is breaking loose from the traditional way of doing business. Recruitment and compensation strategies are being revised to address the creativity imperative. Aspiring candidates with potential will be highly sought. Technology will continue to take over routine and redundant work, freeing knowledge workers to concentrate on human insight and foresight.

- ***Innovation of new ideas:*** It is believed that knowledge management will be an entry requirement for competitive advantage and that the future will belong to innovators, not copycats. This, of course, will be expensive: recruiting intelligence is not cheap or easy. The pressure will increase on human resource managers and recruiters to scout for the right sources of talent and secure a continuing stream of candidates to support the long-term needs of the corporation.
- ***Strategic planning :*** For years, we have been working on the assumption that corporate capital is the enabler of the enterprise. Capital continues to be important, especially when it comes to funding new projects and investing in equipment and technology. However, the trend is toward using corporate knowledge in a global competitive market. Knowledge management requires action, foresight, and focused strategic planning.

Scope and objectives of the paper

Today's knowledge age brings with it an increasingly complex business environment worldwide. Companies, organizations, centers need to address knowledge sharing, knowledge collaboration, and knowledge dissemination to be able to compete in an un-predictable marketplace. In knowledge management environment knowledge sharing means faster processing, no duplication of effort, and reacting more responsively to new organization or business opportunities. The information revolution has placed emphasis on sharing huge amounts of information that is now accessible on the Internet. In this time of "e-everything," information is accessible from business-to-business, business-to-consumer, and consumer-to-consumer. KM is slowly gaining acceptance across industries. Several factors triggered interest in KM:

- *The pace of change has accelerated dramatically during the past decade.* Companies are looking at innovative ways of taking on the competition. Innovation is the one core competency needed by all organizations ***(Drucker 1969).***
- *Globalization and geographic dispersion changed the organization's scope.* More and more organizations are trying to lean on years of experience to manage their global commitment in a timely and profitable fashion.
- *Downsizing and reengineering resulted in staff attrition and knowledge drain.* This prompted organizations to assess their knowledge core and make more effective use of it. Reengineering assumed a one-time fix to a situation. This created a vicious cycle, where solutions became new problems.
- *Networking and data communications made it easier and faster to share knowledge.* Knowledge sharing is becoming the best way to distribute expertise across and around the firm via technology. Technology alone is insufficient.
- *The increasing dominance of knowledge as a basis for improving efficiency and effectiveness triggered many companies to find the means for utilizing the knowledge they have gained from previous experience.*

With these factors, the paper is a theoretical approach which highlights the basic barriers of knowledge sharing and the objectives of the paper is to know how knowledge management works for the survival of the organization. ii. How Knowledge being the core competency are no sharable due to poor managerial commitment; poor technological infrastructure; lack of methodology; lack of organizational structure; lack of organizational culture; lack of motivation and rewards; staff retirement, etc.

Knowledge management barriers: Literaure review

Researchers and authors have approached the issue of barriers to information and knowledge transfer from many different perspectives, and as such there are different, non-contradictory, views.

Kluge et al. (2001) identify two main barriers to developing a knowledge creating and sharing culture: (1) ***Not invented here.*** The 'not invented here' syndrome describes the tendency to negelect or, worst still, disparage knowledge that is not created within an individual's department.This problem can arise from a genuine mistrust of outside knowledge. (2) ***Knowledge is power.*** The 'knowledge is power' syndrome refers to a mindset that place the values of knowledge to the individual ahead of its value to the company. At its most basic, knowledge sharing starts by taking the time to help others. In a successful company there is always time pressure but the extra minutes spent with a colleague explaining something will be repaid later. In spite of this, just as people distrust external knowledge, they also see their own knowledge as a part of their personal competitive achievement. The ideal solution is for employee to share knowledge, as this is where the most significant gains are expected. Conversely, if one decides to hoard knowledge whilst the other shares knowledge then the power balance is shifted in favour of employee who hoards. As no employee wishes to be taken advantage of or if the culture is one where individual performance is rated above team performance, the expected behaviour will be one where both employees hoard. This will maintain a *status quo* where employees are keen to ensure their personal competitive advantage is not eroded. That said, the overall effect within the organization is one where knowledge is selectively shared resulting in modest gains in performance for the organization. If this is the norm, the hoarding process will be counter-productive. This is one of the critical changes that should be targeted by any knowledge management programme, and one that should have positive repercussions beyond purely the exchange of knowledge. ***Kluge et al. (2001)*** acknowledge the importance of technology in delivering information. However, the deciding factor is whether an organization will benefit is down to how the employees pull and share the information and knowledge. Their research shows that successful organizations use a combination of both push and pull. Push systems are top-down in design and dependent on technology for the flow of information. Pull systems are bottom-up in design and more dependent on an individual's innate desire for knowledge. It is this desire coupled with a culture of co-operation that determines how successful the pull delivery mechanism will be. ***Szulanski (1996)*** also supports the view that relationships between employees contribute to knowledge transfer failures. Nevertheless, he points out that prior research suggest ing that four sets of factors likely to influence the difficulty of knowledge transfer: characteristics of the knowledge transferred; characteristics of the source of the knowledge; characteristics of the recipient of the knowledge/information; and context in which the knowledge/information is transferred. Some authors place an almost exclusive emphasis on the attributes of the knowledge transferred—***(Zander and Kogut (1995); Winters (1987).*** Others stress the characteristics of the situation in *which the transfer occurs* ***Arrow, (1969).*** However, all four sets of factors can be used together in a model that allows their relative influence to be measured. ***Szulanski (1996)*** states that contrary to conventional wisdom that places primary blame on motivational factors, the major barriers to internal knowledge transfer are shown to be knowledge related factors such as the recipient's lack of absorptive capacity, causal ambiguity, and an arduous relationship between the source and the recipient. Although Szulanski's research was carried out using manufacturing sites it cannot be assumed his findings will map on to the IBM supply chain. That said, there is no reason to believe that the barriers described will not impact knowledge transfer to a greater or lesser degree. ***Gupta and Michailova (2004)*** found that knowledge sharing among departments within the same organization is in reality not as natural as it may appear. In fact knowledge sharing hostility is a phenomenon that widely dominates organizational reality— ***Husted and Michailova, (2002). Gupta and Michailova (2004)*** identified three difficulties with the process of sharing knowledge: (1) ***Knowledge is developed at a local level.*** By definition knowledge is embedded in a certain cognitive and behavioural context. Without understanding the context one cannot inquire into the reasoning and the assumptions behind the particular piece of Knowledge. (2) ***Knowledge is a symmetricsdiy distributed***. Often those who possess the knowledge are not inclined to invest time and effort to share it without expecting reciprocity, as resources are finite and scarce (***Davenport and Prusak, 1998; O'Dell and Grayson, 1998).*** (3) ***Knowledge sharing is voluntary.*** Efficient knowledge sharing depends on the willingness of individuals to identify the knowledge they possess and to share the knowledge when required. ***Nonaka, (1994).***

Moreover, ***Gupta and Michailova (2004)*** believe that an individual's ability to appreciate new knowledge is a function of their absorptive *capacity*. ***Cohan and Levinthal, (1990); Szulanski, (1996).*** What is interesting about ***Gupta and Michailova's (2004)*** research is that it does not look at the organization as a single entity but as a collection of departments working together, and the different demands they place on knowledge creation. Through their research they identified three aspects of the complex organization that can hinder knowledge creation and sharing:*The nature* of *the different businesses means different knowledge management requirements.* Some departments or business units will operate within different environments; some more stable then others. Therefore, KM systems may need to be modified by each department in order to support the internal knowledge creation process.

The different nature of the different business activities. The nature of the different businesses predispose different requirements to the type of knowledge sought as well as different preferences to how the needed knowledge is obtained.

The way codified and *personalized systems are used within each department or business unit*: Although the common practice is to assess organizations for codified or personalized knowledge systems, at a department level, depending on the mission and expected deliverables of the department, the best fit from a codified or personalised strategy may not fit with the overall organization's assessment.This is an important view as the reality of today's organization, especially a complex supply chain, is that roles and expected deliverables will vary between departments or business units. Therefore, when defining a knowledge strategy, an understanding of how departments, or business units that make up the organization, use information and create knowledge needs to be taken into consideration.Interestingly the literature suggests that when technology is the primary focus of the knowledge delivery system sub-optimal results are achieved ***Barson et al., (2000); Gupta and Michailova,(2004); Marwick, (2001); Pawar et al.(, 2002).*** The assumption that knowledge management relies heavily upon social patterns, practices, and processes goes far beyond computer-based technologies and infrastructures ***Coleman,(1998); Davenport and Prusak, (1998).*** Empirical evidence on barriers to knowledge sharing stresses the importance of behavioural and cultural factors rather than outlining reasons associated with technology ***De Long and Fahey, (2000); Skyrme and Amidon,(1997). Spender (1996)*** and ***Tsoukas (1996)*** also question the value of technology driven approaches, in particular, those directed towards knowledge codification. ***Pawar et al. (2002)*** also question the effectiveness of a purely codified (technology driven) approach to knowledge management. It is their belief that modern management practice has only tended to focus on centralizing, controlling, and standardizing knowledge. Such codification allows the marginal cost of knowledge acquisition to be reduced by economies of scale. This underlying philosophy in the business environment has motivated an immense interest over the last decade in knowledge management. ***Pawar et al. (2002),*** at the same time realize the place technology has within the effective co-ordination of knowledge. Nonetheless, they feel that humans play more of a central role in the identification, acquisition, generation, storage, structuring, distribution, and assessment of knowledge. It is interesting that ***Pawar et al. (2002)*** although taking the softer aspects of knowledge management into consideration, do not really look at how organizations get their employees to 'pull' knowledge. ***Malhotra (2001)*** also believes in line with ***Kluge et al. (2001)*** that there is an overarching need for the building of a KM culture within organizations, and the responsibility for developing this culture does not rest with the information technology specialists. To achieve this ***Malhotra (2001)*** believes organizations should focus on rewarding employees for what they contribute, and ensuring organizations track intellectual assets to show staff that knowledge is regarded as a valuable commodity; views which are supported by ***Kluge et al. (2001).*** A study carried out by KPMG (1998) highlighted that there is not only a lack of understanding about KM and its benefits, but that there is also a lack of skills within people regarding specific KM techniques.***Barson et al. (2000),*** using the TOP (technological, organizational, people) socio-technical systems classification ***(Brandt and Hartmann, 1999),*** investigated knowledge related barriers to change.

This is an interesting perspective, because as many organizations fail to maximize on knowledge management performance due to failure to tackle the softer issues, it can be equally detrimental to performance if technical and indeed organizational issues are also neglected. A common theme that has emerged is that knowledge management must be viewed from a holistic perspective. Failure to do so will result in an organization's failure to realize the potential it has to create and share knowledge. Although the literature reviewed in this paper looks at the barriers to knowledge creation and sharing from slightly different angles there is a lot of commonality in their published findings.

Syndromes to knowledge sharing

There are seven deadly syndromes that hinder effective KM.

1. ***Tall Poppy syndrome:*** Where people are reluctant to share because they fear being "cut down to size" by their peers.
2. ***Shrinking violet syndrome:*** Where people don't believe that they have anything to share.
3. ***On the web syndrome:*** Where people confuse capture with sharing –capture it once,then it's shared forever.
4. ***Communities of practically everything syndrome:*** Where communities are incorrectly perceived as a panacea. Besides these there are other three syndromes which are typical of people not seeking or demanding new knowledge.
5. ***Not invented here syndrome:***Where people believe their culture and company is unique,with unique problems and solutions suggested by external sources will not work.
6. ***Ignorance is bliss syndrome:*** Where lack of curiosity,or inflated self-confidence reduces demands for learning.
7. ***Real men don't ask for directions /Tom Tom syndrome:*** Where asking for help is perceived as a sign of weaknesss.

Cross category barriers

Knowledge can be seen as the entity of cognition and abilities which are used by individuals to solve the problems. This comprises theoretical perceptions as well as pragmatic to –day rules and guidelines and is organized set of statements of facts, or ideas, presenting a reasoned judgment or an experimental result.KM comprises any process or practice of creating ,acquiring, capturing, sharing and using this knowledge ,wherever it resides to enhance the learning and performing in organizations.

1. ***Existing resource***: If an organization wishes to engage in knowledge creation and sharing then the required resource must be available. The organization must also have employees who can implement and develop the knowledge that has been accrued. This is implying *a* 'pull' knowledge culture.
2. ***Need for rewards .Rajan et al. (1998)***: cited by ***Scarborough et al. (1999)*** suggest that employees must be able to see the link between sharing and immediate gains. The need for rewards is a people issue whereas the mechanism for conferring rewards is an organizational one. Organizational goals can't be achieved unless organizations integrate the concept of motivation and re-wards to its employees. Motivation can be provided through recognition, visibility, and inclusion of knowledge performance in appraisal systems and incentives. ***Hariharan (2007).*** The motivation could be either intrinsic or extrinsic. Rewarding and recognizing an employee with tangible form for their knowledge sharing efforts is extrinsic motivation while intrinsic motivation is of intangible nature. ***Bhirud; Rodrigues; Desai* (2007).** Employees share their knowledge easily when motivated. It is critical for sharing of both types of knowledge tacit as well as explicit knowledge. Lack of motivation and reward system is also a barrier because it discourages people to create, share, and use knowledge. Without the establishment of organizational reward and recognition systems, it is very difficult to align the KM and business needs of the organizations. ***Witt (1999).***
3. ***Poor organizational culture***: *A* company's culture may not support sharing and the reuse of knowledge. It is important also to look at culture from a push or pull perspective as this determines largely how employees will access and use the information available. If the culture is predominantly either 'push' or 'pull' this may be seen as a barrier as either the soft aspects of KM are being overlooked or the IT systems are not in place to support information routing and sharing. Organizational culture defines the core beliefs, value norms and social customs that govern the way individuals act and

behave in an organization. It is the sum of shared philosophies, assumptions, values, expectations, attitudes, and norms that bind the organizations together. ***Lekmen; Kahler; & Rittenbruch (2000).*** Lack of organizational culture is a key barrier for successful implementation of knowledge management in an organization. Organizational culture is the largest barrier in creation of a successful knowledge-based organization.***Chase (1997)*** .Culture considers the multiple aspects, mainly collaboration and trust. Trust is one of the aspects of the knowledge friendly cultures that fosters the relationship between individuals and groups, thereby, facilitating a more proactive and open knowledge sharing. ***Alwai; Marzooqi & Mohammed (2007).*** Absence or minimal level of collaboration hinders the transfer of knowledge between individuals as well as of the groups.

4. ***Poor top management commitment*****:** Top management is responsible for each and every activity at all the levels of the organizations. It is instrumental in development of organizational structure, technological infrastructure and various decisions making processes which are essential for effective creation, sharing and use of knowledge. Effective orientation of right people is necessary. Lack commitment of top management is the most critical barrier for a successful KM implementation, particularly in knowledge creation and sharing ***(Knowledge management Research report 1998).***It is also responsible for identifying organizational strength and weaknesses as well as analyzing the opportunities and threads in the external environment. ***Bollinger and Smith (2001).*** The top management has to conceptualize a vision about what type of knowledge should be developed and used into a management system for implementation'. ***Nonka (1995).*** Knowledge creation and sharing require long term commitment and support from top management in recruitment.

5. ***Technological barriers*****:** *Available technology* ***Swartz (1999) and Marwick (2001)*** suggest that technology still is unable to provide a single knowledge solution, and that an organization's codified solutions are usually a combination

of applications cobbled together. As most of the issues of KM are culture based, the role of technology can't be overlooked. Lack of technological infrastructure (TI) is one of the barriers in implementation of KM. TI provides a stronger platform to KM and enhances its impact in an organization, by helping and leveraging its knowledge systematically and actively. ***Singh and Kant (2007).*** The wide varieties of technology such as business intelligence, knowledge base, collaboration, portals, customer management systems, data mining, workflow, etc., support KM activities and the selection of appropriate technology improves the performance of businesses. ***Singh; Narain & Kant (2007).*** IT enables collecting, defining, storing, indexing and linking data, and digital objects in order to support management decisions. ***Carnerio (2001).*** It is able to overcome the barriers of time and space. It also serves as a repository in which knowledge can be reliably stored and efficiently retrieved. ***Chua(2004).***

6. ***Legacy systems*: *Swartz (1999)*** identifies legacy systems as a significant barrier to knowledge management. Connecting the systems of multiple departments, especially when there is no common standard approach to deployment makes it difficult to resolve an efficient knowledge transfer system.

7. ***Poor organizational structure*:** Business organizations should adopt an organizational structure (OS) which matches and supports its strategy. OS includes division of labor, departmentalization and distribution of power which is necessary to support the information and decision process of the organizations. It is defined as the specification of jobs to be done within an organization and the ways in which those jobs relate to one another. There are two types of organizational structure; one is bureaucracy and the other is task force. Bureaucratic structure hinders the flow of knowledge, hence it should be discouraged. Task force structure is flexible and adoptable which brings a team or group together to deal with problems. OS needs to support the knowledge transfer and must contribute towards creation and reuse of knowledge for the successful

implementation of KM in the organizations. It must be capable enough to administer the knowledge related activities. Creating an organizational structure to manage knowledge is by no means enough for the success of KM, but it is an important ingredient of success ***(Devenport & Volpel (2001)***. Lack of organizational structure can discourage the KM activities which certainly hinder the prospect of KM in the organizations.

8. ***Poor targeting of knowledge*: *Scarborough et al. (1999)*** point out that information needs to be targeted if it is to serve knowledge. Therefore, if a knowledge management system is to be effective it must be clear about what information it needs and what it expects to generate by way of knowledge.
9. ***Cost of management of knowledge transfer*: *Farr and Fisher (1992)*** point out that a barrier to inter-organizational knowledge transfer is the cost of managing collaboration.
10. ***Protection of proprietary knowledge*:** Sharing of proprietary information with collaborators leaves an organization open to the risk that the information will be revealed. The consequence of this belief is the resistance within an organization to sharing proprietary information with suppliers.
11. ***Distance*: *Nonaka and Takeuchi (1991)*** suggest the most efficient means of transferring knowledge is through face-to-face communications. However, the distributed nature of today's organization may make this difficult to do, as can cultural, legal, and linguistic factors.
12. ***People barriers internal resistance*:** This is where knowledge is hidden or its flow is restricted in order to protect the interests of the organization.
13. ***Self-interest*:** This is when customers may not be willing to supply information to a supplier for fear that the information will filter through to competitors.
14. ***Lack of trust*:** This impacts the way we perceive received information and the value we place on it, and also the manner in which we share information,

15. ***Risk*:** This is related to both trust and proprietary knowledge barriers. Inter-organizational knowledge sharing inherently involves an element of risk, particularly when proprietary knowledge in being shared.
16. ***Fear of exploitation*:** According to **Lucas** (2000) a fear of exploitation starts with the premise that one expects something in return for sharing. Although ***(Barson et al. 2000)*** see this as a 'people' barrier; the solution for resolving this problem is very much an organizational one.
17. ***Fear of contamination*:** This barrier refers to when organizations with up-market brand issues are nervous about getting together with people they perceive as more down-market ***(Lucas, 2000).***
18. ***Lack of methodology*:** KM is a group of clearly defined processes or methods used to search important knowledge among different KM operations'[38]'. Despite top management commitment, organizational structure and technological support, KM may fail due to lack of methodology. Successful KM implementation requires a set of methodology ***(Singh and Sankar 2006).*** Methodology defines each and every activity which is going to be held during the KM implementation. It is necessary for enhancing KM implementation. Many authors ***Dalkier;Liebowitz (1999)***have suggested the step-by-step methodology for KM implementation. But when it comes to real implementation, they fail. Organizations have to understand those guidelines and transfer them according to their context.
19. ***Staff retirement:*** Staff retirement is the major barrier in the KM implementation. Many organizations are facing lot of problems due to expertise retirement. If any employee retires from his/her job, it is very difficult to get a substitute of that level. His/her experience and expertise will be lost by the organizations. Organizations are less vigilant about protecting their human intellectual capital. Organizations need to focus on knowledge retention and its transfer into their business process management. ***DAlkiier (1999).*** According to **Accenture**, one out of four organizations

makes no effort whatsoever to capture the workplace knowledge of retirees, and a further 16% of organizations expect retirees to have an informal chat with colleagues before leaving. That's more than 40% of the organizations have no formal processes for retaining expertise. ***Parkin (2007).***

20. ***Lack of ownership of problem*:** Lack of ownership of problem is another issue which proves to be a barrier for KM implementation. ***Liebowitz (1999).*** Due to the lack of ownership of problem, no employee is ready to take up the jobs unless it has been properly assigned. This situation is basically due to the absence of culture in the organizations. Employees are not ready to take the responsibility of unassigned jobs. This situation makes difficult to nurture the KM implementation in the organizations.

21. ***Staff defection*:** Increasing staff defection rates are mainly due to the demand for sound trained and skilled personnel. Lack of motivation and reward also contributes in staff turnover. It has much influence on KM implementation. The loss of knowledge through staff defections is a critical driver of KM. ***Martin (2007).*** KM program fails due to staff defection and brings instability to the organization. Staff defection affects the organizations in many ways. One of which is in the knowledge it uses in its day-to-day business. Organizations have to formulate successful strategies for minimizing the staff turnover.

22. ***Language barrier*:** The main concern during knowledge capture is to be able to understand and interpret the expert's verbal description of information, heuristics, and so on. Repeated questioning often clarifies and promotes complete answers. But how well experts represent internal processes varies with their command of the language and the knowledge developer's interviewing skills. For example, take a look at the preceding sentence and review the structure of the sentence: "How well" (how well who? what?), "experts represent" (do they present? summarize?),"internal processes" (what internal processes? what does it mean?). The sentence was written to convey

an idea in words whose meanings the writer hopes the reader understands. Language may be unclear in a number of ways:

- ***Comparative words such as taller or better sometimes are left hanging.*** For example, the expert might say, "This last solution works better for what you're looking for."The question is, better than what? The comparison requires clarification. The knowledge developer might ask, "Better than what?" or "Can you elaborate on that comparison?" or "I don't understand what you mean by *better.*"
- ***Certain words or components may be left out of an explanation.*** Experts sometimes think that certain things are so obvious that they do not need to spoon-feed every detail. A knowledge developer who is not as familiar with the domain as the expert assumes may be lost without these details. The knowledge developer must ask the expert to clarify and to elaborate. If the expert comments, "To me, that is the key point," the knowledge developer might reply "*That* refers to ... ?" or "What makes it a key point?" or "How do you know it is the key?"
- ***Absolute words and phrases may be used loosely.*** For example, be wary when you hear "always," "never." "cannot," or "no way." The expert might say, "This approach will never give you the right combination," "There is no way 1 can explain this procedure in 1 hour," "Your suggestion will never work," or "This procedure cannot be applied." The knowledge developer might probe by asking, "How does this approach make that combination impossible?" "Can you imagine a situation where it might not clear things up?" "Then, can you briefly explain the procedure?" or "What do you mean this procedure cannot be applied?"These questions will gently push the expert to reconsider.
- ***Some words seem to have a built-in ambiguity.*** For example, "The titanium shield of the missile performs a protective function during reentry." The question here is "What is a protective function?" or "protective in reference to what? " The knowl-edge developer should either rephrase the question or ask for further clarification.

The main goal of pointing out these ambiguities is to warn the knowledge developer to be alert to meanings as well as to verbal and nonverbal cues. The success of the subsequent steps in building a KM system is dependent on accurate knowledge capture.

Conclusion

Knowledge management is seen as being passive, in that it is composed of facts and heuristics that can be stored, retrieved, and transferred with little concern for the context in which it will be used. Most of the writings and practices in knowledge management seem to focus on the content of knowledge management systems, overlooking how knowledge is presented or communicated. We believe that knowledge management is more than getting the right information to the right person at the right time. Managing knowledge occurs within a complex structured social context. That is, there must be social and human factors in the creation and exchange of knowledge.The following barriers are to be taken care of for future environment.

Bad news rarely travels upwards in organizations.

- People share information generously peer-to-peer, but be grudgingly upwards, and sparingly downwards in organizational hierarchies.
- People find it easier and more satisfying to reinvent the wheel.
- People only accept and internalize information that fits with their mental models and frames.
- People cannot readily differentiate useful information from useless information.
- The true cost of acquiring information and the cost of not knowing are both greatly underestimated in most organizations.
- People know more than they can tell, and tell more than they can write down.
- People can internalize information presented graphically more easily and fully than information presented as text, and understand information conveyed through stories better than information presented analytically.

- Most people want their friends, and even people they don't know, to succeed, and people they dislike to fail and this has a bearing on their information-sharing behavior.
- People are averse to sharing information orally, and even more averse to sharing it in written form, if they perceive any risk of it being misused or misinterpreted.
- People are generally reluctant to admit they don't know, or don't understand, something.
- People don't take care of shared information resources.
- In some organizations, internal competition mitigates against open sharing of information.
- Some modest people underestimate the value of what they know.
- We all learn differently.
- Rewards for sharing knowledge don't work...

However the problem of capitalizing on organization knowledge can be seen as a cycle determined by four facets. One of the first tasks is to *locate the crucial knowledge:* it must be identified, located, characterized and classified. Next, it must be *preserved,* in other words conceptualized, formalized and conserved. Furthermore, it must be *value-enhanced,* that is, put at the service of the development and expansion of the company. In other words, it must be accessed, *disseminated, used more effectively,* combined, and new knowledge must be created .Finally it must be maintained-evaluated, made updatable,and improved in accordance with rules governing its confidentiality and security.

References

Alawi, A. Marzooqi, Y. Mohammed. Organizational culture and knowledge sharing: Critical success factors.*Journal of Knowledge Management,* 2007, 11(2): 22-42.

Arrow, K.J. (1969). 'Classification notes on the production and transmission of techni-cal knowledge', *American Economic Review,* 52: 29-35.

Barson, R., Foster, G., Struck, T., Ratchev, S., Pawar, K., Weber, R, and Wunram, M.(2000). 'Inter and intra organizational barriers to sharing knowledge in theextended supply chain', e2000 Conference Proceeding.

Bollinger, R. Smith. Managing organizational knowledge as a strategic asset. *Journal of Knowledge Manage-ment, 2, 5(1): 2001.*

Brandt, D. and Hartmann, E. (1999) .'Editorial: Research topics and strategics in socio-technical systems', *Human Factors and Ergonomics in Manufacturing,* 9(3): 241-3.

Chase, R.(1997). The knowledge-based organization: Aninternational survey. *Journal of Knowledge Management,* 1997,38-49.

Carneiro ,A.(2001) . The role of intelligent resources in knowledge management. *Journal of Knowledge Management.* 5(4): 358-367.

Chua. A. (2004).Knowledge management system architecture: a bridge between km consultants and technologists. *Inter-national Journal of Information Management,* 24: 87-98.

Cohan, W.M. and Lovinthal, D.A. (1990) 'Absorptive capacity: a new perspective on learning and innovation', *Administrative Science Quarterly,* 35:128-52.

Dalkir. K (1999). *Knowledge Management in Theory and Practice.* Elsevier Butterworth-Heinemarin., Burlington.

Davenport, T. (2005) *Thinking for a Living.* Boston: Harvard Business Press.

Devenport, T and Volpel. S.(2001) The rise of knowledge towards attention management. *Journal of Knowledge Management,* 5(3); 212-221.

Drucker, P.P. (1994) 'The age of social transformation', *The Atlantic Monthly,* November

Farr,C.M and Fisher ,W.A (1992).Managing In ternational high technology cooperative Projects .Rand D Management,1(2):73-9.

Gupta, A. and Michailova, S. (2004) *'Knowledge sharing in knowledge intensive firms'*,CKG Working Paper No 12/2004.

Husted, K. and Michailova, S. (2002) Management International, 2002, knowledge-boa rd.com.

Kluge, J., Stein, W. and Licth, T. (2001) *Knowledge Unplugged: The McKinsey and Co Survey on Knowledge Management.* London: Palgrave.

Liebowitz, J (199).*Knowledge management handbook.* CRC Press, Boca Raton, FL, Lemken, B, Kahler, H, Rittenbmch. M(2000).Sustained knowledge management by organizational culture, in: *Proc. of the 33rd Hawaii Internationa! Conference on System Sciences,*

Lucas , E.(2000). Creating and giving a culture .Professional Manager,9(3):11-

Martin , B (2007). Knowledge based organizations: Emerging trends in local government in australia. *Journal of Knowl-edge Management Practice,* 2000.

Malhotra, Y. (2001) 'Knowledge management for the new world of business'. Available at http://www.brint.com/km/whatis.htm.

Marwick, A.D. (2001) 'Knowledge management technology', *IBM* Systems *Journal on Knowledge Management.* Armonk, New York: IBM Press.

Nonaka, 1. (1994) 'A dynamic theory of organizational knowledge creation', *Organization Science,* 5(1): 14-37.

Nonaka, II. Takeuchi (1991). *The Knowledge-creating Company.* Oxford University Press, New York, NY,

Pawar, K., Horton, A., Gupta, A., Wunram, M., Barson, R. and Weber, F. (2002) 'Inter-organizational knowledge management: focus on human barriers in the telecommunications industry', proceedings of the 8th ISPE International Conference on Concurrent Engineering; Research and Applications: 271-8.

Rajan, A., Lank, E. and Chappie, K. (1998) *Good Practice in Knowledge Creation and Exchange,* Tunbridge Wells: Create.

Scarborough, H., Swan, J. and Preston, P. (1999) *Knowledge Management: A Literature Review.* Issues in people management. London: Institute of Personnel and Development.

Swartz, J. (1999) 'Collaboration - more hype then reality', *Internet Week,* 25 .October.

Singh, M and Kant. R.(2007). Knowledge management as competitive edge for indian engineering industries, in: *Proc. of the International Conference on Quality and Reliability,* Chiang Mai, Thailand, 2007, 398- -403. 5-7 November , pp. 398-403,

Singh, M and Shankar,R (2006). Survey of knowledge management practices in indian manufacturing industries. *Journal of Knowledge Management,* 2006, 10(6): 110-128.

Singh, M ; Narain, R and R. Kant(2007). Critical factors for successful implementation of knowledge management: An inter-pretive structural modeling approach, in: *Proc. of International conf. on Innovation and Knowledge Management of Social and Economic Issues: International Perspective.* J.N.U., New Delhi, India, January 9-12.

Parkin, G (2007). Knowledge managing the retirement brain drains. 2005. Available at http://parkinslot.blogspot.com/2005/06/knowledge-managing-retirement-brain.htinl

Sulanski, C. (1996) 'Exploring international stickiness: impediments to the transfer of best practice within the firm', *Strategic Management Journal,* 17: 27-^-3.

Winter, S.G. (1987) 'Knowledge and competence as strategic assets', in D. Teece (ed.)

The Competitive Cfiallenge: Strategies for Industrial Innovation and Renewal Cambridge, MA: Ballinger.

Zander, TJ. and Kogut, B. (1995) 'Knowledge and the speed of transfer and imitation on organizational capabilities', *Organizational Science,* 6(1): 76-92.

8

OSS for Libraries

Dr. Pawan Sharma
Librarian, ITM Universe, Gwalior
Dr. Hemant Sharma
Associate Professor, SOS in Library & Information Science
Jiwaji University, Gwalior

Abstract

This article discusses the history, definition of open source software, their need & uses in libraries and criteria of selecting OSS . The OSS authors make all the source code available to users, who can change the software to tailor or more closely to their own requirements. With many OSS applications are now available for library and information management, organizations have a new option for acquiring and implementing systems, plus new opportunities for participating in OSS projects.

History/ Movement of OSS

The free software movement was launched in 1983. In 1998, a group of individuals advocated that the term free software be replaced by open source software (OSS) as an expression which is less ambiguous and more comfortable for the corporate world. Software developers may want to publish their software with an open source license, so that anybody may also develop the same software or understand how it works. Open source software generally allows anyone to make a new version of the software, port it to new operating systems and processor architectures, share it with others or market it. The aim of open source is to let the product be more understandable, modifiable, duplicatable, reliable or simply accessible, while it is still marketable.

The Open Source Definition, notably, presents an open source philosophy, and further defines a boundary on the usage, modification and redistribution of open source software. Software licenses grant rights to users which would otherwise be prohibited by copyright. These include rights on usage, modification and redistribution. Several open source software licenses have qualified within the boundary of the Open Source Definition. The most prominent example is the popular GNU General Public License (GPL). While open source presents a way to broadly make the sources of a product publicly accessible, the open source licenses allow the authors to fine tune such access.

The "open source" label came out of a strategy session held in Palo Alto in reaction to Netscape's January 1998 announcement of a source code release for Navigator (as Mozilla). A group of individuals at the session included Todd Anderson, Larry Augustin, John Hall, Sam Ockman, Christine Peterson and Eric S. Raymond. They used the opportunity before the release of Navigator's source code to clarify a potential confusion caused by the ambiguity of the word "free" in English. The 'open source' movement is generally thought to have begun with this strategy session. Many people, nevertheless, claimed that the birth of the Internet, since 1969, started the open source movement, while others do not distinguish between open source and free software movements (Open Source Software,2008).

The Free Software Foundation (FSF), started in 1985, intended the word 'free' to mean "free as in free speech" and not "free as in free beer" with emphasis on the positive freedom to distribute rather than a negative freedom from cost. Since a great deal of free software already was (and still is) free of charge, such free software became associated with zero cost, which seemed anti-commercial.

The Open Source Initiative (OSI) was formed in February 1998 by Eric S. Raymond and Bruce Perens. With at least 20 years of evidence from case histories of closed development versus open development already provided by the Internet, the OSI presented the 'open source' case to commercial businesses, like Netscape. The OSI hoped that the usage of the label "open source," a term suggested by Peterson of the Foresight Institute at the strategy session, would eliminate ambiguity, particularly for individuals who perceive "free software" as anti-commercial. They sought to bring a higher profile to the practical benefits of freely available source code, and they wanted to bring major software businesses and other high-tech industries into open source. Perens attempted to register "open source" as a service mark for the OSI, but that attempt was impractical by trademark standards. Meanwhile, thanks to the presentation of Raymond's paper to the upper management at Netscape (Raymond only discovered when he read the Press Release, and was called by Netscape CEO Jim Barksdale's PA later in the day), Netscape released its Navigator source code as open source, with favorable results.

Definition

- Open source software is software for which the underlying code has been made available for users. Users are then able to read it or change it as they wish.
  www.open2.net/sciencetechnologynature/computing/glossary.html
- An operating system and/or applications software for which the code is open for alteration by the public. www.girpm.com/articles/glossary.asp
- A program in which the source code is available to the general public for use and/or modification from its original design free of charge, ie, open. Open source code is typically created as a collaborative effort in which programmers improve upon the code and share the changes within the community.
  www.jahadesign.com/glossary.htm
- Free programs created through the collaborative efforts of programmers from around the world.
  www.metromemetics.com/thelexicon/o.asp
- Software that can be copied and redistribute by the user. Many products are also free (FOSS).
  www.timr.ca/RecentArticles/Online/terminology.html
- Open source software allows for anyone with programming experience to revise and change the programming code to suit their individual needs. It allows to fully customize your settings. Many of today's popular software programs once started as an open source software program.
  www.sassyenterprises.com Search_engine_optimization_terms.html

- ***According to Chudnov (1999)*** Open source means several things:

1. Open source software is typically created and maintained by developers crossing institutional and national boundaries, collaborating by using internet-based communications and development tools;
2. Products are typically a certain kind of "free", often through a license that specifies that applications and source code (the programming instructions written to create the applications) are free to use, modify, and redistribute as long as all uses, modifications, and redistributions are similarly licensed; [GPL]
3. Successful applications tend to be developed more quickly and with better responsiveness to the needs of users who can readily use and evaluate open source applications because they are free;
4. Quality, not profit, drives open source developers who take personal pride in seeing their working solutions adopted;
5. Intellectual property rights to open source software belong to everyone who helps build it or simply uses it, not just the vendor or institution who created or sold the software.

The Open Source Initiative (OSI) identified ten criteria for a software product to be called open source. The OSI certifies a software license as an 'OSI Certified License' on the basis of the following 'Ten Commandments' (http://opensource.org/docs/osd).

(1) *Free Redistribution:* The license shall not restrict any party from selling or giving away the software as a component of an aggregate software distribution containing programs from several different sources. The license shall not require a royalty or other fee for such sale.

(2) *Source Code:* The program must include source code, and must allow distribution in source code as well as compiled form. Where some form of a product is not distributed with source code, there must be a well-publicized means of obtaining the source code for no more than a reasonable reproduction cost preferably, downloading via the Internet

without charge. The source code must be the preferred form in which a programmer would modify the program. Deliberately obfuscated source code is not allowed. Intermediate forms such as the output of a preprocessor or translator are not allowed.

(3) *Derived Works:* The license must allow modifications and derived works, and must allow them to be distributed under the same terms as the license of the original software.

(4) *Integrity of the Author's Source Code:* The license may restrict source-code from being distributed in modified form *only* if the license allows the distribution of "patch files" with the source code for the purpose of modifying the program at build time. The license must explicitly permit distribution of software built from modified source code. The license may require derived works to carry a different name or version number from the original software.

(5) *No Discrimination Against Persons or Groups:* The license must not discriminate against any person or group of persons.

(6) *No Discrimination Against Fields of Endeavor:* The license must not restrict anyone from making use of the program in a specific field of endeavor. For example, it may not restrict the program from being used in a business, or from being used for genetic research.

(7) *Distribution of License:* The rights attached to the program must apply to all to whom the program is redistributed without the need for execution of an additional license by those parties.

(8) *License Must Not Be Specific to a Product:* The rights attached to the program must not depend on the program's being part of a particular software distribution. If the program is extracted from that distribution and used or distributed within the terms of the program's license, all parties to whom the program is redistributed should have the same rights as those that are granted in conjunction with the original software distribution.

(9) *License Must Not Restrict Other Software:* The license must not place restrictions on other software that is distributed along

with the licensed software. For example, the license must not insist that all other programs distributed on the same medium must be open-source software.

10. *License Must Be Technology-Neutral:* No provision of the license may be predicated on any individual technology or style of interface.

Why adopt OSS in Libraries

According to the Draft Report (2001) of Digital Library Federation (USA) to consider Open Source Software for Libraries there are three virtues of OSS for the libraries. They are:

1. OSS is an economical alternative to libraries' reliance upon commercially supplied software. That is, despite the real costs involved in the development, maintenance, and use of OSS software, these are lower than those associated with library reliance upon commercial software. Accordingly, OSS economical is not free opens an economical alternative to reliance upon commercial software.
2. OSS is essential if libraries are to develop software and systems that meet their patrons' needs. With OSS the IT infrastructure that is essential to library operations and services can be:
    - Open (that is, built according to open standards and as such potentially inter-operable with other essential software and systems);
    - Ubiquitously available to libraries;
    - Capable of being tailored to suit the needs and circumstances of individual libraries;
    - Documented (and documentation must be available); and
    - Errors can more effectively be identified and corrected ("many eyeballs make bugs shallow") .
3. OSS ensures that library systems and online services will be more functional for libraries and their patrons and as such be good for library patrons. This hypothesis is posited because, through OSS developments, libraries:

- are reinserted into the research and development process that results in systems and software;
- share a stake in software development and as such have greater influence over (and as a result take a greater interest in specification of) the functional and performance requirements associated with particular software tools and systems
- motivate and empower systems librarians and related technical staff by encouraging creativity and positioning them to make a difference; and
- are able more easily to collaborate with other information science communities involved in common research and development area (http://www.diglib.org/architectures/ossrep. htm, 2001)

According to Chudnov (1999) there are three factors pushing the use of OSS in libraries:

- OSS licenses allow libraries to cut budget on software and use it to other issues needing more funds.
- OSS product is not locked into a single vendor. Thus even if a library buys an open source system from one vendor, it might choose to buy technical support from another company or get it from in- house experts.
- The entire library community might share the responsibility of solving information systems accessibility issues.

Criteria for selecting OSS

Frank Cervone (2003) has given the following guidelines for evaluation of Open Source Software. Guidelines for Evaluating OSS all of which follow a single principle: Thoroughly investigate the software before implementing. Some questions to ask include:

- What are the programming language requirements?
- Do you have people on staff who can program in the language in which the software is written?
- If not, do you have ready access to people who can?
- If not, are there alternative packages you can support?
- What is the operating environment?

- Is this software supported on your hardware?
- Does it run on the operating systems you support?
- Is there a large, active user base?
- How is maintenance handled?
- Who is currently supporting it?
- Is there an electronic discussion list, newsgroup, or blog that can be used for support?
- Is there a commercial entity that could provide support?
- Is there a community of peers providing input on enhancements and modifications?
- What sort of functional and integrated testing is performed by the user community?
- Does the software have the necessary functionality?
- Is the product mature? Is it in a greater than 1.0 release?
- Will it require modification? If so, do you have the expertise?
- How will local modifications be folded back into the base product so that the same modifications need not be repeated for each new release?

OSS in Library and Information Management

Open source software has had an increasingly high profile in the library and information management profession since 1999. A September 1999 meeting of 80 senior American academic library managers created three "keystone principles" to set a foundation for future developments of library services. One of these, "libraries are responsible for creating innovative information systems for the dissemination and preservation of information and new knowledge regardless of format" had an action item to "create interoperability in the systems they develop and create open source software for the access, dissemination, and management of information" (Keystone principles, 2000). Members of the profession have continued to have a high level of interest in F/OS software, with more than 200 articles and conference papers published in the last 4 years to describe specific projects. The oss4lib portal (http://www.oss4lib.org), originally set up in 1999, listed over 1090 library-related projects in Nov 2008.

Koha

Koha is an integrated library system (ILS) and was the first open source ILS. Koha was created in 1999 by Katipo Communications for the Horowhenua Library Trust in New Zealand. The first installation went live in January of 2000.

(http://en.wikipedia.org/wiki/Koha_(software)

Greenstone

Greenstone Digital Library Software is a suite of software tools for building and distributing digital library collections. It is a composite tool for building digital library collections. It provides a new way of organizing information and publishing it on the Internet or on CD-ROM in the form of a fully-searchable, metadata-driven digital library. It is an open-source, multilingual software, issued under the terms of the GNU General Public License.

Greenstone is produced by the New Zealand Digital Library Project at the University of Waikato, and has been developed and distributed in cooperation with UNESCO and the Human Info NGO in Belgium. Its developers received the 2004 IFIP Namur award for "contributions to the awareness of social implications of information technology, and the need for an holistic approach in the use of information technology that takes account of social implications." The company DL Consulting provides Greenstone commercial consulting, customization, support, maintenance and hosting services.

Greenstone is easy to use software that can be used to build up large sets of digital documents into searchable collections. It provides a Greenstone Librarians Interface (GLI) to help the librarians or information professionals to build up collections without knowing the hassles of computer programming. Installation, creation and customization of digital library collections by using Greenstone can be learnt by anyone familiar with computer usage within a few days time. Training courses are regularly conducted at various places in the world.

Greenstone is capable of building up multi-media digital documents such as text, pdf, audio, video, etc. very easily. The text, pdf , html and similar documents are converted into Greenstone

Archive Format (GAF) which is an xml equivalent format (***Greenstone (software)***).

DSpace

DSpace is an open source software package that provides the tools for management of digital assets, and is commonly used as the basis for an institutional repository. It is also intended as a platform for digital preservation activities. Since its release in 2002, as a product of the HP-MIT Alliance, it has been installed and is in production at over 240 institutions around the globe, from large universities to small higher education colleges, cultural organizations, and research centers. DSpace supports a wide variety of data, including books, theses, 3D digital scans of objects, photographs, film, video, research data sets and other forms of content. It is shared under a BSD licence, which enables users to customize or extend the software as needed. The first version of DSpace was released in November 2002, following a joint effort by developers from MIT and HP Labs in Cambridge, Massachusetts. In March 2004 the first DSpace User Group Meeting (DSUG) took place at Hotel@MIT, and it was there that the first discussions concerning the DSpace community and its future governance were discussed in earnest. The DSpace Federation formed a loose grouping of interested institutions, while the DSpace Committers group (see Community Development Model below) was formed shortly after, consisting of five developers from HP Labs, MIT, OCLC, University of Cambridge, and University of Edinburgh. Later two further developers from Australian National University and Texas A&M University also joined this group. DSpace 1.3 was released in 2005, and at around the same time the second DSpace User Group Meeting was held at the University of Cambridge. Following this, two further smaller user group meetings were spawned, the first in January/February 2006 in Sydney, and the second in April 2006 in Bergen, Norway. In March 2008, the DSpace Community released DSpace 1.5 ***(DSpace)***

EPrint

EPrints is an open source software package for building open access repositories that are compliant with the Open Archives Initiative Protocol for Metadata Harvesting. It shares many of the features commonly seen in Document Management systems, but is primarily used for institutional repositories and scientific journals. EPrints has been developed at the University of Southampton School of Electronics and Computer Science and released under a GPL license.

The EPrints software is not to be confused with "eprints" (or "e-prints"), which are preprints (before peer review) and postprints (after peer review), of research journal articles: "eprints" = preprints + postprints.

EPrints was created in 2000 as a direct outcome of the 1999 Santa Fe meeting that launched what eventually became the OAI-PMH.

The EPrints software was enthusiastically received, became the first and one of the most widely used free open access, institutional repository software, and it has since inspired many emulations.

Version 3 of the software was officially released on the 24th January 2007 at the Open Repositories 2007 Conference and was described by its developers as "a major leap forward in functionality, giving even more control and flexibility to repository managers, depositors, researchers and technical administrators ***(EPrint).***

GNUTECA

GNUTECA is a Free, Open Source Software for Library Automation, including a Loan System, Catalog Collaboration, MARC Editing among others. It has a Web and GTK (graphic) interface. http://gnuteca.codigolivre.org.br/

Avanti Circulation System

The Avanti circulation system is a simple, scalable, networkable, client/server circulation system that can be deployed in small to medium scale libraries. The end product will be modular: consisting of a system core, circulation module, minimal OPAC, and network and user interfaces. The entire system is written in Java. Avanti 0.3.1 was developed using the Blackdown JDK v1.1.7 on a Linux system with the servlet classes being developed using the Apache Jserv servlet engine. http://www.avanti librarysystems.com/index.html

Karuna

This project is a library management system designed to automate a library. Taken into consideration all the aspects of a library like search, issue/retrieval, acquisition and other aspects of a library. http://sarovar.org/projects/karuna/

CERN Document Server Software (CDSware)

The CERN Document Server Software (CDSware) is the software developed by, maintained by, and used at, the CERN Document Server. It allows you to run your own electronic preprint server, your own online library catalogue or a document system on the web. It complies with the Open Archives Initiative metadata harvesting protocol (OAI-PMH) and uses MARC 21 as its underlying bibliographic standard. The CDSware is free software, licensed under GNU General Public Licence (GPL). http://cdsware.cern.ch/

Ibero-american and Caribbean Digital Library Project

Ibero-American and Caribbean Digital Library Proyect is an initiative between UNESCO, University of Colima on and other experts of the region. The methodology that the registry of resources of information (metadatos) of any type of digital object "books, journals, thesis, music, images, audio, video, etc. As well as the formats and techniques for the digitalization, Design and development of the Z39.50 standard for the exchange of information. The objective is to create a great digital library of the region that this free one of author rights. In order to obtain software http://bdigital.ucol.mx consults the page or the version in CD-ROM to ask for a copy to the person in charge. http://bdigital.ucol.mx

Learning Access ILS

The LearningAccess ILS is a full-feature Open Source library automation system developed for use by public and school libraries throughout world. The Institute will make this system available free to libraries that, because of cost, have been unable to achieve the benefits of automation. The system fully supports MARC21, Z39.50, Unicode andother critical lirbary standards as identified by IFLA. www.learningaccess.org

Museolog

Museolog is a web-driven software system for cataloging museum information. It's software for managing information about museum artefacts collection written using Java/JSP. This software is licensed by GPL license. Museolog has been initially developed by EUROCLID within UNESCO HeritageNet project. This system used in museums of Kazakhstan and Kyrgyzstan republics. Currently Museolog has one developer. http://museolog.sourceforge.net

Open Archives Harvester

The PKP (Public Knowledge Project)Open Archives Harvester is a free metadata indexing system developed by the Public Knowledge Project through its federally funded efforts to expand and improve access to research. The PKP OAI Harvester allows you to create a searchable index of the metadata from Open Archives Initiative (OAI)-compliant archives, such as sites using Open Journal Systems (OJS) or Open Conference Systems (OCS). Harvester version 2.0 includes the following features: (1) Ability to harvest OAI metadata in a variety of schemas (including unqualified DC, the PKP (Open Journal Systems/ Open Conference Systems) Dublin Core extension, MODS, and MARCXML). Additional schema are supported via plugins. (2) Flexible search interface that allows simple searching and advanced searching using crosswalked fields from all harvested archives. Advanced searching of archives that share the same schema will be possible using fields as defined in the schema. When creating crosswalks for searching, admins can define elements are text, date, or HTML multiple select interface widgets. (3) Ability to perform granular harvesting using setSpec and timestamps. (4) Ability to perform post-harvest and pre-indexing filtering/normalization on metadata. (5) User Interface with CSS and template-based HTML for easy customization. (6) Searching is highly scalable (creates an inverted index for searching). http://pkp.sfu.ca/?q=harvester

The Open Source Digital Library System Project (PYTHEAS)

PYTHEAS1 (Powerful Yet Tactfully Helpful Electronic Arranger of Sources) is designed to be a multi-tier ILS (Integrated Library System). The two major building blocks for providing server-based metadata and information retrieval capabilities in PYTHEAS are MARC (MAchine

Readable Cataloguing) and RDF (the Resource Description Framework), standards that define a format for describing objects and can package highly structured metadata for describing content and content relationships in physical and digital objects. The client environment for PYTHEAS can best be described as "web-centric". The objective is to provide a platform and language neutral environment for accessing and manipulating the information in PYTHEAS. http://web2.uwindsor.ca/library/leddy/people/art/pytheas/index.html

ABCD

ABCD is web-based integrated library management software comprising the main basic library functions. This kind of library application is a long held aspiration for the ISIS community, since the first MS-DOS version came out more than 20 years ago. Several library automation systems were developed during this period and are still in operation worldwide. BIRME EMP previous system was limited to the circulation services. The main characteristics of ABCD are the coverage of the main library functions, its web centrality and its development and maintenance under the methodology of Free and Open Source Software. http://reddes.bvsalud.org/projects/abcd/

NewGenlib

One of the most important aspects of using a Integrated Library System is support services. Support services may be

- Support for installation or re-installation.
- Training on the system to use it effectively.
- Migrating data from older systems.
- Clarifying simple and complex doubts.
- Emergency trouble shooting and system recoveries.
- Get newer updates/versions with enhanced functionalities and bug fixes.

Conclusion

OSS has much potential for libraries and information centers, and there are a number of projects, including Greenstone, Koha, and Dspace, etc. that demonstrate its viability in this context. It gives library staff an option to be actively involved in development projects, and this involvement can take many forms, such as reporting bugs, suggesting enhancements, and testing new versions. Organisations adopting OSS will need to provide their staff with additional development and training to enable them to take on these new roles effectively, and will need to have a long-term commitment to the projects. Systems librarians and library managers should watch this trend for future developments.

References

Cervone, Frank (2003). The open source option. Accessed on 01-1-2011. http://www.accessmylibrary.com/coms2/summary_0286-23848225_ITM

Chudnov, Dan (1999). Open Source Library Systems: Getting Started. Accessed on 01-1-2011. http://www.oss4lib.org/readings/oss4lib-getting-started.php

Dspace. Wikipedia: The Free Encyclopedia. Accessed as on 101-1-2011.http://en.wikipedia.org/wiki/DSpace

Eprint. Wikipedia: The Free Encyclopedia. Accessed as on 01-1-2011.http://en.wikipedia.org/wiki/Eprints

Greenstone (Software). Wikipedia: The Free Encyclopedia. Accessed as on 01-1-2011. http://en.wikipedia.org/wiki/Greenstone_Digital_Library_Software

Open Source Software. Wikipedia: The Free Encyclopedia. Accessed on 01-1-2011. http://en.wikipedia.org/wiki/Open_source_software

The Keystone Principles: an action plan for values-based librarianship. 2000. College & Research Libraries News 61 (2):103-104.Accessed on 01-1-2011. http://www.ala.org/ala/mgrps/divs/acrl/publications/crlnews/2000/feb/keystonepri nciples.cfm

9

Cloud Computing
Emerging Technology for Libraries

Manish Kumar Jadiya
UGC-JRF, New Delhi
E-mail: sagar143soni@gmail.com
P. S. Rajput
UGC-JRF, SOS Library & Information Science
Jiwaji University, Gwalior (M.P.)
E-mail: prabhat.t82@gmail.com

Abstract

Gives the meanings of Cloud Computing and brings out its importance. Explains the functioning of Cloud Computing. Gives its architecture. Various types of Clouds—Public, Private, Hybrid, and Community—are explained. Discusses various types of Cloud Services—Saas, Infrastructure, and Platform. Gives advantages of Cloud Computing. Stipulates possible effects of Cloud Computing on libraries. Says that Cloud Computing is the future of computing.

1. Introduction

One of the major components of this digital age is a move towards "cloud computing". In simple terms, this means the replacement of packaged software generally bought on CD load onto PC's, with a variety of applications in the "cloud". Software-as-a-service (SaaS) applications are examples of cloud computing. Google, Amazon, salesforce.com, and others all have successful SaaS offerings.

Web 2.0 applications have already shifted much of the personal computer usage to the cloud. It has facilitated millions of the users to get rid of bookmarks from the desktop by storing them on social bookmarking websites such as Delicious. It also allows uploading and sharing videos on YouTube, use the services, such as Slide share to host presentations, work collaboratively on Google Docs, and adopt web-based email services, such as Gmail. It even enables to design applications for popular platforms, such as Facebook.

2. Functioning of Cloud Computing

Cloud computing is a set of technologies that allows computing applications and data to be exposed as a set of services from a pool of underlying resources. The user does not have to worry about the technologies in the pool. This is similar to running an electrical or electronic device by plugging it to a wall socket. You do not have to worry about how the power is generated in the power plant. You just want the right voltage to be made available so that you can power your device and use your device. Similarly, in Cloud Computing, users simply focus on the services they would like to use, and not worry about how to implement the software that provides these services. Even the IT staff that provides these services can easily pull out the resources required by the users from this pool of resources, and put it back when the services have been consumed.

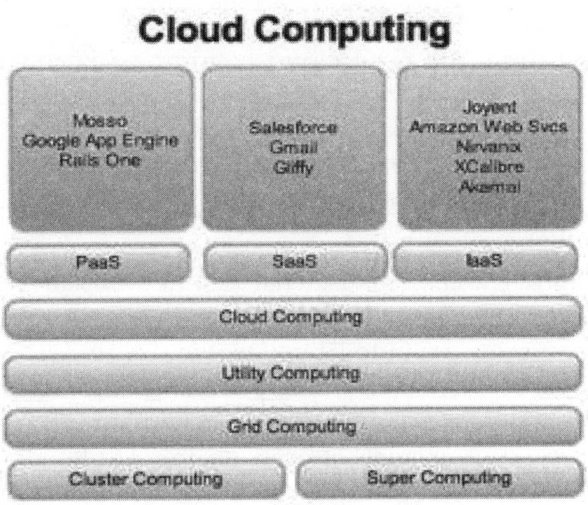

Figure 1: Functioning of Cloud Computing

3. Architecture of Cloud Computing

The foundation of cloud computing comprises of data centers (servers, storage, networking), the business/library applications and middleware, virtualization software and of course operating systems. This foundation provides all the applications to the users on a 'pay as you go' basis. So the entire workload shifts to the cloud i.e. local computers are not burdened with running hundreds of applications anymore. All that users need is system interface software, like a simple web browser to be run on their side.

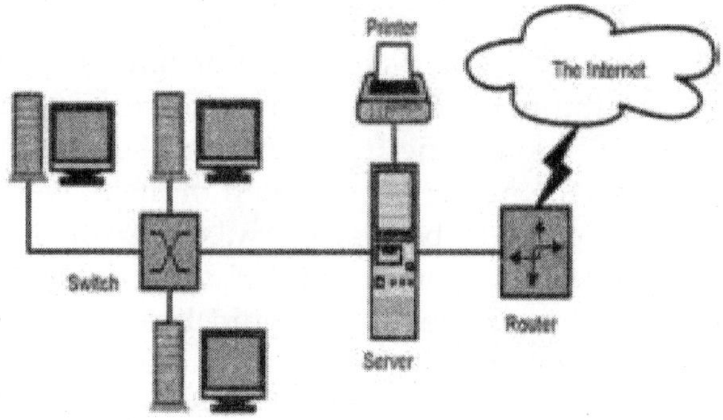

Figure 2: Architecture of Cloud Computing

4. Types of Cloud

Most of the time, the term cloud computing is confused with the Internet cloud. It is very important to understand this difference if one desires to use the cloud more effectively. There are basically three types of cloud—public, private, and hybrid. Community cloud is one more type of cloud, which can also be considered as an important type of cloud.

4.1 Public Cloud: This is what people normally end up talking about whenever the term cloud computing comes up. This is essentially an external cloud, provided by a service provider. It refers to the resources (hardware, software, applications) that a service provider offers over the Internet. Email, if hosted with an ISP is the most basic and oldest type of service offered on the public cloud. Now, just about every kind of service one can think of is available in the public cloud. The public cloud follows the 'pay as you go' model. One only pays for the services he consumes. The benefits of moving to a public cloud are many: (1)One is not to worry about managing the underlying IT infrastructure; (2)No security patches or updates to apply;(3) No software upgrades, etc. All these are the service provider's headache.

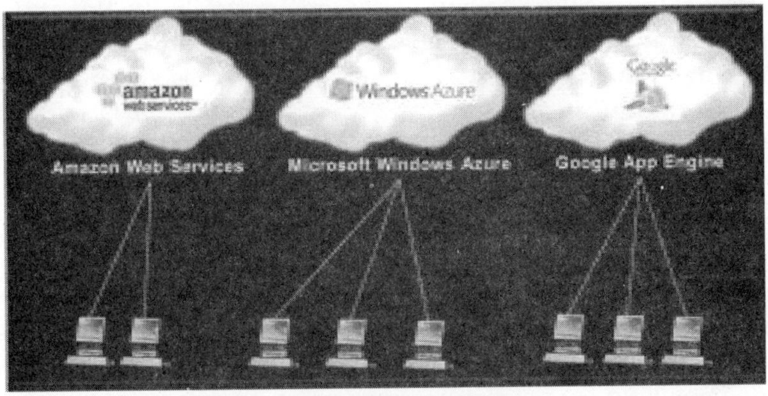

Figure 3: Public Cloud

*4.2 **Private Cloud:*** A private cloud refers to having your own, private cloud computing infrastructure. Therefore, instead of relying on an external, public cloud service provider's infrastructure, one would have his own. A private cloud is more suited for a large enterprise because it has already invested heavily in its IT infrastructure, data center, apps, etc. A private cloud typically involves optimizing the existing IT infrastructure, so that it can deliver services to the users faster and more effectively. A private cloud would allow

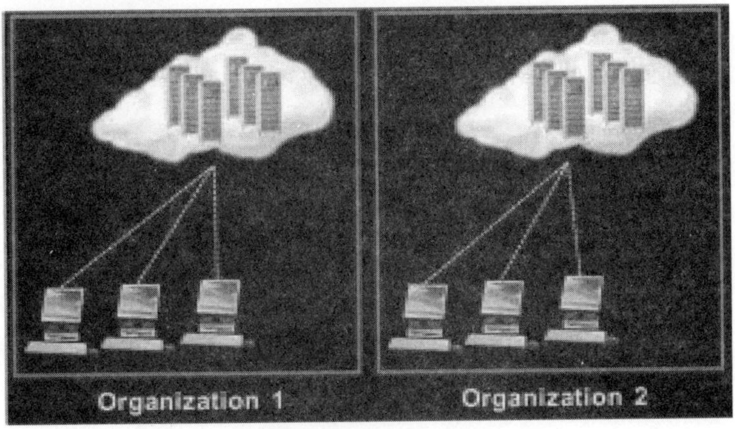

Figure 4: Private Cloud

the IT team to provision for new hardware, software, and services for users as and when required. It would provide better control over the entire process of information processing. This helps reduce costs, improves response time, and provides greater flexibility. Private Cloud borrows some of the best practices of Public Cloud but is limited to an organizational boundary. Private Cloud can be setup by using a variety of offerings from vmWare, Microsoft, IBM, SUN and others. There are also some of the Open Source implementations like Eucalyptus and Ubuntu Enterprise Cloud.

4.3 Hybrid Cloud: As the name implies, it is a cloud computing environment that consists of internal/ external providers, viz. a mix of private and public clouds. Secure and critical applications are hosted by organizations in the private cloud while not so critical ones are hosted in the public cloud. This combination is known as a hybrid cloud. The cloud infrastructure remains as a unique entity, which is bound by a standard technology thus enabling data and application portability. A very good example of this is cloud bursting, wherein the organization for its normal usage uses its own infrastructure but moves to the cloud for peak loads. Realizing the importance of hybrid cloud, Amazon Web Services has announced Virtual Private Cloud (VPC) that securely bridges Private Cloud and Amazon Web Services. Microsoft's announcement of Windows AppFabric brings the concept of Hybrid Cloud to Microsoft's future customers.

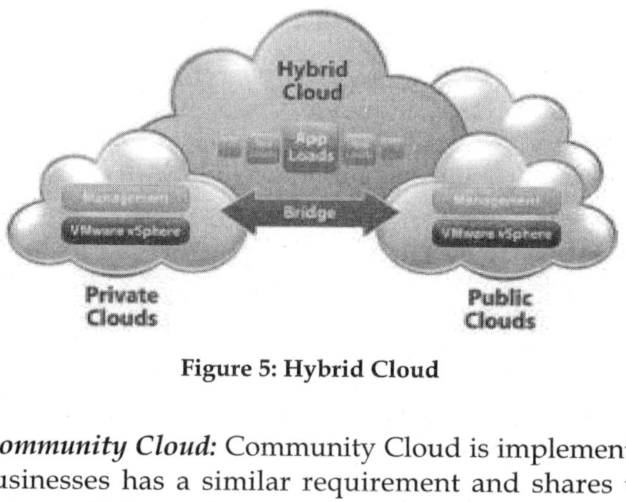

Figure 5: Hybrid Cloud

4.4 Community Cloud: Community Cloud is implemented when a set of businesses has a similar requirement and shares the same context. This would be made available to a set of select organizations.

For example, the Government of India may decide to setup a government specific Community Cloud that can leverage by all the Indian States. Through this, individual local bodies like state governments will be freed from investing, maintaining and managing their local data centers. Similarly, the National Library of India may setup a Community Cloud for all the public libraries that share common goals and requirements. Therefore, a Community Cloud is a sort of Private Cloud but goes beyond just one organization.

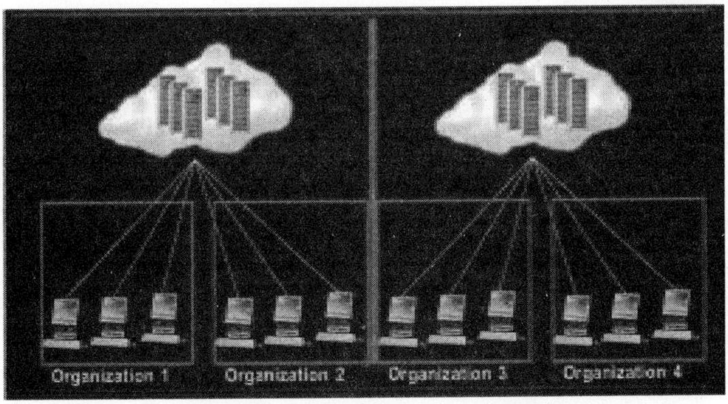

Figure 6: Community Cloud

5. Types of Cloud Services

Whether it's public, private, or hybrid, one could run a range of services in a cloud computing environment. These can be divided into three parts-SaaS, IaaS, and PaaS.

5.1 SaaS (Software as a Service): This is the most familiar and prolific cloud service of all. As the name suggests, it provides any software application as a service through the cloud. We have all been using software as a service for years in the public domain, with the free email services being the most classic example. Today there is a whole range of software applications available through SaaS, be it ERP, CRM, workflow systems, document management, and much more. The cloud service provider offers these services, and the users pay as they use the same. This could be on a subscription model, wherein they pay an annual or a monthly fee for the services. Some of these Web-based applications are free such as Hotmail, Google Apps, Skype, and many 2.0 applications. There is usually little customization or control available with these applications. However, subscribers benefit from low initial costs, have access to (usually 24/7) support services, and need not worry about hosting, installing, upgrading, or maintaining the software. Everything is accessible from a web browser, so the users do not need anything more than that.

*5.2 **Infrastructure as a Service:*** As the name implies, IaaS is a service delivery model in which an organization is given control over different resources and applications. These resources comprise of storage, hardware, servers, networking components, etc. The consumer need not manage or control the underlying cloud infrastructure in this service model. On demand principle is used in this case as the infrastructure is provided to the user as per his requirements. It often takes the form of virtualized computing environment thus giving freedom to consumers wherein they can configure and deploy the applications in a virtual image locally. Then without the need to worry about the network infrastructure they can also execute it within the remote environment. Some of the prime examples of it are Amazon's Elastic Compute Cloud [EC2] that provides computing resources, and Simple Storage Service (S3) for data storage.

*5.3 **Platform as a Service:*** This component of cloud computing can be defined as a set of software and product development tools that allows developers to create applications on the provider's platform. In other words it allows you to build applications that are delivered to users through the Internet and are run on the provider's infrastructure. Cost effectiveness is one of the prime benefits of PaaS as organizations do not need to spend extra bucks for buying and managing the underlying hardware and software. PaaS offerings include facilities for application development and design, testing, deployment and hosting. Web service integration, database integration, security, storage, etc. that come under application services are also included. The prime examples are Salesforce.com's Force.com , Microsoft's Azure and Google's App Engine.

Google's App Engine is a way for developers to run their web applications on Google's infrastructure. With Google App Engine, developers can write web applications based on the same building blocks that Google use, such as the Google File System (GFS) and BigTable (its distributed storage system for structured data).

6. Advantages of Cloud Computing

Cloud Computing promises to provide all what most of the organizations have been asking for years, but have not been able to achieve. Some advantages of cloud computing have been discussed below:

6.1 Scalability: Cloud Computing allows an organization to scale up or down its IT requirements quickly and efficiently without hampering productivity. It cuts down the time involved in buying and setting up additional hardware, software and other necessary resources every time a new service is required.

6.2 Reduced infrastructure cost: 'Pay as you go' is the mantra of Cloud Computing. One pays only for the duration that he uses the service. This helps cut down unnecessary capital expenditure. Since the resources can be pulled out and restored dynamically, a lot of cost related to maintenance, administration, etc. is reduced.

6.3 Usability: As the IT infrastructure is nothing but a pool of resources, it reduces wastage and improves resource utilization. It also cuts down the downtime.

6.4 Reliability: Reliability is improved if multiple redundant sites are used, which makes well designed Cloud Computing suitable for business continuity and disaster recovery. Nonetheless, many major cloud-computing services have suffered outages, and IT and business managers can at times do little when they are affected.

6.5 Maintenance: Cloud Computing applications can easily be maintained since they do not have to be installed on each user's computer. They are easier to support and to improve since the changes reach the clients instantly.

6.6 Portability: Cloud Computing enable users to access systems using a web browser regardless of their location or what device they are using (e.g., PC, mobile). As infrastructure is off-site (typically provided by a third-party) and accessed via the Internet, users can connect from anywhere.

7. Possible Effects on Libraries

So far libraries are far away from cloud computing, but one or more of the following effects of cloud computing will probably impact libraries and other small-to-mid-sized organizations:

7.1 Cost savings: In an era of shrinking budgets, especially in Indian context, it gets harder with each passing year to justify the purchase and maintenance of servers that are not in use almost all the time. Cloud computing offers price savings due to economies of scale and the fact that you are only paying for the resources you actually use.

7.2 Flexibility and Innovation: Organizations of all sizes can take more risks when it comes to creative, innovative technology ideas when the new application will run on someone else's infrastructure. Libraries do not have to decide between devoting their limited server resources to the OPAC's overflow traffic and a new mobile web application that one of your colleagues wants to develop. If they are both hosted in the cloud, the resources devoted to each will shrink and expand as traffic rises and drops. Furthermore, creating and configuring new virtual server instances is fast and easy in the cloud.

7.3 Cloud OPAC and Cloud ILS: Over the past years, more and more ILS vendors have started offering cloud-hosted versions of their products. OCLC joined several other vendors when they began offering a cloud-based ILS tools that complement their existing cataloging tools (e.g. WorldCat and FirstSearch). As individuals and members of organizations, we are already choosing between desktop applications and cloud applications when it comes to e-mail, RSS, file storage, word processing and other simple applications. Sooner or later we will have to make this choice for mission-critical enterprise applications too.

7.4 Private, Hybrid and Community Clouds: Libraries may soon be building and managing their own data centers. In addition to all the hype and optimism surrounding cloud computing, there are still significant fears and doubts. In particular, the major cloud computing vendors have not yet fully addressed concerns about security, privacy and reliability. These concerns are leading some companies to build their own private or hybrid clouds. A hybrid cloud is primarily based in a privately-owned and operated data center, but it can shift some of its traffic and data processing requests to public cloud vendors, such as Amazon or Rackspace, on an as needed basis. This hybrid model would let libraries maintain more control over the applications and data stores that contain sensitive and private information about patrons.

Moreover, libraries can continually adjust and fine-tune the balance between the tight control of a private IT infrastructure, and the flexibility and savings of cloud-hosted infrastructure. If reliability or security of one vendor becomes a concern, you are not committed to one company or one model of computing services. Moreover, if the thought of "building and managing your own data center" sends chills down your spine, you might consider a community cloud. As this explains, Google plans to launch a government-only cloud to address government concerns about security and privacy. Just as libraries presently cooperate with one another to buy IT equipment, bandwidth and the services of IT professionals, libraries may soon cooperate in the building and management of data centers. Alternately, if enough libraries express interest, a company such as Google, Amazon, Microsoft or another cloud vendor might create a Library Cloud similar to Google's Government Cloud. On the other hand, a library vendor with deep IT resources (e.g. OCLC or SirsiDynix) might build library-centric cloud services on top of cloud infrastructure leased from one of the more established players.

8. Conclusion

There is no doubt that Cloud Computing is the future of computing. Though presently there is a dearth of cloud vendors, after a few years every one in the society will consider Cloud Computing as an important aspect of IT. Cloud market will definitely occupy the whole IT world. Personally we have step into the world of cloud by using Facebook, Flicker, YouTube, Google's doc, etc. In the field of library services Cloud Computing will definitely be a key player as commonly there is a financial constraint for all types of libraries specially in India. Building of Community Clouds by the government in the different areas such as education, commerce, agriculture, banking, finance, etc. will definitely be economical, will increase cooperation among different organizations, and also bring transparency in the governance.

References

1. Kroski, E. (2009). Library Cloud Atlas: A Guide to Cloud Computing and Storage: Stacking the Tech, Library Journal. Available on http://www.libraryjournal.com/article/CA6695772.html (Access on 11 April, 2011).

2. Chawla, M. (2010). Demystifying Cloud Computing. Available on http://www.pcquest.com/content/search/showarticle1.asp?arid=122142. (Access on 23 April, 2011).

3. Hane, Paula J. (2008). Reports on Libraries, Cloud Computing, and Better Mapping Tools. *Information Today*. Available on http://www.allbusiness.com/professional-services/librarians/11463718-1.html (Access on 10 May 2008).

4. Peters, Chris. (2010). What is Cloud Computing and How will it Affect Libraries. Available on http://www.techsoupforlibraries.org/blog/what-is-cloud-computing-and-how-will-it-affect-libraries. (Access on 01 May, 2011).

10

RFID: An Innovative Technology for Library and Information Centers

Bharat Kumar
Assistant Librarian
Management Development Institute, Gurgaon-122 007
E-mail: Bharat.Kumar@hotmail.com
Bharatkumr@gmail.com

Abstract

The paper describes Radio Frequency Identification (RFID), gives its objectives and traces its history. Elaborates basics of the technology and its components in detail with figures. States standards of the technology and cost of instillations. Paper also discusses key features, advantages and limitations, and ROI of the technology.

0 Introduction

Radio Frequency Identification (RFID) – a technology to identify objects wireless and remote - has been around for decades. Recently, however, has the convergence of lower cost and increased capabilities made organizations take a hard look at what RFID can do for them. It is being used in organizations for long time for various operations – identification of items, inventory control, anti-pilferage of material, stock verification, etc.

1. What is Automatic Identification?

Automatic identification, or auto ID for short, is a broad term given to a host of technologies that are used to identify an object. Auto identification is often coupled with automatic data capture. That is, organizations want to identify an object, capture information about them and somehow get the data into a computer without human intervention. The aim of most of the auto ID systems is to increase efficiency, reduce data entry errors, and free up the staff for more value-added functions/services, such as providing customer service. The technologies that fall under the auto ID umbrella include bar codes, smart cards, voice recognition, Optical Character Recognition (OCR), and Radio Frequency Identification (RFID).

2. What is RFID?

RFID is a generic term for technologies that uses radio waves to automatic identify an object. There are several methods of identification, but most common is a unique identification number that identifies an object, and perhaps other information, on a microchip that is attached to an antenna. The antenna enables the chip to transmit the identification information to a reader. The reader converts the radio waves reflected back from the RFID tag into digital information that can be passed to computers to make use of it.

3. Today's Challenges for Librarians: Dimnishing Resources and Increasing User's Expectations

Check in / out of documents and their re-shelving is one of important activity in a library and a lot amount of manpower is required for it. Most libraries use barcode technology and traditional security systems for it and have reached their limit in current library management operations. This is even more important because of the demand on libraries to:

(i) Increase productivity as diminishing budgets;

(ii) Reduce document handling time;

(iii) Perform more frequent and accurate shelving for better management of collections;

(iv) Improve ergonomics of repetitive tasks; and

(v) Improve service(s).

4. Objectives

Every library's needs and objectives are different, so purpose of implementing RFID technology will vary from one library to another. Thus it is not possible to state each and every objective for implementation of the technology, but the author tries to explain the major common objectives as follows:

(i) To improve operational efficiency;

(ii) To achieve accuracy;

(iii) To reduce operational cost; and

(iv) To make stock verification an easy process.

5. History

Radio frequency identification has been around for decades. It evolved in World War II, radar systems to today's hottest supply chain technology. The Germans, Japanese, Americans and British were all using radar to warn of approaching planes while they were still miles away. The problem was that there was no way to identify which plane belonged to the enemy and which was a country's own pilot returning from a mission.

Advances in radar and RF communications systems continued through the 1950s and 1960s. Scientists and academics in the United States, Europe and Japan did research and presented papers explaining how RF energy could be used to identify objects remotely. Companies began commercializing anti-theft systems that used radio waves to determine whether an item had been paid for or not.

6. How does RFID System Work?

An RFID system consists of a tag made up of a microchip with an antenna, and an interrogator or reader with an antenna. The reader sends out electromagnetic waves. The tag antenna is tuned to receive these waves. The chip then modulates the waves that the tag sends back to the reader and converts into digital data.

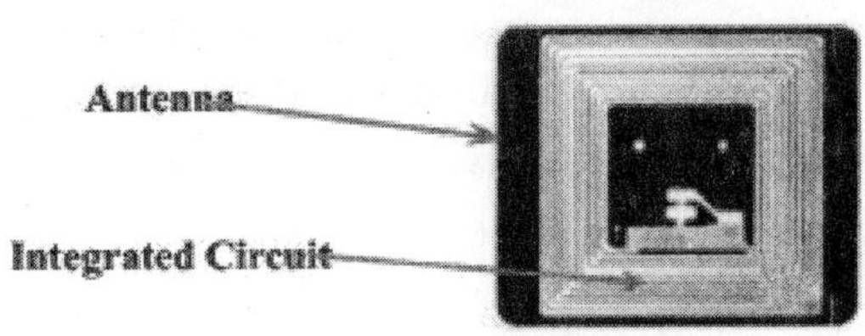

Figure - 1: RFID Tag

7. First RFID Patents

Mario W. Cardullo claims for the first US patent for an active RFID tag with rewritable memory on January 23, 1973. That same year, Charles Walton, a California entrepreneur, got a patent for a passive transponder used to unlock a door without a key. A card with an embedded transponder communicated a signal to a reader near the door. When the reader detected a valid identity number stored within the RFID tag, the reader unlocked the door. Walton licensed the technology to Schlage, a lock maker, and other companies.

Sarma and Brock changed the way that people thought about RFID in the supply chain. They turned RFID into a networking technology by linking objects to the Internet through the tag. For businesses, this was an important change.

Between 1999 and 2003, the Auto ID Center gained the support of more than 100 large end-user companies, plus the US Department of Defense and many key RFID vendors. It opened research labs in Australia, United Kingdom, Switzerland, Japan, and China and developed two air interface protocols (Class 1 and Class 0), the Electronic Product Code (EPC) numbering scheme, and a network architecture for looking up data associated to RFID tag on the network. The technology was licensed to the Uniform Code Council in 2003, and the Uniform Code Council created EPC global, as a joint venture with EAN International, to commercialize EPC technology. The Auto ID Center closed its doors in October 2003, and its research responsibilities were passed on to Auto ID Labs.

8. Basics of RFID Technology

RFID is a technology that connects objects to Intranet, so they can be tracked, and organizations can share data about them. The concept is simple: place a transponder - a microchip with an antenna - on an item and use a reader - a device with one or more antennas - to read data of the microchip using radio waves. The reader passes the information to a computer, so that the data can be used to create business value.

9. RFID System Componenets

Deploying RFID system involves a lot more than purchasing the right tags and installing the right readers. To get business value from the all of the information collected, organizations will need middleware to filter the data. They may need to upgrade enterprise applications and integrate it with RFID middleware. Each component will have up-front costs and some unexpected costs.

9.1 RFID Tags

The vast majority of RFID tags use a silicon microchip to store a unique identification number and usually some additional information. There are two broad categories of RFID tags - *active* and *passive* tags. Passive RFID tags do not have a transmitter; they simply reflect back radio waves coming from the reader antenna. Active tags have their own transmitter and a power source, usually - but not always - a battery (active tags could draw energy from the sun or other sources). They broadcast a signal to transmit the information stored on the microchip.

An RFID tag is often confused with an RFID label. A tag is a transponder mounted on a substrate. It can be embedded in packaging or struck on with adhesive. A RFID label is a transponder sandwiched between a layer with adhesive and paper that can be printed on.

9.1.1 Active Tag

Active tags are used on large assets, such as cargo containers, rail cars and large reusable containers, which need to be tracked over long distances for example in a distribution yard. They usually operate at 455 MHz, 2.45 GHz, or 5.8 GHz, and they typically have a read range of 60 feet to 300 feet (20 meters to 100 meters) and can be read reliably because they broadcast a signal to the reader. The cost of active tag depends on the size of the battery, the amount of memory on the microchip and packaging around the transponder. There are two types of active tags: transponders and beacons.

9.1.1.1 Transponders

Active transponders woke up when they receive a signal from a reader. These are used in toll payment collection, checkpoint control and other systems. The transponder broadcasts its unique ID to the reader. Transponders conserve battery life by having the tag broadcast its signal only when it is within range of a reader.

9.1.1.2 Beacons

Beacons are used in most real-time locating systems (RTLS), where the precise location of an asset needs to be tracked. In an RTLS, a beacon emits a signal with its unique identifier at pre-set intervals (it could be every three seconds or once a day, depending on how important it is to know the location of an asset at a particular moment in time). The beacon's signal is picked up by at least three reader antennas positioned around the perimeter of the area where assets are being tracked. RTLS are usually used outside, say, in a distribution yard but automakers use the systems in large manufacturing facilities to track parts bins.

9.2 Passive Tags

Passive RFID tags have no power source and no transmitter. They are cheaper than active tags and require no maintenance, which is why retailers and manufacturers are looking to use passive tags in the supply chain. They have a much shorter read range than active tags (a few inches to 30 feet). A passive RFID transponder consists of a microchip attached to an antenna. The cost of passive tag depends on its frequency, the amount of memory, design of the antenna and packaging around the transponder.

9.3 Reader

Reader can be internal or external antennas. Reader with external antennas can have one or more ports for connecting reader antennas (the newest readers have up to eight antenna ports). Readers can also have input/output ports for connecting to external devices. An input port might be connected to an electric eye that runs on the reader when something breaks its beam. An output port might connect to a program logic controller, conveyor sorter or other device controlled by the reader. Reader also has ports for connecting to a computer or network. Older reader use serial ports. Newer reader has Ethernet, Wi-Fi or USB ports. The reader's price depends on its features and functionality. The list price of readers may not include the price of antennas and cabling. Organizations should also consider the price of installing readers and the price of running electric cables to areas where readers will be installed.

9.4 Middleware

Middleware is a generic term used to describe software that resides between the RFID reader and enterprise applications. It is a critical component of any RFID system, because the middleware takes the raw data from the reader—a reader might read the same tag 100 times per second—filters it and passes on the useful event data to back-end systems. Middleware plays a key role in getting the right information to the right application at the right time.

There are many RFID middleware products in the market. All do some basic filtering, but many also perform additional functions. Some middleware manage RFID readers: monitor their health, configure them, send software updates and so on. Other middleware may manage the data recorded in databases for enterprise applications to use.

The cost of middleware varies from vendor to vendor and is usually based on the number of locations where it will be installed, the complexity of the application, and many other factors.

9.5 Server

Server is the communication gateway among the various components. Organizations will also need to purchase server to run middleware within a warehouse, distribution center or production facility. This server is sometimes called edge server, because they are close to the edge of the network where the digital world meets the real world. Edge server is a standard computer server, typically do not have any special hardware, and they connect to readers using serial or USB ports.

9.6 Enterprise Applications

The goal of any RFID system is to generate data that can be acted on to boost efficiency, cut costs or provides other business benefits. It means companies will need to invest in enterprise applications that can make use of RFID data. Warehouse management software providers, such as Manhattan Associates and RedPrairie, have upgraded their applications to manage the unique serial numbers in RFID tags. Enterprise resource planning software providers, such as SAP and Oracle, are also working to upgrade their applications. It's likely that software will evolve as RFID adoption spreads and companies learn how to use RFID data to improve their operations. The cost of these applications varies depending on the number of "seats" - how many users will access the application - the number of locations, and other factors.

10. Standards

There are several RFID standards exit, and their applications are under debate within the RFID development community. These standards cover:

- (i) identification, the coding of unique item identifiers or other data on the RF tag;
- (ii) data and system protocols, effectively the middleware of an RFID system;
- (iii) the air interface, that is, the wireless communication between the reader and the tag;
- (iv) application support, which provides advice about how to implement the technology;
- (v) testing compliance, and health and safety, that is, the rules that govern RFID operations; and
- (vi) terminology.

The International Standards Organization (ISO) has three standards for RFID:

- (i) ISO 14443 (for contact less systems),
- (ii) ISO 15693 (for vicinity systems such as ID badges), and

(iii) ISO 18000 (to specify the air interface for variety of RFID applications).

A non-profit organization EPC global, has developed a widely accepted standard for the product identification. The Electronic Product Code (EPC) standard covers the air interfaces, the format of product identification data stored on a RFID tag, and the middleware and the databases sorting information about tags.

11. RFID System Cost

It is not possible to provide a list of every element that every organization will need and the cost of those systems, but the author tries to explain each of the major components and point out where there might be some hidden costs. Keep in mind that every organization's needs - and every application - are different, so costs will vary widely from installation to installation. Organizations will also need to invest in training for their employees particularly IT staff who will work on the system that manage RFID data.

Most organizations will need to hire a systems integrator to install the readers, determine the right placement of tags for products and make sure that they are feeding data to the middleware in the right format. RFID system can be tricky to install in a way that provides accurate reading because many factors affect the ability to read a tag, including the placement of the tag, placement of antenna and type of antenna.

As the technology improves and is more widely adopted, costs will come down and the technology will be easier to install.

12. RFID: Key Features

The key features of using RFID technology are as listed below:

(i) **No Line of Sight:** RFID tags can be read without line of sight. This reduces material handling and makes activities fast, easy, and accurate.

(ii) **Self Charging / Discharging:** This technology enables patrons to issue / return documents themselves. Thus, library staff is relieved for more productive work.

(iii) **Reading Multiple Items:** Number of items can be read at the same time without contact. This can not be done as easily with visual identifiers.

(iv) **Read Speed:** Tags can be read from significant distances and can also be read quickly. It is especially useful when the items need to be identified.

(v) **Robust:** Tags need not be visible and can be wrapped with rugged materials protecting them from the environment they are being used.

(vi) **Security:** The information contained in a tag may be protected through the use of passwords. This ensures a much higher level of security than barcodes or magnetic cards.

13. Advantages

The use of RFID technology increases efficiency and speed of operations. There are several multiple and multiplicative improvements possible as listed below:

(i) improves:

(a) efficiency of the staff; (b) quality of services;

(ii) improves the image of the organization;

(iii) provides reliable statistics for Management Information System (MIS) and management control;

(iv) enhances elegance and aesthetics of the front office and its activities;

(v) ensures perfect entry and retrieval of data;

(vi) improves information availability;

(vii) helps in strengthening security;

(viii) improves shelf collection management; and

(ix) makes library professionals to focus on value added services.

14. Limitations

Some of the limitations in implementations of RFID technology are:

(i) high cost of RFID system;

(ii) lack of standards;

(iii) chances of removal of exposed tags; and

(iv) lack of technical knowledge and exposure.

15. Return on Investment (ROI)

Installation of an RFID system is comparatively more costly than the system using barcodes, primarily because the tags themselves are many times more expensive than the barcode labels. The cost of software and hardware is additional. However, other factors, such as the reduction in staff time for check out and check in of documents, the elimination of the need for "tattle tape" inserts in items for security purposes, and the less tangible savings that could accompany the greater ability to perform inventories and identify missing and miss-shelved documents, may compensate the cost of the RFID. Some estimation of expected savings could be done based on the experience of other libraries, but the fact is that the data on ROI for library RFID systems is still scarce due to the early stage of implementation of this technology.

16. The Road Ahead

Now the standards are starting to appear, the cost of tags will reduce over the time. Industrial experts predict a substantial growth in this. RFID will be next technological wave for the automatic data capturing industry.

17. Conlusion

RFID technology existing for many years has potential uses in a variety of applications. It has been developing into a mature product to provide new solutions to identify an object. Its application increases productivity, and eliminates human error, improves speed of operations and services. The main barrier to implement the technology is cost justification for the application. The magnitude of expected improvement of the introduction of the technology in a library is directly proportional to the size of its collection, the number of patrons, and the number of transactions per day. Application of this technology will definitely improve the image of the library and develop a positive attitude of patrons towards the library. Its application is a step forward towards satisfying the Fourth Law of Library Science – 'Save the time of users'.

References

1. BOSS (R W). PLA Tech Notes (May 14, 2004) RFID Technology for libraries. Available at: www.ala.org/ala/pla/plapubs/technotes/rfidtechnology.htm (Accessed on 19/07/2006)
2. DAVIES (Linda) and ROBERTS (Lindsay). Set your library staff free with RFID: a case study from Cardiff University. *SCONUL Focus*. 45, 2009; 117 – 22. Available at http://www.sconul.ac.uk/publications/newsletter/45/32.pdf (Accessed on 22/11/2009)
3. FAQ RFID Journal. Available at: http://www.rfidjournal.com/faq (Accessed on 27/01/2006)
4. KERN (Christian). Radio-frequency-identification for security and media circulation in libraries. *The Electronic Library*. 7, 4; 2004; 317 - 24.
5. KONERU (Indira). RFID Technology: A Revolution in Library Management. 2004. Available at: http://dspace.inflibnet.ac.in/bitstream/1944/362/1/04cali_54.pdf (Accessed on 22/10/2009)
6. PRABAKARAN (D). RFID tags to track objects. *Electronics for You*. 35, 7; 2003; 97 - 101.
7. Radio frequency identification. Available at: http://www.rfidjournal.com/article/ (Accessed on 27/01/2006)
8. RFID and San Francisco Public Library. 2005. Available at: http://www.sfpl.org/librarylocations/libtechcomm/RFID-and-SFPL-summary-report-oct2005.pdf (Accessed on 22/10/2009)
9. RFID: a revolutionary technology for library management. Available at: http://www.tech-logic.com/pdf/understanding%20rfid.pdf (Accessed on 27/01/2007)
10. RON (Weinstein). RFID: a technical overview and its application to the enterprise. *IT Professional*. 7, 3; 2005; 27 - 33.
11. SHAHID (Syed Md) .Use of RFID technology in libraries: a new approach to circulation, tracking, inventorying, and security of library materials. *Library Philosophy and Practice*. 8, 1; 2005.

11

Implementation of an Innovative RFID Technology in Central Library, IIT Delhi

Dr. Neeraj Kumar Chaurasia
Assistant Librarian & Head, Reader Services
Central Library, Indian Institute of Technology Delhi, New Delhi
Pankaj Chaurasia
Assistant Librarian
National Institute of Public Cooperation and Child Development (NIPCCD), New Delhi

Abstract

The paper provides information about the Radio Frequency IDentification (RFID) technology, its importance and working. It describes the basic and optional components and procedures required for successfully implementing and working of the system. Shows a vivid picture about how RFID technology is acting as a boon for libraries thereby highlighting the key benefits like self charging-discharging, renewing, high speed inventorying, theft detection, automated materials handling, reliability, etc. Besides, it outlines various issues and challenges involved in the process of implementing RFID applications in libraries. Also, it outlines various issues and possible solutions involved in the process of implementing RFID applications in Central Library, Indian Institute of Technology Delhi.

Keywords: RFID Technology, Tag, Transponder, Reader, Radio Frequency Identification, Library Automation, Library Authentication System, Tagging, Smart Card System.

1. Introduction

In their quest for serving the patrons better, the libraries are continually adopting newer and most advanced technologies. RFID is an innovative automated library system for automatic identification and tracking of library material. It is combination of radio-Frequency-based technology and microchip technology and can be used to identify, track, sort or detect library holdings. This is an effective way of managing collections of the library and providing enhanced services to the users having benefits like: to control increasing theft, to find misplaced reading material, inventory accuracy, stock verification, security control, etc. It is an automatic data capture technology that uses tiny microchips and miniature antennas affixed to products. RFID technology offers great potential for broadening access to library services and security in ways never before conceived. RFID plays a vital role in redefining the library processes to make everyone's job easier right from the users to library staff. It provides a platform to automate most of the processes performed by the library staff like check in-check out, sorting, stock management, etc.

Radio Frequency IDentification (RFID) is an exciting and fast growing technology for increasing efficiency, improving profitability and is an important area of study in today's information environment.

According to *Lindquist (2003)*: [. . .] new technologies have always been of interest for libraries, both for the potential of increasing the quality of service and for improving efficiency of operations. At the present time, when libraries of all kinds [public, research, special] are facing economic hardships the overwhelming reason for considering new technologies is the potential for cost savings in the operations and the management of material flows.

Any library's priority is to add interpretive and educational value to its basic resources, and to highlight the importance of the library's contributions to the institution's well-being and future progress. The most significant time savings are attributable to the fact that information can be read from RFID tags much faster than from bar codes and that several items in a stack can be read at the same time.

The implementation of RFID technology certainly improves service efficiency for libraries and enables more diversified applications and service modes. However, as stated by *Yu (2008)* "regulating necessary standards, processes, and interfaces to fit in with current information systems and extend automatic library operations requires continuous effort".

2. Components of an RFID system

A comprehensive RFID system has following components:

2.1 RFID tag (or transponder): The chip and the antenna together are called RFID tag (or transponder). These are paper-thin smart labels which are electronically programmed with unique information. Tags are the electronic chips consisting of an integrated circuit and antenna coil that communicates with a reader by means of a radio frequency signal. These tags are available as labels with adhesive backings and ability to reel through a label printer. After sticking RFID label on the book, its vital bibliographical data, including unique Accession Number is registered in the chip of the label. This function allows writing such information on chip either from the library database or by scanning existing barcode labels and helps to identify each book. Two types of RFID tags are available viz. Active or Passive. Passive tags do not have their own power supply so the device is quite small. These have practical read ranges that vary from about 10 mm up to about 5 meters. Active RFID tags, on the other hand, must have a power source and may have longer ranges and larger memories than passive tags as well as the ability to store additional information sent by the transceiver. Active RFID tags can be about the size of a coin and have practical ranges of tens of meters, and a battery life up to several years. Many libraries are making use of passive tags because of their lower cost and appropriate size. The tags can be read at a distance of up to two feet by each of two parallel exit sensors. The devices used for circulation are usually called "readers" while the ones used at building exits are usually called "sensors".

Figure 1: RFID Tag

There are three types of tags: "read only", "WORM," and "read/ write" *(Boss, 2005)*. "Tags are "read only" if the identification is encoded at the time of manufacture and not rewritable. "WORM" (Write-Once-Read-Many) tags are programmed by the using organization, but without the ability to rewrite them later. "Read/

write tags," which are chosen by most libraries, can have information changed or added. In libraries that use RFID, it is common to have part of the read/write tag secured against rewriting, e.g., the identification number of the item.

2.2. RFID reader (or interrogator): RFID reader consists of a transmitter, receiver, antenna, and a decoder. They communicate with RFID tags, identify them and receive data stored on the tag. It provides a contact less data link which means books can be issued/ retuned without opening. A typical RFID system includes four different kinds of readers, also known as sensors or scanners. These devices are designed to detect and read tags to obtain the information stored thereon.

2.2.1 ***Staff workstations*** for circulation desk charging and discharging. The equipment can easily be connected to a network or single workstation PC or notebook and the application can begin functioning thereon. It also supports all RFID functions like anti collision feature allowing to identify multiple labels simultaneously, present in the reader field and full read/write capability. It is used at the issue/return counters at the library and also for label personalization.

Figure 2 : RFID based staff workstation

2.2.2 ***Self check-in/check-out stations*** for allowing users to borrow books without assistance from the library staff. It is an interactive station/kiosk with touch screen which prompt the user to enter library card. The validity of the library card is checked and user is prompted to place the books on to the deck of the Borrowing Station. The status of each book as checked-out is automatically updated on the Library Management database. The theft detection system of the RFID tag for that book is deactivated to enable smooth passage from the security gate. A receipt may be issued to the user confirming details of borrowed books along with due date.

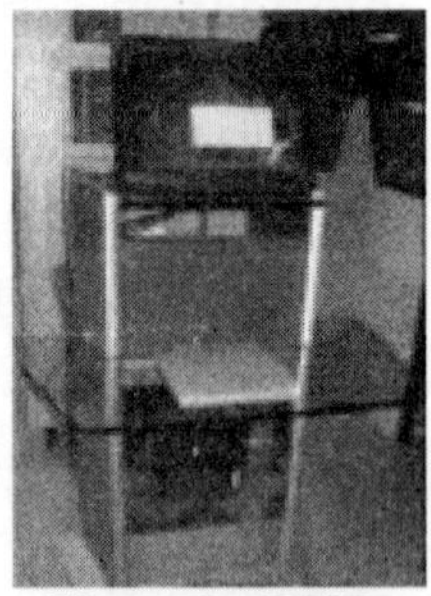

Figure 3 : RFID based self check-in/ check-out

2.2.3 ***Exit sensors*** at exit are of two types; one reads the information on the tag(s) going by and communicates that information to a server. The server, after checking against the circulation database, activates an alarm if the material is not properly checked-out. Another type relies on a "theft" byte in the tag that is turned on or off to show that the item has been charged or not. It is then not necessary to communicate with the circulation database. The security system will work even though the online library server is not working. This gates security system composed of the desired number of pedestals i.e. generally 2 to 4. It may also be used to count the incoming/outgoing people with a facility to record their movement.

2.2.4 ***Shelf management system or Portable shelf scanner*** allows library staff to take inventory and find wrongly shelved books without having to pull the books off the stacks. It is very useful for stock verification purpose.

2.2.5 ***Book drop kiosk*** checks in books when users drop them in the bookdrop. Libraries can offer a distinct service that is very useful for users, such as the ability to return books when the library is closed. An external book return is a machine with a slot with a chip RFID reader integrated into the wall. It works the same way as the self checkout station. The user identifies himself/herself (if required by the library), and then puts the book(s) into the slot. Upon completing the return, the user will receive a receipt showing how many and which books were returned. The theft detection system into the smart labels is simultaneously activated. Since the books have already been checked in and RFID tags activated, they can go directly back onto the shelves.

Figure 4 : RFID based book drop kiosk

2.3 Application software is used for the reader to transmit or receive data from a tag. Software integrates the reader hardware with the existing Library Automation Software for seamless functioning of Circulation Counter.

2.4 Server/Docking station is one on which the software that interfaces with the integrated library software is loaded. The server is the heart of some comprehensive RFID systems. It is the communication gateway among the various components. It receives the information from one or more of the readers and exchanges information with the circulation database. Its software includes the APIs (Applications Programming Interface) necessary to interface it with the automated library system. The server typically includes a transaction database so that reports can be produced.

2.5 RFID Smart Card are used for RFID based library transactions. These cards can also be used for other purposes for the institute. RFID is increasingly used with biometric technologies for security.

Figure 5 : RFID based Smart Card

3. RFID implementation at Central Library, IIT Delhi

The IIT Delhi Library System comprises of a Central Library and 18 departmental libraries that collectively support the teaching, research and extension programmes of the Institute. All students, faculty and employees of the Institute are entitled to make use of the library facilities. The alumni, industrial establishments, faculty-students of outside organizations, wards of IIT faculty and staff can also avail the library facilities as per the prevailing rules. The collection of the library has grown to 3,66,501 as on 31st March, 2011 including 1,87,845 books, 1,03,942 bound volumes of journals, 26,923 standards, 2,261 microfilms, 3,800 theses, 13,430 technical reports, 1,800 video cassettes and 5,000 CDs.

In 1999, in order to provide a better service and to promote the research activity of the Institute, the library started using the LibSys library management system package, developed by Info-Tek Consultants in New Delhi (www.libsys.co.in/). Almost 1,50,000 records have been added to the bibliographic database since then. Following figure shows the opening page of the online public access catalogue (OPAC) at the Central Library, IIT Delhi.

The Central Library, IIT Delhi implemented barcode technology in 2002 to assist the circulation of its stock. The barcode technology adopted in the library was not efficient enough to detect the theft of documents in the library. Library staff were investigating technology as a way to save staff time, reduce personnel costs, improve security and inventory control, but before implementation of RFID, library staff checked the feasibility and planning of this technology.

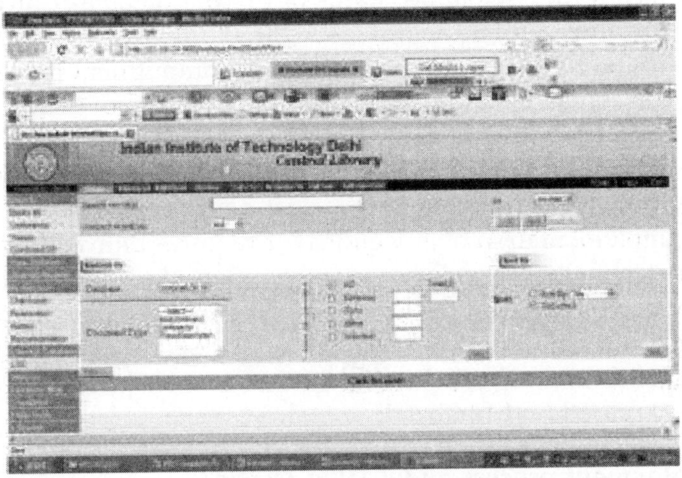

Figure 6: Opening page of the OPAC at Central Library, IIT Delhi.

3.1 Feasibility and planning

The initial task of any feasibility study is to establish the aims of the project, which need to be derived from some form of users' needs assessment in the beginning. *Vaishnaav and Bapat (1995)* have outlined three areas of feasibility study, namely: technical feasibility; social feasibility; and economic feasibility. The central endeavour of any feasibility study is a cost-benefit analysis of the various alternatives, although a full cost-benefit analysis is unlikely to be appropriate in a library situation, particularly when the system under analysis has not yet been instituted. However, a partial analysis can yield useful insights *(Rowley, 1980)*.

Before implementation of this technology in a library, it is necessary to study the feasibility of the system. A committee may be constituted with experts and administrators who may have knowledge of RFID systems and other administrative procedures. The committee may assess the requirements for the institution, budget availability, required hardware and software, cost effectiveness, availability of manpower, time line, etc. The methodology for implementation can be divided into many phases taking into consideration of budget provisions, the types of document holdings, number of volumes, types of items meant for circulation, status of present database/automation and the number and types of users that the institution has. To implement the RFID, gaining management commitment may be a big challenge as it may look into the Return On Investment (ROI) to assess RFID investment before it commits to its implementation. A challenge that institutions face with is the high cost of implementation. To justify the adoption of RFID technology, cost-benefit analysis is a must. Smooth implementation of any endeavor requires thorough planning. Since the technology is still not very common, the committee should see some demos and visit the libraries where the system is successfully running. Data validation is most important before actually starting the tagging work. A feasibility report on the basis of all this exercise may be prepared and finalized.

3.2 Deployment process and related issues

Tendering is the most important and difficult process for the implementation of the system. A good tender document should look into all the minute details of the technical, administrative and functional aspects. If the tender document is fool proof then there may not be any problem in its implementation. The feasibility report prepared by the committee may help in this regard. Some of the things which should be considered for the deployment of RFID system and for preparing the tender document and to select the vender may include:

i. Proven capability of vender to integrate the proposed solution with multiple LMS for future safety. The bidder should have sufficient successful practical experience of supply, installation, testing, commissioning, and post-commissioning.

ii. The items to be supplied should be of proven good quality with makes having globally accepted presence and compatible with global standards.

iii. Supplied equipment should allow forward compatibility with anticipated new standards.

iv. Robustness of the system (scalability, accuracy).

v. Judge vendors' technology know-how for products to be supplied.

vi. Ask for customer reference & arrange site visit and discuss your concerns with them.

vii. Librarians should compare overall benefits vs cost involved while adopting a particular automation technology.

viii. The tender may have two parts; Technical Bid and Financial Bid. The Financial bid should only be opened once the Bidder qualifies for the Technical bid.

ix. Incomplete, vague and conditionally submitted bids should not be considered.

x. The validity of the successful bid should clearly be desired by the Institute with a clear delivery schedule. Payment should be made after satisfactory installation and commissioning.

xi. Issues related to onsite training, warranty, service and AMC should have been clearly mentioned.

xii. The Institute may also think to retain some security money for the post-commissioning period for a couple of years.

3.3. Impact of RFID system on library

The implementation of the RFID systems has impacted the Library in various ways as follows:

3.3.1 Saving time at the circulation counter

Central Library, IIT Delhi has around 9,000 registered users, with different member "categories" being defined in the LibSys member database. Library members can borrow twelve books at a time whereas others can borrow up to 2-5 books. In the circulation module of LSmart, the maximum limit set for one transaction is five books and the software allows for the charging or discharging of five books in one click.

The use of RFID reduces the amount of time required to perform circulation operations. This technology helps librarians eliminate valuable staff time spent scanning barcodes while checking out and checking in borrowed items. For the users, RFID speeds up the borrowing and return procedures. Library employees are released for more productive and interesting duties. Staff are relieved further when readers are installed in book drops.

Circulation includes check-out, check-in and renewal of the documents. It usually takes 1-2 min to complete a single transaction when the task is performed manually, while the same transaction takes place within 1-2 seconds with the RFID system. A further advantage is that if the user has five items to check-out or check-in the transaction can be easily completed with a single stroke.

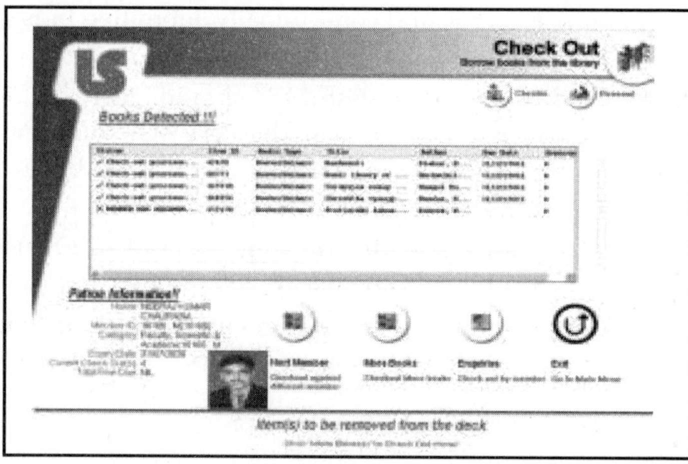

Figure 7: Charging of five books in one click

In the case of barcode systems the circulation staff have to scan the barcode of the user's card and then the barcode of every item to complete a single transaction, whereas using RFID five transactions are possible in one click. This has resulted in saving the time of the users at the circulation counter and also the time of the staff. After comparing the circulation using RFID with that of a manual and barcode system one can conclude that now the circulation system has become much faster than any previous system by implementing RFID.

3.3.2 *Theft detection*

The two security gates, i.e. theft detection pedestals, have been installed at the entrance and exit gates of the library. These gates are independent of each other and also have overlapping protection zones providing additional security. Before the implementation of RFID in the library many items were not traceable, and, apart from books being misplaced on the shelves, one of the main reasons was theft.

Figure 8 : Exit Gates (EAS Pedestal) installed at the entrance and exit of Central Library

Now, since most of the users know that the system is in place and is capable of detecting theft, none is trying to take items out of the library without charging them. The EAS exit gates have option to keep record of incoming and outgoing library users with recording.

3.3.3 *Tracing missing books using RFID hand reader*

Previously it was very difficult to trace misplaced books because of the size of the collection and also because of the Universal Decimal Classification (UDC) scheme used in IIT Central Library to shelve items. To locate a book it sometimes used to take 2-3 hours or even two to three days, however, using the RFID hand reader library staff are able to trace any item in a few minutes. The RFID hand reader allows accession numbers of missing books to be stored and when staff scan though the stacks with the hand reader an audible "beep" indicates the location of the missing item.

Figure 9 : Shelf/ Inventory

3.3.4 *Shelving of books using RFID*

Once the sequence of books is defined and stored in the software (IPAQ) installed on a Tablet PC/Note Book PC, it becomes very easy, with the RFID hand reader, to shelve books. Discharged books can easily be separated according to the rack number and location number.

3.3.5 *Stock verification*

Taking stock every year is an important function in all libraries and is a major challenge for those, such as Central Library IIT Delhi, with a large collection. Performing stock verification manually is practically impossible for this Library. Prior to implementing the RFID system, Central Library IIT Delhi was performing sample stock verification, but now with the help of the hand reader the Library can regularly do its stock verification. The PDA-based hand reader can scan thousands of books lying on shelves without even a single book being pulled out, as would be the case with a barcode reader. Data is then updated instantly on the server for stock verification with the database. At the end it shows a list of matched and unmatched items. This device also helps in sorting shelves and searching for specific items.

4. Stepwise implementation of RFID system in libraries

4.1 Procurement of hardware: Sourcing for the hardware required need to be done before anything else. Quotations/tenders may be called with detailed specification of each item required so as to compare the rates quoted for different items. The libraries should procure the best hardware that includes Readers, Tags, Antenna, etc.

4.2 Retrospective conversion of already existing stack requires a "programmer" or "conversion station." The conversion of existing bar coded items, including affixing the tags to library materials, takes 15-30 seconds per item depending on the amount of information added to the tag and the skill of the person doing the tagging. Pre-programmed tags, which are used for new acquisitions in libraries that want only identification numbers on the tags, take even less time because they do not involve scanning of existing barcodes. The speed of conversion can be increased by dividing responsibility for removing and replacing library materials, converting the barcodes, and inserting the tags among at least three people. It is essential that the tasks be rotated so that no one repeats the same motions over an extended period of time. Also, library might consider doing the tagging of new acquisitions at the time of receipt in Acquisition Section itself so as to avoid losses of unprocessed material from other sections of the library.

4.3 Tagging books: Each document need to be tagged. The fixing of tags to documents can be initially outsourced then in house arrangement can be done after proper training. The tags can be over layered with the self adhesive sticker containing the logo of the library or the institution for longer life. It is also important to select a consistent location for book tags. The inside of the back cover is the recommended location because it is the fastest for right-handed tag installers to reach. One vendor recommends near the spine approximately three inches above the bottom. That avoids possible interference from metal shelves when inventorying. However, a library should consider placing the tags inside the front cover under a bookplate or with a bookplate printed on the tag. That may make the tag less apparent and, therefore, improve security.

4.4 Integration with library management software: With the preset Library Management Software. Care should be taken to integrate the library automation package while detailed tender specifications are drawn.

4.5 Performing test cases: Predefined set of test cases will be performed in scenario based format to examine unit level and system level performance for accuracy and greater throughput. With this the verification of hardware and software can be checked completely.

4.6 Training of staff: Train the staff on various aspects of RFID technology. Since the technology is new to Indian library environment, proper demonstration of the system can be arranged and librarian should visit the library where the system is successfully running. Each and every member of library should be well aware of the technology and the guidelines given for the entire process. Training Session should be organized to make the staff of understand the technology.

4.7 Process improvement: The errors found out from the test cases will be revisited to make the system perform accurately. Until sufficient confidence is gained with the system, old system in practice should be continued.

5. Barriers faced while implementing the technology

The LibSys software package includes a number of modules, e.g. LSPremia, LSmart, and LSdigital. According to its web site "LSmart is a suite of applications harnessing RFID technology for use in libraries. It is the result of integrating the power of LibSys software with RFID hardware equipment from different vendors" (www.libsys.co.in/lsmart.html). Thus, it was appropriate to use LSmart for implementing RFID in the Central Library, IIT Delhi and following shows details of this module. While implementing RFID with the help of LSmart, the Library has come across following barriers.

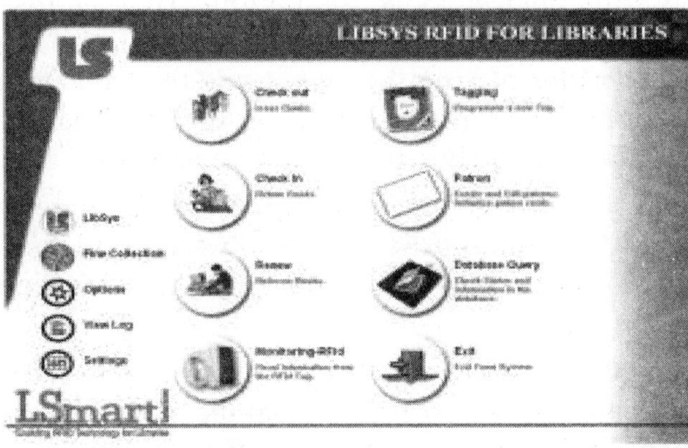

Figure 10 : LSmart module of LibSys software

5.1 Resistance of the users towards change

Initially, when the library started implementing the RFID technology in parallel with the manual charging and discharging system, there was resistance from the users in the adoption of the new technology. Also they were afraid that, while discharging the book if both the records were not cleared by the library staff from both the systems then they might be liable to pay fines. Also, as the users were well versed in the old charging and discharging system they were not ready to switch over to the new system.

5.2 Lack of technology experts

RFID, being new technology, brings about a situation of lack of expertise and professional advice as it has yet not been implemented in many libraries in India and sub continent. When the RFID technology was implemented in the Library it was new for the library staff and a few staff members had appropriate knowledge of it. The lack of any technology expert in the library was a major barrier in the implementation. In order to overcome this barrier the Library arranged various training programmes for the Library staff.

5.3 Technology literate users

The technology literate users have also created many problems in the Library. These users knew the function of the tags and so they removed the tags from the documents and tried to take the books out from the library without getting these charged in the proper way. Once the tags are removed from the documents the RFID gates were not able to detect the theft of the documents and this helped some users to steal items from the Library. Few such cases were recorded in the library after the implementation of this technology.

5.4 Moisture barrier

The moisture present in the atmosphere, especially during rainy days, affects the RFID tag. A tag, which contains moisture, does not respond to the RFID system. The users can take advantage of this by taking items out of the library without charging. Users can pass through the antennae without getting the book charged by putting their palm on the tag, because the RFID signal cannot pass through a liquid medium.

5.5 Problems of tagging and un-tagging

Tagging involves the coding of bibliographic data in the RFID tag attached to a particular book or item. Once data is entered in the database it is essential to perform the tagging function. For this the LSmart tagging function is used to write, or feed, the accession number of the item on to the chip of the label. In some cases this tagging function was not performed correctly by the data-entry operators, as some wrong accession numbers were entered. This resulted in failure to retrieve the correct bibliographic details of the item at the circulation counter. Also, sometimes due to the moisture present on the tags it stops functioning. In such cases the library staff have to perform an "un-tagging" function first and then the tagging function or, in some cases, have had to replace the tag.

5.6 Problems encountered at the circulation counter

Staff at the circulation counter have encountered many problems while using the RFID technology. For instance, users may come to the counter with an item, which does not have an RFID tag, or the tag is removed due to heavy usage. In such cases the message such as "no book found" used to flash on the screen of the computer. Alternatively, when the bibliographic details of an item had not been entered correctly in the database the message "no accessioned book found" used to flash on the screen when a user wished to borrow the item. All such problems have been identified and remedial action for individual problems such as adding tags to the documents, or adding bibliographic details of the document in the database, were communicated to all circulation staff to overcome these problems.

6. Disadvantages of RFID technology

Some of the disadvantages in using the RFID technology are as follows:

6.1 RFID tag

The RFID readers are fairly easy to use but the key failing is the lack of security of the tags themselves. RFID is a wireless technology and is therefore subject to third-party interception unless the signal is secured *(Hodgson, 2004)*. Only a very restricted amount of security can be incorporated in current library RFID tags due to the limited amount of data they can hold and no library tags today employ password or read access control *(Molnar and Wagner, 2004)*.

The tags used by library RFID vendors are not compatible even when they conform to the same standards because the current standards only seek electronic compatibility between tags and readers. The pattern of encoding information and the software that processes the information differs from vendor to vendor. Therefore, a change from one vendor's system to the other would require retagging all items or modifying the software *(Boss, 2005)*.

When the distance among the tags is very close, interference between them may be made or erroneous access may occur. For example, if one patron is taking books to initiate the loan process under self-check in/out equipment (RFID reader), and another patron is standing too close to the first patron, the reader doing the self check in/out may detect the tags of books which are held by the other patron.

6.2 High cost

The major disadvantage of RFID technology is its cost. The readers and sensors used to read the information are comparable in cost to the components of a typical electro-mechanical or radio-frequency theft detection system *(Boss, 2005)*. The price of hardware (per unit) varies extensively from different suppliers, however, the infrastructure requirement also varies. While RFID tags are falling in price they are still more costly than barcodes, however they do offer long-term reliability. The cost is one of the major factors influencing acceptance of RFID system in libraries. At present, the cost of RFID adoption comprise the major investment in hardware, application software, middleware, tags, cost of integrating the RFID-based system with the legacy system, etc.

6.3 Patron privacy concerns

Privacy concerns associated with item-level tagging is another significant barrier to library use of RFID tags. The problem with today's library RFID system is that the tags contain static information that can be relatively easily read by unauthorized tag readers. This allows for privacy issues described as "tracking" and "hotlisting" *(Ayre, 2004)*. Tracking refers to the ability to track the movements of a book (or person carrying the book) by "correlating multiple observations of the book's bar code" *(Molnar and Wagner, 2004)* or RFID tag. Hotlisting refers to the process of building a database of books and their associated tag numbers (the hotlist) and then using an unauthorized reader to determine who is checking out items in the hotlist.

6.4 Accessibility to compromise

It is possible to compromise an RFID system by wrapping the protected material in two to three layers of ordinary household aluminum foil to block the radio signal*(Boss, 2005)*. The system may also be compromised by placing a normal coin on RFID tag or two items against one another so that one tag overlays another. That may cancel out the signals. Some interference from metallic material does occur and tag reading may not be correct. Physical damage to the tags removal by the library users is also un-avoidable. The moisture present in the atmosphere, especially in rainy days, affects the RFID tag. There may be some other factors as well that can influence the read/write efficiency of RFID as well like metal, mist, distance, and incorrect positioning of antennas.

6.5 Chances of removal of exposed tags

RFID tags are typically affixed to the inside back cover and are exposed for removal. This means that there would be problems when users become more familiar with the role of the tags *(Boss, 2005).* In Indian libraries, it is a major challenge to keep the tags intact.

6.6 Exit gate sensor (Reader) problems

While the short-range readers used for circulation charge and discharge and inventorying appear to read the tags 100 per cent of the time *(Boss, 2005),* the performance of the exit gate sensors is more problematic. They always do not read tags at up to twice the distance of the other readers. There is no library that has done a before and after inventory to determine the loss rate when RFID is used for security.

6.7 Reader collision

The signal from one reader can interfere with the signal from another where coverage overlaps. This is called reader collision. One way to avoid the problem is to use a technique called time division multiple access, or TDMA. In simple terms, the readers are instructed to read at different times, rather than both trying to read at the same time. This ensures that they do not interfere with each other. But it means any RFID tag in an area where two readers overlap will be read twice *(Shahid, 2005).*

6.8 Tag collision

Another problem readers have is reading a lot of chips in the same field. Tag clash occurs when more than one chip reflects back a signal at the same time, confusing the reader. Different vendors have developed different systems for having the tags respond to the reader one at a time. Since they can be read in milliseconds, it appears that all the tags are being read simultaneously *(Shahid, 2005).*

6.9 Lack of Standard

The tags used by library RFID vendors are not compatible even when they conform to the same standards because the current standards only seek electronic compatibility between tags and readers. The pattern of encoding information and the software that processes the information differs from vendor to vendor, a change from one vendor's system to the other would require retagging all items or modifying the software *(Shahid, 2005).* All existing RFID systems use proprietary technology which means that if Company A puts an RFID tag on a product, it can't be read by Company B unless they both use the same RFID system from the same vendor. Standards are emerging *(RFID Journal, 2003)*, but according to the industry watchers, the absence of a global standard for RFID deployment has resulted in interoperability issues and a technology that is still too expensive to acquire *(Yu, 2005).*

6.10 Lack of RFID compatible software in India

Software that is available in the Indian market which is RFID compatible includes LibSys, LibSuite, New GenLib and VTLS. Libraries that are using other than these software solutions need to change their software or modify the software as per RFID requirements. In either case libraries need a lot of time and money, which is not economically feasible in an Indian scenario. Apart from the above listed Indian software there are some international products which are compatible with RFID namely: 3Me Detection System, BiblioChip RFID library system, ELiMSw and Civica.

Unlike default availability of free barcode integration module in premium LMS like VTLS, Alice, LibSys, etc, LMS vendors not only charge separately for allowing integration of RFID solution with their software using NCIP V2.0 or SIP2 protocol but sometime integration is also difficult.

7. How library RFID system works?

The technology works through flexible, paper-thin smart labels (RFID tags), which allows it to be placed inconspicuously on the inside cover of each and every document in a library's collection and on the other collections like CDs. DVDs, etc. Complete information about each document is entered into the software installed in Server or Docking station. Now whenever a user brings the book for issue/return purpose, the RFID reader from the tag reads the information pertaining to that book and transmits the data into the software and book is smoothly issued in a few seconds with a minimum of manual intervention. As the user takes the book outside the library, the antenna placed at the exit gate automatically read the information contained on the RFID tag to verify whether the book is properly issued or not. In case the book is not issued to the user as per the library norms or it is being stolen from the library, the antenna senses it and give an instant alert. Thus the technology results in successful theft reduction of documents. The technology is also used for stock taking/inventory management purpose.

8. RFID standards for library

The International Organization for Standardization (ISO) and EPC Global has been very active in developing RFID standards. The AutoID center and their commercial offshoot EPC Global have also defined specifications and standards. There are two important ISO standards pertinent to library RFID systems: ISO/IEC 15693 Standards & ISO/IEC 18000-3. These standards works on 13.56 Mhz (HF). The tags and the equipments used may carry the FCC certifications. They may follow the NCIP V2.0 or SIP2 protocol (http://www.iso.org ; http://www.iec.ch).

9. RFID in Indian libraries

Several libraries have successfully installed the RFID solutions in India. The products of many manufactures of library RHO systems are available in India through their business associates or direct. RFID technology has been introduced in a number of Indian libraries like: Anna University, Chennai; Bank of Baroda, Mumbai; BCL, Chennai; BCL, New Delhi; IGCAR, Kalpakkam; JIM, Indore; IIM, Lucknow; IISc, Bangalore; IIT, Chennai; IIT Delhi; IIT Roorkee (Commissioning stage); IIT, Kharagpur; NASSDOC, New Delhi; NCL, Pune; Nirma University, Ahmedabad; NIT, Rourkela; NIT, Surat; Parliament Library, New Delhi; Punjab University, Chandigarh; Sapru House, New Delhi; University of Pune.

10. RFID vendors in India

There are many vendors of RFID components all over the world and nowadays India is also producing RFID components. A list of some of the RFID vendors with presence in India and Indian sub-continent is given below (*Vasistha, 2009*; http://libsys.co.in/customers.html): 3M Library Systems, New Delhi; Bartronics India, Hyderabad; Capgemini India, Chennai; Ecole Solutions, Bangalore; Edutech, Chennai; Gemini Traze, Chennai; Grandeur Technologies, Chennai; GreenFuturz Software Solutions, Chennai; HCL Infosystems, Noida; IDCUBE Identification Systems, Noida; I-Tek, Pune; LibSys Corporation, Gurgaon; Modular Technologies India, Chennai; Netlink Information Systems, Gurgaon; R.S. Barcodes, New Delhi; RapidRadio Solutions, Ahmedabad; RFID lnfotek, Mumbai; Total IT Solutions, New Delhi; TS Informatics, Delhi; VTLS Software, Noida;

11. Global scenario

The RFID in libraries was first proposed in the 1990s as a technology that would enhance workflow in the library settings. Singapore was certainly one of the first to introduce RFID in libraries and Rockefeller University in New York may have been the first academic library in the United States to utilize this technology, whereas Farmington Community Library in Michigan may have been the first public institution, both of which began using RFID in 1999. In Europe, the first public library to use RHO was the one in Hoogezand-Sappemeer, the Netherlands, in 2001. The University of Connecticut Library; University of NevadalLas Vegas Library, the Vienna Public Library in Austria, the Catholic University of Leuven in Belgium, and the National University of Singapore Library are among the few sites that appear to have tagged more than 500,000 items each. The most ambitious RFID program is that of the Nederlandse Bibliothek Dienst (Netherlands Library Service). It envisions implementing RFID in all of the public libraries of the country, with an item able to travel among libraries that are equipped to read the tags of all of the books, not just their own. Worldwide, RFID is used most in the United States, followed by the United Kingdom and Japan. The largest RFID implementation in academic libraries is in the University of Hong Kong Libraries which has over 1.20 million library items tagged;

whereas the largest implementation for public institutions is in Seattle Public Library in the United States.

12. Conclusion/The Future

RFID is a technology that is booming in libraries due to increased productivity in library processes. It is quite clear from the above discussion that an RFID system may be a comprehensive system that addresses both the security and materials tracking needs of a library. RFID in the library is not a threat if best practices guidelines followed religiously, that it speeds up book borrowing and inventories and frees staff to do more user-service tasks. The technology saves money too and quickly gives a return on investment.

Implementing RFID technology has provided major benefits for Central Library, IIT Delhi. Because of the growth in its collections the functions like stock verification and tracking of missing books was becoming almost impossible for the library. This Library serves a large clientele, and RFID technology has enabled the Library to provide a quick, accurate and timely service to the users. Quick circulation of books means no queuing in front of the circulation counter, and tracking and shelving of the books has become much easier. The manpower required to perform all these functions is now being reduced and is being utilised for providing some extra services. Most importantly the system has already put a check on the theft and misuse of documents, as users understand that the system is in place and capable of detecting theft.

Although, the RFID technology is quite expensive, still it has yielded excellent results for many libraries throughout the world. It is taking off in libraries at an increasingly rapid pace. It has the capability of making the management processes in the library more convenient. The only barrier in the journey is the high cost of it, but every new technology implementation is somewhat dearer. Moreover, RFID applications lead to significant savings in staff costs, enhance services and provide efficient results, which leads to almost fool proof security and access control. It not only provides a constant update of library collections, proper holding management, but also accomplishes real-time services. The bottom line is that the synergy between the latest technology like RFID and libraries can create wonders resulting in empowerment of both users as well as librarians. Also, it is recommended that smaller and new libraries should adopt RFID at an early stage since initially costs and resources involved in adopting & implementing the technology are lower compared to significant benefits it provides. Now-a-days, there are book distributors who supply new books tagged with RFID tags at no extra cost, saving recurring expenses to the institution. In nutshell, RFID can be taken as a boon because of its benefits over other technologies in libraries.

The traditional security systems have proved to be less effective than libraries desire them to be and RFID is more effective in material management. RFID is one of the most demanded and employed technologies in large successful enterprises such as Wal-Mart, Dell, automobile part makers, airlines, supermarkets, computer stores, bookshops, etc. The types of operations that can be done by RFID technology and the benefits offered by that match the needs of libraries as well. Currently, only about 8 percent of libraries world-wide are using RFID, but this figure is rapidly increasing as libraries understand the benefits and convenience of incorporating RFID into their system *(Mehrjerdi, 2011).*

The library of the not too distant future may be assumed to be very different with what we have today. It may work with a combination of computer hardware/software, RFID technology, robots, conveyor belts, computer experts, and few librarians. This is a big picture of the RFID-based system for large libraries where a combination of technologies may be used for wisely managing situations better and more efficiently using the robots to take books off for patron or librarian; and use conveyor belt to send book down the line. A good Material Handling System (MHS) as it is used in large warehouses can be tremendously helpful in RFID based libraries. Since the use of MHS can be quite expensive for large libraries, it is possible to set-up such systems in a portion of the library having large demands on the hourly and daily basis. Using RFID-based systems, it is possible to determine where the material is currently located and then with the help of robots, the material can be brought to the conveyor belt and routed easily to the patron or circulation desk. This is quite possible with the aid of the current technology if the working system at the library is an RFID- based system. In addition to that, it must include a dynamic automated moving robot that can go in search of materials somewhere in the shelves in the limited surrounding that it has authority to work *(Patil, 2008).*

Since RFID technology for the libraries in India is new and the future of Indian libraries depends on this technology, there is an urgent need to develop Indian libraries with RFID enabled technologies, to face global competition. The only barrier in the journey is high cost, but, "every new technology comes at a cost" *(Ayre, 2006)*. As *Mossop (2008)* rightly said, "there's never a 'best time' to adopt any new technology - today's facilities are always better, cheaper and faster than yesterday's, but whatever you buy today is almost guaranteed to have been superseded by something even more ideal by the time tomorrow comes". To conclude, the future of libraries lies in RFID technology and it is expected that in the coming years the cost will come down further and soon we will see mass adoption of this technology in many libraries in India. Regardless of these potential future developments, and of existing problems, the rate of growth in the use of RFID technology by libraries in India continues to increase rapidly, to the extent that, while still clearly developing and adapting to the demands made of it, "it is no longer seen as a novelty, but much more as a significant tool that enables library managers to transform and modernize their services in a way that meets the needs of their 21st century customers" *(Palmer, 2009, p. 135)*. Therefore, despite its limitations, it has become imperative for libraries to use it as it would give definite benefits and solve many tedious, mundane and complex problems easily. The benefits of RFID technology cannot be ignored in today's tight staffing and funding climate in recession.

Finally, we can say that despite all its limitations, the RFID technology is the future of libraries but we should also remember that it is a supporting technology and not a competing one.

References

1. Bhuptani, M. and Moradpour, S. (2005). RFID Field Guide: Deploying Radio Frequency Identification Systems, Sun MicroSystems, Prentice-Hall PTR, Upper Saddle River, NJ.
2. Boss, R.W. (2005). RFID technology for libraries. Available at: www.ftrf.org/ala/mgrps/divs/pla/plapublications/platechnotes/RFID-2007.pdf (Accessed 24 November 2010).
3. Butters, A. (2007). RFID systems, standards and privacy within libraries. *The Electronic Library, Vol. 25 No. 4*, pp. 430-9.

4. Coyle, K. (2005). Management of RFID in libraries. *Journal of Academic Librarianship, Vol. 31, No. 5,* pp. 486-9.

5. Galhotra, M.K. and Galhotra, A.M. (2009). Application of Radio Frequency Identification technology in libraries. *DESIDOC Journal of Library and Information Technology, Vol. 29,* pp. 59-64.

6. Hodgson, C. (2004). RFID in libraries: are we ready. *Information Standards Quarterly, Vol. 16, No. 4,* pp. 1-4.

7. Lindquist, M.G. (2003). RFID in libraries : Introduction to the issues. Paper presented at 69th IFLA Conference, 1-9 August, Berlin. Available at: www.ifla.org/IV/ifla69/papers/161e- Lindquist.pdf (Accessed 24 November 2010).

8. LSmart solutions- http://www.libsys.co.in/offerings-Ismartsolutions.html (online) (Accessed on Sept. 16, 2011).

9. Mehrjerdi, Yahia Zare (2011). RFID: the big player in the libraries of the future. *The Electronic Library, Vol. 29,* pp. 36-51.

10. Mittal, A., et al. (2010). RFID: a complete security system for libraries. In Proceedings of 2nd International Symposium on *"Emerging Trends and Technologies in Libraries and Information Services"*. (ETTLIS-2010). Solan: JUIT: 327- 331.

11. Molnar, D. and Wagner, D. (2004). Privacy and security in library RFID issues, practices, and architectures. In, Atluri, V., Pfitzmann, B. and McDaniel, P.D. (Eds), Proceedings of the 11th ACM Conference on Computer and Communications Security, Washington, DC, USA, pp. 210-9. Available at: www.cs.berkeley.edu/,dmolnar/library.pdf

12. Mulla, K.R. and Chandrashekara, M. (2006). Application of RFID in libraries for physical information security – a view. In, Murthy, T.A.V. et al. (Eds), Dynamic Interoperable Web Based Information System, INFLIBNET, Gulbarga, pp. 500-6.

13. Nagalakshmi, L. Rasha (2011). Development of RFID (Radio Frequency Identification) at Indian academic libraries: issues and best practice. *International Journal of Library and Information Science, Vol. 3.* pp.34-37.

14. Patil, A., et al. (2008). Bluebot: asset tracking via robotic location crawling. *Computer Communications, Vol. 31,* pp.1067- 77.

15. Radio-frequency Identification http://en.wikipedia.orglwikilRadio-frequency_identification#Libraries (online) (Accessed on August 25, 2011).

16. RFID Journal (2003). ISO moves on RFID standards. *RFID Journal.* Available at : www.rfidjournal.com/article/articleprint/297/-1/1/ (Accessed on 24 November 2010).

17. RFID library solutions http://www.tagsysrfid.com/Marketsf Tndustries/Library (online) (Accessed on August 8, 2011).
18. Rowley, J.E. (1980). Computers For Libraries. Clive Bingley, London.
19. Shahid, S. (2005). Use of RFID technology in libraries: a new approach to circulation, tracking, inventorying, and security of library materials. *Library Philosophy and Practice, Vol. 8 No. 1*. Available at: www.webpages.uidaho.edu/,mbolin/shahid.pdf (Accessed on 24 November 2010).
20. Strickland, L. and Hunt, L. (2005). Technology, security, and individual privacy: new tools, new threats, and new public perceptions. *Journal of the American Society for Information Science and Technology, Vol. 56 No. 3*, pp. 221-34.
21. Tagsys (2008). RFID tags. Available at: www.tagsysrfid.com/systems/flexible-hf-tags.cfm
22. Vaishnaav, A.A. and Bapat, N.G. (1995). Library automation - a feasibility study. DESIDOC *Bulletin of Information Technology, Vol. 15 No. 2*, pp. 11-16.
23. Vasistha, Seema (2009). Roadmap for RFID implementation in central library, PEC University of Chandigarh. In Proceeding of *"International Conference on Academic Libraries"*. (ICAL-2009). New Delhi: University of Delhii, pp. 300-306.
24. Yu, E. (2005). RFID interoperability still problematic. p. 3. Available at: www.news.cnet.com/
25. Yu, S.C. (2008). Implementation of an innovative RFID application in libraries. *Library Hi Tech, Vol. 26 No. 3*, pp. 398-410.

12

UNICODE and Information Storage in Hindi Languages
A Critical Study

Dr. R.G.Garg
Head, S.O.S. Library & Information Science
Jiwaji University, Gwalior
Dr. Prem Prakash Pant
Faculty, S.O.S. Library & Information Science
Jiwaji University, Gwalior

Abstract

Unicode provides a unique number for every character, no matter what the platform, or the program, or the language is. Unicode enables a single software product or a single website to be targeted across multiple platforms, languages and countries without re-engineering. It allows data to be transported through many different systems without corruption. Present paper discusses every significant aspect related to Unicode, which is useful to understand the emergence , importance , technical problems and prospects, language and script related problems, complication in Hindi language, encoding and procedure, etc. It also provides a step-by-step user guide to handle the font related problem to display documents/ web pages, to send and receive e-mails, etc. in Hindi language a in comprehensive manner.

Keywords: UNICODE, Encoding ASCII , True type font , Unicode based font, Brahmi script, In script, Key board, change software, TBIL software, UNICODE consortium.

1. Language of Computer

Fundamentally, computers just deal with numbers. They store letters and other characters by assigning a number for each one. Before Unicode was invented, there were hundreds of different encoding systems for assigning these numbers. No single encoding could contain enough characters. For instance, the European Union alone requires several different encodings to cover all its languages. Even for a single language like English, no single encoding was adequate for all the letters, punctuations, and technical symbols in common use.[7]

2. Why Encoding is Needed

Various encoding systems also are having conflict with one another. It is because two encodings can use the same number for two different characters, or use different numbers for the same character. Any given computer (especially servers) needs to support many different encodings, yet whenever data is passed between different encodings or platforms, that data always runs the risk of corruption.[1]

3. UNICODE Encoding Forms

Character encoding standards define not only the identity of each character and its numeric value, or code point, but also how this value is represented in bits.

The Unicode Standard defines three encoding forms that allow the same data to be transmitted in a byte, word or double word oriented format (i.e. in 8, 16 or 32-bits per code unit).

UTF-8 is popular for HTML and similar protocols. UTF-8 is a way of transforming all Unicode characters into a variable length encoding of bytes. UTF-16: It is reasonably compact and all the heavily used characters fit into a single 16-bit code unit, while all other characters are accessible via pairs of 16-bit code units. UTF-32: Each Unicode character is encoded in a single 32-bit code unit when using UTF-32.

All three encoding forms need at the most 4 bytes (or 32-bits) of data for each character. [4]

4. Principles of the Unicode Standard

The Unicode Standard was created by a team of computer professionals, linguists, and scholars to become a worldwide character standard, one easily used for text encoding everywhere. To that end, the Unicode Standard follows a set of fundamental principles: [3]

- Universal repertoire
- Efficiency
- Characters, not glyphs
- Semantics
- Plain text
- Logical order
- Unification
- Dynamic composition
- Stability
- Convertibility

5. Platform of Unicode

The Unicode Standard has been adopted by such industry leaders as Apple, HP, IBM, JustSystems, Microsoft, Oracle, SAP, Sun, Sybase, Unisys and many others. Unicode is required by modern standards such as XML, Java, ECMAScript (JavaScript), LDAP, CORBA 3.0, WML, etc., and is the official way to implement ISO/IEC 10646. It is supported in many operating systems, all modern browsers, and many other products. [2]

6. Characteristics of Hindi languages

Devanâgarî is part of the Brahmic family of scripts of India, Nepal, Tibet, and South-East Asia. It is a descendant of the Gupta script, along with Siddham and Sharada.Eastern variants of Gupta called Nâgarî are first attested from the 8th century. From c. 1200 these gradually replaced Siddham. An early version of Devanagari is visible in the Kutila inscription of Bareilly dated to Vikram Samvat 1049 (i.e. 992 CE).

The Devanagari script is a Brahmi-derived writing system used originally to write Sanskrit. It is used in India and Nepal to write many languages, including the followings:

- Konkoni: The state language of Goa, India.
- Hindi: The official language of the Indian government and the state language of Bihar, Chhattisgarh, Delhi, Haryana, Himachal Pradesh, Jharkhand, Madhya Pradesh, Rajasthan, and Uttar Pradesh.

- Marathi: The state language of Maharashtra.
- Nepali: The national language of Nepal, also used in parts of India and Bhutan.
- Classical Sanskrit. [7]

7. Words in Hindi

There are five principal categories of words in standard Hindi:

- **Tatsam** words : These are words that were borrowed from Sanskrit in the middle Indo-Aryan or early New Indo-Aryan stages. Such words typically have undergone sound changes subsequent to being borrowed.
- **Tadbhav** words: These are words which are spelled differently from Sanskrit but are derivable from a Sanskrit prototype
- **Deshaj** words: These are words that were not borrowings but do not derive from attested Indo-Aryan words either. Belonging to this category are onomatopoetic words.
- **Videshî** words: These include all words borrowed from sources other than Indo-Aryan. The most frequent sources of borrowing in this category have been Persian, Arabic, Portuguese, and English. [1]

8. Official Status of Hindi

The Constitution of India, adopted in 1950, declares Hindi in the Devanagari script as one of the official languages in India. The other 22 Indian languages are recognized as co-official National Languages of the Union (Article 343(1)). [7]

9. Indian Standard Code for Information Interchange (ISCII)

Indian Standard Code for Information Interchange (ISCII) is the character code for Indian languages that originate from Brahmi script. ISCII was evolved by a standardization committee under the Department of Electronics during 1986-88, and adopted by the Bureau of Indian Standards (BIS) in 1991. Unlike Unicode, ISCII is an 8-bit encoding that uses escape sequences to announce the particular Indic script represented by following a coded character sequence. The ISCII Standard can be found on the web.

Devanâgarî is the main script used to write Standard Hindi, Marathi, and Nepali. Since the 19th century, it has been the most commonly used script for Sanskrit. Devanâgarî is also employed for Bhojpuri, Gujari, Pahari, (Garhwali and Kumaoni), Konkani, Magahi, Maithili, Marwari, Bhili, Newari, Santhali, Tharu, and sometimes Sindhi, Dogri, Sherpa and by Kashmiri-speaking Hindus. It was formerly used to write Gujarati. [6]

10. UNICODE Working in Hindi (step-by-step user guide)

Unicode enabls a Computer to avoid font related problems to display documents/ web-pages, send & receive e-mails, etc. in Hindi.

Procedure to enable use of Unicode to work in Hindi on computers having Windows 2000 or later version Operating Systems:

For Windows XP

1. **Step - 1**

   Go to **Start-> Control Panel > Regional & Language Options** >Click on **Languages Tab** (the following screen will appear)

   Tick the Check box to **Install files for complex scripts...** and click **OK.**

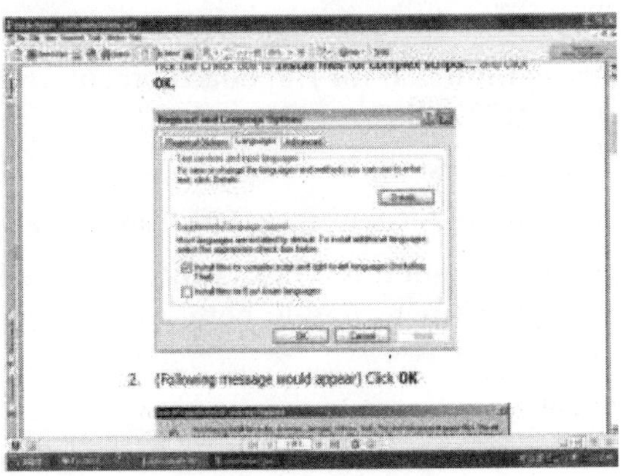

2. The following message would appear. Click **OK**

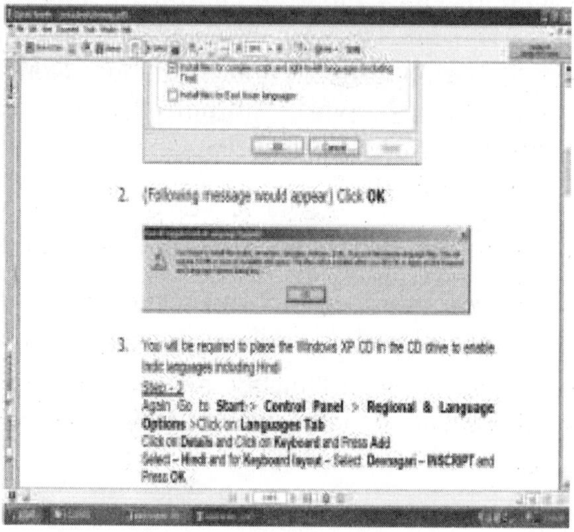

3. You will be required to place the Windows XP CD in the CD drive to enable Indic languages including Hindi.

   Step - 2

   Go to **Start-> Control Panel > Regional & Language Options** >Click on **Languages Tab**

   Click on **Details** and Click on **Keyboard** and Press **Add**

   Select – **Hindi** and for **Keyboard layout** – Select **Devnagari – INSCRIPT**and Press **OK**

   Reboot the System

   In the bottom System tray, **EN** icon will appear.

   From the System tray Click on **EN** or Press Keyboard's left side ALT+Shift to toggle between **EN (English) and HI (Hindi).**

For Windows 2000

1. Go to **Start->Settings->Control Panel->Regional Options**

   The following screen would display

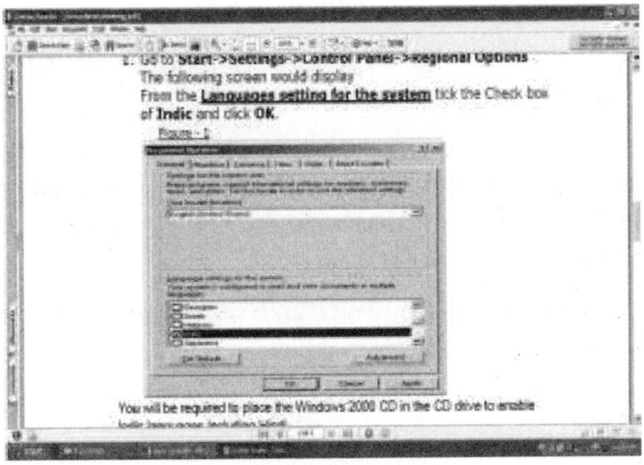

Figure - 1

From the **Languages setting for the system** tick the Check box of **Indic** and click **OK**.

You will be required to place the Windows 2000 CD in the CD drive to enable Indic languages including Hindi.

2. **Go to Start->Settings->Control Panel->Regional Options** The above screen (Figure -1) would display.

   Click on **Input Locales Tab**

   For Input Language Click on

   Add Select - **Hindi** and for **Keyboard layout** - Select **Devnagari - INSCRIPT**

   Reboot the System

   From the System tray Click on **EN**or Press Keyboard's left side ALT+Shift to togglebetween **EN (English) and HI (Hindi)**

For Windows VISTA

The following screen would display:

- Go to the Control Panel and then click to the Regional and Language Option. Choose the Country - India.
- Click on the Key-board and Languages Tab and choose the Hindi and for Keyboard layout - Select Devnagari - INSCRIPT

From the System tray Click on **EN** or Press Keyboard's left side ALT+Shift to toggle between **EN (English) and HI (Hindi).**

With the enabling of Unicode in your system, the INSCRIPT key-board driver and Unicode supported Mangal and Arial Unicode MS fonts will be installed in your system.

For typing using Typewriter/Remington, Phonetic/ Roman Keyboard layouts

Solution No. 1

http://www.ildc.in .

- Choose the language. (Hindi)
- Click on the 'Download'
- Click Option No. 4 (Unicode supported key-drivers)
- A zip file will be downloaded.

Unzip the folder and run setup.exe file. Gist-OT-Typing Tool will be installed in your system. With the help of Gist-OT-Typing Tool, you can type in Remington and Phonetic keyboard layout.

Solution No. 2

http://www.bhashaindia.com .

- Click on Downloads >> INDIC IME >> Indic IME 1 (Hindi)
- A zip file will be downloaded.
- Unzip the folder and run setup.exe file.

How to Use

Go to Control Panel >> Regional and Language Option >> Click on Language Tab

Click on Details and Click on Keyboard and Press Add

Select - Hindi and for Keyboard layout - Select Hindi Indic IME 1 (V 5.1)

For Fonts Convertor (Non Unicode fonts like Akshar, ISM, APS, Akruti, KrutiDev etc. to Unicode)

http://www.ildc.in .

- Choose the language. (Hindi)
- Click on the 'Download'
- Click Option No. 5 (Universal hindi font code and storage converter)
- A zip file will be downloaded.

Unzip the folder and run setup.exe file. Parivartan software will be installed in your system. With the help of Parivartan, you can convert non Unicode fonts Hindi files to Unicode's Mangal font. [3]

11. Interpreting Characters and Rendering Glyphs

The Unicode Standard does not define glyph (is a visual representation of the character images) . The Standard defines how characters are interpreted, not how glyphs are rendered. The software or hardware-rendering engine of a computer is responsible for the appearance of the characters on the screen. The Unicode Standard does not specify the size, shape, nor style of on-screen characters. Following illustration shows the exercise of Indian languages in Unicode [5]

12. Unicode and ISO/IEC 10646

The Unicode Standard is very closely aligned with the international standard ISO/IEC 10646 (also known as the Universal Character Set, or UCS, for short). Close cooperation and formal liaison between the committees has ensured that all additions to either Standard are coordinated and kept in synch, so that the two Standards maintain exactly the same character repertoire and encoding.

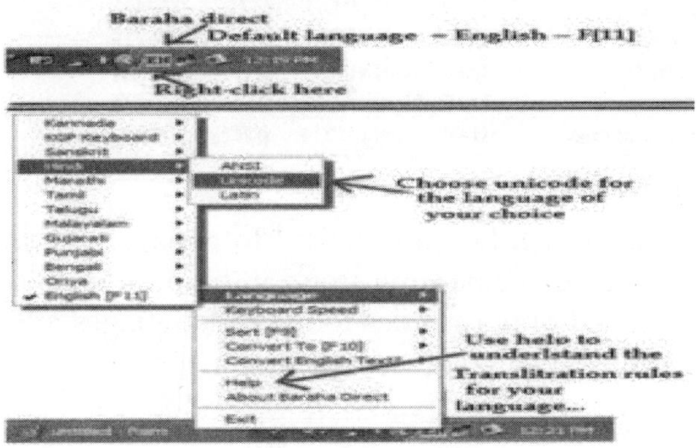

Version 6.0 of the Unicode Standard is code-for-code identical to ISO/IEC 10646:2003 plus amendments. [2]

13. Unicode Consortium

The Unicode Consortium is a non-profit organization founded to develop, extend and promote use of the Unicode Standard, which specifies the representation of text in modern software products and standards. The membership of the consortium represents a broad spectrum of corporations and organizations in the computer and information processing industry. [4]

14. Conclusion

The Unicode Standard provides the capacity to encode all the characters used for the written languages of the world. Unicode enabling on Computer to avoid font related problems to display documents/ web-pages, send & receive e-mails, etc. in Hindi. Unicode also works in Hindi on computers having Windows 2000 or later version Operating Systems.

Table 1: The Unique numbers to the scripts allocates by the Unicode Consortium

Script	Assigned unique number by Consortium	
Arabic	U+0600-U+06FF	(01536-01791)
Devnagari	U+0900-U+097F	(02304-02431)
Bengali	U+0980-U+09FF	(02432-02559)
Gurumukhi	U+0A00-U+0A7F	(02560-02687)
Gujarati	U+0A80-U+0AFF	(02688-02815)
Oriya	U+0B00-U+0B7F	(02816-02943)
Tamil	U+0B80-U+0BFF	(02944-03071)
Telugu	U+0C00-U+0C7F	(03072-03199)
Kannada	U+0C80-U+0CFF	(03200-03327)
Malayalam	U+0D00-U+0D7F	(03328-03455)

Source- Google (image)

Present paper will be quite useful to enhance the awareness of librarians towards this emerging trend in librarianship, Unicode also provides the global opportunities to Hindi languages which is one of the largest speaking language of the world.

References

1 Malhotra, Vijay Kumar. Computer par hindi bhasha ke liye unicode ki bhumika.http://tdil.mit.gov.in

2 McClure, Wanda L. and Hannah, Stan A. Communicating Globally: The Advent of Unicode Information today and Tommorow. May 1995.

3 www.unicode.org

4 www.cdac.in

5 http://www.ildc.in

6 http://www.bhashaindia.com

7 Wikipedia (the largest online encyclopedia)

13

Digital Preservation
Issues and Challenges

Dr. Bhaskar Mukherjee
Assistant Professor, DLIS
Banaras Hindu University, Varanasi
Email: mukherjee.bhaskar@gmail.com

Rapid changes in information technology have unleashed the production and distribution of digital information. There is a continuous increase in the ability of individuals to become self-publisher. In recent years, the core activities of any organization- from government to individuals— have increasingly depended on digital objects. However, storage of such gigantic volume of information for long term use has become a serious challenge for those who are involved in preservation process. The continuous change in the format for storage digital contents, and the technologies for read/use the digital data arises a variety of challenges, including policy questions, institutional roles and relationships, legal issues, intellectual property rights, and metadata. Danny Hills, Vice-President of R&D at Walt Disney Imagineering once mentioned:

> *We're very fortunate that civilization of thousands of years ago recorded things on media like stone tablets that lasted for thousands of years. And we are fortunate that people of hundreds of years recorded things of acid-free paper that lasted for hundred years. And... we're fortunate that people 10 years ago stored things on media like magnetic tapes that lasted at least 10 years..... But our good fortune is running out ... because we're in a period now where we are storing things that will not last even our own life time.*

Certainly, the concept of preservation, especially digital preservation, has now become one of the greatest challenges among us. To address challenges, let use first understand what does preservation mean? Preservation is defined as the activities required for keeping materials in usable form for a long period of time. Generally, the activities discussed in the context of scientific and technical information are identified as "long-term preservation". Long-term has no specific time limit; it is long enough to be concerned with the impacts of changing technologies, including support for new media and data formats, or with a changing user community. As technology grasp our life, everything now becomes digital - from birth to death certificate. The traditional concept of hard-copy becomes obsolete day-by-day. Many types of digital information can and do exist in other forms, such as books, reports, correspondence, and lists. But many forms of digital information cannot be expressed in traditional hard-copy or analog media; for example, interactive Web pages, geographic information systems, and virtual reality model. Broadly speaking, there are two types of digital objects: born digital and digitized. The term born-digital refers to the materials that originate in a digital form. Most of the literature of present days is born-digital. This is in contrast to digitization or digital reformatting, through which traditional form of materials become digital. The word 'digitised' refers to those that are copied or translated into digital form from some other medium, such as paper or film. The word digitisation was previously used to represent conversion of analog media to digital form, but now this term is widely used for conversion of traditional paper form into digital form. It is often used in relation to digital libraries, and the issues such as digital preservation and intellectual property are mostly associated with these types of digitized materials or objects.

Digital Preservation—Concept

Generally, digital preservation means transforming, storing, archiving various forms of media that has been transferred to a digital format and getting a long-term access to it. "Digital Preservation" refers broadly to the series of managed activities necessary to ensure continued access to digital materials for as long as necessary, such as collection, description, migration and redundant storage. The materials subject to digital preservation may be born digital or be the products of digitization projects. Digital preservation activities are undertaken by a range of preservation institutions, including libraries, archives and museums. Such institutions may operate independently or may be located within other bodies, such as educational institutions or government entities.

Traditional preservation strategies, such as providing appropriate storage and environmental conditions, are still necessary in the digital environment, but they are not enough to ensure that digital information is preserved.

Some of the major advantages of digital preservations as identified by Abby Smith are:

a) **Increasing Access:** Content created in other media can be digitized through scanning, keying text, photographing with digital cameras, or otherwise capturing in digital form. Digital data can be accessed through a number of computers in network mode, so that more than one user can share the same data simultaneously to satisfy Ranganathan's First Law in present context "Information is for use".

b) **Democratization**: Despite various positive sides of paper based information communication, issues like time loss between literature production and its absorption by journals, postal delay, and the perceived problem for peer reviewing process has been much criticized these days. But with the help of gigantic Internet communication now author can communicate easily with the peers by using digital files. Author can host his/her thought content to some website without the loss of time and not being bothered by others.

c) **Feasibility:** One of biggest assets of digital information is flexibility. It is easy to edit. easy to handle different type of data i.e. text, graphics, etc. easy to reformat and to commit to print in a variety of iterations without the effort required to produce hard copy from a typewriter. It is easy to summon up quickly a number of variations of values, shapes and placement to see, rather than to imagine, what different visual options look like. Furthermore, one can create an endless number of identical copies from a digital file, because the file does not decay by virtue of copying.

Despite many advantages of digital preservations, there are some challenges too.

A) Various Formats of File

In order to handle the issue of archiving, storing of digital object, it is better to discuss first what a fomat or digital format is? 'Format' has been defined by the Global Registry of Digital Formats as: "... a fixed, byteserialized encoding of an information model." (Global, 2006) The LC-NDIIPP format sustainability assessment defines a 'Format' as "packages of information that can be stored as data files or sent via network as data streams (aka bitstreams, byte streams)." (Arms & Fleischhauer, 2006 - Formats, Evaluation Factors and Relationships). Preservation formats are those file formats that provide the best chance to achieve preservation, including the ability to capture the material into the archive and render and disseminate the information now and in the future. In some cases, this may be only a few years, while in other cases it may be for the life of the republic.

With the fast-paced technological revolution, as we move further from paper-based media to electronic media, the sharing of electronic resources becomes increasingly important. But, there is no single standard for all electronic files to ensure this process. In fact, the number of different electronic formats is quite large. In most cases one type of file containing different styles of information are not supported by other formats. In some cases, software companies intentionally do this for maintaining competitive advantage. For users requiring to share electronic files it can sometimes be a challenge to move their files between different applications, i.e., between different software, and across platforms [Lynn-George, 1996].

In a report written for the National Archives (UK) in 2003, Adrian Brown summarises:

> *The selection of file formats for creating electronic records should ... be determined not only by the immediate and obvious requirements of the situation, but also by longer-term considerations. An electronic record is not fully fit-for-purpose unless it is sustainable throughout its required life cycle. ... It is therefore highly desirable to identify the minimum set of formats which meet both the active business needs and the sustainability criteria below, and restrict data creation to these formats.*

Some major Formats are:

Tagged Image File Format (TIFF or. tiff)

TIFF is a widely used high-resolution raster image file format for graphic applications and photographic productions. It is a wrapper format capable of containing various image bitmaps, pixel-by-pixel representations of scanned pages or pictures. It supports RGB, CMYK, greyscale and bitmap images. One of the most common TIFF bitmaps is a bitonal (pure black and white) document image. Such images are produced by scanners and have been used to reproduce documents from at least the 1980s forward. It is a platform independent and can be exchanged among different computers. TIFF does not use file compression in the base standard. However, it does work well with certain types of loss-less compression schemes such as LZW (Lempel-Ziv-Welch is a proprietary loss-less data-compression algorithm used in GIF and TIFF files.). The current specification of TIFF is version 6 TIFF images faithfully reproduce the scanned page, but the text can neither be searched nor manipulated. Adobe Systems Incorporated owns and publishes for open use the TIFF file format specification in the same manner as it owns and publishes the PDF format specification.

Portable Document Format (PDF or .pdf)

Adobe Acrobat's PDF is now becoming a standard viable text exchange format, which is highly compatible across virtually all platforms. PDF documents are compact, and can be viewed by anyone with the free Adobe Acrobat Reader software available from the Adobe Web site. PDF is used when documents have to look exactly the same across all computer platforms and browsers. It is a highly configurable format that can provide from low-to-high compression results depending on the fidelity of the match required for the exchange. In professional print production, high fidelity requirements generally result in large file sizes. Acrobat uses a font substitution scheme that may allow for some variation in appearance for the sake of file size. PDF is rapidly becoming a new preferred standard for dealing with professional pre-press work but has some limitations. It has a limited ability to edit or modify files once created — a very important aspect of print production workflow. It is not a recommended format when you need someone to be able to edit your file. PDF was originally based on Postscript to make it possible to print across a variety of computers and printers. Adobe enhanced the technology so that it would provide the look and feel of a document across platforms.

Portable Document Format/Archival (PDF/A-1)

PDF/A-1 is a published International Standards Organization (ISO) standard. It is a specification or set of rules for what should NOT be included in a PDF 1.4 file in order to be able to read it later and what is allowed or required in PDF/A-1 and how to implement those objects. This specification can be implemented by Adobe and other vendors.

Extensible Markup Language (XML or .xml)

XML (Extensible Mark-up Language) is an ASCII-based format that includes tags to accommodate both the mark-up of the meaning of fields and the display of the information. Using either DTDs or schema, XML requires declaration of the structure so that the information is more portable and interoperable. The comparative picture of various file formats is given in Appendix.

Format Assessment Factors

Choosing the best format for long-term preservation is a difficult task. However, there are certain criteria through which one can choose the best format. Library of Congress suggests certain criteria for evaluation of format:

Technical Factors - Under technical factor each format is analyzed against the following factors for sustainability:

Disclosure - existence of complete documentation

Adoption - degree to which the format is already in use

Transparency - degree to which the digital representation is open to direct analysis

Self-documentation - digital objects that contain basic descriptive, technical, and other administrative metadata

External Dependencies - degree to which the format is dependent upon specific hardware, operating system, or software for rendering or use and the complexity of dealing with those dependencies in future technical environments

Impact of Patents - degree to which the ability of archival institutions to sustain content in a format will be inhibited by patents

Technical Protection Mechanisms – implementation of mechanisms that prevent the preservation of content by a trusted authority

Quality and Functionality: This factor is related to the importance of content for reuse versus layout and presentation

Striking a Balance: This means between the technical factors and the quality and functionality factors, which may compete with one another and may change over time.

Similarly, the NDIIPP program has chosen seven factors to evaluate the sustainability of any given format. (Arms & Fleischhauer, 2006). These are:

Disclosure: Degree to which complete specifications and tools for validating technical integrity exist and are accessible to those creating and sustaining digital content. A spectrum of disclosure levels can be observed for digital formats. What is most significant is not approval by a recognized standards body, but the existence of complete documentation.

Adoption: Degree to which the format is already used by the primary creators, disseminators, or users of information resources. This includes use as a master format, for delivery to end users, and as a means of interchange between systems.

Transparency: Degree to which the digital representation is open to direct analysis.with basic tools, such as human readability using a text-only editor.

Self-documentation: Self-documenting digital objects contain basic descriptive, technical, and other administrative metadata.

External Dependencies: Degree to which a particular format depends on particular hardware, operating system, or software for rendering or use and the predicted complexity of dealing with those dependencies in future technical environments.

Impact of Patents: Degree to which the ability of archival institutions to sustain content in a format will be inhibited by patents.

Technical Protection Mechanisms: Implementation of mechanisms such as encryption that prevent the preservation of content by a trusted repository.

B) Obsolescence of Storage Media

Obsolesce means the process by which a product or component becomes unusable and cannot be maintained. With the passage of time and technological development physical storage media become obsolete. The storage world has gone through transmission from 8 inch floppy to 5½ inch and then to 3¼ inch, and then to CD-ROM, DAT, ZIP, DVD, etc. But these storage devices become obsolete very quickly and today it is very difficult to find a driver with contemporary peripherals. Rothenberg [18] mentioned that average life span of digital media is only five years. In general, technology offers the solution to copy a file onto a new physical storage media as old media becomes obsolete [22], but how far it is possible and how much cost involved in the conversion is also a matter of concern. Because of these characteristics, preservation of digital materials must begin at or shortly after production or acquisition.

Although there is no "permanent" digital storage medium that meets standards of longevity and durability established for "permanent paper" or microfilm, transferring older digital information to new media brings additional advantages, such as increased media capacity and faster access which offset the costs of copying. Established repositories and most digital library designers accept the need for systematic maintenance of digital materials and periodic replacement or "refreshing" of the underlying storage media. Some recent research is developing automatic methods for detecting and repairing damage from media failure and deterioration (Copper, 2000, LOCKSS). Media deterioration and loss remain a problem when digital materials are not integrated into systematic management and maintenance programmes and where there is no adequate system of security and back-up.

Libraries are increasingly paying for access to information held remotely. If libraries do not physically own digital material, they cannot preserve it. Publishers may or may not have a commitment of preserving their own information; this is likely to depend to an extent on the type of publisher and its mission. However, to preserve the digital contents there should be some sound strategies.The strategies for digital preservation may include:

Migration: The act of moving data from one hardware and/or software configuration to another. It is more than copying, refreshing, or replicating the data. Simple example is: Creating a new version of an MS Word 2003 document by "migrating" it to the newer MS Word 2007 document format. MS Office software programmed to (presumably) faithfully render the old document into the newer format without information loss, including both data and style attributes.

While refreshment and media migration ensure that a reliable bit stream of the digital object is maintained, migration strategies may result in a loss of data, or changes in functionality and look and feel of the digital object. Wheatley has discussed different types of migration and the specific types of activities associated with each type (Wheatley, 2001). These may include stripping down information into its most basic form for ease of access to the intellectual content. It may involve conversions between formats or recreation of the software aspects of the resource. The look and feel and functionality of digital resources may be recorded in some way to provide a record. Migration on demand may minimize the frequency of intervention because "All the migration from an obsolete format to an appropriate current day format happens at the point of request."(Cedars Project). However, this approach will require the maintenance of migration tools.

Normalization: The act of moving data from one hardware and/ or software configuration to another configuration that adheres to a published standard. It is typically more than migration. Simple example of it is: Importing ISO-2709 format data into Dublin core metadata standard.

Emulation: Replicating a hardware and software environment in which the data object is accessed. The hardware and software environment conforms in nearly all characteristics to an environment in which the data object may have been originally accessed. There is likely to be some sort of encapsulation of content, software and metadata. Metadata could include a specification for an emulator (Rothenberg, 1999). Alternatively, emulators could be designed and then updated over time. Emulation will involve refreshing or migrating media over time to keep the encapsulated material safe. Reengineering of software may also be necessary to specify or create emulators.

Redundancy: Redundancy is a part of traditional preservation management and creating backups is part of good security practice for digital data.

Technology Preservation: Preserving the original hardware (and software - operating systems and applications) needed to access an archived data object. This is a strategy for gaining access to old data, not for preservation of data.

While maintaining obsolete technologies might be the only possible option in some circumstances, because of the associated need to keep every version of every piece of software and hardware, operating systems and manuals as well as personnel with relevant skills, it is not generally considered to be a feasible alternative. Emulation shows considerable promise. However, it is largely untested in the context of digital preservation. While migration is generally regarded as being the most promising digital preservation strategy currently, the difficulty in predicting the timing, nature and costs of this approach match the unpredictable nature of technological obsolescence itself.

C) Device Dependency

Another important trade-off of digital format is that it requires special equipment to read, which involves an extra cost. Paper based information are 'eye legible' requiring no special equipment. But digital information is not 'eye legible', without technical capabilities to run or display the content, it is lost.

D) Degradation

Many analog materials remain stable for long periods of time and require only intermittent interventions for purposes of preservation. Moreover, degradation of an analog work is usually gradual enough to provide advance warning that preservation efforts are required. For instance, one can perform a fold test to determine if the paper on which a book was printed has become brittle, or smell the vinegar that signals degradation of films. Digital materials, in contrast, cannot be unattended for long: their preservation requires regular intervention. They may suffer from "bit rot," a degradation that usually cannot be discerned by the naked eye and therefore may not be discovered until someone tries to use the work. Bit rot often renders the entire digital copy useless.

E) Lack of Standards

In the area of digital preservation, standards issues primarily concern encoding, data formats, and representation schemes. Archivists and librarians tend to favour open standards over *de facto* or proprietary standards for two reasons. First, open standards are published and readily available whereas *de facto* standards (e.g. standards by virtue of common use or marketplace dominance) tend to be proprietary. If a digital preservation strategy depends on proprietary standards, then the long-term future of digital resources in that proprietary standard is dependent upon the longevity of the firm that owns the standard or on its continued market dominance. Second, open standards are developed through a consensus process where various parties with an interest in the standard have opportunities to contribute to or comment on its merits. In an ideal world, institutions that are building digital libraries and individuals with particular expertise in this area would participate actively in standards developments that affect the ability to preserve digital information and lower the costs of doing so. However, in the absence of open standards for many aspects of digital objects, proprietary standards become the *de facto* standard. Even where open standards exist, they may not be effective because a proprietary standard is technically superior to an open standard or because a few or no vendors produce products that conform to the open standard.

In order to overcome the challenges of media obsolescence various initiatives have been taken place. Reference Model for an Open Archival Information System (OAIS), produced by an international group of digital preservation researchers and practitioners convened by the NASA Consultative Committee for Space Data Systems (CCSDS) develops a standard for sustainable preservation. OAIS is an ISO standard (ISO 14721:2003) that provides the functional framework for sustaining digital objects in managed repositories. Another possible alternative to clearing rights could be including rights information in metadata associated with digital material. The OCLC/RLG Working Group on Preservation Metadata21 has developed a preservation metadata framework that includes a rights-related element.

F) Copyright

The copyright issues surrounding published works are similar for digitizing as for reproducing any protected work. Although library, archives and museum associations have tried to make the case for preservation because of its great importance to society, copyright law plays an important role in this debate, sometimes furthering the ability of a library to preserve a work and sometimes hindering it. In discussing the problems with archiving the web, Berkeley Professor of Information Management and Systems, Peter Lyman says:

In the past, important parts of our cultural heritage have been lost because they were not archived – in part because past generations did not, or could not, recognize their historic value. This is a cultural problem. In addition, past generations did not address the technical problem of preserving storage media – nitrate film, videotape, vinyl recordings – or the equipment to play them. They did not solve the economic problem of finding a business model to support new media archives, for in times of innovation the focus is on building new markets and better technologies. Finally, they did not solve the legal problem of creating laws and agreements to protect copyrighted material yet at the same time allow for its archival preservation

Making copies of digital items and adapting them in various ways are generally the first steps of preservation. Previously, copyright only prevailed with the works in hard-copy form and libraries purchased them for long-term preservation. But now, many works are never in hard-copy form, some are available on internet and are not available for acquisition. Those work can not be preserved unless they can be copied or acquired with the purpose of managing and maintaining long-term preservation. Some other types of materials, like e-journals are accessible through authentication, but the terms of use may not permit the creation or retention of archival copies. Additionally digitizing retrospective materials is a form of publishing. The original format is being changed, but copyright laws still apply to the items. The duplicity and wide spread access to literary output also sometimes violate copyright issues and also violate intellectual property act. It is necessary to obtain permission from the copyright owner before digitizing works under copyright protection.

Digital preservation necessarily involves the exercise of one or more of the exclusive rights of the author or other right holder. In an increasingly digital world, libraries and archives must develop policies to preserve and provide access to e-books, online journals, magazines, and newspapers. However, libraries of the world have different legal landscape for digital contents. Although use of digital assets may not be governed by copyright, but they are controlled by contract. This threatens the ability of libraries to lend copies, to make copies, to keep copies and to preserve copies of digital assets. So, there is a need to create new legal rights for all non-profit libraries and archives. Only with correct legal buttressing can libraries make digital preservation an established practice.

There are some examples of countries that have legislation that looks more amenable to copying for digital preservation. In the United States, the Digital Millennium Copyright Act (DMCA) expressly allows authorised institutions to make upto three digital preservation copies of an eligible copyrighted work in certain circumstances. The new UK legal deposit legislation acknowledges this by providing for amendments to rights legislation so that "copyright, publication right, database right and any similar right" is not infringed by deposit libraries which need to copy for preservation or the provision of access or uses making temporary copies for access purposes. The Swedish Government issued a decree authorising the Royal Library to not only collect Swedish web sites on the Internet but also to allow the public access to it within the library premises. The French Government has adopted a law requiring every French web site to be archived, allowing preservation organisations to harvest material at regular intervals. The UK's Joint Information Systems Committee (JISC) and the Wellcome Trust recently commissioned a study on legal issues related to Internet archiving in the UK, European Union, the USA, and Australia.

Under the copyright act of India, 1957 section 14, it has been mentioned that "to reproduce the work in any material form including the storing of it in any medium by electronic means is infringement of copyright act". So digital preservation have narrow scope in Indian context. Whereas, under the US Copyright Act, Section 108: It is not an infringement of copyright for a library or archives, or any of its employee acting within the scope of their employment to reproduce no more than one copy or photo-record of a work, except as provided in subsection if-

1. The reproduction or distribution is made without any purpose of direct and indirect commercial advantage.

2. The collection of the library or archives are: i) open to the public, ii) available not only to researcher affiliated to library or archives or with the institution of which it is a part, but also to other persons doing research in a specialized field.
3. The reproduction work should be provided with copyright notice mentioning the sections too.

There is need to re-think of copyright act in order to preserve our culture for future use. Information Technology Act, 2000 (IT Act, 2000) which basically Cyber Law of India, also provides a "Digital Framework" for ensuring Digitilisation, Electronic Documents Creation and their use in Government Departments. The Section 7 of the IT Act, 2000 deals with retention of electronic records. Section 7(1) of the Act provides that where any law provides that documents, records or information shall be retained for any specific period, then, that requirement shall be deemed to have been satisfied if such documents, records or information are retained in the electronic form, if-

(a) The information contained therein remains accessible so as to be usable for a subsequent reference;

(b) The electronic record is retained in the format in which it was originally generated, sent or received or in a format which can be demonstrated to represent accurately the information originally generated, sent or received;

(c) The details which will facilitate the identification of the origin, destination, date and time of dispatch or receipt of such electronic record are available in the electronic record.

Indian Scenario

Digital preservation in India is in its infancy stage. Till now, India has no well defined legal framework for digital preservation. Major preservation challenges include non-availability of standard formats for the image, lack of updated software for compatibility with new hardware, shortage of skilled personnel and lack of management and preservation policy. In reality, digital preservation framework in India is missing as we do not have a "dedicated" techno-legal digital preservation laws in India. Although, laws like Public Records Act, 1993, Right to Information Act, 2005, proposed Electronic Services

Delivery Bill 2011 (Bill), etc. mandate digital preservation and digitalization of records in "Electronic Form". However, the scope of such laws does not solve the real problems. Additionally, it becomes more complicated with the enactment of laws like Digital Millennium Copyright Act (DMCA). Efforts, however, are in the pipeline for the adoption of an efficient digital rights management (DRM) system in India. But the Intellectual Property Rights (IPRs) are generally found conflicting with the digital preservation initiatives.

The Indian Government in general and the Ministry of Culture in particular has initiated certain projects to improve the situation. Centre of Excellence for Digital Preservation is the flagship project under the National Digital Preservation Programme of the Department of Information Technology, Government of India. This project is awarded to Human-Centred Design & Computing Group, C-DAC Pune. It's objectives are to:

- Conduct research and development work in digital preservation to produce the required tools, technologies, guidelines and best practices.
- Develop the pilot digital preservation repositories and provide help in nurturing the network of Trustworthy Digital Repositories (national digital preservation infrastructure) as a long-term goal
- Define the digital preservation standards by involving the experts from stakeholder organizations, consolidate and disseminate the digital preservation best practices generated through various projects under National Digital Preservation Programme, a nodal point for pan-India digital preservation initiatives.
- Provide inputs to Department of Information Technology in the formation of national digital preservation policy and strategy by identifying and selecting the activities for the National Digital Preservation Programme.
- Spread awareness about the potential threats and risks due to digital obsolescence and the digital preservation best practices.

There is also a need to look various models that exist in this field. For instance, National Digital Information Infrastructure and

Preservation Program (NDIIPP) of USA, Open Archival Information System (OAIS) and European Model of Cultural, Artistic and Scientific Knowledge for Preservation, Access and Retrieval (CASPAR) are examples of the digital preservation models. It is necessary to develop a National Policy for digital preservation of data and when formulated, an effective implementation of this policy.

References

1. Cedars Project. *Cedars guide to digital preservation strategies.* Available at: http://www.leeds.ac.uk/cedars/guideto/dpstrategies/dpstrategies.html
2. Cooper, B., Crespo, A. and Garcia-Molina, H. (September, 2000) "Implementing a reliable digital object archive." *Proceedings of the Fourth European Conference on*
3. *Digital libraries (ECDL).* Available at: http://www-diglib.stanford.edu/~testbed/doc2/ArchivalRepositories/
4. Digital Preservation in India. Available at: http://ictps.blogspot.com/2011/06/digital-preservation-in-india.html
5. Hirtle, P.B. (2003). Digital preservation and copyright. Available at: ttp://fairuse.stanford.edu/commentary_and_analysis/2003_11_hirtle.html
6. Lots of Copies Keep Stuff Safe. Available at: http://lockss.stanford.edu/
7. Lynn-George, J. (1996). *Digitization: technical processes, applications and issues.* John A. Weir Memorial Law Library, University of Alberta Libraries,
8. Rothenberg, J (1999). *Avoiding technological quicksand: finding a viable technical foundation for digital preservation: a report to the Council on Library and Information Resources.* CLIR, 1999. Available at: http://www.clir.org/pubs/reports/rothenberg/contents.html
9. Smith, Abby (1999). *Why digitized?* New Work, Council on Library and Information resources.
10. Wheatley, P. (2001). Migration: a CAMiLEON discussion paper. *Ariadne,* 29. Available at: http://www.ariadne.ac.uk/issue29/camileon/intro.html.

14

E-Publishing
A Boon for Writers of Twentyfirst Century

Prof. Krushna C. Panda
Head, DLIS, Chairman, BoS, Dean, Faculty of Arts
Sambalpur University, Jyoti Vihar-768 019
E-mail: krushna52@yahoo.co.in

Abstract

Electronic publishing has become common in scientific publishing where it has been argued that peer-reviewed paper in scientific journals are in the process of being replaced by electronic publishing. Although distribution via the Internet (also known as online publishing or web publishing when in the form of a website) is nowadays strongly associated with electronic publishing, there are many non- network electronic publications such as Encyclopedias on CD and DVD, as well as technical and reference publications relied on by mobile users and others without reliable and high speed access to a network. The term "electronic publishing" is primarily used today to refer to the current offerings of online and web-based publishers; the term has a history of being used to describe the development of new forms of production, distribution, and user interaction in regard to computer-based production of text and other interactive media. This paper unfolds the concept, basic steps and services, criteria for selecting an e-publisher, economics and applications of e-publishing, classification of e-publications and their contents, selected technology vendors, the merits and pitfalls of e-publishing trade.

Keywords: E-Publishing, Online Publishing, Wireless publishing, Web-publishing, E-Books, POD.

1. E-Publishing: The Concept

E-publishing is short for electronic publishing, referring to a type of publishing that does not include printed books. E-publishing instead takes the format of works published online, on a compact disk, emailed, or provided in a file format compatible with handheld electronic readers. E-publishing is an alternate form of publication especially attractive to new writers. There are advantages and disadvantages to e-publishing over traditional printed books(http://www.wisegeek.com/what-is-e-publishing.htm accessed on 17.10.09) E-publishing infact, is a very broad term that includes a variety of different publishing models, including electronic books (e-books), print-on-demand (POD), email publishing, wireless publishing, electronic ink and web publishing, and so on (http://www.writerswrite.com/epublishing/info.htm accessed on 21.10.09).

Electronic publishing or e-Publishing includes the digital publication of e-books and electronic articles, and the development of digital libraries and catalogues. Electronic publishing has become common in scientific publishing where it has been argued that peer-reviewed papers in scientific journals are in the process of being replaced by electronic publishing. Although distribution via the Internet (also known as online publishing or web publishing when in the form of a website) is nowadays strongly associated with electronic publishing, there are many non network electronic publications such as Encyclopedias on CD and DVD, as well as technical and reference publications relied on by mobile users and others without reliable and high speed access to a network(http://en.wikipedia.org/wiki/Electronic_publishing/accessed on 18.10.09). While the phrase, "electronic publishing" is primarily used today to refer to the current offerings of online and web-based publishers, the phrase has a history of being used to describe the development of new forms of production, distribution, and user interaction in regard to computer-based production of text and other interactive media(A good example of this use of the phrase can be found in the work of Walter Bender and his Electronic Publishing Research Group at the MIT Media Lab.)

Some known examples of electronic version of traditional media includes:

CD-ROM

- E-book
- Electronic journal
- Online newspaper
- Online magazine

New media:

- File sharing
- Podcast
- Collaborative software

2. Why E-Publishing?

E publishing gives authors the opportunity to reach a global audience in a cost- effective manner. Also, E publishing is the recent phenomenon in the present day knowledge economy! For an author, this is a promising, cost effective manner of publishing his/her work and reaching out to a large global audience(http://www. chillibreeze.com / articles_various/epublishing / E-publishing.asp/ accessed on 19.10.09) in least efforts, cost, and time.

After an article is submitted to a journal for consideration, there can be a delay ranging from several months to more than two years (B.G. Ellison (2002). "The Slowdown of the Economics Publishing Process". Journal of Political Economy 110 (5): 947-993) before it is published in a journal, rendering journals a less than an ideal format for disseminating current research. In some fields such as astronomy and some parts of Physics, the role of the journal in disseminating the latest research has largely been replaced by preprint repositories such as arXiv.org. However, scholarly journals still play an important role in quality control and establishing scientific credit. In many instances, the electronic materials uploaded to preprint repositories are still intended for eventual publication in a peer-reviewed journal.

There is statistical evidence that, electronic publishing provides wider dissemination (Online Or Invisible? by Steve Lawrence of the NEC Research Institute). A number of journals have, while retaining in their peer review process, established electronic versions or even moved entirely to electronic publication.

Electronic publishing is increasingly popular in works of fiction as well as with scientific articles. Electronic publishers are able to provide quick gratification for late-night readers, books that customers might not be able to find in standard book retailers (erotica is especially popular in e-Book format, and books by new authors that would be unlikely to be profitable for traditional publishers.

3. Basic Steps and Services in E-Publishing

E-publishing is akin to conventional publishing. Only the final product is in the digital form instead of paper. Therefore, any book to be published has to undergo all quality checks and mandatory registrations, like:

- Editing
- Cover page design
- E-book design
- ISBN registration
- Copyright certification
- Marketing

4. Questions to be answered Before Deciding and Selecting an E-Publisher?

There are some crucial questions that need to be answered before selecting an e-publisher:

4.1 What does the author will do to publish his work?

The authors need to fill in the e-publishing enquiry form available on the web and the concerned publisher will get in touch with the author and take this forward.

4.2 What will it cost to the Author?

The price which the author is going to pay depends on the services he/she intends to avail. For example, editing, cover page design, book layout, ISBN, copyright registrations and internet marketing- an author can opt for one or a combination or all the services. Pricing is based on services, length of text, kind of graphics and amount of tabulated information in text, etc.

4.3 How will the Author know that people have bought his/her books?

The e-publishers have a content management system in place which ensures that all data on sales, downloads, enquiries are available. The author (s) will be informed biannually on sales status along with the royalty payments ,if any, made there of.

4.4 Will the Author get the copyright?

Normally, the author gets the copyright for the content. The copyright for the design and the version of the e-book that e-publisher publish will be with them (publishers). The e-publisher will discuss this with the author ahead of publishing.

4.5 Can the author publish the same work on other sites too?

For instance, the Chill breeze e-publisher says no to this question. The author will have to give the e- publishing rights to Chill breeze.

4.6. Do the author need to have the full manuscript ready before he/she approaches the e-publisher? What will happen, if the publisher does not like it?

Not necessary. If the author has a good idea then the author can approach the concerned e-publisher and the e-publisher can help the author in the matter.

4.7. If an author can't wait to publish on the website of the concerned e-publisher, then what he/she has to do next?

The answer is the author has to go ahead and click on e-publishing enquiry to find out his name on an e-book, for example, on the Chill breeze e-publishing website!

5. Economics of E- publishing

The e-publisher might save costs associated with paper, printing and distribution, but if he wants to put out quality content, he continues to incur fairly high costs in terms of the editorial and technical staff. To capture the true value that e-publishing can deliver, he has to choose the business model that enables him to cast a wider net and garner more customers to cover total cost so that each customer needs to pay for a smaller fraction of the total.

Total costs include support function costs like HR, accounting and legal, operational costs including editorial and technical staff for activities like design and typesetting, and lastly the chunk constituting advertising, promotions and distribution. Of these, costs incurred on editorial and technical staff engaged in bringing out quality products, however, will remain significantly high, but the costs incurred on paper, printing and actually mailing individual copies could drop considerably.

The revenue spectrum would range from subscription rates, to licenses to special groups (universities / corporate entities, industry bodies, libraries) and pay-per-look options. Advertising and selling rights for reprinting are additional sources of revenue. Advertising, however, tends to be limited in the online versions, and take the form of either related advertising or affiliated links. And if an online vendor distributes the e-book, the revenue is lower on account of greater revenue splitting. Some strategies that could be adopted by e- publishers to counter the fall in revenues are:

- Increase member services (retain specialized content for members);
- Increase pay-per-look charges;
- Increase charges for group users like libraries, corporate entities, etc.; and
- Bundling of information to charge more.

6. Applications of E-publishing

What started out as a trend to provide printed material in a digital format, has today become an alternative in itself.

While e-publishing has existed for over 7 years, debate over its use and acceptance has reached a feverish pitch in the last few years.

6.1 Where can it find use?

Simply put, almost everywhere. It is most ideally suited for publications like journals, research reports or resource bases and newsletters. It is also suited for all information that is dynamic or constantly changing, it could be ongoing research or even news.

It finds great use and acceptance in academics, in the online publishing of educational books or tutorials. With an increase in distance learning programs, the need for quality educational material is on the rise. These e-books and study materials need to recreate an active learning atmosphere as can be found in a class full of students and a teacher. The content and the product, therefore, have to be interactive. This can be done through open assignments, online debates, chats and discussion forums. These products also have to provide for a feedback mechanism. Naturally, in order to be effective these products have to be more colorful and interactive, and at the same time also be concise and crisp to match the attention span of the student reading online. Electronic-Publishing is also used extensively in large academic institutions and libraries for their periodicals and journals.

E-Publishing could also help in bringing out industry journals / periodicals, megazines and newsletters. Authors and publishers gain when they publish e-books. Costs are lower and royalties could be higher. Working papers on ongoing research helps unleash the power of collaborative work through networking. E-publishing is very effective here as different sets of people can work with data so varied and complex, with charts, tables and images of amazing complexity made accessible in digital formats replete with animation and sound almost instantaneously.

7. Types of E-Publishing Models

There are several models in e-publishing ranging from commercial e-publishing, print-on-demand and subsidy e-publishers, no fee distributors and self publishers. In addition to these, there are agent vendors who package on-line journals, books and sell the database to industry bodies, universities, etc. with a mark-up over their cost, incurred for procuring rights. These costs would vary depending on whether the vendor has procured exclusive rights or has to share them with a competitor. As a variation of the above, there are online bookstores.

7.1 Commercial E-Publishers are almost like their traditional counterparts. These publishers choose to publish books that are most likely to be sold – a good mix of quality and subject matter is what they look for and rejection rates are pretty high. While their websites serve as effective storefronts, they also sell through other online bookstores like Amazon.com, etc. By and large, e-publishers do not pay an advance, but royalty payments are higher than what traditional publishers offer, often as high as 40%. The editorial and technical work that the e-publishing team puts in is no different from that what is done in print publishing.

7.2 Subsidy E-Publishers differ from commercial publishers in several ways. For one, they accept most manuscripts and publish them on an "as is" basis. These are not edited or proofread or even formatted. They have a virtual rate card for add-on charges for these services, should the author opt for it. Everything, from adding images or graphics to copyright registration, is offered at add-on rates. They publish books for a flat fee and pay the authors a royalty that is comparable to what they would receive from the commercial e-publishers. However, they are more likely to sell through online stores than through their own websites. Likewise, they pass on the added cost of selling through online stores to the author who receives higher royalties for books sold through the publisher's website and lower royalties if they were sold through, say for instance, Amazon.com.

7.3 Another interesting model is the **"print-on-demand" (POD) model**, which is a mix of electronic and print publishing. The book is held by the publisher in electronic form and is printed out in the hard copy form only on order. This is also done for a flat fee. While many commercial publishers also offer the POD format, this is a model more often followed by the subsidy e-publishers.

7.4 The **No-fee "Distributors"** accepts manuscripts and publishes them on an "as is" basis, in a sense, simply providing these authors with a bookstore. They do not charge a fee, but take a slice of the royalties. Price setting is usually the author's prerogative. The no-fee distributors do not offer services like editing or formatting. This works well for the authors who prefer the self publishing model, but want to offload the task of setting up their own "store front" or website. This also does away with the need to register as a retail business as they get paid royalties by the distributors as opposed to revenues on sales.

As an alternative, several authors prefer to self publish their books. This is not only inexpensive, but also offers them total control over the various processes. The author usually does all promotional and marketing work on the Web. Unless the author wants to offer the e-book in multiple formats like downloads, CD-ROMs or floppy disks, distribution costs are also very low. Again, offering only a download-able format makes it possible for the author to register only as a publisher and not a retail business, which entails the procurement of a license.

The spectrum of cost recovery models covers pay-on-download PDF files (research reports), subscription (newsletters), membership (where members get value-added content over the free subscription content), payment in small installments and annual payments for an agreed upon amount of information downloads. Accordingly, the information can be restricted to those that pay through logins and passwords.

8. Selecting the Business Model

As mentioned earlier the choice of business model would depend on the kind of information that the e-publisher wants to publish. Several academic institutions, industry bodies and individual authors prefer to be self publishers. The models that do not offer editing or marketing services work best for information that has a small, informed and ready market. On the other hand, e-books that require promotion and marketing, where the market has to be segmented and targeted, where the authors need help with editing or proofreading, are best handled by the commercial e-publishers.

Whatever the information or delivery model, there is a corresponding e- publishing model. And for those that require unique business models, the good news is that the industry is still evolving. With a little bit of tweaking and a liberal dose of innovation, a new business model can be rustled up, say some experts.

9. Classification of E-Publishing

We are only beginning to see the ramifications of e-publishing. A variety of different publishing models, including electronic books (e-books), print-on-demand (POD), email publishing, wireless publishing, electronic ink and web publishing. More types of e-publishing are sure to be developed in the near future. Here are some descriptions of the different methods of electronic publishing.

9.1 E-books

E-books are electronic versions of books which are delivered to consumers in digital formats. There are a large number of devices being developed to make reading e-books easier for consumers. Special software, which makes documents or pages of a book easier to read on a screen, is also being developed by software companies. A standard for e-book software, known as the open-e-book standard, or OEB, has been developed as a standard format for e-books, but competing standards such as Adobe's PDF exist. The potential market for electronic books (and shorter length content) is extremely large. Although presently there is some sales resistance to the idea of abandoning paper books for a handheld electronic reader, certain sectors of the buying public are already recognizing the benefits of e-books over paper books. Students who are tired of lugging around forty pounds of textbooks (which become obsolete quickly) and consumers or business people who travel a great deal are two groups who seem thrilled with the idea of downloading 10 or more books into a small, portable reader. E-books are already starting to be trendy. Recent issues of top women's magazines such as *Vogue* have recently featured e-book readers as the latest must-have fashion accessory. This market could develop faster than expected because leading publishers and technology companies are pouring money resources into e-book technology. It remains to be seen, however, exactly which electronic devices and which software will succeed and exactly how long it will take people to convert to e-books. When the price of handheld readers comes down to under $50.00, one can be sure that, these devices may quickly become ubiquitous.

9.2 Print-on-Demand(POD)

Print-on-Demand is a new method for printing books (and other content) which allows books to be printed one at a time, or on demand. This method helps free publishers from the process of doing a traditional print run of several thousand books at a time. The technology involves complex laser printing systems and electronically formatted text which the printers can read. Many publishers include web upstarts, are hoping this method will allow them to more effectively print smaller numbers of a book and still make a profit. The technology is currently very expensive and the *New York Times* recently reported that Lightning Source, Inc., a leading provider of e-book fulfillment, charges publishers over $4.00 per book, which is a higher cost per unit than that of small print run. Prices should come down as more publishers and retailers purchase the technology. POD is very hot right now; in a sense, it is a good intermediary step between the regular method of printing paper books and electronic books. However, because POD is still a method that uses paper and can not be delivered as cheaply and quickly as electronic books, in the long run, POD could decline in popularity when consumers become comfortable with electronic reading software and e-book reading devices.

9.3 Digital Content

Digital Content generally refers to the electronic delivery of fiction which is shorter than book-length, nonfiction, documents and other written works of shorter length. Publishers of digital content deliver shorter sized works to the consumer via download to handheld and other wireless devices. Technology used for delivering digital content includes Adobe PDF, XML, HDML, WAP (Wireless Application Protocol) and other technologies. The security of the data being delivered is the major concern of publishers who want to ensure they can deliver digital content without the risk of someone copying the work and selling or giving away the works. The market for wireless content, which is being developed to deliver content to everything from phones, handhelds, microwaves and even clothes, is a potentially enormous market. This fact has the major media companies and publishers scrambling not to be left out of the digital content arena.

10. Data Conversion Services in E-Publishing

Westech Data Conversion Services is a Data Management and Conversion provider focused on offering a full range of Data Conversion, e-publishing and e-commerce solutions from conceptualization to full life-cycle development, implementation, maintenance. We leverage technology to help clients achieve competitive advantage in their businesses. At Westech Data Conversion Services, we provide organizations with turn-key Data Conversion, Management and e-commerce solutions along with a full range of development and technical support services(http://www.westech.co.in/accessed on 21.10.09)

11. Taxonomy of E-Publishing Contents & Domains

The demand for e- publishing content is driven by the surge in digital storage means and use of internet for information search, business and entertainment. E- publishing content has *four basic aspects*- editorial, interactive, visual appeal and accessibility to the user and an infinite range of subjects to be addressed. An OECD report (2005) points to the variety of subjects which topped e book sales across countries. In France it was literature, Germany and Japan read non fiction, in UK it was scientific and technical books, South Koreans focused reference books and Australians on educational books. The top e-publishing content types are summarized below (http://www.chillibreeze.com/articles_various/epublishing/E-Publishing-Content.asp, accessed on 24.10.2009):

11.1 Scientific, Technical and Medical (STM)

The use of electronic journals, publications, archives and datasets have become popular across various disciplines for research. STM publishing includes scientific, technical, medical subjects as well as social sciences, humanities and arts.

A 2002 study by Morgan Stanley revealed that, scientific publishing was one of the fastest growing media sectors. By 2003, seventy five percent of scholarly journals were available online (Cox and Cox) According to the EPS Market Monitor, the global market for STM publishing and information services grew by 7.0% from? $8.7 billion in 2003 to $9.3 billion in 2004 .

Reports indicate that, 50%-80% researchers in biological, physical sciences, law and engineering use online sources. The customers include academic institutes, medical institutes, practitioners and corporates.

11.2 Legal, Tax and Regulatory (LTR)

Legal, Tax & Regulatory topics constitute the other subject for high value publishing content. According to Electronic Publishing Services Ltd (EPS), Asian markets will dominate intellectual legal and tax publishing, law firm advertising and marketing services.EPS expects the sector's compound annual growth rate through 2006 to increase to 4.5%, spurred by growth in international markets.

11.3 Education and Training

Creating educational aids for schools and colleges is another major segment for content creation. Instructional design focuses on high quality digital content to facilitate class room teaching. The categories range from pre kindergarten to senior high school and colleges.

A 2003 study EPS market study on revenues generated in education and training content publishing in America and Europe were estimated to be $ 23.9 billion.

Keeping in perspective the technological changes and the manner in which information is sourced and viewed, this sector has tremendous business potential in developing countries of Asia and Africa. Established international publishing giants are hoping to capitalize on growth in new markets like China and India.

11.4 Travel

User behavior is indicative that more and more people access the net for travel information and online bookings. The travel portals and websites is considerably increasing e-business transactions. Market research firms estimate that, nearly one third of travel bookings were made online in USA during the last year. Travel providers are targeting the college students in the USA for online bookings. This trend is expected to further increase and also pick up globally.

On the Indian internet scene, five new online travel portals are soon to be launched and the travel business is expected to draw major venture capital investments. (Business World, Feb 2006). Providing updated, relevant and interesting travel content to a global diverse audience is an emerging content segment. Consumer created content is becoming a practice in the travel world.

11.5 Finance and Market Research

Relevant and quick information is what business needs. There is an increasing practice of selling reports, sections and data by web based companies to academic researchers, business organizations and news agencies. The reports are sourced from different specialty and general publishers on different industry sectors, country profiles, global markets, technologies, economic and financial sectors, etc. Firms like, marketresearch.com, ecnext.com and mindbranch.com are selling customized information to users as well as personalized inputs on industry trends, etc.

11.6 News

News and weather search is the most important topic searched on the internet. Newspaper web sites attracted 32% more users in 2004 over the previous year (World Association of Newspapers). As newspapers and magazines go online, the quality of content and analysis will determine viewer ratings and success.

11.7 Entertainment & Sports

US online consumer spending on sports and entertainment sector has recorded phenomenal increase. The main components contributing were music, dating sites and game purchases. (EPS). As internet and other forms of media move towards overlapping zones, the demand for entertainment and recreational content for different age groups, gender and community profiles is expected to increase substantially.

11.8 Health Care

According to the Journal of Medical Internet Research, 'e-health is an emerging field in the intersection of medical informatics, public health and business, referring to health services and information delivered or enhanced through the Internet and related technologies'(http://www.jmir.org/2001/2/e20/). The need for reliable, factual, easy to understand, medical jargon free information will be the focus for content providers. As health tourism becomes an important component of diversifying economies, medical and health service related content mostly will be sought for.

11.9 Advertising

As internet companies try to reach out to new markets, the content for online advertising becomes a potential business area. For example, India has a $35 million online advertising market, of which search engine marketing constitutes about $6 million, expected to double by year end. (Business World, Feb 2006). Other niche segments for content inputs includes online classifieds, jobs, retail, industry trading.

12. Why E-Publishing?

(i) **Increase Sales**

CMS + eCommerce + Community

(ii) **Attract New Customers**

SEO built in; optimize all content

(iii) **Save Money, Increase ROI**

No expensive hardware or staffing

(iv) **Be Nimble**

Add sites, integrate other platforms

(v) **Take Charge**

Deliver content with intuitive tools

(vi) **Rest Easy**

24 X 7 service & support

(v) **Grow**

World Class Technology Infrastructure
(http://www.epublishing.com/ Accessed on 17.10.2009)

13. Technology Vendors

Some of the leading technology vendors in the field of E-Publishing industry who acclaim popularity at international-level are as follows:

- Issuu
- eMeta Corporation
- Ingenta
- Safari Books Online
- Eastgate Systems
- InformIT
- Pressmart Media

14. E-Publishing Tools

(a) WebWorks Publisher for Word

WebWorks Publisher Professional enables you to author in Word and ePublish in multiple formats, including HTML Help, JavaHelp, WinHelp, and WebWorks Help 3.0 .Live Linx provides custom templates for WebWorks, training, customization and support.Live Linx is the exclusive distributor in Israel for all Quadralay products, including WebWorks.

(b) WebWorks Publisher for Frame maker

WebWorks Publisher Professional enables you to author in Framemaker and ePublish in multiple formats, including HTML Help, JavaHelp, WinHelp, and WebWorks Help 3.0. Live Linx provides custom templates for WebWorks, training, customization and support.Live Linx is the exclusive distributor in Israel for all Quadralay products, including WebWorks.

(c) Framemaker to XML/SGML

Live Linx enables conversion from FrameMaker to XML or SGML (conforming to your DTD) as well as publishing for special needs such as Interactive Electronic Technical Manuals (IETM), distance learning and interactive training.

(d) Frame Script

Live Linx delivers FrameScript training, support, implementation, customization and sales (we are the exclusive FrameScript reseller in Israel). By supporting FrameScript together with FrameMaker consulting and WebWorks, Live Linx delivers end-to-end productivity and single source solutions for FrameMaker users.

FrameScript enables customizing Adobe FrameMaker, automating repetitive tasks and adding new capabilities to Adobe FrameMaker. FrameScript macros deliver benefits similar to those delivered by Microsoft Visual Basic for Applications (VBA) for Microsoft Word and other Microsoft Office applications.

FrameScript facilitates the creation of new FrameMaker functions that previously required C language programming in the Frame Developer's Kit (FDK). FrameScript empowers non-programmers to combine multiple FrameMaker functions into a single command, speed display of and response to standard FrameMaker dialog boxes, and perform many other functions. Today, anyone can use FrameScript and maximize the power of FrameMaker. Find out more about FrameScript (http://www.livelinx.com/contentmanagement/e-publishing-tools.html).

15. E-Publishing: Merits

Electronic publishing has spun the information delivery model on its head to allow for information, in formats like books, journals, newsletters, magazines and research papers, to be distributed faster, better and most importantly, in a dynamic and interactive way. Perhaps the biggest advantages of e publishing are the cost saving in printing and paper as well as better data storage and maintenance (http://www.chillibreeze.com/articles_various/epublishing/Electronic-Publishing.asp accessed on 21.10.09). The following are some of the key advantages of e-publishing:

(i) Negligible investment by the publisher translates to a greater willingness to take on untried writers and non-traditional characters, story lines, and manuscript lengths.

(ii) Faster publishing time for accepted manuscripts. Rather than waiting up to two years for a manuscript to see print, e-publishing generally publishes work within a few weeks to a few months after acceptance.

(iii) Greater flexibility within the writer/publisher relationship. E-publishing affords more say to writers in preparing works for publication. A paper publisher might ask a writer to change a character, plot line, or other features of a story to make it more marketable. An e-publisher might also make suggestions, but the writer will generally have more say. The writer might also be instrumental in providing graphics for the work, such as an electronic jacket.

(iv) Writers have the ability to update text often and easily at virtually no cost. This is particularly handy for works related to fast-moving industries such as computer technology. Since the e-publisher does not have an investment in printed books already lining shelves, text can be electronically updated in seconds.

(v) E-publishing offers greater longevity for works with slower sales. While paper publishers will remove slow movers from active status (print), electronic storage affords unlimited archiving. This gives new writers time to build a following by having their entire catalog available over extended periods of time.

(vi) Works published electronically have an ISBN number, just like printed books. This means anyone can walk into a storefront bookstore and order an electronic copy of the book.

(vii) Writers get a higher percentage of royalties through e-publishing because the initial financial layout for the publisher is so much less than for a paper publisher. Some writers receive as much as 70% of the profits in royalties.

(viii) With e-publishing writers normally retain all other rights to the work, such as the option to go to a paper publisher later, adapt a screenplay, or use the work in some other capacity. Paper publishers, on the other hand, tend to covet as many rights as possible from the writer in the initial boilerplate contract.

16. E-Publishing: Pitfalls

If this all sounds a little too rosy, one may note the key disadvantages of e-publishing:

(i) To date, electronic works sell far fewer copies than paper books. Many people are not aware of e-publishing and others prefer reading a book from print rather than electronically. Good sales, according to one e-publisher, amount to 500 copies for a successful manuscript.

(ii) Writers are responsible for providing their own ongoing marketing for e-published work. A book might be great, but if nobody knows about it, it won't sell. Authors also can't count on the public seeing their books on shelves or in store windows.

(iii) If interested in building credentials, e-published works do not carry the same weight as traditional paper publishers. The sense is that the bar is somehow lower for e-published works than for printed works. However, this may change with time as e-publishing becomes more established.

(iv) Writers do not receive an advance. This is not just a financial disadvantage, but might disqualify e-published authors from participating in certain organizations where membership requirements include works paid by advance. That said, sales royalties are often paid more frequently by e-publishers, such as quarterly rather than annually.

(v) Piracy is another concern in the e-publishing industry. It is a fairly simple thing, technically speaking, for a recipient of an e-work to edit the file, make several copies, and sell the work out from under the nose of the e-publisher and author. Some e-publishers counter that the relatively small market for e-works provides little impetus for this.

(vi) Prices are not always significantly cheaper for e-works, despite the lower overhead. This might be a deterrent to sales.

Despite the disadvantages, e-publishing can be a good way for a new writer to gain a following. Romance, science fiction, murder mystery and fantasy are all possible genres for e-publishing. It is also ideal for *How-To* books that must be updated frequently. Businesses can also save money on employee manuals and training materials by e-publishing them. An added advantage here is that works can be clickable. Table of contents and indexes can all make navigating through technical e-books a breeze.

References

1 (http://www.wisegeek.com/what-is-e-publishing.htm accessed on 17.10.09)

2. (http://www.writerswrite.com/epublishing/info.htm accessed on 21.10.09)

3. (http://en.wikipedia.org/wiki/Electronic_publishing/accessed on 18.10.09)

4. (http://www.chillibreeze.com/articles_various/epublishing/E-publishing.asp/ accessed on 19.10.09)

5. (http://www.westech.co.in/accessed on 21.10.09)

6. (http://www.chillibreeze.com/articles_various/epublishing/E-Publishing-Content.asp, accessed on 24.10.2009)

7. (http://www.chillibreeze.com/articles_various/epublishing/Electronic-Publishing.asp accessed on 21.10.09).

8. (http://www.jmir.org/2001/2/e20/)
9. (http://www.livelinx.com/contentmanagement/e-publishing-tools.html)

15

Electronic Books in Digital Age
An Overview

Dr. Rajesh Kumar Singh
Assistant Librarian
Central Library, Banaras Hindu University, Varanasi
E-mail : rksb17@yahoo.com

Abstract

The past few years have seen a growth in the provision of electronic resources in both academic libraries and everyday life, still there is a lot of confusion about them, even with regard to the basic definition of what an e-book is. The objectives of this paper is clear the concept of e-books in digital age. It explores some interesting data regarding to e-books. The hardware and software (format) of the e-books have been narrated. Describes the comparison of commercially available e-readers and different formats of e-books. Advantages and disadvantages of print and electronic books in tabular form are given.

Keywords: E-books, Digital age, Digital Library, Information Communication Technology (ICT)

1.0 Introduction

Electronic book is the digital representation of the printed material; the medium may vary from a computer to a digital eBook reader like PDA, Kindle, iPod, mobile phone, etc. Usually the content is available in PDF, HTML, ePUB/ XML, etc. formats. This makes the content much more versatile and flexible than the traditional print book. An eBook is a digital object with textual and / or other contents, which arises as a result of integrating the concept of a book with features that can be provided in an electronic environment; and eBooks typically have in-use features such as search and cross reference functions, hypertext links, bookmarks, annotations, highlights, multimedia objects and interactive tools.

While any book-length electronic document could be considered an eBook, a true eBook reader and software is optimized for reading rather than developing contents, and most eBook readers attempt in some way to simulate the experience of reading a paper book. The eBook makes it possible to take reading with you, without the mess of lugging dozens of books around with you. Perfect for traveling, trips or even the long commute to work. Readers can find these books through search engines (such as Google), the library catalog (OPAC) or the publisher platform. Overview of digital world before further exploring the world of eBooks, it will be interesting to present an overview of the current digital world which is given below:

> *"Email 294 billion- Average number of email messages sent per day 1.8 billion- Number of email users world wide websites 25million- Number of websites as in Dec. 2010 21.4 million- Added new websites in 2010 Social media 600 million- People on face book at the end of 2010 Internet users 1.9 billion- Internet users worldwide as in June 2010 14%- increase in Internet users since previous year The Federation of Indian Publishers: there are about 11,000 publishers producing nearly 60,000 titles a year."*
>
> **(Information taken from different Speeches of Conference on Publishing in India: Challenges and Opportunities, January 17-18, 2011, Ambedkar University Delhi, New Delhi).**

2.0 E-Books

The idea of e-books is not new - ever since there have been computers; people have envisioned using them to store and access individual titles or vast libraries. Over the last two decades, a number of important factors have influenced the need for and development of e-books, such as the advent of desktop publishing; the growing importance of paperless publishing; the ease with which electronic information can be created, updated, copied, shared, distributed and searched; more wide spread availability of both local and global computer based communication networks; and the incipient onset of electronic information explosion (Barker, 1999). The significant factors that have converged to make e-books popular and offer the promise of succeeding in the consumer marketplace are: advances in computer hardware and software; the internet which has made it possible to exchange text and data electronically; and the world wide web which has made it easy to publish/refer/transfer content with enabling technologies such as HyperText Markup Language (HTML), eXtensible Markup Language (XML) and Portable Document Format (PDF) as underlying standards.

E-books are the third wave of electronic publishing. First, indexes from secondary publishers became searchable databases via online information systems such as Dialog in the 1970s and then on CD-ROMs in 1980s. Second, when the web became popular, primary journals began converting to PDF format for local printing or to the Standard Generalized Markup Language (SGML) format for enabling users to provide hot links to other references for further study (Luther, 1998). The web has made publishers realize that they need not choose between print and electronic publishing. Publishers are more commonly re-purposing the electronic files used in the production of print and some are re-engineering their editorial and production processes to produce files better suited to electronic products in first place. Currently, several modes of electronic publishing are available. Journals are commonly delivered by subscription over the web; reference, legal and medical books are on CD-ROM or DVD-ROM and are becoming more web based. E-books are more often referred to a consumer product as a single volume, such as a trade book that can be bought over the web and read in a laptop, a desktop computer, a personal digital assistant (PDA), or a dedicated e-book reading device.

According to (Rao, 2001)

> *"The e-book as a text in digital form or a book converted into digital form or digital reading material or book in a computer file format or electronic file of words, images with unique identifiers, metadata to be displayed on computer screen or read on a computer through a network or view on a desktop/notebook/ dedicated portable device or read on all types of computers or formatted for display on e-book readers."*

3.0 Types of E-books

The concept of an e-book is not attached to one single medium in the way that DVDs or CDs are. Therefore, it is appropriate to introduce a classification of various types of e-books. Hawkins (2000) and Crawford (2000) have attempted to identify various concepts, products and models. Hawkins has identified four types based on content availability and access, while Crawford identified nine types based on proprietary formats, standards, media form, length of contents and access.

- Downloadable e-books Contents are available on the internet for downloading to the user's PC. No special reading device is required Bartleby (www.bartleby.com), Librius (www.librius.com), Glassbook (www.glassbook.com), Project Gutenberg (www.promo.net/pg)
- Dedicated e-book readers Contents are downloaded to a dedicated hardware device with a high quality screen and specialcapabilities for book reading Gemstar's REBs (www.ebook-gemstar.com), Franklin's eBookman (www.franklin.com/ebookman)
- Print-on-demand books Contents are stored in a system connected to a high-speed, high quality printer and bound copies are produced on demand Xerox, IBM, Sprout, Lightning Source (www.lightningsource.com), Hewlett Packard
- Web-accessible e-books Published on the provider's web site and may be accessed for a fee or purchase the books to receive indefinite access
- Proprietary e-book devices Text is downloaded in proprietary formats that are locked to a single reader Portable hardware devices from Gemstar's REBs (www.ebook-gemstar.com), Franklin's eBookman (www.franklin.com/ebookman)
- Open e-books XML based standard that allows any text to reside on any reader. Potential reading devices include PCs,notebooks, palmtops and proprietary e-book devices Open Ebook Forum Specifications Free books or public domain e-books Digital copies of books available or texts placed in public domain for free downloading, printing and circulation Project Gutenberg (www.promo.net/pg),

Internet Public Library (www.ipl.org), Bartleby (www.bartleby.com)

- Pseudobooks Titles bought by libraries or consortia and loaned out to users to download to their own PCs. Users can borrow one title at a time, unless libraries paid for more than one copy netLibrary (www.netlibrary.com)
- Instabooks Books printed and bound on-demand from fully marked up digital texts or scanned page images stored digitally Lightning Source. (www.lightningsource.com), Replica Books (www.replicabooks.com)

4.0 E-Book Readers

An e-book reader, also called an e-book device or e-reader, is a portable electronic device that is designed primarily for the purpose of reading digital books and periodicals.

4.1 Hardware

A number of portable e-book devices in a range of shapes, sizes and prices are available. They have little or no inter-operability. Some involve attaching reader to the computer and require proprietary software, plus purchasing and downloading of titles from vendor's library on the internet. Others allow connection directly to their libraries through communication links. The specifications of select commercial e-book readers are listed in Table 1.

4.2 Software (Formats)

E-book titles are not just readable on any software or reading device. Most are device or software dependent. Hence, matching of e-book title's format to the reading device or software is a pre-requisite. Some of the most popular e-book reader software (formats) available in the market i s provided in Table 2 along with their characteristics.

Table 1: Comparison among commercially available e-readers (Wikipedia, 2011)

Features	1	2	3	4	5	6	7	8	9	10
	Kindle 3	Nook Simple Touch Reader	Kindle DX	Nook Color	Sony Reader Touch Edition	Sony Reader Daily Edition	BeBook Neo	Nook 1st Edition	Kobo Wireless eReader	Pandigital Novel

Design										
Screen Size (diagonal inches)	6	6	9.7	7	6	7	6	6	6	7
Touch Screen		✓		✓	✓	✓	✓	✓		✓
Screen Type	E-Ink	E-Ink	E-Ink	LCD	E-Ink	E-Ink	E-Ink	E-Ink	E-Ink	TFT LCD
Resolution	600 x 800	600 x 800	824 x 1200	600 x 1024	600 x 800	600 x 1024	600 x 800	600 x 800	600 x 800	600 x 800
Overall Size (inches)	7.5 x 4.8 x 0.335	6.5 x 5 x 0.47	10.4 x 7.2 x 0.4	[illegible]	[illegible]	[illegible]	[illegible]	[illegible]	[illegible]	[illegible]
Weight (ounces)	8.7	7.48	18.9	[illegible]	[illegible]	[illegible]	[illegible]	[illegible]	[illegible]	[illegible]
Content										
Dedicated Content Service	✓	✓	✓	✓	✓	✓		✓	✓	✓
Newspaper/Magazine	✓	✓	✓	✓	✓	✓	✓	✓	✓	✓
Blogs	✓		✓				✓	✓		
eBooks in Bookstore		2.5 million		2.5 million	[illegible]	[illegible]		2.5 million		[illegible]
Magazines in Bookstore		100		100	[illegible]	[illegible]		100		[illegible]
Newspapers in Bookstore		16		[illegible]	[illegible]	[illegible]		[illegible]		[illegible]
Memory/Battery Life										
Internal Memory	[illegible]	2 GB	[illegible]	[illegible]	[illegible]	[illegible]	[illegible]	[illegible]	[illegible]	[illegible]
Removable Memory		Up to 32GB		Up to 32GB	Up to 32GB	Up to 32GB	[illegible]		Up to 32GB	Up to 32GB
Battery Life (Page Turns)			Up to 7500		[illegible]	[illegible]	[illegible]	[illegible]	[illegible]	
Additional Features										
Text to Speech	✓		✓							✓
Grayscale Levels	16	16	16	[illegible]	16	16	[illegible]	16	[illegible]	[illegible]
Recharge Time	4.5 Hrs.	3 Hrs.	4 Hrs.	[illegible]	[illegible]	2.5 Hrs.	[illegible]	3.5 Hrs.	[illegible]	4 Hrs.
Audio Formats	MP3, Audible, AA, AAX		MP3, Audible, AAX	MP3, AAC	MP3, AAC	MP3, AAC	MP3	MP3		MP3, AAC, WAV
Document Formats	Kindle (AZW), PDF, TXT, MOBI, PRC, HTML, DOC	EPUB, PDF, ADE	Kindle (AZW), PDF, TXT, MOBI, PRC	EPUB, PDF, XLS, DOC, PPT, PPS, TXT, DOCX	ePub, PDF, BBeB Book, Text, RTF	ePub, PDF, BBeB Book, Text, RTF	EPUB, [illegible], PDF, TXT, HTML, RTF, MOBI, CHM, PDB	EPUB, PDB, PDF	EPUB, PDF	EPUB, PDF
Image Formats	JPEG, PNG, GIF, BMP	BMP, JPG, GIF, PNG	JPEG, PNG, GIF, BMP	JPG, GIF, PNG, BMP	JPEG, PNG, GIF, BMP	JPEG, PNG, GIF, BMP	JPEG, PNG, GIF, BMP, TIFF	JPEG, GIF, PNG, BMP		JPEG, BMP, PNG, GIF
Internet Capabilities										
Wireless	Wi-Fi	Wi-Fi	3G, Whispernet	Wi-Fi	Wi-Fi	Wi-Fi, 3G	Wi-Fi	3G, Wi-Fi	Wi-Fi	Wi-Fi

Table 2: Comparison among different types of formats (Wikipedia, 2011)

Format	Filename extension	DRM support	Image support	Table support	Sound support	Interactivity support	Word wrap support	Open standard	Book-marking
Arghos Reader	.aeh	Yes	Yes	?	No	No	Yes	No	Yes
DjVu	.djvu	?	Yes	Yes	No	No	No	Yes	Yes
EPUB (IDPF)	.epub	Yes	Yes	Yes	Yes	Yes	Yes	Yes	Yes
FictionBook	.fb2	No	Yes	Yes	No	No	Yes	Yes	?
HTML	.html	No	Yes	Yes	No	No	Yes	Yes	No
Kindle	.azw	Yes	Yes	Yes	Yes	No	Yes	No	Yes
Microsoft Reader	.lit	Yes	Yes	?	No	No	Yes	No	Yes
Mobipocket	.prc, .mobi	Yes	Yes	Yes	No	No	Yes	No	Yes
Multimedia EBook	.exe	Yes	Yes	?	Yes	Yes	No	Yes	Yes
eReader	.pdb	Yes	Yes	?	No	No	Yes	No	Yes
Plain text	.txt	No	No	No	No	No	Yes	Yes	No
Plucker	.pdb	Yes	Yes	Yes	No	Yes	Yes	Yes	Yes
Portable Document Format	.pdf	Yes	Yes	Yes	Yes	Yes	No	Yes	Yes
PostScript	.ps	No	Yes	?	No	No	No	Yes	?
[illegible]	[illegible]	?	Yes	Yes	No	No	Yes	No	No
TealDoc	.pdb	Yes	Yes	?	No	No	Yes	Yes	Yes
TomeRaider	.tr2, .tr3	Yes	Yes	?	No	No	Yes	No	?
WOLF	.wol	Yes	Yes	?	No	No	No	No	?

5.0 E-Books Versus Print Books

In Most of the aspects, eBooks offer more positive attributes, features and benefits to academic and professional users than print formats. EBook users can book contents concurrently, and search the full text of any title. Multiple libraries can share in a small number of copies. EBooks offer remote access outside of traditional library hours. EBooks are subject to no transportation, storage, or processing costs, nor do they suffer from physical degradation or damage. Users can also add and save their own notes to the contents and cut and paste the selected text, illustrations and diagrams. This means that medical illustrations, scientific and technological formulas and charts can be copied easily by users for own files to make their own courseware or ppt, paper. Multiple libraries can easily negotiate and manage shared use of eBooks, rather the engaging in the costly and time- consuming inter-library loan programs required for books in print. The real cost of providing library users with effective access to contents via eBook is clearly far lower than in traditional print formats. The usability of contents in eBook format is also far higher. The major benefits of eBooks over printed books are summarized below through Table 3:

Table 3: Comparison between e-book and printed book (keel, 2011)

Attribute	Ebook	Printed Book
Concurrent users	Yes	NO
Full text searchable	Yes	NO
Shared access	Yes	NO
Remote access	Yes	NO
User can add notes	Yes	NO
Cut and Paste function	Yes	NO
Cost of transportation	NO	Yes
Cost of storage	NO	Yes
Processing cost	NO	Yes
Risk of damage	NO	Yes
Inter-library loan	NO	Yes

6.0 Conclusion

The arrival of eBooks presents many opportunities for users in new, convenient and cost effective ways. At the moment viewing technology, contents and pricing models are important limiting factors but in future, contents will become paramount. The success or failure of eBooks depends not only on their acceptance by users, but also on the publishing industry's ability to see beyond traditional business models and recognize that eBook readers are still even now at an early stage of development and the hope is that generally accepted industry standards will soon be adopted. EBooks are yet to become a major form of publication, even for students to consume and enjoy in addition to improving the quality and reducing the cost. The eBook industry should make more relevant, popular, and interesting titles available.

References

1. Barker, P. (1999), "Electronic libraries of the future", in Kent, Allen, Williams, James G. and Hall,Carolyn M. (Eds), Encyclopedia of Microcomputers, Vol. 23, Supp. 2, Marcel Dekker, Inc, New York pp. 121-52.
2. Crawford, W. (2000), "Nine models, one name: untangling the e-book muddle", American Libraries, Vol. 31, pp. 56-9.
3. Hawkins, D.T. (2000), "Electronic books: a major publishing revolution. Part 1 – general considerations and issues", Online, Vol. 24 No. 4, pp. 14-28.
4. Keel ,V.(2011)available at: http:// meemimasin. blogspot.com /2009/ 11/ comparision-of-e-books-with-printed.html

5. Luther, J. (1998), "E-books – the next electronic frontier", available at: www.informedstrategies.com/Pub_eBook.html
6. Rao, S.S. (2001), "Familiarization of electronic books", The Electronic Library, Vol. 19 No. 4, pp. 247-56.
7. Wikipedia (2011), available at: http://en.wikipedia.org/wiki/Comparison_of_e-book_readers
8. Wikipedia (2011), available at: http://en.wikipedia.org/wiki/Comparison_of_e-book_formats

16

Expediency of Search Engines
Researcher's Opinion of Banaras Hindu University

Dr. Vivekanand Jain
Deputy Librarian, BHU, Varanasi - 221005
Email: vivek_digora@rediffmail.com
Dr. Sanjiv Saraf
Deputy Librarian, BHU, Varanasi - 221005
gyanshrisanjiv@rediffmail.com

Abstract

Search engines are the main search tool for getting the information from Internet or online information sources. Researchers are using general as well as subject specific search engines as per their information needs. In the present paper, research scholars of Banaras Hindu university opine their views on different aspects of internet search engines. It includes search strategy, preferences to search engines, their expectations and suggestions to improve the retrieval efficiency of Internet search engines.

Introduction

A search engine is an information retrieval system designed to find information, and it serves as a tool that web surfers use to search the Internet. Search engines are databases that contain the reference to thousands of resources available in network environment over the internet.

Search engine provides an interface between the user and the database. The interface presents the user with an opportunity to type in a search string which may be a word, a phrase, a date or some other criterion, and then submit the request to find the results.

Definition of Search Engine

1. "Search engine is a tool for finding information, especially on the Internet or World Wide Web. Search engines are essentially massive databases that cover wide swaths of the Internet." (Britannica Concise Encyclopedia).
2. Search engine is a program that indexes documents, and then attempts to match documents relevant to a user's search requests.

We conducted user study of research scholars working in different disciplines with the help of a questionnaire. We are able to get information regarding type of information users searched from Internet, search strategy, preferences to search engines, their expectations and suggestions to improve the retrieval efficiency of Internet search engines.

Objectives

The objectives of the present study are to study the retrieval efficiency of Internet search engines and identify the search engine for retrieval of scholarly information.

Figure 1: Online Information Access via Search Engine

Population of the Study

To get the user's opinion on Internet search engines, total 104 questionnaires were distributed among the research scholars of 10 teaching departments of the Banaras Hindu University and received back 100 questionnaires duly filled. The research scholars belonged to the departments of Biochemistry, Biotechnology, Botany, Chemistry, Economics, Law, Library & Information Science, Mathematics, Physics and Zoology.

Analysis of Questionnaire

Internet is used for various purposes. The BHU researchers use the Internet in the following manner:.

Table 1 : Aspects of Internet Search

Purpose	Total response	Yes	%	No	%
General Information	83	80	96.4	3	3.6
News/ Views / Current Information	81	73	90.1	8	9.9
Research Articles	98	98	100	00	00
Academic Information	93	91	97.8	2	2.2
Health / Medical Information	57	39	68.4	18	31.6
Music/ Entertainment	68	50	73.5	18	26.5

The research scholars of Banaras Hindu University availed the Internet service for retrieving the research articles (100%) and academic information (97.8%), besides this, they used Internet for general information (96.4%); for news, views and current information (90.1%); for music/ entertainment (73.5%) and health / medicine information (68.4%).

Search Strategy

Users are applying simple as well as advanced search applications for getting the required information. Researchers are well aware of Boolean operators (and, or, not) and applied in their search string.

Table 2: Query Formulation: Advanced Search

Yes	78
No	22

Majority of researchers (78%) applied advanced search features for information retrieval and rest of the users (22%) did not use the advanced search features. This means they used simple basic search without operators.

Table 3: Search String Analysis

Operators used	No. of User	%
AND	64	82.05
OR	38	42.71
NOT	18	23.07
Phrase "..."	40	51.28
Truncation	14	17.94
Range search	10	12.82

Out of advance search users (78) most of them applied Boolean operators: AND (82.05%), OR (42.71%), NOT (23.07%); phrase search (51.28%), truncation (17.94%) and range search (12.82%). These operators were helpful to get the precise information from the web. It also saved the time of researcher.

Relevancy of Information

Researchers are able to get their desired information with the help of search engines as mentioned in Table 4.

Research scholars were able to get the 55.68% relevant information, 36.55% partially relevant information and 7.75% non relevant information from web after putting queries related to their research topics in various Internet search engines.

Table 4: Search Results Analysis

Name of Department	Number of Search Queries	Relevant Output	Partially Relevant Output	Non - Relevant Output
Biochemistry	53	37	15	01
Biotechnology	74	36	32	06
Botany	78	57	18	03
Chemistry	54	46	07	01
Economics	42	09	29	04
Law	62	33	18	11
Library & Info. Science	57	22	26	09
Mathematics	36	17	18	01
Physics	58	30	24	04
Zoology	66	36	25	05
Total	580	323	212	45

Fondness of Search Engine

Researchers were using a variety of search engines from the general to subject specific. These included popular search engines like Google, yahoo, AltaVista, Rediff, MSN and subject specific search engines and databases like: AOL, Nothern- light, NCBI, Goodtree, All-the-web, Scirus, Science-direct, Pubmed, Scifinder, Highwire, Answer.com, JSTOR, Emerald, SOSIG, etc.

Table 5: Number of Search Engines Used

Number of Search Engines	%
1-2	51
3-5	40
>5	09

As per analysis most of the users (51%) applied one or two search engines for specific search and 40% users applied three to five search engines. Only 9% users applied above five search engines for their specific information need.

Table 6: Search Engines Preference

Search Engines	No. of Users	%
AltaVista	29	29
Google	100	100
Indiatimes	19	19
Lycos	5	5
MSN	21	21
Rediff	39	39
Yahoo	57	57

Ranks provided by users to search engines, it was found that Google was the first choice of 90.8% users; Yahoo was the second choice of 38.9% users; Rediff was the third choice of 35.4% users; AltaVista was the fourth choice of 22.9% users; Indiatimes was the fifth choice of 30.1% users; MSN was the sixth choice of 25.8% users and Lycos was the seventh choice of 36.6% users.

On the basis of above analysis Google was the most popular search engine and Lycos was the least preferred search engine as ranked by the users.

Analyses of User's Opinion

User's opinion was sought regarding the available information on Internet and its usefulness to academicians.

Table 7: General User's Opinion

User's Opinion	Yes	No	No any remarks
Information on internet should be reviewed and authentic.	92	05	03
Information on internet should be subject categorized	85	07	08
Separate search engines for academic information	84	09	07
Commercial advertisement should not be on academic website	79	09	12
Information for academic purpose should be free	89	02	09

Table 7 continued...

Training program should be organized by the Library for effective information retrieval	80	07	13
Online training program should be provided by search engines for effective information retrieval	86	06	08

Information available on Internet should be reviewed, authentic (92% users) and subject categorized (85%). Users were expecting access to academic and research information free of cost (89%).

Users were expecting separate search engines for academic information (84%) which should not have commercial advertisements with academic websites (79%)

In users' opinion library could play an important role by organizing the user's training program regarding information retrieval (80%). But more users (86%) believed in online training program by search engines for effective information retrieval.

Discussion

Results of present study corroborate the findings of earlier studies of Bayers (2001) Stevenson (2001) in which Google is popular among users because of its simplicity and easy to use features. In the present study user's opinion revealed that Google is preferred by 90.8% users in BHU. It means Google is the most popular search engine and Lycos is the least preferred (36.6% users) search engine.

Google page rank system is useful to get most relevant results in the beginning and it helps the users to select appropriate items without a long search. Google Scholar is the new addition on Google for academicians for getting web-based scholarly documents. Google Scholar provides a simple way to broadly search from many disciplines and sources: articles, theses, books, abstracts and court opinions, and all these from academic publishers, professional societies, online repositories, universities and other web sites.

Conclusion

Search engines have opened a door to the world's information to provide effective and efficient information services. Search engines have enabled access to information like – government publications, statistics, health information, curriculum support materials, etc. Search engines provide opportunity to use catalogues and portals of other libraries.

Search engines studied are significantly different from each other in precision, recall and in general search features. Users are advised to read the suggestion or search tips provided by search engines and use the search engines as per their information needs.

Like a library catalogue, search engines are very useful tools for library professionals to provide effective information service and ready reference service to the users. We should explore the web resources with the help of search engines and provide best possible information service to our patrons.

References

1. Jain, V. and Saraf, S. (2006) Recent developments in Google search engine and its usefulness to library professionals. *DESIDOC Bull. of Info. Tech.* 26(5). pp.23-28.
2. Search Engine: http://www.marketingterms.com/dictionary/search_engine/
3. Review of Google: www.searchengineshowdown.com
4. Vise, David A. (2008) Google story. Rev.Ed. London, Pan Books.
5. Chowdhury, G G. Introduction to modern information retrieval. Library Association, London, 1999.
6. Hou-Ming (1998) Comparison for three Internet search tools: Yahoo, AltaVista, Lycos: http://vered.rose.utoronto.ca/people/ming/Three_Internet.pdf
7. Search engines definition from Britannica Concise Encyclopedia: http://www.answers.com
8. Google scholar : http://scholar.google.com/intl/en/scholar/about.html
9. Stevenson, V (2001) Search engine update. *Legal Information Management*, 1(3), pp.29-31.
10. Jain, Vivekanand (2011) Retrieval efficiency of Internet search engines. Saarbrucken (Germany) LAMBERT Academic Pub.
11. Bayers, C (2001) Google's secret formula. *Wired* 9(10), pp.88-92.

17

Web Analysis of National Libraries of SAARC Countries

Bhupendra Ratha
Lecturer, School of LISc
Devi Ahilya University, Indore (M.P.)
E-Mail : bhu261@gmail.com
Dr. G. H. S. Naidu
Librarian, Central Library, Devi Ahilya University
Indore (M.P.)
E-Mail : ghsnaidu@gmail.com
Ravi Silawat
M.Phil. Student, School of LISc, Devi Ahilya University, Indore
E-Mail : rsilawat99266@gmail.com

Abstract

The paper presents an analysis of design and structure of websitesthe of National Libraries of SAARC countries. It is found thatthere exist significant differences in respect of some important points such as the user supporting link, staff information, number of hyperlinks on home pages and whole websites, number of images, location of images, In-active links and web pages, etc. The contribution finally looks at the design and structure of the national library websites.

Keywords: Web sites, Web analysis, SAARC, National library websites.

1. Introduction

Billions of computers around the world are connected to the web and offer a tremendous variety of information and services. Now the libraries are also connected to the network or Internet with their own websites. Libraries are also going to library 3.0 because many libraries are using Web, Blog, RSS, Instant messaging, FAQ, Web OPAC, Chat referencing to providing recent and important information. Libraries have embraced the Internet fairly recently and are therefore still struggling to overcome Internet-related challenges such as the construction and development of library websites, online resources, the implementation of Online Public Access Catalogs, online communication with patrons, suppliers, etc. online library acquisitions, library networking. All these services require online connectivity on the part of libraries. Thus library websites are increasingly fetching tool that enables libraries to offer and market their services online. It is crucial to periodically audit the libraries websites in order to measure their web presence, structure and impact.

2. Need of study

- To determine the web structure of national libraries of SAARC countries.
- To know the length of national library web sites of SAARC countries.
- To know the retrieval service on the national library websites of SAARC countries.
- To determine the location and number of Images.
- To determine the E-Resource service through the library websites.

3. Objectives

As stated in the Need above, the objectives of the study are:

- To analyse the information presentation method in the National Library websites
- To analyse the services offered by the national libraries through their website.
- To analyse the layout, graphical presentation and the information provided on different pages of the websites.
- To analyse an in-active links and web pages in the websites of national libraries.

4. Hypotheses

We have some hypothesis about this study like:

a. This study may be useful in designing and improvement of National Library web sites.

b. This study may be useful for LIS professionals and web designer.

5. Methodology of Study

To achieve the desire result for the present study the observational method has been adopted. First we observed all the national library websites of SAARC countries then collected the primary data from same websites. After that the primary data input on the MS-Excel sheet according to some point of view in the table format then analysis the each table with their graphs. The secondary data was collected from the books, journals, Internet, conference proceedings, etc.

6. Scope and Limitations of Study

The present study focus on the design and structure of national library websites of SAARC countries which include Afghanistan, Bangladesh, Bhutan, India, Maldives, Nepal, Pakistan, and Sri Lanka.

Only seven countries have been covered because the website of Afghanistan National Library is not available on the Internet. There are all URLs or Web addresses of the National Libraries of SAARC countries.

- National Library of Bangladesh / www.nanl.gov.bd
- National Library of Bhutan / www.library.gov.bt
- National Library of India / www.nationallibrary.gov.in/
- National Library of Maldives / www.nlm.gov.mv
- National Library of Nepal / www.nnl.gov.np
- National Library of Pakistan / www.nlp.gov.pk
- National Library of Sri Lanka / www.natlib.lk

7. Review of Literatures

The paper of Arakaki, Monica and Peter, Willett (2009). [1], reports an analysis of the websites of the departments of library and information science of U.K. Paper of Jeyshankar, R. Babu, B. Ramesh (2009).[2] is a webometric study of the websites of 45 universities in Tamil Nadu comprising of 27 state and 18 private universities. The paper of Amagad, Elgohary (2008)[3] investigates the web impact factor of Arab universities. Walia, P. K. and Kaur, Prabhjeet (2008)[4] report the results of a webometrics investigation done on the websites of selected library association websites of India. Junping Qiul, Quan'eRen (2006)[5] employ the web link analysis method to evaluate the web influence for enterprise web Sites.

8. Introduction to SAARC

The South Asian Association for Regional Cooperation (SAARC) is an economic and political organization of eight countries in Southern Asia. It was established on December 8, 1985 by Bangladesh, Bhutan, Maldives, Nepal, Pakistan, India and Sri Lanka. In April 2007, at the Association's 14th summit, Afghanistan became its eighth member. The objectives of the Association as defined in the Charter are: [6]

- to promote the welfare of the people of South Asia and to improve their quality of life;
- to accelerate economic growth, social progress and cultural development in the region and to provide all individuals the opportunity to live in dignity and to realize their full potential;
- to promote and strengthen collective self-reliance among the countries of South Asia;
- to contribute to mutual trust, understanding and appreciation of one another's problems;
- to promote active collaboration and mutual assistance in the economic, social, cultural, technical and scientific fields;
- to strengthen cooperation with other developing countries.

9. Web Analysis and their Graphical Presentation

Table 1: User Supporting Link

S.No.	Name of National Library	OPAC	Feedback	Search Bar	FAQ
1	National Library of Bangladesh	No	No	Yes	No
2	National Library in Bhutan	yes	No	No	No
3	National Library of India	No	No	No	No
4	National Library of Maldives	No	Yes	Yes	Yes
5	National Library of Nepal	yes	No	Yes	No
6	National Library of Pakistan	yes	No	Yes	No
7	National Library of Sri Lanka	No	No	yes	No

Table 1 gives the web analysis of different National Libraries. National library websites are compared using four essential services: Provision of Online Public Access Catalogs (OPAC), Feedback , Search Bar, and FAQ (including training and orientation resources), as shown in Table 1. 3(42.85%) national libraries provide OPAC facility on their websites, while 5(71.42%) national libraries provide Search Bar options on their web site. Only 1 library provide Feedback and FAQ facility.

Table-2: Contact addresses of National Libraries

Name of National Libraries	Address	Phone	Fax	Email Add.
National Archives & National Library of Bangladesh	32, Justice S.M. Murshed Sarani Agargaon , Sher -E-Bangladesh	0088-02-9129992	0088-02-9118704	nabdirector@gmail.com
The National Library of Bhutan	GPO PO Box 185 Kawang-jangtsa Thimphu , Bhutan	9752322885, 9752322693	9752322693	Library.bhutan@gmail.com
National Library of India	National Library, Belvedere Kolkata -W. Bengal .	91-33-2479-1381	913324791462	nldirector@rediffmail.com
The National Library of Maldives	The National Library 59,Majeedi Magu Male Republic of Maldives	3323945/ 3323943/ 3323485	3313712	nlm@nlm.gov.mv
Nepal National Library	Nepal National Library, P.O. 182 Lalitpur , Nepal	977-1-5521132	97715530061	nnl@nnl.wlink.com.np
National Library of Pakistan	National Library of Pakistan, Islamabad	92014523/ 92026436	9221375	nlpiba@isb.paknet.com.pk
National Library of Sri Lanka	14, Independence avenue, Colombo 7 Sri Lanka.	094 11 2687583	094 11 2685201	isu@mail.natlib.lk nldsb@mail.natlib.lk

Table 2 displays correspondence information about the National Libraries of SAARC countries. This consists of the name of library, its address, contact details, etc. Mostly this information is available on the websites of the respective library.

Table 3: Staff Information on Website

S. No.	Name of National Library	Staff Information
1	National Library of Bangladesh	No
2	National Library in Bhutan	Yes
3	National Library of India	Yes
4	National Library of Maldives	Yes
5	National Library of Nepal	Yes
6	National Library of Pakistan	Yes
7	National Library of Sri Lanka	Yes

Table 3 shows the staff information on the national library websites. This information is available on the web site of all the National Libraries, except that of the National Library of Bangladesh.

Table 4 : Home Page Link

S.No.	Name of National Library	No. of Link on Home Page	Percentage
1	National Library of Bangladesh	12	05%
2	National Library in Bhutan	38	16%
3	National Library of India	16	07%
4	National Library of Maldives	67	27%
5	National Library of Nepal	37	15%
6	National Library of Pakistan	21	09%
7	National Library of Sri Lanka	50	21%
	Total	241	100%

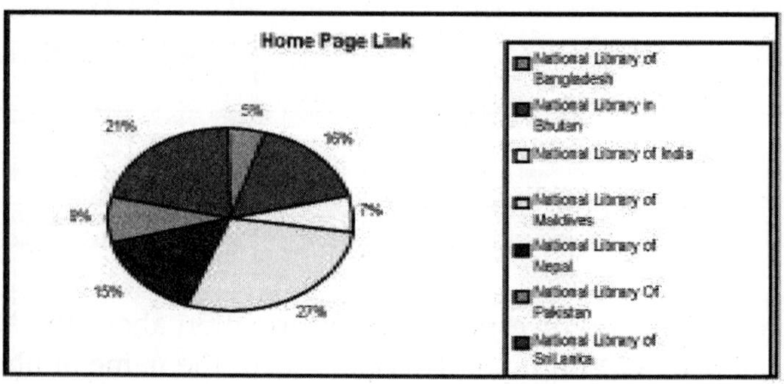

Figure- 1

Table 4 and Figure 01 give the analysis of total number of links available at the home pages of websites of the national libraries. The National Library of Maldives leads with 67(27%) home page links, followed by National Library of Sri Lanka 50(21%), National Library of Bhutan 38(16%), National Library of Nepal 37(15%), National Library of Pakistan 21(9%), National Library of India 16(7%) and the National Library of Bangladesh 12(5%). Thus there are 241 total links at the home pages of websites of national libraries and an average of 34 links per home page of each national library website.

Table 5: Home Page Image

S.No.	Name of National Library	No. of Image on Home Page	Percentage
1	National Library of Bangladesh	1	05%
2	National Library in Bhutan	3	16%
3	National Library of India	4	21%
4	National Library of Maldives	0	00%
5	National Library of Nepal	3	16%
6	National Library of Pakistan	2	11%
7	National Library of Sri Lanka	6	31%
	Total	19	100%

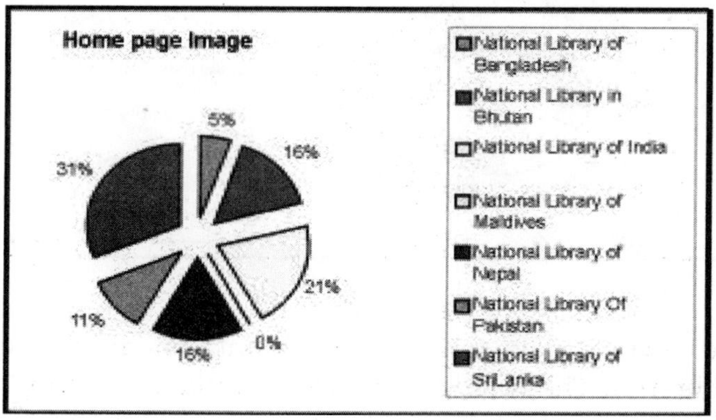

Figure- 2

The total number of images on the home page of national library website is analysed to find out the most graphical home page. Overall the National Library of Sri Lanka comes first with 6(31%) images, followed by National Library of India 4(21%), National Library of Bhutan 3(16%), National Library of Nepal 3(16%), National Library of Pakistan 2(11%), National Library of Bangladesh 1(5%) and National Library of Maldives 0(0%).

Thus there are 19 total images at the home pages of national library websites and an average of 2 images per home page of each national library websites.

Table 6: Link on Whole Website

S.No.	Name of National Library	No. of Link on Website	Percentage
1	National Library of Bangladesh	006	01%
2	National Library in Bhutan	397	51%
3	National Library of India	133	17%
4	National Library of Maldives	039	05%
5	National Library of Nepal	026	03%
6	National Library of Pakistan	151	19%
7	National Library of Sri Lanka	032	04%
	Total	784	100%

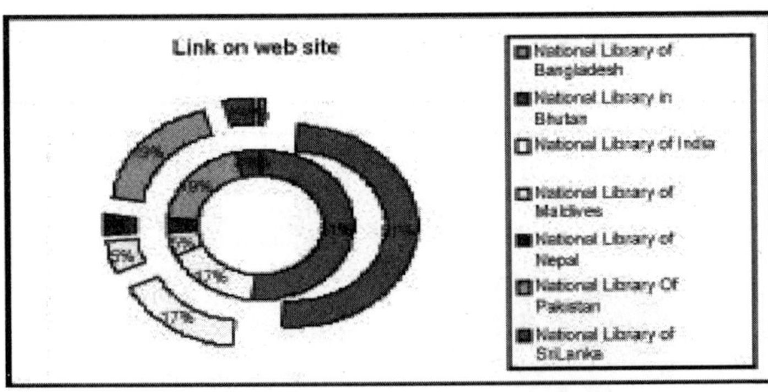

Figure- 3

Table 6 indicates the total number of links on all the websites of national libraries. The National Library of Bhutan is on the top with the 397(51%) total links, followed by the National Library of Pakistan 151(19%), National Library of India 133(17%), National Library of Maldives 39(5%), National Library of Sri Lanka 32(4%), National Library of Nepal 26(3%) and National Library of Bangladesh 6(1%).

Thus there are 784 total links at the websites of the National Libraries and an average of 112 links per websites of each national library website.

Table 7: Web Page on Website

S.No.	Name of National Library	No. of Web Page on Website	Percentage
1	National Library of Bangladesh	14	02%
2	National Library in Bhutan	400	56%
3	National Library of India	58	08%
4	National Library of Maldives	36	05%
5	National Library of Nepal	19	03%
6	National Library of Pakistan	134	19%
7	National Library of Sri Lanka	50	07%
	Total	711	100%

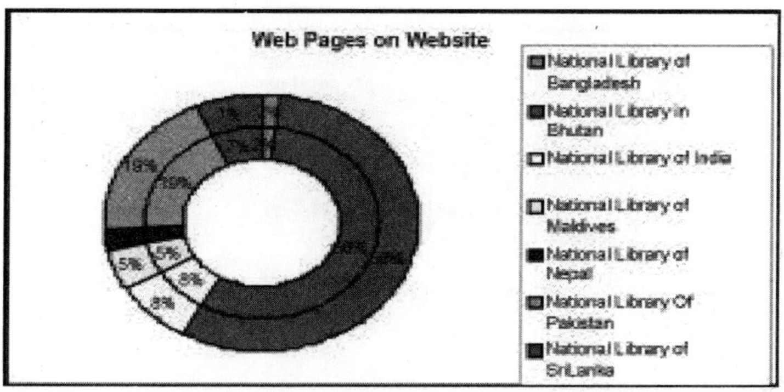

Figure- 4

Table 7 describes the total number of web pages on the websites of national library. There are 711 web pages on all the national library websites. The National Library of Bhutan is at the first rank with 400(56%) web pages, followed by National Library of Pakistan 134(19%), National Library of India 58(8%), National Library of Sri Lanka 50(7%), National Library of Maldives 36(5%), National Library of Nepal 19(3%) and National Library of Bangladesh 14(2%).

Thus there are 711 total web pages at the website of national library website and an average of 102 web pages per website of each national library websites.

Table 8: Image on Website

S.No.	Name of National Library	No. of Image on Website	Percentage
1	National Library of Bangladesh	65	22.88%
2	National Library of Bhutan	65	22.88%
3	National Library of India	61	21.47%
4	National Library of Maldives	11	03.87%
5	National Library of Nepal	29	10.21%
6	National Library of Pakistan	24	08.45%
7	National Library of Sri Lanka	29	10.21%
	Total	284	100%

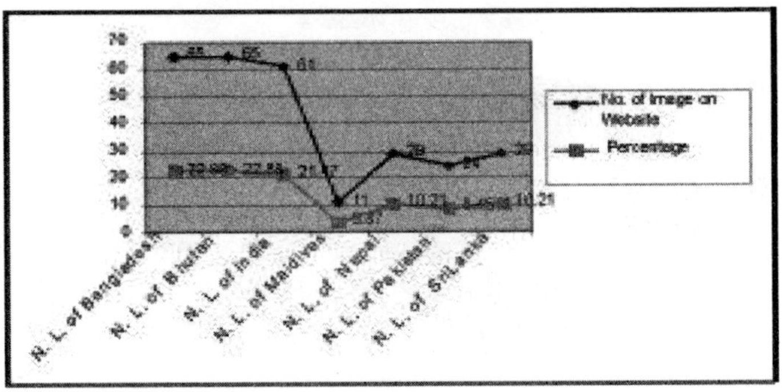

Figure- 5

Table 8 shows the total number of images on the websites of the National Libraries. The National Library of Bangladesh 65(22.85%) and National Library of Bhutan 65(22.85%) has equal images on their websites, followed by the National Library of India 61(21.47%), National Library of Nepal 29(10.21%), National Library of Sri Lanka 29(10.21%), National Library of Pakistan 24(8.45%), National Library of Maldives 11(3.87%). Thus there are 284 total images at the National Library websites, and an average of 41 images on the each national library website.

Table 9: Never Display Image on the Website

S.No.	Name of National Library	Never Display Link	Percentage
1	National Library of Bangladesh	5	10.63%
2	National Library in Bhutan	0	0%
3	National Library of India	0	0%
4	National Library of Maldives	42	89.36%
5	National Library of Nepal	0	0%
6	National Library of Pakistan	0	0%
7	National Library of Sri Lanka	0	0%
	Total	47	100%

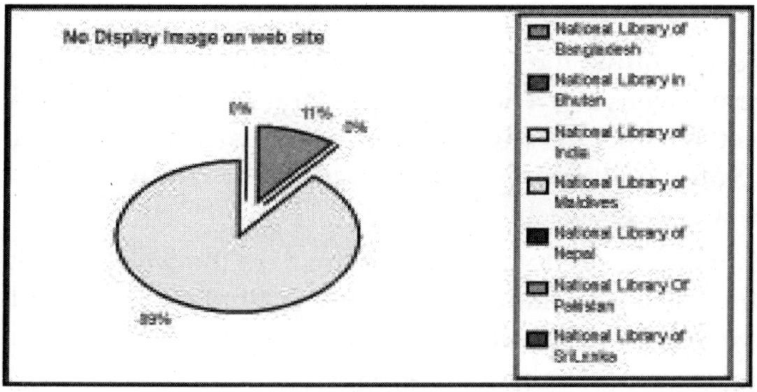

Figure-6

Table 9 exposes the total number of never display images on the website. The National Library of Maldives 42(89.36%) and National Library of Bangladesh 5(10.63%) have no display images on their websites.

Table10: In-active Link on Website

S.No.	Name of National Library	In-active Link	Percentage
1	National Library of Bangladesh	1	09%
2	National Library in Bhutan	0	00%
3	National Library of India	0	00%
4	National Library of Maldives	1	09%
5	National Library of Nepal	0	00%
6	National Library of Pakistan	6	55%
7	National Library of Sri Lanka	3	27%
	Total	11	100%

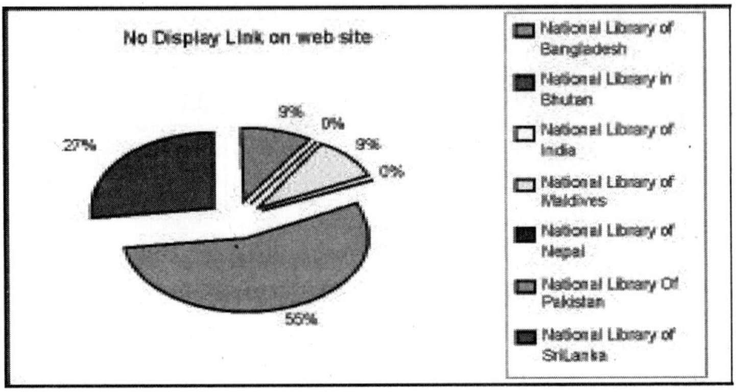

Figure-7

Table 10 shows the total number of In-active links on the national library websites. The National Library of Pakistan 6(55%) has total In-active links, followed by the National Library of Sri Lanka 3(27%), National Library of Bangladesh and National Library of Maldives with1(9%) each.

Thus there are 11 total In-active links on the website of national library websites. The national libraries of Bhutan, India and Nepal don't have any In-active link on their websites.

Table11: In-Active Web pages on Website

S.No.	Name of National Library	In-Active Web Pages	Percentage
1	National Library of Bangladesh	1	07%
2	National Library in Bhutan	1	07%
3	National Library of India	0	00%
4	National Library of Maldives	0	00%
5	National Library of Nepal	5	33%
6	National Library of Pakistan	0	00%
7	National Library of Sri Lanka	8	53%
	Total	15	100%

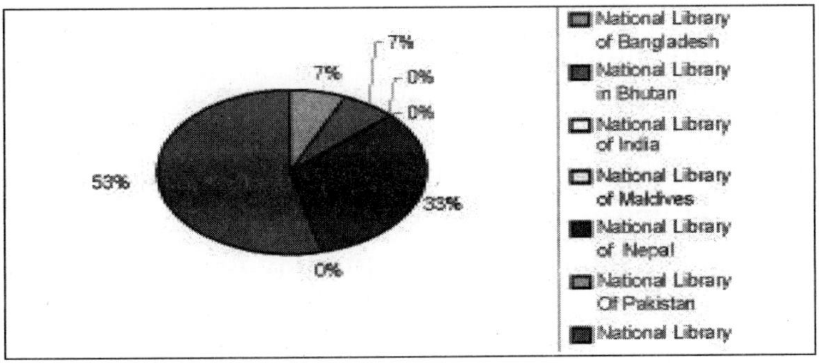

Figure-8

Table 11 shows the total number of In-active web pages on the national library web sites. The National Library of Sri Lanka 8 (53%) has inactive not display pages, followed by the National Library of Nepal 5(33%), National Library of Bangladesh 1(7%) and National Library of Bhutan 1(7%) with the same results.

10 Findings with Suggestions

- Some of the libraries are also providing library services through their websites, such as the National Library of Maldives provides user supporting services like Search Engine, FAQ and Feedback, and the National Library of Nepal provides the facility of Web OPAC and searching, etc.
- The national library website of Maldives is providing brief information with the maximum link on their home page to linking other web pages related to the different aspects of the library. If we see graphically this web has 42 never display image so graphically it is so poor but all the Information is arranged in a proper manner.
- Some of the libraries expose the descriptive information about their collection, infrastructure, system and services on their websites such as the National Library of India. It has descriptive information about all the aspects of the Library.
- The National Library website of Bhutan is the biggest and more Informative because it has 400 web pages and 397 total

links on the whole website. It is also proving the OPAC facility on their web.

- Most of the national libraries like Bangladesh, Bhutan, India, Maldives and Pakistan do not update their websites while the website of National Library of Nepal and Sri Lanka are being updated from time to time.
- All the National libraries provide the staff information, except that of Bangladesh. The National Library of Nepal is providing the staff information with images and brief information about the library staff.
- All the national library websites are well-designed for the purpose of navigation and facilities for jumping to appropriate pages.
- National library website of India provides the full version of website in both Hindi and English. The National Libraries of Bhutan and Nepal are also using other Languages on the few WebPages. But national library websites of Bangladesh, Pakistan and Sri Lanka are using only English Language.
- National Libraries of Bangladesh and Sri Lanka do not provide the link or webpage of news/event on their websites while National Libraries of Pakistan, India, Bhutan, Maldives and Nepal do provide.
- The web search bar is available on the national library websites of Nepal and Maldives only, while other library websites do not have this type of service.

11 Suggestions

- The National Library website should choose a common layout for each and every page.
- Images location, size and style should be standard on the websites.
- All the national library websites of SAARC countries should be well designed and should not have any never display image or graph.
- The national library websites should be measured and updated by web designer and web editor.

- The national library websites create the fulfillment of library users while there are only few services available on the national library websites. So, all the national library websites must be created for its users.
- All the national libraries of SAARC countries should be provided with more user supporting services on their web to use and retrieve the information for the user.

12. Conclusion

This study shows that the National Libraries of SAARC countries are well aware about their websites and future benefits and the high opportunities of Internet and WWW. At presents all the national library website of SAARC countries are available on the Internet except that of the National Library of Afghanistan.

References

1. Arakari, Monica and Willett, Petar (2009). Webometrics analysis of departments of librarianship and information science: A follow-up study. Journal of information science, 1 (April); 143-152. DOI: 10.1177/0165551508094051, retrieved from sage journals online. (Accessed Jan 23, 2010).
2. Jeyshankar, R. Babu, B. Ramesh (2009). Websites of universities in Tamil Nadu: a webometric study. Annals of Library and Information Studies, Vol.56 No.2 (June); 69-79.
3. Elgohary, Amgad (2008). Arab Universities on the web: a webometrics Study. http://www.emeraldinsight.com/Insight/viewcontentItem.do?contenttype= Article&Action= Inkhtml &contentId= 172864&dtype= SUB history =false (accessed May 13, 2010).
4. Wallia, P.K. and Kaur, Prabhjeet (2008). Webometric analysis of library association's websites of India. IASLIC Bulletin, 53(3);131-143.
5. Junpin, Qiul and Quane, Ren (2008). Link analysis and web influence evaluation for enterprise websites. Springer link, 10 (April):300-30.DOI:10.1007/978-0387-75466-6-34.springerlink.2008.12.007. http://www.springerlink.com/contentm3x26132v41635h2 (accessed Apr 15, 2010).
6. http://en.wikipedia.org/wiki/South_Asian_Association_for_Regional_Cooperation (accessed March 21 , 2010)
7. www.library.gov.bt (accessed April 13 , 2010)
8. www.nanl.gov.bd (accessed April 13 , 2010)

9. www.natlib.lk (accessed April 13 , 2010)
10. www.nationallibrary.gov.in/ (accessed April 13 , 2010)
11. www.nlm.gov.mv (accessed April 13 , 2010)
12. www.nlp.gov.pk (accessed April 13 , 2010)
13. www.nnl.gov.np (accessed April 13 , 2010)

18

Usefulness of Automation and E-Resources in Agricultural Libraries and Information Centers

Dr. Madhav Pandey
University Librarian
Indira Gandhi Agricultural University
Raipur 492006, C.G.

Abstract

Library and information centers today are playing a great role in meeting the quality development in every institution. Usefulness of e-resources in agriculture research and teaching is studied.The views of users regarding necessity of e-resources are brought out. These are essential for providing teaching and research support to its users. The sharing of knowledge from various libraries and information centers are possible only through networks or consortium. They are working as information hub to provide e-resources and online information on large scale to the end users of teaching and research community throughout the country. CeRA is useful to avoid budgetary constraints of agricultural libraries and Krishiprabha like theses repository is useful to avoid duplicity of research work. Similarly various networks, e-resources, e-book, e-journals, CD ROM Databases and OPAC of libraries are useful in developing e-culture among the researchers for having better results in research.

Keywords: DTR, ICT, CeRA, , Krishiprabha, Electronic Resources, Electronic Databases.

Introduction

Agricultural libraries are playing an important role in improving agriculture scenario of our country. Existence in terms of usefulness of any library mainly depends on its physical, human and e-resources and its services. In this context user satisfaction is the paramount component of library services. To know the satisfaction level of users of IGKV Library, the present study was undertaken.A brief detail of the Nehru Library of IGKV is given as under.

Library, Indira Gandhi Krishi Vishwavidyalya, Raipur

The Nehru Library founded in 1987 after separation of IGKV from JNKVV Jabalpur. Before this, it was a college library of the College of Agriculture, Raipur. The present status of Nehru Library has been attained by the help of grant received from Indian Council of Agricultural Research through National Agricultural Technology Project, National Agriculture Innovation Project and the State Government for its infrastructural development and required services. The Library is equipped with latest communication media and information technologies like web based information, CD Rom search and internet browsing as it is well connected through LAN/ BSNL leased line. The Library is linked with various consortiums for online journals. Nehru Library maintains around >50000 collections of books, reports, theses, monograph, journal volumes, CD ROM Databases and other reference material. Library subscribes > 250 journals in physical and/or in electronic forms. The Nehru Library is the Central Library of Indira Gandhi Agricultural University catering to the needs of constituent libraries of colleges/faculty and research stations viz. College of Dairy Technology, Raipur, Faculty of Agricultural Engineering, Raipur, College of Vety. & Animal Husb., Anjora, Durg, TCB College of Agriculture & Research Station, Bilaspur, RMD College of Agriculture, Ambikapur, SG College of Agriculture & Research Station, Jagdalpur, SK College of Agriculture & Research Station, Kabirdham, BRSM College of Agril. Engineering & Technology, Mungali, Bilaspur.

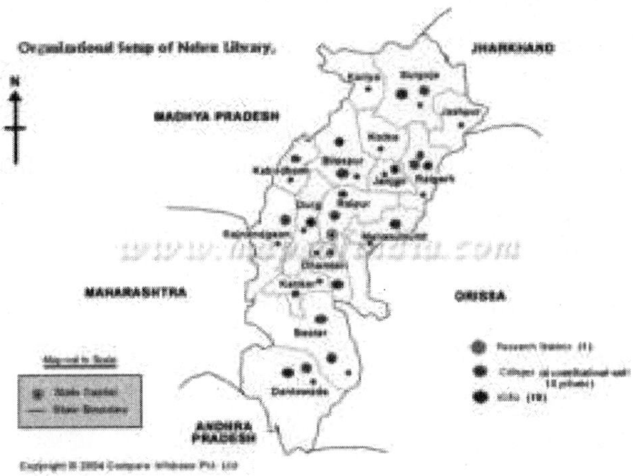

Library and Information Services of Indira Gandhi Krishi Vishwavidyalya, Raipur

University libraries generally provide its services to its users on very broad level. Library users are generally students, research scholars, faculty members and non-member visitors. To make library services more effective, availability of good resource/collections are a must and in addition, efficiency of the library staff and duration of library timings are also important. The library must have a rich collection / e-resources on the subjects in which teaching and research is being conducted. Efficiency of the library depends mainly on up-to-date OPAC. The staff must be technically sound to provide the following library services in an efficient manner.

e-Services

- Online Public Access Catalogue (OPAC)
- Online library information
- Internet Browsing
- Online Journals
- CeRA
- Online Theses Repository
- CD-ROM data bases :Abstracting Services

- Web based institutional information
- Barcode based circulation

Others

- Collection development
- Loan privilege
- Book Bank
- Documentation services
- Abstracting and Indexing Services
- Reference services
- Translation services
- Photocopy service
- Awareness programme /training and library course, etc.
- Organization of book exhibitions
- Scientific information exchange services

Objectives of the Study

The main objectives of the study are to know the view of users regarding library services, to know how to strengthen libraries and increase their efficient use and how to maintain significant relationship among the users.

The population of this study consists following categories of users undergraduate students, post-graduate students, research scholars and faculty members, etc. This study is concentrating on only users of university library main campus Raipur but presently the strength of student's users of various colleges i.e. College of Agriculture, Raipur is 576, College of Dairy Technology, Raipur is 126, Faculty of Agril. Engineering, Raipur is 17, College of Vety. & Animal Husb., Anjora, Durg is 262, TCB College of Agriculture & Research Station, Bilaspur is 212, RMD College of Agriculture, Ambikapur is 189, SG College of Agriculture, Jagadalpur is 210, SK College of Agriculture & Research Station, Kabirdham is 150, College of Fisheries, Kabirdham is 31 and BRSM College of Argil. Engineering & Technology, Mungali is 105.

Methodology

In the present study a survey was conducted to study the awareness of use of e-resources in agriculture among library users. The survey was conducted among 100 users during 2010 in Nehru Library, IGKV, Raipur. In the present survey reprenstative users from all the groups vig. Students, research scholar and faculty members were selected to know the impact level of library services. The data obtained from the study was analyzed.

Automation in Nehru Library

The Nehru Library has followed the following steps while converting into an automated system: Retrospective conversion of theses, rare documents, extension publications, proceedings of National and International Seminars held at IGAU. Computerized Data entry pertaining to bibliographical details of available books, journals, theses, CD-ROMs, etc. in LIBSYS. Generation of bar-codes and its labeling on all available books, journals, theses and important reports. Establishment of one CD mirror image computer server (Tulsient CDH) and one Linux server for LIBSIS. Establishment of LAN for connecting different computer systems in the library. Generation of bar-coded E-library cards for all the library users.Creation of OPAC.Circulation of all reading material through barcode reader.Establishment of BSNL-ISDN/dedicated lease line in the library.Subscription of online E-journals/resources. Linked with CeRA and Krishi Prabha Theses database. Organizing regular training course for readers for effectative use of electronic data base and information retrieval system. Teaching course "Library and Information Services" offered for PG and Ph.D. students.

Impact of Automation in Nehru Library IGKV, Raipur, Chhattisgarh

1. Reading environment in Nehru library has been considerably improved.
2. Availability of world wise agricultural information possible through various databases on campus network.
3. Users are also retrieving the OPAC on each corner of library.
4. Researchers are verifying their library account from entry gate of library.

5. Chances of damage are minimized due to retrospective conversion of theses, rare documents, extension publications, proceedings of National and International Seminars held at IGAU.
6. In Nehru Library via LAN so many users are utilizing the multi-user retrieval system.
7. Readers are well-acquainted with the automated library system following the regular training on 'Effective use of electronic data base and information retrieval system'.
8 Web browsing, internet, e-mail, data transformation, dissemination of latest information and new arrivals are possible through group mail, etc.

Library Services

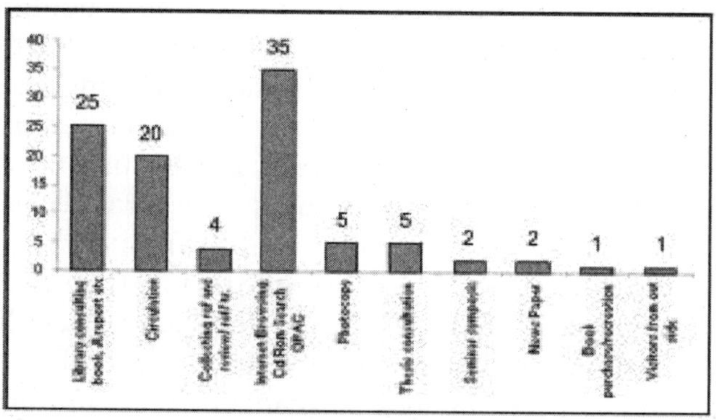

Fig. 1: Analysis of library services

Results of analysis of library services are presented in the above Figure 1. Results revealed that the maximum user percentage (35%) were concentrated towards use of net based library services CeRA / Krishiprabha/internet browsing and uses of CD ROM Database abstracting services, etc. because these services serve the actual needs of users.

Retrieval Method

Figure 2 indicates that majority of the users use direct web browsing or consult OPAC for retrieval of information for quick search without wastage of time. Remaining 16% of users conduct manual search information, because they believe in practical due to generation gap.

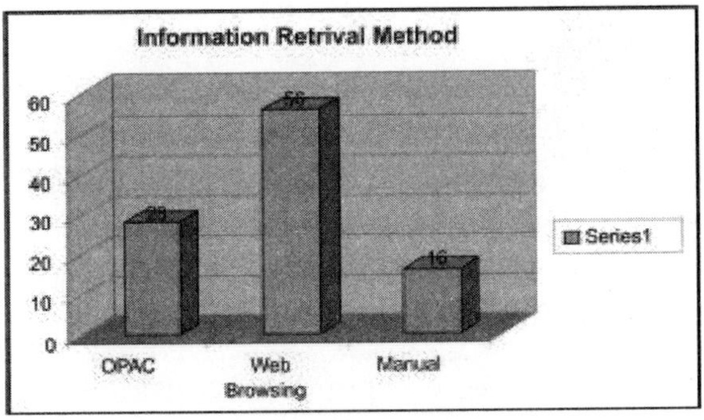

Fig. 2: Information retrieval method

Usefulness of CD ROM Database

Figure 3 indicates that the actual users of CD ROM facility are 81%.16% of the respondents depend on other persons to get information, but only 3% of respondents are not interested in computer service.

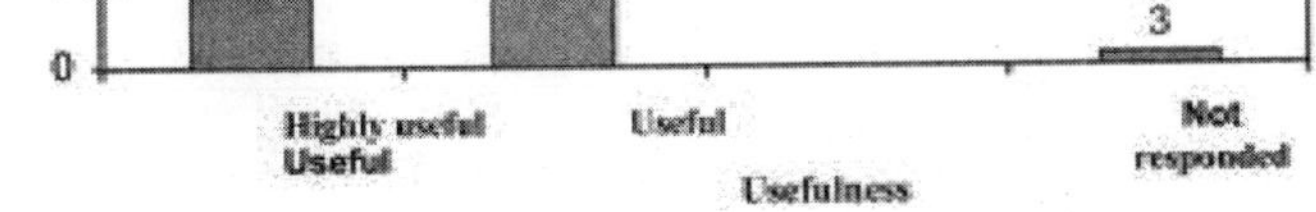

Fig. 3: Usefulness of CD ROM database

Internet Users

Internet connectivity: Whole Library system is connected through LAN using BSNL-ISDN/dedicated lease line. Fig. 4 indicates that 90% of respondents are regular users of internet browsing and only 10% are occasional or rare users due to lack of time or computer knowledge.

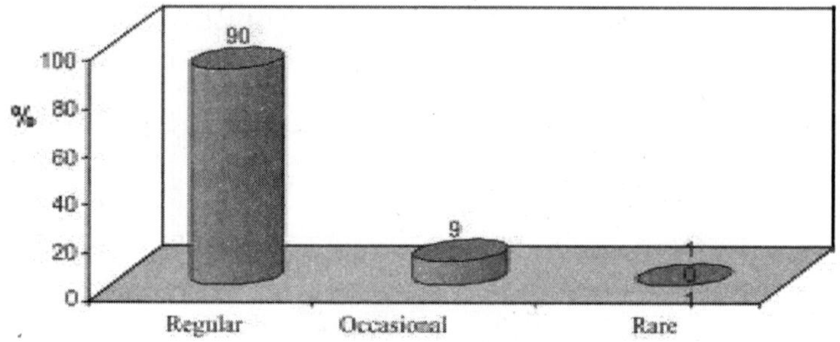

Fig. 4: Internet users

Necessity to subscribe online journals

Figure 5 indicates that 63.75% of respondents consider online journals necessary but remaining 36.25% of them show that online journals are highly necessary because they are actual browsers of online journals.

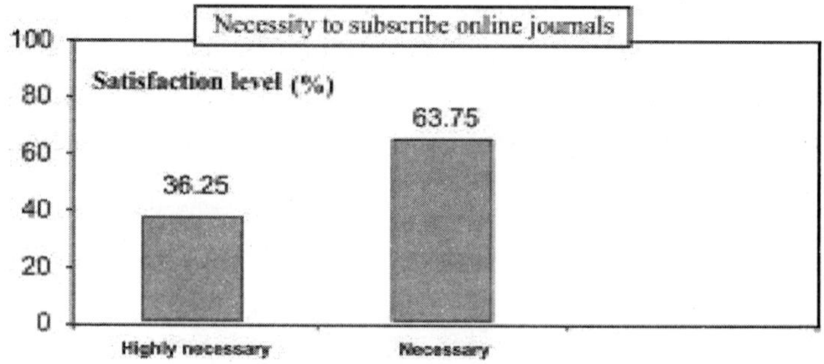

Fig. 5: Necessity of online journals

Consortium for e-Resources in Agriculture (CeRA)

More than 3000 scientific research journals are available online through Consortium for e-Resources in Agriculture (CeRA) on request. 124 libraries are the member of this consortium. Objective of this consortium is to develop the existing R & D information resource base of ICAR institutes/universities, etc., comparable to that existing in world's leading institutions/organizations. Its purpose is: To subscribe e-journals and create an e-access culture among scientists/ teachers in ICAR institutes/agricultural universities, to develop a Science Citation Index (SCI) Facility at IARI for evaluation of scientific publications, to assess the impact of CeRA on the level of research publications measured through SCI. It is a customized solution for accessing and sharing journal literature subscribed by all the 124 participating libraries in the consortia, individually and collectively, through CeRA Consortium. It gives full text access to 1343 journals to all the libraries from 3 consortia subscribed publishers –Annual Reviews, CSIRO (Australia) and Springer. In addition it gives access to metadata of journals from 635 publishers for those journals which libraries subscribe and also Open Access Journals. The Consortium consists of the following organizations under NARS, Deemed Universities, 3 ICAR Headquarters and Krishi Anusandhan Bhawans, 5 National Bureau, 42 Institutes, 21 National Research Centres, 9 Project Directorates, 38 State Agricultural Universities. Documentary delivery systems are to be developed at IARI, NDRI, IVRI and CIFE to enable those Consortium partners who do not have the print versions of particular scientific articles. Periodic reporting of the activities of the Consortium from time to time is done. CeRA is Consortium of e-journals being subscribed by NAIP, ICAR and provided access to 124 libraries of Agriculture (NARS). IGKV Raipur is also one of the Libraries among 124. Through this service the user can access the following three major on-line Portals and Bouquet of Journals from Publishers with full text of articles. CeRA consist with following gateway i.e. **Springer link:** It is a platform of Springer and product of bouquet of e-journals on different subjects published by Springer. Through this Bouquet user can access the full text of around 1100+ journals since 1996. **Annual Reviews**: Annual Reviews are authoritative, analytic reviews in 34 focused disciplines within the Biomedical, Life, Physical, and Social Sciences, etc. Through this product user can access the full text of an articles from 1990 onwards.. **CSIRO (Australia):** Australia's Commonwealth Scientific and Industrial Research Organization (CSIRO): Through this product users can access full text of complete package. **JCCC (J-Gate Custom Content for Consortia):** It is an Contents database collected from journals being subscribed by all 123 Libraries individually for the year 2008 (Not through Consortium) under NARS. This database is customized product of M/S Informatics, Bangalore and covers the contents of only periodicals which have electronic version and also given link to approximately 4000+ open access journals since year 2000..Jccc@cera covers in all 2199 journals.

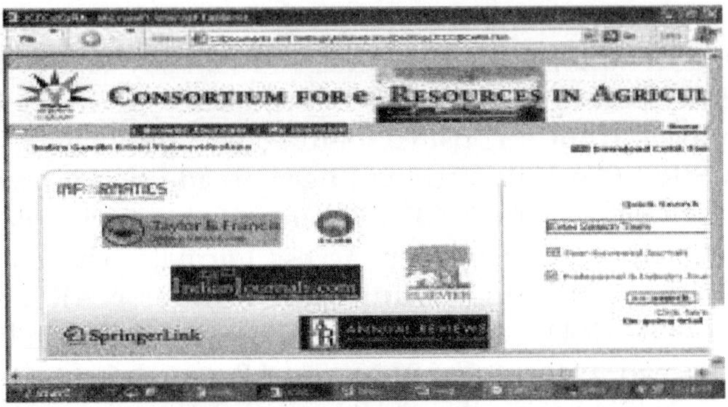

Fig. 6: Nehru Library IGKV is linked with Consortium for online e- Resources in Agriculture.

Recent improvement in journals through CeRA

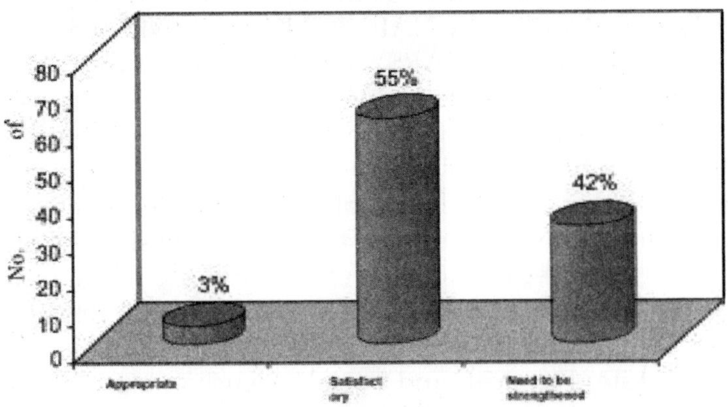

Fig. 7: Journals through CeRA

Figure 7 indicates that 55% of readers response is satisfactory for e-services in Nehru Library 42% respondent need to be strengthened i.e. more workstation and connections required other campus network also for CeRA facility and only 3% say appropriate due to lake of computer knowledge.

Krishiprabha Doctoral Theses Repository (DTR)

DTR covers 45 Agricultural Universities/Deemed Agricultural Universities in India which award Doctoral Degrees in agriculture and allied disciplines. These doctoral dissertations are one of the very important and valuable original sources of information. Indian agricultural repository of doctoral thesis is open for the members/ IP Users through eResource 'Krishiprabha'. Objectives of Krishiprabha are to develop, organize and sustain knowledge base of Indian Agricultural Dissertations in digital form and make it accessible online. To develop a standard format for submission of theses to the SAUs/ DAUs. To upgrade skills of human resources of SAUs/DAUs. To publish a journal in electronic form from the Database. The objective of this Project does not terminate with the establishment of the Digital Library and the Repository of hard copies.

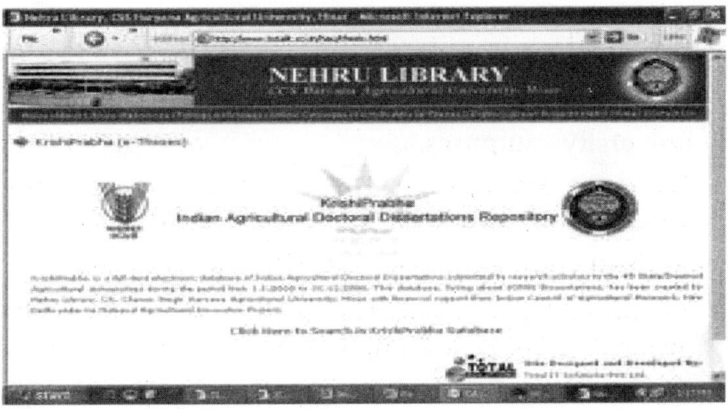

Nehru Library linked with Krishipr- abha Database for Indian agricultural repository of docto-ral theses. 73% users of PG and PhD scholar are actual users. Response is very useful but 24% respondent ask for include PG theses also in Krishiprabha database and 3% not respondent due to not avail this facility in his campus network.

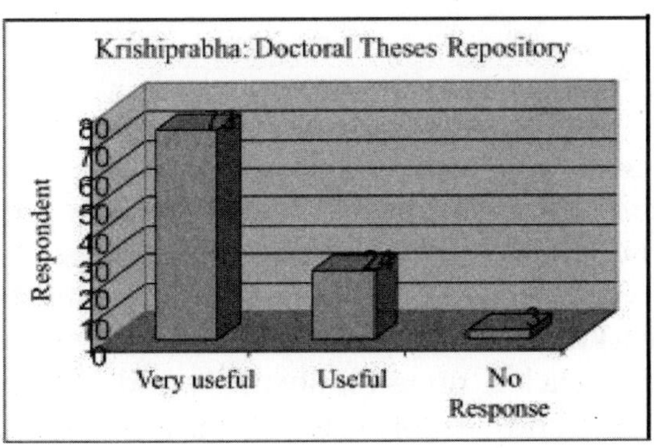

Awareness programme for use of e-Resources

In spite of this survey, recently library organized an awareness programme for use of e- Resources in Agriculture on 15-29th September 2010 for the user of Nehru Library. Results shows that 72% respondent took keen interest in awareness programme and suggest necessity of awareness programme on regular intervals. But 28% of respodents informed that e-resources like CeRA , Krishiprabha and full text journal is not available in outside campuses. They also demanded increase in the connectivity of internet in remote areas also.

Feed back regarding e-Resources

- CD- ROM database facility should be increased to all the university campuses.
- Need to strengthen the e-journals and e-book by subscription/purchase.
- Accessibility and use of CeRA be strengthened.
- Krishiprabha: Doctoral Theses Repository should be made available to outside campuses also.
- PG theses should also be included in Krishiprabha repository.
- Increase speed and connectivity of internet.
- More work stations should be established for browsing the internet.
- Awareness programmes for eResource Orientation are to be organized at regular intervals.
- Library timing is should be increased to 8.0 pm.

Conclusion

Presently, necessity of automation and e-resources in agricultural libraries is necessary to provide teaching and research support to its users. Only, the way is seeing that is resource sharing of knowledge among various libraries and information centers. It is possible only through networks or consortium. In field of agriculture CeRA is useful consortium working as information hub to provide e-resources i.e. online journals, articles, reviews, abstracts and other e resources on large scale to the end users of teaching and research community throughout country. CeRA is useful to avoid budgetary constraint of libraries. Similarly Krishiprabha like theses repository is very useful to avoid duplicity of research work. Certainly theses repositories save the time and energy of researchers and develop e-culture among the researchers for encouraging better results in research. Availability of information of library resources on website, OPAC like search engines has increased the quality of library services except some barriers like lack of e-literacy, connectivity in remote areas, and delaying of automation of libraries.

References

1. Pandey, Madhav, 2010. Impact of Automation in Agricultural Libraries and Information System. Paper presented and published in National Conference on Knowledge Management in the Globalized Era. 21-23 April 2010. Organized by Association of Agricultural Librarians and Documentalists of India in association with Indian Council of Agricultural Research Library and Indian Agricultural Statistics Research Institute Library, New Delhi. Lead paper:501-506
2. Indian Agricultural Research Institution, 2008. Consortium for e-Resources in Agriculture (Project under National Innovation Programme: Folder. 2009 Pub. Unit of Simulation and Informatics, IARI, New Delhi. 4p.
3. Pandey, Madhav, 2008. Perspective and potential of automation in agricultural libraries of Chhattisgarh. *Indian Journal of Agricultural Library and Information Services,* 24:66-72
4. Pandey, Madhav, R.N. Sharma, and U.K Watti,. 2007. Automation of agricultural libraries: Perspective and potential. *Research Digest,* 1 (3):140-42.
5. Choudhary Charan Singh Haryana Agricultural University, 2008 Krishiprabha: Indian Agricultural Doctoral Dissertation Repository: Brochure. Pub. Nehru Library CCSHAU, Hisar.6p.
6. Pandey, Madhav, Anil Kumar Kulshrestha and N.S. Pakhale, 2003. Role of IARI library and development of agriculture Paper presented and published in the National Seminar cum workshop on Role of Libraries in the development of Chhattisgarh, 6th February 2003 organized by Indira Gandhi Krishi Vishwavidyalaya, Raipur. pp. 5-9.

19

Networking of Agricultural Libraries and Information Centres of India

A necessity

Dr. Ashish Kumar Sharma
Assistant Librarian, Central Library, Gurukul Kangri University
Haridwar (Uttarakhand)
Ashish1077@yahoo.co.in

1. Introduction

Like other libraries and information centers, the agricultural libraries and information centres are the institutions with the responsibility of meeting the information needs of the users of their respective organizations. India is mainly an agricultural country and agriculture is the main source of her economy. Supply of information pertaining to agriculture is vital for the development of farming and rural economy. The rapid growth of publications, decreasing ability of libraries to go in for comprehensive acquisition of documents, escalating prices of reading materials, regular devaluation of Indian currency, growing demands of the ever-increasing users of agro-biological literature and their multifaceted information needs are some of the challenges presently faced by the library and information professionals in India. Resource sharing through networking is the only way to overcome the above challenges and to enhance the library resources for providing better services to its users. In the present age of information explosion, no library is self-sufficient to provide comprehensive service to its users. The advent of information technology has added new dimensions to the concept of networking towards cooperation among the agricultural libraries. The supply of information on agriculture is vital for the development of well-informed agriculture community. The library networks aim at providing requisite reading materials, need-based information and services to its general as well as the specialist users.

2. Network

A network, in simple words, refers to two or more computers connected together. There are a number of reasons to connect computers into networks, but important two are:

- Allowing human beings to communicate.
- Sharing of the resources.

Library network may be defined as "a distribution system composed of two or more libraries and/or other organizations engaged in a common pattern of information exchange, through communications for some functional purpose" (Sujatha, 1999). The National Commission on Libraries and Information Science (NCLIS), in its National Programme Documents (1975) also gives the same definition and adds, "A network usually consists of a formal arrangement whereby materials, information and services provided by a variety of libraries and other organizations are available to all potential users. Libraries may be under different jurisdictions but agree to serve one another on the same basis as each serves its own constituents. Computers and telecommunications may be among the tools used for facilitating communication among them."

According to Vilentchuk (1975), " An information network may be defined as a system integrating institutions—libraries, documentation centres, information centres, analysis centres—into a coordinated whole, to provide a community of users with relevant input data, irrespective of its origin, format or physical location". Miller has defined it as "a cooperative system established by libraries and information centres which are brought together by common subject, geographic proximity to share information resources and all other elements essential for providing effective information service" (Ramaiah, 1977).

According to United Nations Information System for Science and Technology (UNISIST), "Networking is a set of inter-related information system associated with communication facilities, which are co-operating through more or less formal agreements and institutional agreements with a view to pooling their resources for better serving the users. They generally follow identical or compatible rules and procedures" (Satyanarayana and Rajan, 1984).

A network in information field means a systematic organization and coordination of inter-connected libraries, documentation and information centres for achieving greater economy and efficiency (Subbaiah, 1988).

It is clear from the above definitions that network is a cooperative system of sharing resources among two or more libraries through a formal institutional agreement, common pattern of exchange of information among the libraries with the help of communication system.

3. Need for Networking Agricultural Libraries and Information Centres

It has been an accepted fact that no library in the world can be self-sufficient in the collection of published literature in any branch of knowledge to meet the requirement of its users. Each and every library has to depend on its counterparts to meet the demand of its users. This dependence on other libraries has been solved through different methods at different periods of time like inter-library loan, resource sharing, networking of libraries, etc. Networking of libraries has become possible after the application of computers in library activities and the development in communication technologies. Following are some of the needs (Natraj, 2003) for networking of libraries:

- To promote sharing of resources among the libraries of agricultural institutions and research organizations by collecting, storing, disseminating information, and by offering computerized services to the users;
- To co-ordinate efforts for suitable collection development and reduce unnecessary duplication wherever possible;
- To enable the users to acquire reading materials not available in their library from other libraries participating in the network system;

- To establish a referral centre for maintaining a central on-line union catalogue of books, serials and non-book materials of all participating libraries;
- To develop bibliographic database of books, serial and non-book materials for search and access;
- To possess and maintain electronic and mechanical equipment for fast communication of a information delivery;
- To evolve standards and uniform guidelines in techniques, methods, procedures, hardware, software and services for adoption by the participating libraries to facilitate pooling, sharing and exchanging resources and services;
- To coordinate with other national and international networks for exchange of information and documents;
- To create a database of projects, specialists, and institutions for providing on-line information service to those who seek it;
- To locate out-of-print materials and to facilitate fast retrieval in special areas; and
- To take initiative for promotion of agricultural research, development and innovation of information technology in agriculture.

4. Functions of Agricultural Libraries and Information Centres Network

Following are some of the important functions of agricultural libraries and information centres:

- To co-ordinate and communicate the resources and services within the network;
- To facilitate efficient and economic inter-lending and exchange of information resources;
- To provide reprographic and translation facilities;
- To establish centralized data bank for providing quick information service;
- To formulate standards for information techniques, procedures, processes and services for the use of participating libraries in the network;

- To establish co-ordination with other regional, national and international centres, engaged in information handling.

5. Agriculture Information and Resource Sharing in the Existing System

The voluminous growth of published documents in agricultural information, increasing cost of information sources, technological advancements that offer newer methods of information processing, retrieval and dissemination are some of the factors which have made resource sharing a possibility.

For resource sharing the participating libraries need to come together and co-operate in two broad areas:

- Developing the collection on shared basis; and
- Developing services for exploiting such collection.

Developing the shared resources is of great importance and central to the concept of resource sharing. In developing the shared resources the first and foremost focus in eliminating duplication in the acquisition of source material in agriculture by participating libraries to the extent possible. Thereafter, the focus is on the selection of such publications as the participating libraries agree to share, and later on their acquisitions. However, modern information technology has made the task of resource sharing simple, quick and convenient. The new technology brings forward new products and services in the information field, which has changed the nature of fundamental library objectives and operations. There are two technologies—computer and telecommunication technology— which have contributed to these revolutionary changes. Impact of these technologies on the library services can be further enhanced by the following means:

- Use of computer and communication networks for resource sharing and;
- Use of national and international databases through communications networks.

6. Networking Model for Agricultural Libraries and Information Centres

A network can be local, regional, national or international. It is for the electronic transfer of information between two or more points irrespective of distance. The model that may be used for networking as well as for resource sharing in the agricultural field is as follows:

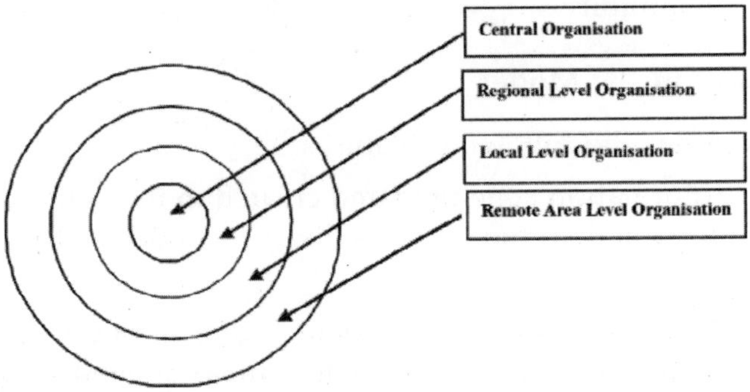

Networking Model for Agricultural Libraries & Information Centres

Above model can be discussed according to the stages of occurrences:

Stage I

The Model of resource sharing includes:

- Interlinking between national and international level organizations related to agricultural field.
- One of the national level institutes of agriculture must act as a hub/a central organization for coordinating all networking activities.
- A central organization is supposed to get information from the national level institutions as well as international institutions in the field of agriculture studies.

Stage II

Central node accumulates the information from all participating institutions of national and international level and disseminates to regional level points. To make this process of information dissemination more effective and useful, the two-way communication should be encouraged.

Stage III

Regional level centres will disseminate information at the local level points, institutions/universities/public libraries/community information centres, including non-government organizations also.

All the participant institutions in the above network model must have motivation and clear aims to provide efficient services to the farmer's community.

7. Features of the Model

The model has the following features:

- Information generated and created in the field of agriculture anywhere in the world is disseminated speedily at the grass root levels.
- Participating institutions and organizations arrange for their own money from different sources related to agricultural information product and services.
- Institutes/universities are fully equipped with computer and other related equipment for giving document delivery services.
- To make the networking efficient, the skilled and experienced human resource is to be deployed.
- To make the use of electronic form of publications for sharing resources.
- Duplication of costly and highly used journals need be avoided by mutual agreement and the same can be shared through the network.

Developing such a network requires a proper cooperation and understanding. Network enables the participating libraries to obtain materials from each other. It may be the list of books, indexes and abstracts of required articles, facsimile copies of required pages or documents, charts, figures, drawings by using computer terminals attached to a large network system, data bases coupled with visual display units (VDUs) and attached with printing facility. Information can be scanned first on the screen, and if required, relevant information can be obtained in the print form. It is important that the attitude of staff of the participating institutions should be very co-operative. In addition, learning about the technical aspect of information technology and the attitudes of its users is also essential for its users in the resources sharing. There is also a need to make an effort for the attitudinal change among the human resources in the libraries. The training programme related to the development and human resources in the libraries and information centres should be devised keeping in view this aspect. As more and more institutions related to the field of agriculture are willing to be participants in the network, they can be included.

8. Implementation Plan

Considering the existing infrastructural facilities, financial resources, manpower and technological aspects, the implementation of the model can be made in three successive phases (Uddin and Rashid, 2002) The phase-wise implementation tasks is to be undertaken are as follows:

Phase I

- Introduction of computer culture in the agricultural libraries and information centres.
- Procurement of hardware and software as also site preparation by the individual libraries.
- Setting up of communication infrastructure.
- Creating of machine-readable catalogue as per the standard format, Common Communication Format (CCF).

Computerization of internal procedures/systems of each library.

In the first phase, all the infrastructures for automation of library activities and networking will be created and the personnel will be trained in automation and computers. The libraries will create a machine readable database (catalogue) of their holdings as per standard format and automate all their house keeping services and be ready to join the network.

Phase II

- Setting up of the network.
- Linking of the individual libraries into the network.
- Introduction of various user services through network.

The second phase will culminate into the setting up of formal network, linking all the participating libraries into the network, and introducing various services through network.

Phase III

- Bringing all the agricultural universities, college libraries, libraries of the research organizations and public libraries/ community information centres into the network.
- Joining hands with other local, national and international networks.

In the third phase, it is proposed to bring all the agricultural university libraries, college libraries, libraries of research organizations and public libraries/ community information centres into the network. The network will join hands with local, national and international networks.

9. Conclusion

It can be concluded that in a developing country like India, steps are being taken to disseminate information pertaining to agriculture to its user community. With the explosion of information and constraints on the financial resources, the resource sharing networking has emerged as an important alternative. Information Technology with computer and telecommunication has facilitated the resources sharing among the institutions located in different geographical area. It is also necessary to prepare the library staff through appropriate IT training. The great libraries of the future will not be those with great collections, but with good staff because knowledge must be acquired and understood in the library before it is put to use. Rediscovery may be as important as the creation of knowledge itself in view of the developments in information technologies that are taking place continuously.

There is no alternative for the institutions that are engaged in teaching and research as well as generating information on agriculture, but to come together under a formalized network in order to develop strategies for effective communication, resource sharing and information dissemination. The agricultural scientists and researchers require relevant information from wherever it can be found.

For the growth and development of our country, the needed information is an essential input for the agriculture community. Resource sharing and networking among the agricultural libraries in India is therefore a must. For this the participating libraries shall have to co-operate to make networking programme a success.

References

1. NATIONAL COMMISSION ON LIBRARIES AND INFORMATION SCIENCE. Towards a national progress for libraries and information services: goals for action. 1975; Govt. Printing Office; Washington; p 82.
2. NATRAJ (B Vibhuti). Need for networking agriculture libraries and information centres. *ILA Bulletin*. 39(3); 2003; 33.
3. RAMAIAH (L S) et al. Public library system: services and networking. 1997; Ess Ess; New Delhi; p 173.
4. SATYANARAYANA (R) and RAJAN (T N). Information networks: structure and operation with reference to India. *International Information Communication and Education*. 12; 1984; 156.
5. SUBBAIAH (R). Agricultural Librarianship in India: an overview. 1988; Metropolitan; New Delhi; p 218.
6. SUJATHA (G). Resource sharing and networking of University libraries. 1999; Ess Ess; New Delhi; p 4.
7. UDDIN (M H) and RASHID (M H). Networking of agricultural information system in Bangladesh (BD-AGRINET): a model. *Library Herald*. 40(1); March 2002; 16.
8. VILENTCHUK (L). Guide lines on the conduct of National Infentory of Scientific and Technological Information on Documentation facilities. 1975; UNESCO; Paris; p 137.

20

Information Access and Use of ETD in Social Science

Dr. K. C. Das
Head, P.G. Dept. of Library & Information Science
Utkal University, Bhubaneswar-751004,Orissa

Introduction

The access to information without technological barriers is one of the gospels of the information society. The society that has been responsible for transforming information into knowledge and that knowledge is now being strongly considered as the basic resource in all human activities.

Access to information is one of the prime objectives of librarianship, since libraries have been providing access to vivid forms of documentary sources of information since time immemorial. Development in the area of Information Communication Technology (ICT) comprising of the concept of super highway, WWW, Internet, Electronic Library and Virtual library, etc. has made great impact upon all walk of life and dynamic practice of modern librarianship. The exponential growth in Information Technology (IT) sector has paved the way to unprecedented phenomenon of access to information. The current information landscape is experiencing tremendous growth in the quantity of information with multiple and overlapping types and format of information, redundancy in the information produced, and the ambiguity about the future of traditional text-based publishing. Open access for global information from a remote place is present day's fashion or a necessity. Libraries need to understand the essence of service delivery in IT driven world and should opt for making a good balance between print and electronic resources.

1.0 Information Access

Information access refers to the means or modes through which information is made available, or to an entire range of possibilities for making information and information services available to the users. Campbell (1984) defines information access as the *"ability to quickly and easily find what you want and need in a pool of information"*.

Faculties, students and research scholars in Social Sciences, largely depend on electronic resources for timely and for instant access to information. A library's survival depends upon its capability to understand the users' need and responding fast to satisfy the needs of the clienteles effectively and efficiently.

2.0 Role of Librarian as Facilitator of Information Access

The role of librarian as facilitator of information access and disseminator of information is well-established. This role of intermediary is expanding and becoming more and more demanding to facilitate information access and use. These developments are assigning a central role for libraries in the educational process and exciting range of opportunities for librarians to be innovative educators. They also strive to arm the learners with the knowledge and skills necessary to take full advantage of new information resources influenced by technology. The change in search strategies for accessing information from Internet, demand different skills, different from retrieving information either from CD-ROM databases or online information retrieval systems. This demands the learners to work independently on computers; therefore they must be familiar with:

i. How to identify relevant databases in relation to a query;
ii. How to interconnect such databases;
iii. How to differentiate between an index and a search engine;
iv. How to use different search strategies on the Internet like advanced search;
v. How to build Web catalogues;
vi. How to serve as intermediary for Internet access to remote users; and
vii. How to download, cut and paste, and so on .

3.0 Information Users

Theoretically speaking user of a digital library may be anyone living anywhere in the world. This is especially true for those digital libraries that aim to offer information access to a global audience, for example, the Networked Digital Library of Theses and Dissertations (NDLTD), the Networked Computer Technical Reference Library (NCSTRL) or the Greenstone Digital Library.

Users of these digital libraries may vary in terms of their information need, characteristics, and capabilities and so on. Some digital libraries aim to cater to a rather homogeneous group of users though they may not be bound by any geographical boundary. Example of such digital libraries includes the Association of Computing Machinery (ACM) digital library and Institute of Electrical and Electronic Engineers (IEL) digital library. Yet there are other digital libraries that are designed specifically to support a defined group of users. Most university digital libraries, for example the California Digital Library and Headline belongs to this category. However, as Nicholas and Dobrowolski (2001) argue, the characteristics and role of user in a digital environment vary significantly from those in a traditional library environment. Users in a digital environment need not only have adequate information literacy skills, but also some ICT skills to help them make optimum use of the digital resources. The SCONUL position paper (SCONUL, 1999) identified seven information skills that are considered necessary in a digital environment:

- The ability to recognize a need for information;
- The ability to distinguish ways in which the information need may be addressed;
- The ability to construct appropriate information strategies;
- The ability to locate and access appropriate information;
- The ability to compare and evaluate information obtained from various sources;
- The ability to organize, communicate and apply information in problem solving tasks or in decision making; and
- The ability to synthesize and build upon existing information, and to contribute to the creation of new information (Chowdhury & Chowdhury, 2003).

Information Needs

Information needs and how to provide access to information has remained a central theme of study among information and computer science researchers for many years. It is commonly agreed that the provision of information begins when a user has an information need. Information need is a stage where the user senses that it may be useful to know something that they don't know at that particular point in time. Marchionini (1995) comments that information seeking is a fundamental human process that is closely related to learning and problem solving. According to Borgman(2000b) a need is a psychological construct, and it can be observed by a researcher, a librarian or an intelligent agent; only indicator or manifestations of needs can be observed. The information needed by a user to accomplish a goal—to resolve a problem, to answer a specific question or to satisfy a curiosity—may be quick and brief factual data or exhaustive and detailed. Figure 1: Basic Information Access Model (Source: Baeza and Ribeiro, 1999) shows a simple model of information access. Users often learn during the information search process. For example, they may come across some information that influences their information need.

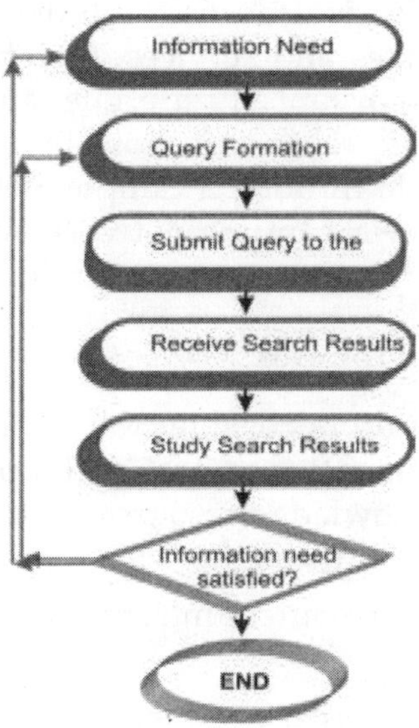

Basic Information Access Model

Access to Information Resources

Access to information and information resources has been one of the objectives of the libraries and librarians and this is fairly exemplified by Ranganathan's famous Five Laws of Library Science. While libraries have been doing a good job of providing access to traditional documentary sources for a number of years, the application of ICT to the generation, processing, storage, retrieval, and dissemination / transmission of information has Information Access radically changed the situation, and has altered, for example, the objectives and strategies, the nature of sources and services, operational/ organisational structures, and the ways in which service is delivered. In recent times, increasingly, some of the libraries have been providing access to electronic resources which have expanded from a few dozen computerized bibliographic databases to include the overwhelming information available on the internet (Fecko, 1997). In addition, thanks to electronic publishing, authors including academics are producing scholarly papers and teaching materials which are being placed in the institutional (if not public) domains without resorting to the traditional publishing process. Furthermore, the accelerated growths of institutional internets or intranets have facilitated access to information. Thus, one can see efforts underway to facilitate all types of access, bibliographical access, physical access, intellectual access, and networked access to resources and services, thereby enhancing use of information. In the not too distant a future, one can envisage various levels of access to electronic resources those in great demand are made permanently accessible through a campus network and others can be accessed remotely via campus network when needed, for example, through the internet (Lancaster & Sandore, 1997).

4.5 Information Access in Libraries

In an academic setting, the users consider the library as their prime source of information. As mentioned earlier library is reservoir of both print and non-print knowledge resources. The library provides information access to its users through:

1. Conventional print resources indexed and catalogued (Print Resources);
2. Micro documents with reader/printer facility (Micro Resources);

3. Collection of networked CD- ROMs, both bibliographic and full text; tape–loaded database available on a computer (Electronic Resources);
4. Subscriptions to online services and own website;
5. Staff's direct interaction (Ref. services);
6. Sharing of database and other resources with neighboring institutions(Resource Sharing); and
7. Interlibrary loan and document delivery services (ILL).

People frustrate when they know that a potentially useful resource or service exists, but they are not to use it in the timeframe in which it is needed. The conventional library with its massive weight of paper gathering dust and restricting efficient searches is another paper-based institute that sets fingers at the keyboard. The sense that information is "there" somewhere, but cannot be found can drive anyone to digitize (Brown and Duguid, 2000). IT applications are erupting and moving faster than one's imagination resulting in information explosion and the libraries are forced to meet the challenges of users' increasing need for electronic resources. While providing access to electronic resources through campus-wide networks, it is desirable and necessary for library professionals to be knowledgeable and subsequently to streamline their efforts to optimize the use of resources.

4.6 Information Access in Digital Libraries

The two basic modes of accessing information in digital libraries are browsing and searching. Most digital libraries provide facilities for browsing and searching. Hence we will take a look of the user interfaces of some digital libraries highlighting their features for supporting and browsing, query formulation and display of search results. A number of portals and subject gateways have been developed over the past few years to facilitate access to digital information. These gateways are not digital libraries per se; some prefer to call them virtual libraries since they provide organized and systematic access to information resources on the web. Examples of such gateways include BUBL, EEVL, SOSIG, Biz/ed and BIOME. Chowdhury and Chowdhury (2001b) provide useful discussion on the characteristics of these subject gateways.

4.7 Role of Library in Information Accessibility

Although technologies provide resources for full and richer learning experience, the improved learning outcomes through information technology do not happen by chance. Librarians must be the part of the process to inform and empower learning with technology that enables faculties to access and interact effectively with information in its many forms and formats - real and virtual - and use it responsibly and purposefully. The libraries have been conducting library and information use programmes under the broader umbrella of User Education consisting of, user orientation, freshmen initiation and bibliographic instruction programmes. The emergence of Information Society transforming into Knowledge Society, has increased the complexities of information accessibility, reliability and dependability. In the digital world of information highway, there are stresses on *three* things:

1. Awareness of information
2. Awareness of technology, and
3. Awareness of needs.

The awareness of information gives the breadth of vision; awareness of technology gives the power to make the vision manifest; and awareness of needs gives the insight to use professional skills and talents to the greater effect (Krishan Gopal, 2005).

4.8 Factors Influencing Access to Information

Borgaman (2000b) comments that the concept of access to information has its roots in different areas such as library services, telecommunication policies, and so on. She defines access to information as connectivity to a computer network and to the available content, given that the technology is usable; the user has the requisite skill and knowledge and the content is in usable and useful form. Thus, the three major factors influencing access to information are:

the technology, content and above all the users.

The software issues in examining the information access can be separated into two areas:

- *Content* : What is the medium of the information and how is it presented to the user once it has been located (e.g. a video clip displayed by a browser plugin)

- *Access :* How are searching and browsing accomplished to enable the user to locate information (e.g. full text searching with ranked result lists of document titles)

Although the type of content can influence the access mechanisms (e.g. image thumbnails, query by humming) this broad division is useful as it highlights a potential consequence of current interface design practice. Namely, that useful content can be rendered inaccessible by access mechanisms that require print literacy.

Conclusion

On the whole, information access largely depends on how effectively and efficiently information is primarily managed by libraries and information centers. Since, Digital Libraries do not have any physical presence; users do not get a view of the collection and the contents as they do in a printed library. In fact, users of a digital library may not know much about its content, and thus find it difficult to formulate a query to get access to the required information. Users may not know how exhaustive the collection is in the area of interest or the size of the entire collection. Hence it may become difficult for them to assess how exhaustive to retrieve information set at the end of a search is, and how precise the search results are. Determining how much information to show the users of a digital library is a major design choice in information access interfaces (Hearest, 1999) that pretext a challenge before the information professionals of electronic generation to redesign and reform the whole gamut of information set up.

References

1. Borgman, C.(2000b), "From Gutenberg to the global information infrastructure : access to information in the networked world", New York, ACM press.
2. Brown, J.S. and Duguid, P (2000), "The social life of information", Boston: Harvard Business School Publishing, pp. 171-200.
3. Campbell, J.D. (2006), "Changing a cultural icon: The academic library as a virtual destination".Educause Review, Vol.41 No.1, pp. 16-31.
4. Chowdhury, G. G. and Chowdhury, S. (2003), "CD- Rom and online information sources and searching", London, Library Association Publishing.

5. Gopal, K(2005), "Information literacy in digital era : a gate way to learning, in SIS 2005, 23rd annual convention & Conference volume, 27-29 Jan, ed. Shasikala.C & others; pp. 691-699.

6. Hearst, M. (1999), "User interface and visualization", In Baeza - Yates, R. and Ribeiro - Neto, B, (Eds), Modern information retrieval, New York, ACM Press, pp. 257-323.

7. Patra, Manaswini and Das, K.C.(2011). Information Access and Management in Digital Era. New Delhi, SSDN Publishing

8. Nichols, D.et al. (2000), "DEBORA: developing an interface for support collaboration in a digital Library". In Borbinha, J. and Baker, T. (eds) proceeding of the 4th European Conference on Research and Advanced Technology for Digital Libraries (ECDL, 2000), Lisbon, Portugal, 18-20 Sept, 2000, Berlin, Springer, pp. 239-248.

9. SCONUL. (1999), " Information skills in higher education", SCONUL position paper, available at www.sconul.ac.uk/publications (accessed 14 April, 2010).

21

Failure of ICT Applications in Libraries in Developing Countries

Harish Kumar Tripathi
Librarian
Indian Council of Agricultural Research
Krishi Anusandhan Bhavan, New Delhi

Abstract

ICT (Information and Communication Technologies) is playing a significant role in house keeping activities and information retrieval in libraries and it has brought a lot of varieties of changes of traditional concept in libraries, for instance, books to electronic documents; catalogue cards to database, corresponding mail to e-mail and traditional libraries to digital or virtual libraries and so on. The impact of ICT has been amply charted on libraries over few decades, but the result of majority of ICT development in libraries in developing countries like India, are not satisfactory due to lack of planning, allocated budget to library, proper training to library professionals, professional ICT ethics and other unavoidable causes. So in this paper, an attempt has been made to discuss the causes of this failure and to suggest solutions.

Keywords: ICT; Information Technology; Communication Technology, Failure; India

Information and Communication Technology (ICT)

ICT consists of three terms—Information, Communication and Technology. Information has been one of essential needs to progress in the life of a nation during the 21st century, in addition to basic human needs. Information, has no value if it is not communicated, so it is also very necessary that information should be communicated to the person who requires it. Various media of communication like authors, speakers, books, journals, newspapers, news channels, publishers, print media, mass media, libraries, Internet and its allied services like e-mail, world wide web, web-blogs, face book, chatting, etc. are playing their vital role in the society and through these useful and required information is being communicated to individuals or a group of users or all common users.

ICT may be defined as technology, which is used to store, process and communicate the required information on demand or in anticipation. ICT is a very broad term in the field of information technology that includes all technologies, which are brought to use in information and it communication. For instance, computer or CDs, DVDs, magnetic disc or telephone, microphone, loud speakers, mobile phones or radio, television or Internet. Information and Communication Technologies (ICT) are making their significant contribution in the development of libraries.

Major components of ICT and their use in libraries

Key components of ICT, which are needed in the library towards library automation, are as follows:

1. Computers
2. Printers
3. Xerox machine
4. Scanners
5. Library Management Software
6. Mobile technology
7. Telephone and fax machine
8. Local Area Network
9. CD Roms and Online databases
10. Internet
11. Audio and Video Conferencing
12. Consortia

13. Web 2.0 technology including blogs, facebook, twitter, etc.
14. Trained Library Professionals

Benefits from ICT cannot be derived without creating the proper technical infrastructure, which provides the platform for delivery of applications and services and access to them. So it is necessary to create proper ICT infrastructure in the library, keeping view user's needs and parent organization's objectives.

ICT is used in libraries in two ways:

1. For house keeping activities.
2. In information retrieval and communication

House keeping activities involves the followings:

a. Official works in library: like preparing office orders, supply orders, library circulars, reminders, etc. by using computer;
b. To make available prints out of required document for readers
c. To make available the required document by scanning and sending to the user through e-mail
d. To create institutional repository, by scanning the rare documents.
e. Other house keeping operations like acquisition, circulation, cataloguing, serial control, article indexing, stock management, inter-library loan services by using Library Management Software.
f. Simultaneously house keeping works can be done on various nodes by establishing LAN (Local Area Network) in the library.

Information retrieval means to make retrieve the required information on demand and in anticipation by using ICT components

a. To make available the required information by using various searching technologies on Internet.
b. To make available the required publications to users by Consortia.

   Consortia is the new concept in ICT. These are being used by many libraries. CeRA (Consortium of electronic Resources in Agriculture) is the sub-project under NAIP (National Agricultural Innovative Project) of ICAR (Indian Council of Agricultural Research). Agricultural libraries are getting utmost benefits, by making available the articles through CeRA.

c. OPAC or Web-OPAC (Online Public Access Catalogue) facilitates to provide the information about the availability of the publications in the library.

d. Library blogs, a new concept of web technology which is used to publish information about library and its resources.

e. Advanced Add-on features in Library Management Software; mobile technology facilitates users by providing information about new arrivals, reminders for the borrowed books, and reservation of required book.

Causes of failure of ICT in Libraries

The major causes for failure of automation or ICT projects in the libraries of developing countries are as follows:

1. Selection of Library Management Software without analytical study

There are various commercial and open source library software available in market. However, the selection procedure of LMS is a very complex process. Normally library professionals or libraries go with either renowned library software or that is imposed by Competent Authority.

We should have an analytical study of all the Library Management Software, about which we read in published papers, keeping in view the user's needs and parent organization objectives.

2. Lack of searching technologies among library professionals

Lack of expertise in searching technologies among library professionals, results into incorrect approach. So it is necessesary to give more attention to such important issues as to integrate with curriculum and training library professionals in the use of technologies in an effective way.

3. Lack of adequate fund allocation for library

Investment on ICT in libraries is highly expensive is beyond any doubt. But the libraries in the developing countries like India are not given adequate budget by its parent organization. So it is not easy to implement ICT component in libraries.

Compromise on low cost ICT equipment can also result in performance and longevity of the equipment. So low budget libraries should seek the alternate of brand name like assembling computer or any hardware, without compromising on the performance and longevity of the computer or any ICT equipment. Competent authority should be convinced to make available the required ICT equipment for the library. There are many open source software available in market, so professionals should be made aware about them. But they should do the exercise of analytical study before adopting any open source software; so open source software having advanced and add-on features could perform house keeping activities and information retrieval in the library in an effective way.

4. Lack of adequate competent library professionals

In the developing countries like India, libraries don't have adequate competent ICT skilled professionals. Library professionals cannot be IT specialists, so they should be encouraged to join short-term course or capsule ICT course so that the ICT technologies could be implemented in libraries. The availability of adequate and sufficient competent library professionals is the primary requirement to plan, implement, manage and use of ICTs in libraries.

Nowadays, it is a fashion to appoint low salary professionals on contract basis. Their performance is poor. There is no use of investment in ICT training for them.

5. Lack of interest of learning process among library professionals

Since continuous learning activities result in advanced technical knowledge and skills among library professionals, so they should be addicted to make themselves aware about the latest Information and Communication Technologies (ICT) and their maximum use in effective way. Library professionals should also be encouraged to attend seminars or workshop cum training programmes, in order to create interest for ICT among them.

6. Sharing of thought among library professionals

Sharing of thoughts is the best way of anchoring learning in any field. It helps both sharer and receiver. So library professionals should continue to share their professional thoughts and ICT ethics by attending conferences or seminar, and creating social networks, facebook, blogs. Twitter, orkut, messangers, e-mails. Library professionals should also have interest to learn about these communication channels and their effective use.

7. Lack of training for library professionals

Well qualified library professionals are the back-bone of Library System, so successful introduction of ICTs in library requires their involvement and support. Training is essential part in ICT environment for both library professionals and end users, so that utmost use of ICT like Internet, e-mail, online resources could be made possible, in order to get their required information. Proper training to library professionals reduces the fear among library professionals for ICT implementation in libraries.

8. Lack of professional ethics

Ethics refer to the moral standards or human values in such a way what should be done or not be done in term of behaviour, laws, social habits, responsibility, accountability, rights and benefits to all. ICT ethics and general moral ethics cannot be separated or differentiated from one another. ICT doesn't have only technological aspect, it is also used for the benefits of library users and nation. The integration between ICT advances and professionals ethics is the most primary key factor for implementation and sustainable management of ICT in libraries. Library professionals should use innovative methods of introducing ICTs to enhance the library and information services in the library in effective way, so that maximum number of users could get their required information.

9. Lack of communication between library professionals and competent Authority

It is very necessary to fill the communication gap between library professionals and competent authority, by taking some initiatives for providing the required information at the earliest. Library professionals should convince the competent authority about CAS (Current Awareness Service) and other services provided, and assure better services for coming time, on condition of making available the required facilities in the library.

10. In-adequate planning for ICT implementation

Adequate planning for ICT implementation is the foundation of ICT Resources Management (IRM). Technologies are being changed rapidly, so adequate planning is very necessary to avoid incompatibility and inaccessibility, keeping in view of limited availability of financial and managerial resources. Sometimes it has also come into notice, librarians and funding projects do prepare their plans and projects to implement in the library without proper or sufficient knowledge of hardware, software and analytical study of other factors and they are imposed on libraries. Adequate planning about ICT implementation results into something positive.

Sustainable management of ICT Resources ensures reliability and efficiency of the system. Library professionals should therefore need to think about the followings:

a. Escalating cost of ICT components rapidly.

b. Library professionals should be made aware about latest technologies by organizing various workshop-cum-training programmes.

c. ICT professional should be available at all stages in the library.

d. There must be a provision of allocating the budget for AMC (Annual Maintenance Contracts) for ICT equipment like Library Management Software, Printers, Xerox machine, Computers and other hardware.

e. Library users or member should be trained for proper and optimum use of ICT resources.

11. Lack of language command

Very interesting and funny, but real thing in some Asian developing countries like India, is the lack of good command of English language.

They do not follow the literature or information published on Internet in English language. This results into depriving them from learning of ICT knowledge, use of information resources and sharing these among other library and information professionals at national and international level.

12. Lack of speed of communication network

ISPs (Internet Service Provider) are chosen for offering high speed transmission technologies. Most of ISPs offer ISDN and 56 K Modem services. The new modem technology facilitates 56kbp speeds over standard analog phone lines. Earlier it was necessary to have at least one phone line for every Internet connectivity. Now ISDN facilitates and provides multiple connectivity through the same phone line. Sometimes it come to notice, due to slowness of Internet or computer, it is not easy to retrieve the required information soon. Bandwidth explores the speed of communication network. Good bandwidth is the backbone of good ISP. Most ISP maintains bandwidth on the basis of available subscribers and charges. So before taking the connectivity, library or parent body should have the agreement to make available the required bandwidth.

Similarly, we should also think about the reason of slowness of computer, which results into the barrier to provide the information. The main causes to make the computers slow are viruses, hardware problems, less than 10% space in hard drive, small page files, miscellaneous files during installing and uninstalling the application software, poor security software, fragmentation of hard drive and file system, corrupted or overloaded windows registry. We should seek the solutions to causes of slowness of computer , in such way by removing the useless and temporary files, space can be increased hard disc to limited extent; by installing latest anti-virus software to remove the viruses, using trusted hardware to remove hardware problems, pirated software should not be used because it corrupts the computer hardware and software, and other problems can also be solved by contacting ICT professionals or calling to AMC contractor. Library professional should also have keen interest to learn such things so as to find out the solution of the problem.

Need to think more about ICT

1. Why Information can not be retrieved via Single Library Network, like Indian Railway Network, LIC Network, Many Bank Network -SBI (State Bank of India) Network, ICICI network?
2. Why all libraries are not inter-connected to each other, in all repects, even libraries belong to same parent organization are not inter-connected to each other?
3. Why a reader runs from one library to another library for his information requirement.

Conclusion

Library professional should have a positive attitude towards use and implementation of ICT in libraries. The sufficient knowledge, learning process and training about ICT, promote and encourage Library Professionals' attitude in positive direction, since it is assumed that a qualified and trained library professional can make a better use of ICT and can provide services in effective way. Library professionals should also have their keen interest and moral responsibility to keep uptodate themselves with ICT developments so that they may give effective information services to users.

References

1. Ali Salman. (2010). ICT, The new media (Internet) and development. The Innovation Journal 15(1). p.1-5. site: http:// www.innovation.cc/ scholarly-style/salman_internet_ malaysian3final5.pdf (Accessed on 30/8/2011)
2. Augereau, Angelique and Greenstein, Shane (2001). The need for speed in emerging communications markets: upgrades to advanced technology at Internet service Providers. International Journal of Industrial Organisation. 19. 1085-1102.
3. Chauhan, Buddhi Prakash. ICT Enabled Library and Information Services.. In Winter School of ICT enabled Library and information Services Patiala, India. December 27-31, 2004, organized by INFLIBNET
4. Eguavoen, OEL (2011). Attitudes of Library staff towards the use of ICTs : the case of Kenneth Dike Library, University of Ibadan, Nigeria. Ozean journal of social sciences. 4(1). 347-350

5. Goldfinch, Shaun () The four sinthusiasms of ICT failure, problem of control and information system development in the public sector work in progress. Site http://www.pacis-net.org/file/2007/1340.pdf (Accessed on 30/8/2011)
6. Guideline for Sectorial ICT policy and Planning: a consultant document. Commonwealth Network of IT for development and Common wealth Secretariat. Ottawa. 67p. site http://www.ictdevlibrary.org/downloads/comnet-it_guidelines.pdf
7. Mabel K. Minishi-Majanja. Integration of ICTs in Library and Information Science Education in sub-Saharan Africa. Available at website http://archive.ifla.org/IV/ifla73/papers/083-Minishi-Majanja-en.pdf (Accessed on 3/9/2011)
8. Narayan, A, Sanjay Singh and Somasekharan, M. Implementing RFID in libraries. Available at website: http://library.igcar.gov.in/readit-2005/conpro/lgw/s5-8.pdf (Accessed on 3/9/2011)
9. Prasad, H N and Singh, Suchitra (2008). Blog applications in developing library and information services. International Caliber. 452-461
10. Prashar, R G (1991). Information and its communication (pp34-35). Delhi: Today and tomorrow.
11. Sembok, Tengku Mohd T. Ethics of Information and Communication Technology (ICT). Regional Meeting on Ethics of Science and Technology, Bangkok, held on 5-7th November, 2003. site http://www2.unescobkk.org/elib/publications/ethic_in_asia_pacific/239_325ETHICS.PDF (Accessed on 2/9/11)
12. Sharma, Parul, Singh, Mahesh and Kumar, Pankaj. Approach To ICT in Library Training, Education and Technology :Issues and Challenges. Available at website http://crl.du.ac.in/ical09/papers/index_files/ical-116_104_236_2_RV.pdf (Accessed on 1/9/2011)
13. Tusubira, FF, et al () ICT implementation Challenges and strategies for Enterprises in Africa.Site http://www.fftusubira.com/publications/ict_implementation_challenges.pdf (accessed on 4/9/2011)
14. Zhuang, Yue-Ting(2005). Digital libraries: a testbed for multimedia technology. Journal of Jhejiang University Science. 6A(11); 1201-1203

22

E-governance: Libraries and Rural Development in India

Dr. R.P. Bajpai
Associate Professor of Library & Inf. Science
MGCGV, Chitrakoot
E-mail: rpbajpai@gmail.com
Dr. M.P. Upadhyay
SPA
Ramanujan College
E-mail: upadhyay.mangala@yahoo.com
Dr. B.K.Mal
I/c Librarian
P.V.university
E-mail: bidyutmal@gmail.com
Mukta Tailang
Librarian
CIC,Chitrakoot
E-mail: omsainathmukta@gmail.com

Abstract

E-governance means utilizing the internet and practising World Wide Web for delivering government information and services to citizens. It has become a buzzword in post-liberalization India, with the belief that information technologies can be used to make government practices more accessible, transparent and responsive. The evolution and rapid expansion of Information and Communication Technologies (ICTs) has affected whole society. The use of ICTs like computers and internet have entered into various ways and in every aspect of our lives; from defence to education; environment to research business, health, banking, media, land record, civil administration and so on. In the fast changing scenario, e-governance has become not only necessary but essential in a set-up where people are the biggest stack holders. E-governance is the name given to I T driven public and development administrative system, which essentially means delivery of government services and information to people using electronic means.

Introduction

Information Technology has been a compelling force for the government to get online government services. The use of information and communication technology has become a powerful tool for good governance. E-governance refers to the ability of the government to provide access to services and information twenty- four hours and seven days of a week. E-governance, broadly, is the use of information and communication technologies (ICTs) in governance mechanisms. It is widely perceived as essential for efficient governance. But, beyond the obvious necessity for any society to absorb technological change and anecdotal reports of success in some projects, the actual impact of e-governance on citizens needs to be presented carefully to facilitate a systematic adoption. Subhas Bhatnagar[1], a member, on the National Advisory Group on E-governance, notes that a 2003 survey suggested that only 15 percent of e-governance projects the world over were successful and that, in India, in spite of massive spending, hardly five percent of government agencies provide e-governance services, and the failed projects are rarely documented thoroughly. Bhatnagar emphases that e-government cannot be a panacea for social ills like poverty and corruption, but he places enormous faith in its ability to act as a catalyst and as one of the drivers of development. Although most e-government schemes have an urban focus, he asserts the political and social commitment to rural development can be accommodated in them.

1. Definition of E-Governance

E-governance is an emerging trend to re-invent the way the government work and a new model of governance would be based upon the transactions in virtual space, digital economy and dealing with knowledge oriented societies. [2]

In simple words, it is the application of ICTs to governmental functioning to accomplish simple, accountable, speedy, responsive and transparent administration in government. [3] But, E-governance does not mean mere computerization of all government office operations or government web-sites on the internet. With the new tools, a networked society's government must completely rethink and re-engineer itself. It is complete transformation of the existing style. Although conventionally the prefix 'e' suggests that an activity is electronic but 'e' also denotes efficiency, effectiveness, and empowerment, economic and social development and enhanced services. [4]

2. Development of Good Governance

Good Governance and its basic determinants have been defined by various scholars, international agencies and reports. In 1989, the World Bank in its documents on sub-Saharan Africa mentioned four key dimensions of good governance: (i) public sector management, (ii) accountability, (iii) legal framework for development and (iv)information and transparency. Further, the World Bank in its document, Governance and development (1992) defined governance as "the manner in which power is exercised in the management of a country's economic and social resources for development." [5] The views of some important bodies on governance are:

a. Organisation for Economic Cooperation and Development (OECD)

The concept of governance as per OECD, denotes the use of political authority and exercise of control in a society in relation to the management of its resources for social and economic development.

b. Commission on Global Governance

The Commission, in 1995, considered governance as the totality of management of affairs by individuals and the public and private institution affecting them. It is a continuing process though conflicting or diverse interest may be accommodated and cooperative action may be taken. This is made possible through formal institutions and informal arrangements of the people and their institutions. [6]

c. United Nation Development Programme (UNDP)

Governance, according to UNDP, is viewed as the exercise of economic, political and administrative authority to manage a country's affairs at all levels. It comprises mechanisms, processes and institutions, through which citizens and groups can articulate their interests, exercise their legal rights, meet their obligations, and mediate their differences (United Nations Development Programme, 1997). [7]

d. United Nations Educational, Scientific and Cultural Organisation (UNESCO)

UNESCO laid emphasis on making citizen contribute to the positive social and economic development of society. It defines governance as, a political process that encompasses the whole society and contributes to the making of citizens and active continuously to the social contract that binds them together. Their sense of political efficacy is one of the indictors of democratic government. The UNESCO working document on Higher Education in the 21st Century: Vision and Action, observed the advent of the communication society that has many consequences for the world of work: decision- making is increasingly becoming remote from the areas of production.. IT makes different types of remote consultation (stock exchange, business, health indicators, list of potential customers, list of sub-contractors, price indexes, etc.) possible. Money no larger circulates in paper, but in virtual form; book keeping is becoming increasingly delocalized; areas of production, distribution and research are becoming increasingly separate geographically but increasingly linked by new technology. IT has enabled more and more individuals to have simultaneous access to information, thus, shrinking the world into a global village. IT is also a vehicle for the internationalization of culture and a tool for defending cultural identity; a major challenge to which higher education cannot remain indifferent. [8]

e. Report on Human Development in South Asia

This report, more than any other, focuses on human governance. It defines human governance as good governance dedicated to secure human development. It requires effective participation of people in state, civil society, and private sector activities that are conclusive to human development. Human governance must lead to broad based economic growth and social development which in turn would bring about greater human development. Governance must be seen by the people as operating in their interests only—transparent and accountable to all its constituents, and conclusive to building a society in which all believe they are treated fairly and decently. [9]

In its simple dictionary meaning, good governance refers to the well-being of people. The Oxford Dictionary defines governance as the act or manner of governing, or the way of control. Today, good governance has entered that development lexicon, where the focus has shifted from 'maximizing the quality of development founding to maximizing of development outcomes and effectives of public services delivery.' (Mid term appraisal of 9th Five Year Plan.).

3. Dimensions of E-governance

This multinational activity includes e-society, e-democracy, e-republic, e-business e-administration, etc. It encompasses a wide range of activities, and integrates people and information technology for meeting governmental goals.

4. E-Governance Model

The present model of e-governance does not aim to reduce the role of government in the life of citizens but to serve them more timely and efficiently. Now it is the government, which tries to adopt itself to the life of a citizen particularly the under privileged as against the traditional model, which is just the opposite of it. The emphasis is to make the user in charge of affairs and in command of situation. The government's role is to be limited as facilitator only. [10]

5. Right to Information

According to Cheria A. [11] poverty and inequality are maintained by the political, economical, social, patriarchal and religious systems. Unless all are addressed condignly, poverty can not be eradiated. Stratification and inequality being legitimized as a key of religion, democracy can only be created from the secular space. In carrying out rights to restoration and inclusion activities there can not be various strategies such as capacity and perspective building through training, workshop and seminars, organizing and mobilizing people and federations, networking on common issue, lobbying and advocacy for pro-poor policy changes, documentation and dissemination of information communication and fund raising. Obviously Govt. needs to develop a positive programme to ensure the value of information and facilitate use of such information by the public to renew, modify and change the lifestyle. Pathak [12] describes, the informed citizens are better equipped to take advantage of opportunities, access services, exercise their rights, negotiate effectively and hold state and non-state accountable. Right to Information (RTI) should be made a fundamental right as soon as possible, so that provision of information is not considered a favour but a right of the public.

6. Objectives of E-governance

The objectives of e-governance are to enhance efficiency, provide total transparency, high responsiveness, accountability, convenience and accessibility of services and information from the point of view of citizens. From governments perspective it is to abolish corruption, cut in costs, an antidote to 'Parkinson's law' i.e. "works expands to fulfill available" [13]. Instant quick reactions in time of crisis, easy access to data bases for officials as well as keeping an eye on subordinates and availability of services to public any time, anywhere.

In fact the purpose of e-governance is to develop "an IT driven system of governance that works better, costs less and is capable of serving the citizens as never before" [14]. It is to promote good governance and democracy by ensuring participation of and feedback from the public and making the administration SMART (simple, moral, accountable, responsive and transparent).

7. Elements in E-governance

There are four elements of e-governance—information, technology, process and people. All technology, process and people of information system are critical to e-governance. If any of the four components of the system is found to be missing, e-governance cannot work.

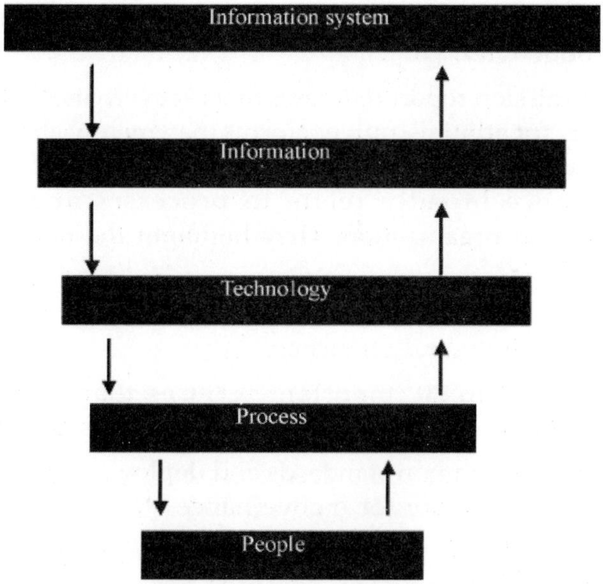

8. NKC's Recommendations on E-governance for better service delivery, etc.

Knowledge services have the potential to simplify many differences at which citizens interact with the State. Traditionally, these points of interaction have been vulnerable to unscrupulous activities and rent-seeking. Technology provides us with an opportunity to ensure accountability, transparency and efficiency in government services. E-governance is one of the ways in which citizens can be empowered to increase transparency of government functioning, leading to greater efficiency and productivity. [15]

E-governance has the potential to ensure speedy delivery, productivity and efficiency of services, making them citizens- centric and ensuring that the right of people is served.

The benefits of E-governance include:

- Reducing the cost and improving the reach and quality of public services;
- Reducing transaction costs and transaction time;
- Empowering citizens and increasing transparency of government function;

- Re-engineering of process for greater efficiency and productivity. [16]

The Commission report reiterates that e-governance is more about an opportunity for administrative reforms than merely about electronic and information technology and infrastructure. The recommendation on e-governance broadly relate to processes and standards, infrastructure and organization. They highlight the new to:

- Re-engineer government processes for first, to change our basic governance pattern for simplicity, transparency, productivity and efficiency.
- Select 10 to 20 important services that make a critical difference, simply they offer them as web-based services.
- Develop common standards and deploy a common platform or infrastructure for e-governance.
- Begin all new national programmes (like Bharat Nirman, Rural Employment Guarantee Scheme, etc.) with well-engineered E-governance implementation and web interface. [17]

9. Role of E-governance

Network technology has made virtual reality possible, wherein a person can work and stop sitting at home. Moreover, in all information processing systems, communication and interaction are facilitated. The application of ICT has been found to be highly useful in governance, which is known as e-governance, or electronic governance. e-governance plays an important role.

1. Increases efficiency by automation, computerization and networking.
2. Supports effective decentralization decision-making by providing an efficient information flow.
3. Increase accountability of the public services to agencies to citizens.
4. Improves resource management.
5. Offers the various departments and agencies involved in public service provision the facility of effective

communication between each other and effective interface with the citizens.

6. Increases the accessibility of individual citizens to information and services and allows them to influence government operations.
7. Provides comprehensive database which helps policy makers to design, formulate and evaluate policies.
8. Facilitates the strategic planning process which helps the organization to clearly lay down the objectives, goals, programmes and projects.
9. Enables reduction of paperwork with the use of e-mail and electronic data interchange
10. Enables marketization by supplying information on related to the market and enhances public service.

10. Libraries and E-governance

Public libraries are called public universities as they play a vital role in informing and educating the public during and after their formal education. By doing so they guard against the tyranny of ignorance, the Achilles heel of democracy. [18] Libraries in a free society always perform the fundamental function of keeping the public well informed which is a pre-condition of e-governance. For quite a long time governments have used libraries to inform people of their work and policies. Libraries are essential to the free flow of ideas and for maintaining, increasing and spreading knowledge. As repositories of books and other printed materials they are key to promote reading and writing.

Libraries can play an important role in the promotion of e-governance.

1. Already established libraries, especially public libraries, can be used as information centers or public kiosks in the absence of basic infrastructure. Internet connections and other equipment can be provided to them on subsidy basis and the public should be allowed to use them by becoming members of these libraries as is done in several advanced countries like U.S.A., Canada, etc. [19]

2. These libraries can work as depositary libraries for all types of government information from where the public can access and monitor the work of its elected officials and policy makers. [20]
3. Libraries can also help to bridge divide in the digital contents by providing special services to the general public. [21]
4. Libraries ensure freedom to speech, the freedom to read, and freedom to view. When the people are better informed, they are more likely to participate in the political process, thus keeping an eye on their elected representatives and making them more accountable.
5. Local and state governments need access to information from comparable jurisdiction in order to do their duty effectively and efficiently. [22]
6. In the field of information literacy, library professionals can play a pivotal role. Besides acting as facilitators and tutors, they can also act as inspirators and help along with teaching community to spread the culture of information literacy. [23]
7. In the worlds of James Madison "Knowledge will forever govern ignorance and that people who mean to be their own governors must arm themselves with the power that knowledge gives. A popular government without popular information or means of accruing it is a prologue to a farce or tragedy perhaps both." [24.]
8. The main thrust in this area should go to the rural public library. A village or a village cluster with an adequate population should have a community library which will also serve as an information centre. Resources of different agencies engaged in the work of public health, adult education, self-government and such others may be pooled to build up this composite centre. [25]
9. The Seventh Plan Working Report of the Planning Commission states that "No community, institution or organization is considered complete without a good library services. The gradual spread of the concept of democracy of socialist pattern of society, the extension of education,

the intensification of research activities, the rapid increase in the production of recorded knowledge both in print and non-print forms, and vast innovations in information and communication technology have led to the expansion of libraries, information centers and systems as well as development of their services."

10. According to the Library Association, Britain, "Community Information Services assist individuals and groups with daily problem solving and with participation in the democratic process. The services concentrate on the needs of those who do not have ready access to other sources of assistance and on the most important problems that people have to face, problems to do with their hoes, their jobs and their rights." [26]

The scheme for the Improvement of Library Service came in to force in 1952. In 1952, the Government of India initiated the Community Development Programme in which social education was assigned an important role. Gradually, the pattern of the social education programme took a clear shape and libraries, including circulating libraries, occupied an integral place in this programme. The community development programme thus gave a fillip to rural libraries.

11. Rural Development Services via the E-governance

Services provided at the villager's doorstep via the e-governance route can presumably cut out the inherent social biases. A computer generating the printout of a land record for a peasant cannot possibly deny service on account of social prejudices or in expectation of a brick. Schemes successful in some states in India have failed in others and he attributes the failure to a host of factors such as the absence of standards and infrastructure, the lack of local language interfaces, the resistance of civil servants to change, the absence of a political will to reform, and the institutional incapacity to absorb change. But beyond such factors, people with a shared background are still needed to operationalise e-government systems designed to replace inefficient manual systems, and there might be no social imperative for the technological change, both causes ultimately resulting in similar effects. Villagers are not enamored of electronic delivery. [27]

India really is a land of contrast. We still have a huge section of the society living in the dire poverty, utter ignorance, and illiteracy. The important task for e-governance is to remain in touch with the concerned authorities in village, Talukas, Districts and even in the Metropolis.

ICT has touched all facets of the life of a common man. Richard Heeks and David Mundy [28] have defined IT as computing and telecommunications technologies that provide automatic means of handling information.

Richard Heeks [29] points out that governance is both, the present and the future of developing countries like India, which still have a long way to go. Currently, more than half of India's villages lack telephone connectivity, let alone internet access. The 26 million phone lines (mostly business-owned) and 2 million internet subscriber that do exist nationwide are concentrated in urban areas, while rural areas are left out of the loop.

ICT has made services amenable to people living in cities and villages. The gyandoot programme in Madhya Pradesh, the e-Seva network in Andhra Pradesh, FRIENDS (Fast, Reliable, Instant, Efficient, Network for Disbursement of Service) in Kerala, the Saukaryam project in Vishakapatnam, the Gramsat project in Orrisa, e-Gram Suvidha in five districts Chhattarpur, Bhopal, Dhar, Mandla and Damoh of Madhya Pradesh, Lokvani Sitapur, Uttar Pradesh, Lok Mitra in Himachal Pradesh are efforts to foster connectivity, accessibility to services and information to people.

Painter and Goodwin [30], who urge that while a regulations approach would lead to the conclusion that: the local state and local governance cannot be fully understood outside their roles (positive and negative) in the ebb and flow of regulation.... neither can they be fully understood within them. The institutions and practices of local government have their own histories and pattern of development. Explaining their changing character thus requires a theory of governance, a theory of the State and empirical... research, as well as a theory of their impact on (economic regulation).

12. Conclusion

E-governance is a step towards reform in government and administration. These reforms focus on bringing improvements in the service delivery, dissemination of information, transparency, public and private partnership, efficiency and accountability. There is an urgent need for sustainable development. In developing countries like India, it is not easy to fulfill all the pre-conditions. But it does not mean we should not go ahead with e-governance. For the successful working of democracy, the empowerment of its citizen is a pre-condition, which can only be achieved by making the people fully informed and aware. E-governance is also seen as a multi-dimensional concept, an IT driven methodology that improves efficiency in administration, brings about transparency and leads to the reduction of costs in running the government. There are three main domains of e-governance: improving governmental processes (e-administration); connecting citizens (e-citizens and e-services); and building external interaction (e-society).

References

1. The Hindu, Tuesday, July 28, 2009. p.13.
2. Vijayaditya, N. facing the citizen: turning G to G by 180: Seventh Annual lecture on e-governance in the information age. Delnet News Letter, 11 (1&2), Dec. 2004, p. 15.
3. Raghvan, Vijaya G Nair, VSM. E-Governance: leveraging IT for reinventing the government. Manorama Year Book 2004. New Delhi: Malayale Manorma, p.130.
4. Pardhasarahi, Y. information technology for governance and efficiency. Indian Journal of Public Administration, 50(1), Jan. mar.2004, pp.272-273.
5. World Bank. Governance and Development, World Bank Ranganathan, Shyam. Assessing the impact of e-governance Publications, Washington, D.C., 1992
6. Commision on Global Governance. Our Global neighborhood, Oxford University Press, New york, 1995.
7. UNDP. A UNDP Policy Paper: Strategy on Governance, (draft paper), New york, 1997.
8. UNESCO, Working Document on Higher Education in the Twenty First Century-Vision and Action, Paris, 5-9, Oct. 1998.
9. Human Development Report in South Asia. The crisis of governance, human development center, Dup, 1999, Karachi, Pakistan.

10. Vijayaditya, N op. cit. p.15.
11. Cheria, A. A human rights approach to Development: a resource book. Banglore: book for change, 2004.
12. Pathak, R. Empowerment and social governance. Delhi: Isha books, 2003.
13. Vittal, N. and Mahalingam, S. information technology: tomorrow. New Delhi: Manas Publishing, 2001, p.306.
14. Kumar, Rupali and Kumar, Ajit. "E-governance and society." In. India's kaul, A.K. and Body, M.D. (Ed.) Library and Information Networking (NACLIN) 2002. New Delhi: Delnet, 2003, p.291.
15. Government of India. National Knowledge Commission. January, 2007, p.24.
16. Ibid. p.24.
17. Ibid. p.24.
18. Kranich, Nancy, C. Libraries, the internet and democrary. In. Libraries and Democrarcy/edited by Nancy C. Kranich. Chicago: American Library Association, 2001, p.38.
19. Ibid. p.91
20. Heanue, Anne. In support of democracy. In Kranich, Nancy C. Op. cit., p.122.
21. Kranich, Nancy C. Op. cit., p.159.
22. Heanue, Anne. Op. cit., p.125.
23. Jagtar Singh. Information democracy and South Asia: Promises and perils of the web. Ludhiana: Medallion Press, 2003, p. 105,159.
24. Madison, James. Writings. New York: Library of America, p.790. Cited in Kranich, Nancy C. op. cit., pp. 121-122. 1999.
25. India. Committee on National Policy on Library and Information System. A Presentation. 1986. Government of India. p. 30.
26. Library Association. Community Information: What Libraries can do. 1980. London Library Association.
27. Ranganathan, Shyam. Op. cit., p.13.
28. Heeks, R. and David, Mundy. Information Systems and public sector reform in the third world. (Ed.). Willy Mac court and Martin Minouge, Edward Elgar, U.K. 2000.
29. Heeks, Richard. Understanding e- governance for development, government working paper series. Working Paper No.11, Institute for

Development Policy and management, 2001, and University of Manchester.

30. Painter, J and Goodwin, M. Local governance and concrete research: investigating the uneven development of regulation, Economic and society. 1995, 24:334-336.

23

Webometrics: Tools and Techniques

Bhaskar Mukherjee
Assistant Professor
Department of Library & Information Science
Banaras Hindu University
Email: mukherjee.bhaskaar@gmail.com

Introduction

Although the application of various statistical techniques in library services and operation was first introduced by Dr. S.R. Ranganathan in 1948, the application became more prevalent after the inception of concept 'bibliometrics' by Allan Prichard in 1969. Subsequently, Vassily V. Nalimov of Russia had coined the term 'Scientometrics' and Jean Tague introduced the concept 'Informetrics'. With the advent of Internet and to perform Web statistics the term "Webometrics' came into existence. The term was born in 1997 (Almind and Ingwersen 1997) and was driven rapidly forward by a number of pioneering researchers and investigations (Rousseau 1997; Smith 1999) Webometrics is such a concept which deals with Web based phenomena, emergence from the realization that methods originally designed for bibliometric analysis of scientific journal article citation pattern. According to Bjornebron and Ingwersen, Webometrics is "the study of the quantitative aspects of the construction and use of information resources, structure and technologies on the WWW, drawing on bibliometrics and informetric approaches" and a later proposed definition is "the study of Web-based content with primarily quantitative methods for social science research goals using techniques that are not specific to one field of study" (Thelwall, 2009). The main four areas of webometric research are: (a) Web page content analysis (by evaluating e-contents), (b) Web link structure analysis (by evaluating linking pattern available in the journal pages and article pages), (c) Web usage analysis (by exploiting log file of users' searching and browsing behaviour) and (d) Web technology analysis (including search engine performance) (Thelwall, 2005).

(A) Web Page Content Analysis

In order to evaluate web page contents of any website it is better to judge the contents of the website by some evaluation techniques. Traditional evaluation techniques applied to reference source evaluation can also be implied for web site with bit modifications. Various criteria like Availability, Authority and Review Policy, Scope and Coverage, Exhaustiveness of Articles, Page Format, Availability of Hyperlinks, Currency, Search facility, etc. can be implied to evaluate web page contents. Some of the common questions through which evaluation can be performed under various criteria are:

Availability

- Whether the web site has independent domain name? If yes, nature of Top-Level-Domain (TLD) and if no, position of the web site's name in respective domain?

Authority and Review Policy

- Nature of Sponsoring/ Technical Supporting body of web site
- Nature of Publishing body
- Authority of that body

Scope and Coverage

- Scope and coverage of the contents, its genuinity, recency, exhaustiveness etc.
- What Updating Policy website follows? Why the all page contents date of modifications?
- How many times the journal was updated during last 2 years? (can be measured by WayBack Machine of Internt Archive)

Page Format

- In which format the web page appears? PHP, HTML, XML or simply TXT (because each format has some limitations)
- In which format most of graphic file appears?
- How much time it takes to load?
- Whether Hyperlinks from one page to another is there?
- Whether there is any link towards any outside of the web site?

Search facility

- Is there any dedicated window for searching database?
- Whether Search Tips provided
- Nature of searching- Basic or Advanced Search
- Whether Boolean (AND,OR,NOT) facility allowed ? if so dDefault Boolean Operator
- Whether the site have specially designed or powered by some other search engines crawler?

Is there any RSS Feed available?

Other issues

- Page ranked (by Google Page rank)
- Whether the Home Page contains advertisement?
- Is there any product marketing?
- Is the site easy to navigate and use?
- Appearance of Home page – Attractive, Moderate, Low

(B) Weblink Structure Analysis

Webslink structure analysis can be categorized into three sub-themes:

(i) Link Analysis

Before discussing the concept of link analysis let us first understand the basic terms associated with the content. A *hyperlink*, or simply a link, is a reference in a hypertext document to another document or other resource. As such it is similar to a citation in literature. Combined with a data network and suitable access protocol, a computer can be instructed to fetch the resource referenced (Wikipedia). A link may be inlink, outlink or selflink. An inlink means a directed link that starts from a page and directed towards some other Web resources, it is analogous with the term reference in bibliometrics. On the other hand, an outlink is a link that comes to a Web page from another Web page, it is analogous with the term cited. Selflink is a link that traverse between the same Web page from which it originates, it is analogous with the term self-citation.

Web consists of number of pages interconnected with hyperlinks. These hyperlinks are inserted not for navigational purposes, but to point to pages with similar and relevant contents. These hyperlinks are generally termed as 'outlink' of the page. Total number of such pages can be measured by using some inbuilt command [site:page address] of search engines. Using this command along with some advanced command one can extract the total page, file format, etc. of the whole site. They add structure to the collection and it is important to explore the ways these links are employed for characterization of the Web. These interconnected structures probably help the search engines rank the pages.

(ii) Web/URL Analysis

Web/URL analysis is different from link analysis because, by this analysis it is possible to know how many pages are inlinked towards the particular Web page. These links are termed as 'inlink' to a page. At present, most of the search engines [e.g. Altavista, Google, All the Web, etc.] provide some in-built command [link:page address] to extract inlink towards a particular Web page but not the whole Web site. Some of the search engines [Microsoft based MSN], however, claim that they have a different string command to excavate total inlinked page of whole Web site [linkdomain:web address]. But it is always recommended to use these results with caution because no search engines is able to fetch all pages of the Web and most of the search engines display duplicate results to attract users towards their coverage. Below mentioned are two well popular search engines where one can imply the commons mention in colum 2 to know information on column 1.

Commercial Search Engines	Commands
Google	
To measure the links that are directed toward the home page of the web site	Link : w w w . host (also interlinking)
To measure the total number of pages that are originating from the host	Site:www.host
To understand the ranking of the page	Page Rank (Google)
MSN	
Total inlinks towards this domain	linkdomain:www.host
Linking towards this site originating from different domain	linkdomain:www.domain –site:www.domain
Links originating from this site	site:www.domain

Similarly Yahoo developed a specially designed exclusive website, Yahoo site explorer for such jobs. Yahoo! Site Explorer is a tool that allow to:

- Find which sites and subpages are indexed.
- Find inlinks or pages that link to any site or any page.
- Submit and track feeds for any sites.

One can get even more detailed information and greater ability to manage a site or its URLs when he/she authenticate the site. One can:

- Monitor the status of one's submitted feeds.
- Delete URLs from the search index.
- Specify content-neutral Dynamic Parameters for the site.
- See the number of Views and Clicks on the Yahoo! Search results for the Top 10 search queries for that site.
- View the "Last Crawled Time" and any problems it reported while crawling the site.

(iii) Web Citation Analysis

Previously, Web link analysis was assumed as successor of citation analysis. But later it was observed that a Web page can be linked (inlinks) from different Web sites or different Web contents. Inlinks may come from journal articles, conference papers, research reports, etc., as also from author's personal Web sites, Web CVs, or simply from a Web page. In terms of citation analysis it is not fair to consider all such inlinks for scholarly impact measurement. So, there is a need to compare inlinks for formal reasons from inlinks for informal reasons. Google and Yahoo are two widely used tools for measuring Web links. However, the newly emerged Google Scholar mostly extracts Web citations from scholarly sources than less-scholarly sources. As mentioned on the Web site of Google "Google Scholar has boosted the worldwide visibility and accessibility of [the] content. [They] work with publishers of scholarly information to index peer-reviewed papers, theses, preprints, abstracts, and technical reports from all disciplines of research and make them searchable on Google and Google Scholar". In addition, Google scholar's "Cited by", "Group of" or "Related sites" are widely used presently for statistical analysis of the Web results.

(C) Web Usage Analysis

Web usage analysis is a new type of statistical analysis to closely track the behavior of web site visitors. These days web usage analysis has been considered as one of the most promising facets to know the characteristics of web users, amount of site visibility, etc. to increase the reputation of the organization. Many companies invest a lot of money in market research. The outcomes of market research contribute to the development and the optimization of products and services. Web sites are important channels for the communication towards customers and prospects. A web site server logs each and every mouse-click. The data reflect visitors' behavior on the site on a microscopic level. The term 'clickstream' denotes the path a visitor takes through a web site. This pathway reflects a series of choices made within a web site. Although expensive market researches are conducted, the free click-stream data of visitor's behavior on the web site are still rarely analyzed.

There are two main technological approaches to collecting the data. The first method, logfile analysis, reads the logfiles in which the web server records all its transactions. The *Webalizer* is a log file analysis program which produces highly detailed, easily configurable usage reports in HTML format, for viewing with a standard web browser The second method, page tagging, uses JavaScript on each page to notify a third-party server when a page is rendered by a web browser. Initially, web site statistics consisted primarily of counting the number of client requests (or hits) made to the web server. These were page views and visits (or sessions). A page view was defined as a request made to the web server for a page, as opposed to a graphic, while a visit was defined as a sequence of requests from a uniquely identified client that expired after a certain amount of inactivity, usually 30 minutes. The page views and visits are still commonly displayed metrics, but are now considered rather rudimentary due to various technical problems like web proxies and dynamically assigned IP addresses for large companies and ISPs, the extensive use of web caches, etc. Log analyzers responded by tracking visits by cookies, and by ignoring requests from known spiders. The other way, i.e. Page tagging concerns about the accuracy of logfile analysis in the presence of caching, and the desire to be able to perform web analytics as an outsourced service, led to the second data collection method, page tagging or 'Web bugs'. In the mid 1990s, web counters were commonly seen, however, in the late 1990s this concept evolved to include a small invisible image instead of a visible one, and, by using JavaScript, to pass along with the image request certain information about the page and the visitor. This information can then be processed remotely by a web analytics company, and extensive statistics generated.

With the increasing popularity of Ajax-based solutions, an alternative to the use of an invisible image, is to implement a call back to the server from the rendered page. In this case, when the page is rendered on the web browser, a piece of Ajax code would call back to the server and pass information about the client that can then be aggregated by a web analytics company. This is in some ways flawed by browser restrictions on the servers which can be contacted with XmlHttpRequest objects. Also, this method can lead to slightly lower reported traffic levels, since the visitor may stop the page from loading in mid-response before the Ajax call is made.

In order to measure web usage present day a number of web analytic tools are available on web. Web analytics tools help to track the site's statistics- how many people are looking at each page, what sites they came from, and other information to develop a picture of the audience. Before discussing some of the important web analyzer let us understand some of the terms associated with the analysis:

- **Hits:** This metric measures the total number of requests for text, images, and files your web server receives for a given page. In fact, hits are virtually meaningless when it comes to actually understanding what users are doing on your site. Because the number of hits a site receives depends on how it is organized rather than how visitors interact with it, this metric is useful only in evaluating such information as server load.
- **Visits:** The most common unit of measurement in site analytics is the number of visitors to a particular site or page. The trend in the overall number of visits to your site over time can give you insight into your site's popularity. Comparing the number of visits to each page is also a good way to identify which parts of your site are most useful to visitors.
- **Unique Visitors:** This is the number of site visits by different users. If two people visit the site three times each, you have six visits by two unique visitors. Comparing visits to unique visitors can help you understand whether users are returning to your site over and over, or whether you are attracting a large number of users who only visit once or twice.
- **Page Views:** This is the number of times any page was viewed by any visitor, and is often divided by visits to give a page-views-per-visit figure that represents the average number of pages each visitor viewed on a single trip to your site. Increased page views can indicate a more interesting site, or simply one that requires people to jump through hoops to find what they need.

While looking for who the visitors to your site are, and what they are doing when they visit - metrics to help understand these factors include:

- **Bounce rate:** Bounce rate is the percentage of single-page visits or visits in which the person left your site from the entrance (landing) page. Use this metric to measure visit quality -for example, a high bounce rate might indicate that site entrance pages are either not relevant or compelling enough to your visitors. On the other hand, if you have a blog or article-based site, it may make sense for visitors to come, view one article, and leave.

- **Top Entry and Exit Pages:** This refers to the pages on which most visitors enter your site--- do not assume it is the home page – and leave it. These pages can be good places to begin when you are optimizing your site. All web analytics tools contain the Top Exit Pages report. In terms of mechanics the web analytics tool take the last page viewed in each visitor session and the report simply shows that pages that appear most frequently (by a raw count) as the last one in visitor sessions.
- **Visitor Information:** Through analytics tools one can study that how many are new to the site, the country or region where they are located, the web browser they are using, and much more.
- **Click Paths:** Also called click tracks, or click trees, these are graphical representations of typical journeys through your site. Click path is the sequence of hyperlinks one or more website visitors follow on a given site. A visitor's click path may start within the website or at a 3rd party website and it continues as a sequence of successive webpages visited by the visitor. For instance, a click-path chart might show you that 20 percent of your home page visitors go on to click the Resources link, while 15 percent visit the About Us page -- and that 60 percent then leave the site and 10 percent go on to the Board page.
- **Conversion:** Conversion analytics is the study of how users convert online. This is a complex-but-valuable statistic that typically needs to be customized in a tool or calculated by hand. Conversion tracks the number of people who did what you wanted them to from a given starting point - for example, the number of users who went from a Donate link on your home page all the way through the donation process, or the percentage of people who viewed your home page and then signed up for your newsletter.

- **Tracking Registered Users:** When a registered user accesses your site, that user needs to identify himself or herself to the Personalization module to ensure that the correct profile is associated with him or her. Typically, this is done by requiring the user to log in. Requiring a log in helps maintain the security of your site. When a user provides such data to log in, a web analytics tool can track exactly what they did during each visit to the site. (Without a log in, it is not practical to link up data for a particular person from one visit to another.) This can allow for more detailed analysis and understanding of what different types of visitors are doing on your site.
- **Site Search:** Some packages allow you to see what people search your site for. This can help you understand what visitors are looking for, and what trouble they are having in finding.

Lastly, it can be beneficial to track where visitors to your site are coming from. This can help you to find similar sites or better understand of the types of things that lead people to you. Metrics include:

- **Referrers:** These are the external links people follow to get to your site. For example, if TechSoup links to Idealware's site, TechSoup would show up as a referrer in Idealware's web stats. This metric can be very useful in tracking a big influx to your site or just in staying on top of who's talking about you.
- **Search Keywords:** Many packages can show the words or phrases people typed into search engines like Google or Yahoo! that led them to your site.

Now let us talk about some of the free web analytics available on web through which one can judge their website.

(i) Alexa: Alexa, developed and maintained by Amazon.com is one of the useful resources for people who want to discover information about websites. You can use Alexa to learn how popular a site is, to find new sites, to learn who owns a site, etc. In order to know or to compare the popularity of any website one has just to put the URL of the site on Alexa. It will then show the basic information on site, Alexa traffic rank, rank of the site on corresponding country and prepare some graphs of the site about its audiences, daily reach, pageview, pageviewer/user, users spent time on that site, etc. Additionally, it also shows the information about where visitors mostly go while looking for that site and for what queries they usually visit that site.

(ii) Google Ad Planner: DoubleClick Ad Planner by Google is a free media planning tool that can be used to identify the audiences who are likely to visit so that one can make better-informed advertising decisions. It defines audiences by demographics and interests, searches for websites relevant to the audience, accesses aggregated statistics on the number of unique visitors, page views, and other data for millions of websites from over 40 countries, creates lists of websites where one may like to advertise and stores them in a media plan, and generates aggregated website statistics for your media plan. It is, however, unable to produce statistics for those sites having less number of traffic volume and robots.text prevents to crawl the site.

(iii) SmartViper: This is another free web tool to track as to how your site is doing, what is working and what is not. It helps to improve the site and attract more visitors. By using this analytics one can study the : Percentage of content changed, Changes to the site's home page, Home page links analysis, Overall site backward links analysis, Site geographical targeting and audience by countries, Possible web duplicates, Related web sites, Home page heatmap changes, Important keyword changes, CMS platform changes, Main page title history layout changes, Popular page changes, Aggregated news - RSS feed, Site contacts changes, Social media changes including what is the trend in social media related to the site at a time of check

(D) Web Technology Analysis

Working of Crawler in Webometrics Research

A web crawler is a computer program that is capable of retrieving pages in a methodical, automated manner or in an orderly fashion from various web sites, extracting links from those pages and following the new links. Sometimes crawler are also named as wanderer, spider, robot, bot, etc. Every crawler starts with a list of URLs to visit, called the seeds. As the crawler visits these URLs, it identifies all the hyperlinks in the page and adds them to the list of URLs to visit, called the crawl frontier. URLs from the frontier are recursively visited according to a set of policies. The crawling policy i.e. which page to visit, in which order and how often, is different in different crawlers. These differencing policies make any crawler differ from other in term of size, coverage and freshness. Revisiting Web pages are necessary for a crawler as web undergoes changes from time to time. After crawling, it forwards results to the indexer. The job of indexer is to extracts words from the pages forwarded to it by crawlers, and turns each document into a list of words. This list of words then inverted into 'inverted index' or 'inverted file', and facilitates the work of the query engines. Sometimes crawler may also decide to save other information about the document such as metadata describing its contents, URLs of page linking to this page.

Every commercial search engines uses a crawler to collect such links. In addition search engines also have another engine - called query engines. The query engine is responsible for receiving request and providing answers to the users. The query engines consult the inverted file and the database of additional information to match the query. The capability to handle various advanced techniques such as phrase search, Boolean expression, domain specific search, time specific search, etc.of various search engines allowing it to display more specified results. But before display, search engines ranks the list of results, with most relevant results (as their policy determine) displayed at the top of the list. Here various ranking algorithms, including classical one based on similarity between the documents and the query (a function of the frequency of the search terms in the document, and the rarity of the search terms in the database), the location of search terms ion the documents (terms in title or headers receive more weight) and algorithms that are applicable to hypertext system (e.g. link analysis, most frequency clicked web pages, most downloaded web pages etc.) Each search engine uses different secret techniques to compute the ranks. In addition to this some search engines provide refined search, suggested search terms, groups, similar pages, cache etc. which make them unique from the others.

In order to overcome this problem of incomprehensiveness of commercial search engines, specially developed crawler (Thelwall, 2001) has used to explore the link pattern. These crawlers are fed with university official home page and interactively downloaded all pages that it could find by extracting links from the anchore tags, client side image maps, meta-tags and HTTP server redirection instruction. Detailed methodology of the crawler and its unique feature has been discussed by Thelwall (2004). Although measurement of inlinks to these universities is not possible through this crawler but this crawler can be extensively used to measure interlinking between the sample, to understand the most prominent page of a given site as well as major page formats used in a web site. Below mention are some of the well known crawlers that re using in webmetric research these days.

SocSciBot: This a type of crawler developed by Statistical Cyberetrics Research Group for link analysis on a single web site or collection of sites, or for text search/analysis on a collection of sites. SocSciBot crawls one or more web sites and analyses them to produce standard statistics about the interlinking and network diagrams of the interlinking. It also runs limited analyses of the text in the web sites. This program runs on Windows only and crawl sites with up to 15,000 pages and has a speed restriction. SocSciBot may not work well on web sites with non-ASCII URLs (e.g., Chinese) and the text analysis does not work well with non-ASCII text. The latest version 4.1 of SolSciBot has launched on April 2011. The software available along with this crawler can process different types of analysis, like:

- Data cleansing to remove unwanted links.
- Extracting subsites (e.g. any sub-domain of whole domain)
- Counting links between sites using the ADMs (Alternative Document Models)
- Counting site inlinks using the ADMs
- Reporting the most frequent link targets
- Removing internal site links.
- Summarizing link targets by domain or top level domain.
- Calculating PageRank statistics
- Calculating topological components (eg. IN, OUT, CONNECTED)

- Finding the link diameter of collections of pages and longest shortest paths.
- Converting link structure files to Pajek and UCINET input files.

Heritrix

Heritrix is a open-source, extensible, web-scale, archival-quality web crawler launched by the Internet Archive's to collect and preserve the digital artifacts for the benefit of future researchers. It is designed to respect the robots.txt exclusion directives and META robots tags, and collect material at a measured, adaptive pace unlikely to disrupt normal website activity. The recent release 1.14.4 is a 'micro' release with various improvement of earlier edition. Heritrix 1.0.0 offers the following key features:

- Collects content via HTTP recursively from multiple websites in a single crawl run, spanning hundreds to thousands of independent websites, and millions to tens of millions of distinct resources, over a week or more of non-stop collection.
- Collects by site domains, exact host, or configurable URI patterns, starting from an operator-provided "seed" set of URIs
- Executes a primarily breadth-first, order-of-discovery policy for choosing URIs to process, with an option to prefer finishing sites in progress to beginning new sites ("site-first" scheduling).
- Highly extensible with all of the major Heritrix components – the scheduling Frontier, the Scope, the protocol-based Fetch processors, filtering rules, format-based Extract processors, content Write processors, and more – replaceable by alternate implementations or extensions. Documented APIs and HOW-TOs explain extension options.
- Highly configurable. Options include:
- Settable output locations for logs, archive files, reports and temporary files.
- Settable maximum bytes to download, maximum number of documents to download, and maximum time to spend crawling.

- Settable number of 'worker' crawling threads.
- Settable upper bound on bandwidth-usage.
- Politeness configuration that allows setting minimum/ maximum time between requests as well an option to base the lag between requests on a multiple of time elapsed fulfilling the most recent request.
- Configurable inclusion/exclusion filtering mechanism. Includes regular expression, URI path depth, and link hop count filters that can be combined variously and attached at key points along the processing chain to enable fine tuned inclusion/exclusion.

Nutch

Nutch is an open source web search engine based on Lucene Java for the search and index component. It is developed by Apache Software Foundation and is coded entirely in the Java programming language, but data is written in language-independent formats. It has a highly modular architecture, allowing developers to create plug-ins for media-type parsing, data retrieval, querying and clustering. It includes feature as:

- Fetching and parsing are done separately by default, this reduces the risk of an error corrupting the fetch parse stage of a crawl with Nutch.
- Plugins have been overhauled as a direct result of removal of legacy Lucene dependency for indexing and search.
- The number of plugins for processing various document types being shipped with Nutch has been refined. Plain text, XML, OpenDocument (OpenOffice.org), Microsoft Office (Word, Excel, Powerpoint), PDF, RTF, MP3 (ID3 tags) are all now parsed by the Tika plugin. The only parser plugins shipped with Nutch now are Feed (RSS/Atom), HTML, Ext, JavaScript, SWF, Tika & ZIP.
- MapReduce ;
- Distributed filesystem (via Hadoop)
- Link-graph database
- NTLM authentication

Link Checker

Link Checker is another web crawling software for errors and possible improvements of website, analyzing links, spell check, etc. of a web site. It runs on Windows 7 / Vista / XP / 2008 / 2003 / 2000. One can even have the link extractor of the crawler engine include Javascript code when it searches for and extracts links. Depending on configuration, redirect and link checking can include references to all file types, e.g. documents, images and videos. The basic feature that this crawler can perform includes:

- *Broken links*: Link analysis and validation ensures whether website has any broken links.
- *HTML errors*: HTML validator ensures whether pages are crawled and shown correctly.
- *CSS errors*: CSS validator ensures whether visual elements render correctly in browsers.
- *Response time*: It can ensure whether the webserver respond to multiple concurrent requests in proper time?
- *Download time*: It also check whether the webserver CPU or bandwidth is too slow at serving files?
- *File size*: It reports optimize bandwidth usage and download time caused by large pages and images.
- *PageRank sculpting*: Analyze how internal link juice flows to important pages one need to rank high.
- *Page titles*: Check if all page titles are optimized and none are duplicated.
- *META description*: Verify page META description and keywords are relevant with no duplicates.
- *Custom search*: Search and check all pages for custom text and code, e.g. Google Analytics.
- *Spell check*: Check websites for spelling errors using a variety of spell checker dictionaries.

JSpider

JSpider is a highly configurable and customizable Web Spider engine, developed under the LGPL Open Source license in 100% pure Java under Java Coding project (2003). This spider can be used to:

- Check your site for errors (internal server errors, ...)
- Outgoing and/or internal link checking
- Analyze your site structure (creating a sitemap, ...)
- Download complete web sites
- Any task you want, if you write a JSpider plugin.

Conclusion

The field of webometrics, a new research area that has grown out of bibliometrics, has established an important independent domain in quantitative research. In the last few years there has been wide applicability of webometric research for Web Impact Assessment, Link Analysis, Blog Searching, Tracking User Actions Online, etc. However, one of the major breakthrough is the application of search engines for measuring impact of web content. In order to measure the Impact factor, h-index, researchers are using Google Scholars, Yahoo Beta, etc. as a supplement tool for impact measurement.

References

1. Almind, T.C. & Ingwersen, P. (1997). Informetric analyses on the World Wide Web. Methodological approaches to 'webometrics'. Journal of Documentation, 53(4), 404-426.
2. Amazon.com (2011). Alexa – a tool for web analytics. Available at: www.alexa.com
3. Apache Nutch wiki. Available at: http://wiki.apache.org/nutch/
4. Internet Archive Web Team (2004). An Introduction to Heritrix: An open source archival quality web crawler. Available at: http://iwaw.europarchive.org/04/Mohr.pdf
5. Mukherjee, B. (2010). Scholarly Communication in LIS The Impact of Open Access Journals and E-journals on a Changing Scenario, Oxford: Chandos Publication, 2010. 200p.
6. Mukherjee, B. (2011). Analysing usability and accessibility of India's three popular commercial websites – Rediff, Indiatimes and Sify, *Annals of Library & Information Studies*, 58(3), 2011,.
7. Rousseau, R. (1997). Sitations: an exploratory study. Cybermetrics, 1(1), Retrieved July 25, 2006 from: http://www.cindoc.csic.es/cybermetrics/articles/v1i1p1.html (Archived by WebCite® at http://www.Webcitation.org/5stBoPIrC).

8. Smith, A. G. (1999). A tale of two Web spaces; comparing sites using Web Impact Factors. Journal of Documentation, 55(5), 577-592.
9. Statistical Cybermetrics Research Group (2011). SocSciBot. Available at. http://socscibot.wlv.ac.uk/
10. Thelwall, M. (2005). Webometrics. In: Drake, M. A. (Ed.) *Encyclopedia of Library and Information Science,* Second Edition, Marcel Dekker, Inc., New York.
11. Thelwall, M. (2009). Introduction to webometrics: Quantitative Web research for the social sciences. New York, NY: Morgan & Claypool.

24

Change Management: A Benchmark for Library and Information Centre

Dr. Hirak Kanti Chakraborty
Associate Professor & Head
Dept.of Library and Information Science
Sampurnanand Sanskrit University, Varanasi

Abstract

Change management is a structured approach to shifting/transitioning individuals, teams, and organizations from a current state to a desired future state. The present paper highlights the principle, advantages and disadvantages of change management. It also deals with framework and models of change management. There has been a paradigm shift in the ways libraries used to be managed earlier. This paper aims at visualizing a broad overview of the concept of change management and its relevancy or validity for managing the transit of traditional paper based library to digital library.

1. Introduction

Change is the only constant

– Heraclitus, Greek philosopher

Change is a common thread that runs through all businesses regardless of size, industry and age. Our world is changing fast and, so organizations must change quickly too. The concept of "change management" is a familiar one in most institutions today and it varies enormously depending on the nature, type and structure of the institution, the change and the people involved. It depends on how far people within it understand the change process. Institutions that handle change well thrive, whereas that do not may struggle to survive.

"**Change management** is a structured approach to shifting/ transitioning individuals, teams, and organizations from a current state to a desired future state. It is an organizational process aimed at empowering employees to accept and embrace changes in their current business environment."[1]

Change management has a wide scope, its not only about transforming from one level to another level. It also includes change management process, communication and communication planning, coaching and manager training for change management, training and employee training development, sponsor activities and sponsor roadmaps, resistance management, data collection, feedback analysis and corrective action. According to Prosci's research, most change management processes contain the following three phases[2]:

- **Phase 1 - Preparing for change** (Preparation, assessment and strategy development)
- **Phase 2 - Managing change** (Detailed planning and change management implementation)
- **Phase 3 - Reinforcing change** (Data gathering, corrective action and recognition)

2. Principles, Advantages And Disadvantages

Achieving change will be more successful if we follow the principles of change and browse through the advantages and disadvantages of change management which are as follows[3, 4]:-

Principles of Change

- Change is a process that can be enabled, not managed.
- The change process must be linked to performance goals.
- Building capacity to change is a strategic and evolutionary process.
- Systematic visualization of organization is essential for effective change processes.

- Effective change processes require a systemic view of the organization.
- The change process involves both organizational and personal transitions.
- Behavioral change is a function of perceived need and occurs at the emotional, not the intellectual level.
- Resistance to change is predictable reaction to an emotional process and depends on a person's perception of a change situation.
- A handful of change enables takes most change processes to success path.
- Change strategies are based on need and urgency.

Advantages

- Change allows organizations to better compete with their rivals and develop new skills or services that will bring glory to the organizations.
- Change management always helps each individual to realize the reason behind the change and gives impetus to move forward.
- Change always enhances innovation and skills.

Disadvantages

- If resistance from employees is not effectively dealt with through communication, it can derail any project.
- If clients are not informed about the change brought then, clients may choose to go to another organization.
- A poor change management plan can also negatively affect an organization.

Thus, Change management is a critical part of any project that leads, manages and enables people to accept new processes, technologies, systems, structures and values. It is the set of activities that helps people transition from their present way of working to the desired way of working. The focus of change management is to address the people and organizational factors that will both drive and obstruct change throughout the organization. The ultimate goal of any change initiative is to ensure everyone in the organization is ready, willing and able to appropriately perform their role in the new environment.

3. Framework For Change Management

Organizational change management begins with a systematic diagnosis of the current situation in order to determine both the need for change and the capability to change. "The Change Management process includes creative marketing to enable communication between change audiences, but also deep social understanding about leadership's styles and group dynamics. Organizational Change Management aligns groups' expectations, communication and integrates teams and manages people training. It makes use of performance metrics, such as financial results, operational efficiency, leadership commitment, communication effectiveness, and the perceived need for change to design appropriate strategies, in order to avoid change failures."[5]

Figure 1: Framework For Change Management
[Source: www.sourcingmag.com]

Figure 1 depicts a basic structure for understanding the change management. The segments in the wheel describe the various components that fit together in order to ensure the success of the organization. The salient features of the segments/components are as under: [6]

- **Culture:** This includes cause for change and its contribution towards organization's strategic goals and evaluating the strength and promptness of both individuals and organization to assimilate change. The blockage must be identified and articulated with accepted strategies and plans so that the initiatives are not derailed.
- **Organization:** This incorporates the operating model, organizational structures, role definitions, competency frameworks, governance and decision-making frameworks. The emphasis should be given on realistic and effective design of the new setup.
- **Leadership:** This activity aims at the leading of organization and leadership roles. The specific activities include defining the role of the leadership team, roles and responsibilities of individual leaders. This activity may need for training of leaders.
- **People Capability:** This activity aims to correlate the skills, competencies required for the new environment and the path to meet the requirements.
- **Execution:** This activity aims to set up a new structure. It incorporates hard deliverables such as project plans, milestones, progress reports and budget analysis, and soft deliverables as communications.
- **Continuous Improvement:** This includes frameworks and processes to measure the effectiveness of the changes and mechanisms for further improvement in timely manner. The expectations of all those impacted must be managed by the shared service initiative, so that they become accustomed to the idea that change will be a constant feature of the new model.

4. Models of Change Management

John P Kotter's 'Eight Steps To Successful Change'

American John Kotter is a Harward Bussiness School professor and leading thinker and author on organizational change management. Kotter's eight steps model helps in understanding the pressures of change on people, and people's reactions to change. Kotter's eight steps change model can be summarised as under:[7]

- **Increase urgency**: A sense of urgency has to be created among people and inspire people to move, make objectives real and relevant. A few questions arise: What do we want to achieve with this change, why, and how will we know that the change has been achieved? Who is affected by this change, and how will they react to it? How much of this change can we achieve ourselves, and what parts of the change do we need help with?
- **Build the guiding team**: Before starting organizational change we have to build up a framework to get the right people in place with the right emotional commitment, and the right mix of skills at all the levels. The initiative taken has to be strong. Responsibility for managing change is with management and executives of the organisation, they must manage the change in a way that employees can cope with it.
- **Get the vision right**: To guide and achieve success in the long run, a simple vision and strategy has to be established, focus on emotional and creative aspects is necessary to drive service and efficiency.
- **Communicate for buy-in**: Involve as many people as possible, communicate the essentials, simply, and to appeal and respond to people's needs. Involving and informing people also creates opportunities for others to participate in planning and implementing the changes, which lightens the burden, spreads the organizational load, and creates a sense of ownership and familiarity among the people affected. De-cluster communications, make technology work for you rather than against you.
- **Empower actions**: Remove obstacles, enable constructive feedback and lots of support from leaders – reward and recognize progress and achievements. Dynamic environments requires dynamic processes, people, systems and culture, especially for managing change successfully, notably effectively optimizing organizational response to market opportunities and threats.

- **Create short-term wins**: Set aims that are easy to achieve. Manageable numbers of initiatives should be in pockets and before starting new ones finish current stages.
- **Don't let up**: Foster and encourage determination and persistence for ongoing change , encourage ongoing progress reporting , highlight achieved and future milestones.
- **Make change stick**: Reinforce the value of successful change via recruitment, promotion, new change leaders. Weave change into culture.

Kurt Lewin's Model

One of the models for understanding organizational change was developed by Kurt Lewin, known as Unfreeze - Change - Refreeze, refers to the three-stage process of change. Lewin, a physicist as well as social scientist, explained organizational change using the analogy of changing the shape of a block of ice.If we have a large cube of ice, but want it to be a cone of ice, what should we do? Firstly, melt the ice to bring it into a liquid state (unfreeze). Then mold the iced water into the shape of cone (change). Finally, solidify it, which takes a new shape (refreeze). To begin any successful change process, you must first start by understanding why the change must take place. As Lewin put it, "Motivation for change must be generated before change can occur. One must be helped to re-examine many cherished assumptions about oneself and one's relations to others"[8].

Unfreeze

This stage involves preparing the organization to accept the change, which involves the breakdown of existing environment to build up a new and creative one. To achieve success, we need to have a strong base and to start at its core. In the beginning it seems to be difficult as we are cutting down the way things are done and everything is getting off balance. The pillars are being modified to make a strong foundation.

Change

In the unfreeze stage, people start to resolve their uncertainty and look for new ways to do things. It is not a matter of overnight. People will take time to move towards new direction and participate proactively in the change. In order to accept the change and contribute to making the change successful, people need to understand how the changes will benefit them. Time and communication are the two keys to success for the changes to occur. People need time to understand the changes and they also need to feel highly connected to the organization throughout the transition period.

Refreeze

When the changes are taking shape and people also start moulding with it. With a new sense of stability, employees feel confident and comfortable with new ways of working. It involves the identification of what supports the change and barriers to sustaining change. In the refreeze step information, support and training is provided. The celebration of success of the change is also a part of the refreezing process as this will make employees recall the struggling and painful time and also help them to believe that future change will be successful.

5. Change Management and its Application in Library and Information Centre

Change management refers to the making of changes in a planned or a systematic fashion where the aim is to implement new methods and systems in an on going organization in a more effective manner. "It is both an area of professional practice as well as a body of knowledge."[9] Change from an existing setup to a new environment has its own set of inherent problems and the problems become multifold when applied in a service institution as library. Libraries have been pioneers in adopting any new technology.

The role of libraries has gradually changed from the traditional storehouse of information to access providers, it is like Google on your fingertips. There has been a paradigm shift in the ways libraries used to be managed earlier. This paper aims at visualizing a broad overview of the concept of change management and its relevancy or validity for managing the transit of traditional paper based library to digital library. The adoption of ICT in library has drastically changed the way of fractioning of library. Today we have both print and e-resources in library and also have web based information services. Hence, the present status may be of hybrid in nature and libraries are referred to hybrid library. Thus, with the help of new converging technologies the libraries are changing towards digital library and they require different skills and strategies of change management.

Introducing a digital library setup has different dimensions depending on the host organization. For instance, the user requirements of the digital library at a university will be different from the users of a school library. In this situation, it is very difficult to suggest a universal change management strategy, it needs to be defined and designed depending on the need of the organization. Different 'skills and strategies are involved in managing change'[10] in libraries such as :

Skills

1. The motivation of people and convincing of management is required for the maximum benefit of the institution and users.
2. The ability to analyze the situation impartially and to act wisely is the foremost requirements of a good manager.
3. The ability to manage people in the groups, those who are part of the change and those who are bringing about the change.
4. Set of skills required for designing of a new system or bringing out balanced renovations in existing systems.
5. The business skills proficiency due to increasing emphasis on the evolution of self-sustaining profit generating information centers.

Strategies

"Change strategy can not be defined in a singular fashion rather it has to be adopted as a mixture of strategy sets, keeping an eye on the ultimate grand vision"[11].

Following factors determine the choice of the strategies:

1. Coupling of power-coercive and environmental-adaptive strategies is for strong resistance whereas an empirical-rational and normative-reductive strategy is for weak resistance.

2. Mixtures of strategy are demanded for large population.
3. Power-coercive strategy is needed usually for short span frame.
4. Management gets ample of confidence by availability of desired expertise.
5. If the organization is dependent on its people, management's ability to command or demand is limited. Likewise, if people are dependent upon the organization, their ability to oppose or resist is limited. Dennis Sparks, (1993)[12], 13 tips can be applied suitably in the case of managing the change from a paper-based library to a digital-library and these are :
   a) The leaders of change must be educated.
   b) To incorporate all aspects of institution at the time of planning and implementing change by system approach.
   c) Team approach ensures higher authorities in change process.
   d) For encouraging the implementation of change, sharing power with each and everybody is essential.
   e) Making, developing and adopting of plans have to be based on needs of change.
   f) For change, management needs to implement new approaches quickly. It should not take so much time and effort that people lose interest and motivation.
   g) Rigorous training and staff development are required.
   h) Innovative practices, approaches that have been already used or researched can help the implementing the proposed change.
   i) The emotional effects of change on educators need to be considered and understood by all involved in the change process.
   j) Experts advise that things can often get worse temporarily before improvement begins to appear, So, preparation is required.
   k) Co-operate with others in developing an "intellectual understanding" of the new practices.

l) For making substantial changes in practice, one may seek guidance from "paradigm shifters" and "idea champions".

m) Change takes time and should not be forced to occur too quickly. So, a long time frame should be taken.

6. Conclusion

The concept of change management can be understood and its relevance has been proved for managing the "*transit of traditional paper-library to digital-library*"[13].Change management entails thoughtful planning and sensitive implementation, above all, consultation with, involvement of, the people affected by changes. If we force change on people normally problem arise. Change must be realistic, achievable, and measurable. For bringing change in an organization successfully, the planning should be done very carefully, a proper foundation has to be build up, then implementation will become much easier, and the chances of success will increase.

Few key points should always be kept in mind such as sense of urgency has to be created, recruitment of powerful leaders, build a vision and effectively communicate it, remove obstacles, create quick wins. Change must involve people; it should not be imposed on them. Workshops are very useful processes to develop collecting information, understanding, approaches, policies, methods, system, ideas, etc. Staff surveys are a helpful way to repair damage and mistrust among staffs. Change needs to be understood and managed in a way that people can cope effectively with it. Change can be unsettling, so the manager logically needs to be a settling influence.

Thus, Organizational change is the alteration of work environment in organization. Organizational change is very important for the organizational development. Any change affect the whole organization, some parts of the organization may be affected more; others less; some parts are affected directly, others indirectly. Change in one system requires complementary change in other subsystems. Organizational change is a continuous process. However some changes which are of minor type may be absorbed by the existing equilibrium; others, which are major ones, may require special change effort. Time and communication are the two keys to success for the changes to occur.

References

1 http://en.wikipedia.org/wiki/changemanagement

2 http://www.changemanagement.com/change-management-toolkit.htm

3 www.citehr.com

4 www.brighthub.com

5 http://en.wikipedia.org/wiki/change_management

6 www.alsbridge.com

7 http://www.businessballs.com/changemanagement.htm

8 http://www.consultpivotal.com/lewin%27s.htm

9 Bennis,W.G.,Benne,K.D. and Chin,R(ed.). (1969).The Planning of change.2nd ed. New York: Holt, Rinehant and Winston.

10 Newell, A. and Simon, H.A (1972). Human Problem Solving . Englewood Cliffs: Prentice-Hall

11 Thomson, J. D.(1967).Organizations in Action . New York:McGraw-Hill

12 http://home.att.net/~nickols/change.htm

13 http://www.themanager.org/Knowledgebase/Management/Change.htm

25

Career Opportunities for Library and Information Science Professionals in India

Dr. M.R. Rawtani
Associate Professor & Head
Department of Library & Information Science
University of Rajasthan, Jaipur
Parveen Babbar
Assistant Librarian
Indira Gandhi National Open University
Delhi-110068
E-mail: parveenbabbar@ignou.ac.in
parveenbabbar@yahoo.com

Abstract

Nearly every human endeavor uses information, and librarians are masters of information. The traditional concept of a library has been redefined from a place to access paper records or books to one that also houses the most advanced electronic resources from internet, digital libraries, repositories to webology.

The paper describes the current status, the different patterns and levels of LIS education programmes being offered by various universities in India. Provides an overview of the institutions providing LIS courses at various levels. It discusses the status, trends and challenges of library and information science and career opportunities in India.

Librarians are becoming information professionals by combining traditional duties with tasks involving fast changing technology. The career in LIS has become multidimensional, emergent and bright, which is significantly enriching the knowledge base of the society for prosperity and progress. The paper identifies the information-related careers that library and information science graduates could enter with specific reference to the Indian situation.

It is important that both LIS faculty and students of library and information science recognize those careers which are related to the information profession to enable the graduates to practice what they learned and hopefully increase the opportunity of more employment in this sector. So the paper discusses in depth various types of recruitment opportunities available to LIS students in India in LIS job market.

Keywords: Library science; Librarianship; Career, Job Opportunities, Career planning, India

Introduction

With the fast changing and expanding information industry, cut throat competition in the employment sector, multiple job skills, and demanding employers, career planning and self-marketing have become crucial. Over the last decade or so many new avenues of employment have become open to library information services (LIS) graduates than our educators are equipped to train for; or that the mid-career library professional has even heard of. Though the profession has always been in flux, these days changes in the profession are really rapid. The LIS profession is becoming more and more profound, pervasive and universal. During the last decade, this process of change has accelerated as new areas of studies have emerged in the LIS studies and many inter-disciplinary academic programs have surfaced that include information management, knowledge management, content management, information architecture, digitization and archival and record systems.

LIS degree has become one of the new hottest post-graduate degrees for current y-generation. As it was earlier, librarianship is no longer a dowdy, old-fashioned profession, but has been reinvigorated by new technologies and new blood stream. With the expansion of internet and online teaching it is now even possible to choose whether to get a library science degree online or in a traditional setting. Whichever option students may choose, the focus within the program will set them on a bright career path. LIS career options are wide-ranging and with a little exploration a student can find a unique job with a library science degree. The scope of librarianship is brighter. Career in LIS is multidimensional, ever-growing, bright and significantly enriching the knowledge base of the society for prosperity and progress.

The objective of this paper is to identify the information-related careers that Library and Information Science (LIS) graduates could enter with a specific reference to the Indian situation. It is important that both LIS faculty and LIS students recognize these careers, as these are related to the information profession, to enable the graduates to practice what they have learned and hopefully increase the opportunity of more employment in this sector.

Library & Information Science Programmes

W. A. Borden and A. D. Dickinson were the first to initiate the formal course of library education in India. Borden established a training course at the Central Library, Baroda in 1911/12 and Dickinson at the Punjab University, Lahore in 1915. After the Columbia School, the training school at Punjab University is the second library school known in the world. Gradually other universities and library associations started setting up library schools. Madras Library Association in 1929 and Bengal Library Association in 1935 started certificate course. Madras University under Dr. S. R. Ranganathan took over the certificate course from Madras Library Association in 1931. These courses were subsequently converted into postgraduate course of one-year duration in 1937. Postgraduate courses also started in other universities subsequently, i.e. Andhra University (1935), Banaras Hindu University (1941) and University of Delhi (1947). University of Delhi in subsequent years started providing facilities for research leading to Ph.D. degree. It was again the first to start M.Phil courses in 1977.

Universities Offering Courses in LIS

At present there are about 80 university departments offering the LIS courses through regular or in distance learning mode. These universities/ institutes include

- Alagappa University, Karaikudi
- Aligarh Muslim University, Aligarh
- Allahabad University
- Annamalai University, Annamalainagar
- Awadhesh Pratap Singh University, Rewa
- Babasaheb Bhimrao Ambedkar University, Lucknow
- Banaras Hindu University, Varanasi
- Bundelkhand University, Jhansi
- Devi Ahilya Vishwavidyalaya, Indore
- Dr. Bhim Rao Ambedkar University, Agra
- Dr. Harisingh Gour Viswavidyalaya, Sagar
- Gulbarga University, Gulbarga
- Guru Ghasidas University, Bilaspur
- Guru Nanak Dev University, Amritsar
- HNB Garhwal University, Srinagar - Garhwal
- Jadavpur University, Calcutta
- Jamia Millia Islamia, New Delhi
- Jiwaji University, Gwalior
- Karnatak University, Dharwad
- Kurukshetra University, Kurukshetra
- Nagpur University, Nagpur
- North Eastern Hill University, Shillong
- Pandit Ravishankar Shukla University, Raipur
- Panjab University, Chandigarh
- Patna University, Patna
- Punjabi University, Patiala
- Rani Durgavati Vishwavidyalaya, Jabalpur
- Sambalpur University, Sambalpur
- SNDT Womens' University, Mumbai
- University of Delhi, Delhi

- University of Hyderabad, Hyderabad
- University of Jammu, Jammu (Tawi)
- University of Kashmir, Srinagar
- University of Lucknow, Lucknow
- University of Madras, Chennai
- University of Mysore, Mysore
- University of Pune, Pune
- University of Rajasthan, Jaipur
- Vikram University, Ujiain
- UP Rajarshi Tandon Open University, Allahabad (Distance Education)
- Indira Gandhi National Open University, New Delhi (Distance Education)

In addition to above two Sanskrit universities, viz., KS Darbhanga Sanskrit University (Bihar), and Sampuranand Sanskrit Vishvavidyalaya (Varanasi) offer 9 months Pustakalaya Vigyan Shastri and one year Granthalaya Vigyan Shastri courses respectively.

The course in LIS range from

- Certificate course in Library and Information Science (CLISc or CLIB) Eligibility: 10+2
- Diploma course in Library and Information Science (DLISc or DLIB) Eligibility: 10+2
- Bachelor in Library and Information Science (BLISc or B.LIB) Eligibility: Graduate in any discipline from a recognized University
- Post Graduate Diploma in Library Information Network (PGDLAN) Eligibility: BLISc or B.LIB from a recognized University
- Master in Library and Information Science (MLISc or M.LIB) Eligibility: BLISc or B.LIB from recognized University
- M.Phil. in Library and Information Science. Eligibility: MLISc or M.LIB from recognized University.
- Ph.D. in Library and Information Science. Eligibility: MLISc from recognized University.

In addition to above, NISCAIR under the Council of Scientific and Industrial Research (CSIR), New Delhi conducts a two-year programme leading to the award of Associateship in Information Science (AIS) and the Documentation Research and Training Centre (DRTC) under the Indian Statistical Institute at Bangalore, offers Associateship in Documentation and Information Science (ADIS).This award is also recognised as equivalent to MLISc degree. In view of the increased use of computer and information technology in libraries, several universities in India also have started various courses focusing primarily on information technology and computer.

The LIS courses are also now provided online. IGNOU under LIVE (Library and Information Virtual Education) has initiative in-house Learning & Content Management System for imparting online education. It is a complete virtual learning environment suite covering all the activities from registration to certification. Under the virtual learning environment Master's Degree in Library and Information Science (MLIS) Online is presently offered by the University.

Course nomenclature and qualifying marks in different courses differ from university to university. Earlier the subject was called library science but now due to information explosion, library professionals are handling information, so the subject has changed into information science. At present most of the universities provide degree i.e. Bachelor in Library and Information Science (BLISc), and Masters in Library and Information Science (MLISc), M.Phil in Library and Information Science and Ph.D in Library and Information Science.

A successful library and information science course must review its philosophy and content continuously, responding to the changing realities of the workplace and to the changing roles and expectations of the information professionals. It is recommended that the course should have atleast five-yearly revisions so as to make it remaining true to its philosophy of teaching the "core areas" of information work, and producing all-rounder graduates, capable of entry into any area of the profession.

It has been seen, that students come on to the course with varied and sometimes vague expectations, often based on old ideas of what the library profession involves, or with a fixed intention to follow down a specific road, e.g. to be a university librarian, school librarian, or to have a career in "the information science". For many, the course confirms or alters their career hopes, but others seem to be uncertain or, perhaps, they take the view that any kind of post will be as good as any other.[1]

LIS Profession Perception vs. Reality

While the popular perception of a librarian is of an old woman, hair in a bun, busily checking out books and shushing people all day, librarians' actual duties, focus, and abilities are much more varied.

In reality the librarian's work may range from creating original cataloging records for items in library collections, classifying them, developing entire taxonomies to organize companies' data to using their expert skills to answer complex reference questions. For the librarians today it has become essential to pursue career paths of technology enabled librarianship, ranging from having responsibility for implementing Web 2.0 technologies, developing and managing an institutional repository, designing portals, maintaining library servers for different applications.

Library and Information Science Sectors

Today there are bright career prospects in LIS. The qualified professionals are employed in libraries and Information Centers. Librarians are now known as Information Professionals because present day libraries have become centers for providing various types of information and they play an important role in research in various fields. The job opportunities in LIS can be depicted in the following sectors:

- **Academic libraries** are School libraries, College Libraries, University Libraries, Institutional Libraries/Information centers etc. and may be either general or focused on one area of specialization, as the health sciences library or law library. Librarians' roles in these institutions include such tasks as working on the reference desk, teaching bibliographic courses, classifying and cataloging incoming materials, selecting materials in particular areas, serving as faculty and departmental liaisons, and maintaining library web pages and online collections.

- **Public libraries** serve communities of all sizes and are distinguished by being open to all; this is what most people think of when they picture both libraries and librarians. Public libraries also employ people in multiple types of positions, which are often defined by department; you can choose a particular area, such as, children's librarianship, reference, technical services, systems librarianship, training, readers' advisory, or collection development. There is large network of public libraries at Administrative levels of governments such as Villages, Panchayats, Block, District, Commissionery and State, etc. Some NGOs are also running various public libraries. In India there is a large number of Public Libraries as shown in the following table:

Penetration of Public Libraries in India [2]

Demography of India	Number	Public Libraries	Number Covered	%
State & Uts	35	State Central Libraries	28	80%
Districts	592	District Libraries	451	76%
Talukas#	3987	Taluka Libraries	501	12.5%
Villages # #	5,87,226	Rural Libraries	28,820	4.9%

(Source:# census of India, 1991, ## Ghosh 2005)

- **Special (corporate) libraries** or information centers are found in corporations and other specialized environments. Many special librarians/information specialists now work with information centres outside the typical library setting and have a non library job title, ranging from Information scientists, Information managers, Database managers, Resource managers, Knowledge workers, Library supervisors, Librarians etc. Special libraries focus in a specific area of study. Hospitals, medical schools, law schools and offices, museums, prisons, publishing houses, and practically any other large corporate or non-profit making organizations have a library that needs a librarian. According to the Special Libraries Association, people in this job build a dynamic collection of information resources based on the organization's needs and use this information to help in making decisions on new products and services. Usually people choose this career option if they have an interest in one of the specific fields. Since special librarianship is so broad, it also encompasses a number of subgroups from medical librarians to law librarians, each with its own typical set of duties and its own association. Any previous experience or specialized degree in the institution subject helps in the profession.[3]

Each of these types of libraries employs librarians in multiple subspecialties. In a public or academic library, for example, one can work in areas such as reference librarianship, answering questions at the reference desk and helping people with research; systems librarianship, working with library technology; or cataloging, creating, organizing, and annotating records for library materials.

Librarianship can also be a great foundation for information-related careers in general; the skills gained are directly transferable to a number of alternative careers, such as knowledge management, data mining, or competitive intelligence. Careers with related organizations; library vendors, for example, often seek people with library and technical or library and training backgrounds. Some librarians choose to work as independent information professionals and run research, indexing, records management, database, training, or other information-related businesses. This option is best for those who have some years of experience as a librarian, though; it takes time to build up the skills and contacts necessary to run and market one's own enterprise.

So a wide variety of options are open to LIS professionals. Beyond traditional options in public, academic, special, and corporate libraries, any organization in the information age needs the people to shape, retrieve, and manage its information. If one thinks broadly about prospects, one will be able to maximize his/her opportunities.

Operational Convergence

Operational convergence signifies the increased use of joint initiatives and cooperation between overlapping or complementary services, while maintaining existing departmental boundaries. Organisational convergence is the emerging trend for library services to combine with other academic support services and undergo internal restructuring to form a large information service department. Both types of convergence place new demands upon the staff - paraprofessional support staff, middle level professionals, and senior managers - working within those services, and bring particular threats and opportunities which have an impact upon potential career progression.

The driving force behind operational and, indeed, organisational convergence is convergence of the technologies underlying both library and computing services. These developments are well-known and have been well rehearsed in the literature. Those which are more responsible for creating the need for changed structures are:

- growth in electronic forms of information;
- growth in the use of IT by academic staff and students;
- changing models of teaching and research.[4]

Career Planning

Career planning means planning for your progress through life or working towards achieving your greatest potential. It is more concerned with encouraging to take a long-term perspective about achievement than about assigning specific targets and attaching dates to them. Career planning should help to focus thoughts. It is about what one would like to do with his/her life and how to go about making it happen. The development of career would not only benefit you, but it is also likely to benefit those around you if you achieve job and life satisfaction.[5]

A Master's in degree in LIS will open a lot of doors in different careers, but graduates with that degree have to be willing to be creative. They must think of all the places that may need someone to organize information, and apply to them. If librarians have managerial or business skill they may even become a library managers or directors, which focuses less on the information side of the job and more on managing people and resources. Library science graduates simply must employ the information gathering skills they gained in library schools and will have to use these in their future careers, and apply them to job hunting.

Librarianship as a profession provides a variety of employment opportunities. Today there are a number of career prospects in LIS. The qualified professionals are employed in various libraries and information centers. Trained library professionals can find opportunities for employment both as teacher and as a librarian. In fact, it is possible to choose the kind of library to suit one's interest and background. In librarianship, designations could be Librarian, Documentation Officer, Assistant Librarian, Deputy Librarian, Scientist (Library Science/ Documentation), Library and Information Officer, Knowledge Manager/ Officer, Information Executive, Director/Head of Library Services, Information Officer, and Information Analyst.

- In School or College or University library;
- In Central Government Libraries.
- In the training centers of banks.
- In National Museums and Archives.
- In NGOs working in different areas.
- In R&D Centre like ICAR, CSIR, DRDO, ICSSR, ICHR, ICMR, ICFRE, etc.
- In Business Houses.
- In Foreign Embassies and High Commissions.
- In International Centers like WHO, UNESCO, UNO, World Bank, etc.
- In the libraries of Ministries and other government departments.
- In National Level Documentation Centers.
- In Library Networks.
- In newspaper libraries.
- In news channels.
- In the libraries of Radio Stations.
- In the databases provider firms.
- In publishing companies for preparing Indexes, abstracts, bibliographies, etc.
- In various digital library projects like 'Digital Library of India'.
- In Training academies.

Types of Recruitment in Library and Information Science

The information related jobs described as follows are not exhaustive because there are still a number of jobs which have not yet been identified and which require multi skills in addition to the LIS education.

(1) *Library Professionals:* This is where most of the librarians in India are concentrated. Library Science graduates can work as librarians or library professionals in school, colleges, and universities or in other academic libraries. Generally assisting the readers is the prime job in these cases. There are some specialized libraries where the professionals provide information on specific topics.

(2) *Faculty/Teaching Library and Information Science*: With the establishment of library and information science programmes in more than 80 universities, polytechnics and colleges of education in India, there is no doubt that the teaching of library and information science holds prospects for librarians who wish to teach as Professors, Associate Professors, or Assistant Professors.

(3) *Information Specialists*: Information centres in diverse organizations such as government ministeries, information divisions of hospitals, embassies, business companies, etc., offer job opportunities for library and information sciences professionals. Work in these information centres largely involves selecting, gathering, preserving and disseminating information about the functions of the organization. Professionals working in such centres are known either as information officers or information specialists.

(4) *Systems Analysts*: A focus in information systems and technology will help a library professional to become a technology expert. Technology experts may build websites, provide computer support, engage in programming and help organizations with storage, management and retrieval of records. This job typically pays more than a library job and is a good option for those who would rather work with the technical side of information services.

(5) *Library consultant*: This is an area where the LIS graduate can also usefully apply his or her professional skill. Writing a proposal for the setting up of a library, establishing a library and advising on the improvement of an existing library are examples of library consultancy services. Some Indian librarians have in the past served as library consultants especially in the establishment of special libraries. Some of these library consultants also provide research to corporations, writers or any other individuals needing information. These professionals are generally freelancers who have developed excellent research and writing skills in their undergraduate and post-graduate studies. Extensive knowledge of a certain area of study may be helpful in this choice.

(6) *Bibliometrics or informetrics*: Bibliometrics is traditionally associated with the quantitative measurement of documentary materials. It refers to a variety of regularities taken from different fields and exhibiting a variety of forms. Although bibliometric distributions differ greatly in appearance, they can be conceptualised as versions of a single regularity, so that we can properly speak of bibliometric laws and their manifestations. Bradford's Law of scattering, Zipf's Law and Lotka's Law are the best known laws dealing with important phenomena or "regularities" found in science communication. Advanced online search facilities and information retrieval (IR) techniques have considerably increased the potential of bibliometric research methodology and are opening up new possibilities for tracking down analytical information in large collections of bibliographic data. Linking the theoretical and practical aspects of information retrieval with the methodological and experimental research programmes in bibliometrics offers integrative and interdisciplinary research approaches - in which LIS professionals are working.[6]

(7) Indexing: There are a number of indexing activities going on in India which have become a full fledge profession. Back-of-the-book indexing is one area that attracts a huge money. This is mostly an area of commercial indexing in which the

indexing of books, newspapers and magazines are done. Presently, web based digital resource indexing has become a market for LIS professionals.

(8) *Abstracting*: Another potential area in which the information professionals in India could apply their skill is in the area of abstracting. Certainly, abstracts are needed in several subject fields and for certain categories of information sources. In this area LIS professionals require subject knowledge and the availability of information sources for abstracting.

(9) *Compilation of bibliographies*: This area continues to attract many librarians in India. Even though several bibliographies exist, there is still a need for more, especially bibliographies that will be available on a commercial basis.

(10) Metadata: At some libraries, metadata librarians or archivists create metadata for a variety of collections having digital format. Various metadata standards have been established. This is not only a huge amount of work, but also needs library and information science professionals to do the job. To facilitate metadata creation, metadata librarians are sought for batch loading or auto-generated metadata to provide access to digital contents with the help of technologies.

(11) *Editing books, journals, newspapers and magazines*: Some information professionals work in publishing houses as editors.

(12) *Proof-reading of books, journals, newspapers and magazines*: This job again requires the information professional to work in publishing houses.

(13) *Records management in business organizations*: The information professional works in organizations, especially business organizations, as records manager.

(14) *Archivist*: Education and training in archives administration enables the information professional to work as archivist in national, state, institutional and religious archives in India and elsewhere.

(15) *Publishing*: The information professional who is knowledgeable in publishing can set up a publishing company which may publish books, journals, newspapers and magazines.

(16) *Cyber Kiosks/Photocopying*: The information professional can also venture into the "copy shop" business. They can open Cyber Kiosks to provide all kind of information related machines ranging from computers, printers, photocopiers, fax, internet facilites.

(17) *Vendor/Dealer in library publications, equipment and materials*: The library and information science graduate can work as a vendor/dealer in library equipment such as shelves, catalogue cabinets, and in library materials such as catalogue cards.

(18) V*endor/Dealer in Online Resources/Databases/E-Journals*: The LIS graduate can work as a vendor/dealer in online journals, online books, databases, reference books available online. This is most popular and growing market at present.

(19) *Audio and video recording/ conversions*: Video recording offers another business option for the information professionals, but it requires major capital inputs. They can take the projects of conversion of video to different media and formats like tapes, dvds, cds etc

(20) *Binding of books and periodicals*: The LIS graduate who has done a course on book production and publishing can set up a bindery to bind books and periodicals. Such a business will thrive rapidly if set up near institutions of higher learning where library books and students' theses and projects need binding.

(21) *Information brokerage*: The information professional can set up a fee-based information service. The professional gathers information and makes this available to the information seeker for a fee. Database vendors come under this category. They are also known as freelance information specialists. Being an information broker affords him or her the opportunity of travelling to several places to gather information and meet people. The information broker not

only supplies information for a fee but also supplies books and other media for a fee.

(22) *Museum documentation*: This information professional works in a museum as a museum-documentalist. The job involves documentation of various kinds of museum objects, preparation and maintenance of information storage and retrieval devices.

(23) *Advertising, publicity and promotions*: The LIS graduate works as the public relations officer of an organization or institution. The job involves gathering information about the activity of the organization, organizing the information and publicizing it.

(24) *Writing*: Writing offers an exciting career for the LIS graduate who wishes to demonstrate his or her talents. Many Indian librarians are already in the writing business, either writing LIS books or books on other subjects.

(25) *Researcher*: Several organizations, institutions and government bodies have research departments. Given the education and training received in research methodology, statistics and the management of projects, the LIS graduate can work in such departments whose activities involve identification of problems, data gathering, data analysis and their interpretation.

(26) *Computer business*: The LIS graduate who specialized in information technology and basic computing courses could work in computer organizations, selling computer hardware and software, as a computer operator or as a programmer. He may set up a computer business centre in which he could mount training courses, development, or software, systems analysis and design, word processing, desk-top publishing, renting of computer printer ribbon, computer stationery, consumables and accessories, book publishing and data analysis and charting, using statistical and graphics packages.

(27) *Book rental*: The LIS professional may rent books for a fee. The system, which is similar to video rental clubs in various parts of India, requires that the customer must be a registered member before borrowing books.

(28) *Bookshops*: Bookselling in bookshops is one area in the business world that readily attracts LIS professionals. It is an area in which some librarians both retired and serving are actively involved.

(29) *Toy Libraries*: Another latest area is toy libraries where kids are issued toys on a membership basis. Many women/ female librarians are independently running this business in India [7]

Perceived need of the Country

Well-trained information professionals are essential in any country, both in the developed and in the developing world. They are employed in libraries of all kinds (school, public, special, academic), in information centres (private, public, government), as consultants to big business, as information managers, etc. Therefore there is a huge market for the graduates of LIS.

In addition to this the National Knowledge Commission set up by the Prime Minister with the challenging mandate to transform India of the 21st century into a knowledge society has especially recommend changes and reforms to address the problems and challenges relating to the LIS sector. Libraries have been given due importance to ensure a holistic development of information services in all areas of national activity. The report has stressed on need for assessing the manpower requirements for different types of libraries and departments of library and information science, keeping in mind job descriptions, qualifications, designations, pay scales, career advancement and service conditions. [8]

Further the emerging market in India, with non-library jobs both in the public and corporate/private sectors, is rapidly growing and requiring high levels of information competency. Essentially, the LIS sector in this sector requires comprehensive knowledge and skills in areas such as information literacy, information and knowledge management, information technology, information searching and retrieval, research, communication skills, customer care, the ability to work both independently and in a team, and positive work-related attitudes. [9]

Conclusion

It is evident that LIS profession has taken the challenges of the changing information environment very seriously, and has adopted its name and its work profile alignments to reflect these changes.

Apart from career opportunities in traditional libraries, there are rapidly growing career opportunities in the non-library sector or the emerging market. The emerging market has forced most LIS professionals to venture into the new market in order to survive. The LIS professionals should work more for information and knowledge management, information storage and retrieval, knowledge organization, knowledge representation, and ICTs.

The process of traditional librarianship has changed over the years, with the advancement of technology. The concept of libraries has also evolved and changed – they are no more considered as storehouse of books, manuscripts, and records. That age-old concept has been redesigned and today libraries are the place to hit if you're looking for CDs, DVDs, Internet access, and virtual databases, Web 2.0, Librarians 2.0, Social Networking and many others.

So library and information professionals have ample opportunities as they can apply their management and research skills outside libraries in database development, reference tool development, information systems, publishing, Internet coordination, marketing, Web content management and design, and training of database users. It is quite evident now that in India the business of having own consulting practices, acting as freelance librarians or information brokers, and providing services to other libraries, businesses, or government agencies is growing at very fast pace. All this provides good career opportunities to LIS professionals.

References

1. Burke, Maria E and Stephen, Peter. (1994) The Learning Experience Student Perceptions and Evaluations. *Librarian Career Development*, 2(3), 11-13
2. Ghosh, Maitreyee. (2005). The public library system in India: challenges and opportunities. *Library Review*, 54(3), 180-191.
3. Special Libraries Association. http://www.sla.org

4. Abbott, Christine M. (1998). Personal career development in converged services *Librarian Career Development*, 6(3), 28-35.

5. Farmer, Jane; Ward, Grainne and Wood, Lawraine. (1996) Taking stock: career planning for isolated, middle-level professionals, *New Library World* 97(1127), 14–22

6. Wormell, Irene (1998). Informetrics: an emerging subdiscipline in information science. *Asian Libraries*, 7(10), 257-268.

7. Afolabi, Michael (1994). Career Opportunities for Library and Information Science Professionals in Africa. *New Library World,* 95(1114), 13-20.

8. National Knowledge Commission http://www. knowledge commission.gov.in / downloads/documents/wg_lib.pdf

9. Ocholla, Dennis and Bothma, Theo. (2007). Trends, challenges and opportunities for LIS education and training in Eastern and Southern Africa University of Zululand, *Africa New Library World.* 108(1/2), 55-78

26

Human Resource Development for Libraries in IT Environment

Dr. T. R. Borse
Librarian and Head
Dept. of Library and Information Science
North Maharashtra University
Jalgaon-425 001

Abstract

Presently the libraries are in the environment of Information Technology. This has impacted all the components of libraries. Human Resource is one of the essential components, without which libraries would not run efficiently to provide better services. This component deals with manpower invariably and requires the capabilities of staff to be developed to such an extent that accomplishes the works of entire library processes. Human Resources Development is the process by which the employees of library are helped in a continuous and planned way to sharpen their abilities to undertake the responsibilities and accountabilities they are charged with.This paper reveals various levels of HRD, its programmes, and role of IT in a library. Also it connotes the need of HRD processes for library as an organization.

1. Introduction

Human Resources Development is an activity by which the employees of an organization are helped in a continuous and planned way to acquire or sharpen the capabilities required to perform various functions associated with their present and expected future roles and to develop their general capabilities and to discover and exploit their own inner potentiality for their own and organizational development. It is also a process that develops an organizational culture in which the relationship of super-ordinates and subordinates is maintained. It also leads the team work among personnel, along with professional contribution[1].

As stated above, HRD in a nutshell, aims to help the personnel of an organization to acquire competencies which are required and are a must to perform various duties related to a job. Another concept getting important is the Information Technology Environment. To understand this concept, it is important to know what of environment. In short, environment is an aggregate of external conditions which affect the life of human being[2]. This connotation helps us to understand its meaning as the totality of human being's surrounding. Surrounding is the physical and external conditions that affect the human life.

The technology involving information which has been stored electronically and retrieved immediately through electronic machine is the information technology[3].

Information Technology Environment means the physical and total surrounding of digitized or electronic technology which is being used to store, retrieve, and to transfer information.

To keep pace with present information technology environment it is imperative for library as an organization to develop its employees to acquire capabilities as are needed to accomplish the works that are related with IT environment.

2. Need of Human Resources Development (HRD)

HRD is needed by any kind of organization that desires to grow and progress continuously. In the fast changing and emerging new technical environment the organization of any kind can scale the new heights of developments through effective and efficient human resources. The right and relevant personnel policies help to maintain the motivation and morale of employees. However, the right and relevant policy alone does not help the organization to achieve the success for progress. To avoid the stagnant position of an organization, the personnel capabilities are a must to be acquired to perform the various jobs. To enhance the improvements in job performance, a continuous training in recent trends in job related environment is necessary to make the employees efficient. They also need be encouraged to take the risks and to undertake the experiments to achieve the goals of the organization. HRD is also required to enhance and develop the qualities in performing the jobs to serve the people better [4].

2.1 Need of HRD in Library

Library is an organization entrusted with the responsibilities of collecting, organizing, preserving and disseminating knowledge available in different forms of documents[5].

A library functions with the help of its personnel. To have the improvements in organizational services towards the library users, it needs the process of Human Resources Development, as other service organizations need. The employees (personnel) of a library also need to acquire the capabilities to perform the various technical jobs in the library. In the present environment of technology in general and in the environment of information technology in particular, the library as an organization needs to enhance the quality of its staff in performing each and every job of library work. The library performs the job of collection of documents, organization of documents, preservation of documents and dissemination of knowledge through documents. To perform all the jobs, library personnel also need to cope with the present environment of information technology. To retain and sustain efficiency among its staff, HRD in a library system is needed.

HRD at Macro Level: Macro level HRD is concerned with the development of people for the well-being of nation. It considers health, efficiencies, skills, attitudes and capabilities of people which are more useful to the development and progress of nation as a whole. While considering the economic growth and per capita income, the HRD concept verifies the potentialities of individuals who are working in organizations. In order to have a continuous growth of nation in general, HRD establishes a concrete base for planning[6].

Macro level HRD is very much applicable to a library because it is a social, educational, and service-oriented organization[7]. The jobs and works related to all these components in a library require a role of macro level HRD. To perform the job well-connected with social developments, educational progress and different services to be rendered nation-wide through the citizens, a library plays a vital role through provision of services. By rendering better services to users, the members of society, and contributing towards its social transformation, a library considers the HRD planning at macro level; though the involvement of a library in the national progress is indirect.

HRD at Micro Level: Micro level HRD is concerned with grass root level developments within organization. This micro level HRD realizes the importance and future of employees and organization that leads to the developments of employees and organization itself. Micro level HRD in particular considers human resources planning, i.e. selection, recruitment, training, placement and welfare; as also it looks to get the good performances of employees by acquiring in them the capabilities and efficencies[8].

Library as an organization needs to implement the concept of micro level HRD, as the library, as an organization, requires certain progress and development by providing timely services, that is, right information to right person at right time.

The macro level and micro level HRDs mentioned above are needed for library to be implemented so that it may operate successfully in current environment of information technology of present society, known as information society. The following components further lead the libraries to implement both the concepts of HRD for national as well as in-house developments.

2.1.1 Changing Role of Library in IT Environment

The role of library has been changing over a period of time. Before the advent of printing press the role of library was custodial and for preserving the records in different physical forms, thus ensuring the continuation of culture and civilization. And with the availability of documents in multiple copies, after the advent of printing, the role of library changed from deposition to the promotion of use of documents.

The society has also been through different stages from agricultural society to cottage industries, to technologies, to industrialization, to information society. Such conditions also led a library to adopt various changes to meet the new requirements. In the present day society the role of library is to communicate the needed information to users, because the information is considered as an economic goods and essential input in the process of decision-making.

The library system is indispensable today to make the nation a knowledge society, where creating, sharing and using of knowledge is a key factor for progress and prosperity, as also for the well-being of the people.

2.1.2 *Libraries' Modernity*

The traditional and conventional practices have been left by libraries and now the use of information is promoted. In the present age of information society the conventional functions of library are replaced by the changed role and new techniques and technologies that crept in the present environment of IT. Automation and computerization process of library have taken over a lot of work which was earlier performed by manual efforts. The walls of a library have become meaningless and information services are provided from all over the world in a timely manner. The modern library system is surely exploiting Information Technology for managing information well and making it available to seekers fast. These developments in the modern libraries are leading to the phase of change in library from its state of repository to the state of centre of poly-media, electronic, digital and virtual.

2.1.3 *Role of IT in Library*

Information Technology is intended to manage the information by processing the data into information.The processed and stored information is retrieved speedily to make it available to the users without the loss of time. Information Technology, as mentioned earlier, denotes all the various activities connected with the location, acquisition, processing, storage and communication of information. It involves an extensive use of electronic and micro-electronic equipment for processing, storing, and communicating information. In fact extensive use of telephone, radio, television, satellite, computer, and micro-processor are well utilized in information communication. Floppies, diskettes, CDs, etc. provide tremendous storage space and these further facilitate the transfer of information from one machine to another. These all are coming under the purview of Information Technology, which is subject to think about in the libraries of the 21st century to keep pace with the present situation.

2.1.4 *Paperless Society*

The total knowledge and information, which is presently available in the libraries in the form of books and other documents can be put on world wide web (www) making libraries web based and with no collections of documents in physical form. Knowledge and information of all types can be accessed through network terminals, through personal computers and through fax machines. If required the information is also made available in print. The technological advances have made it possible to provide library services and access to information even outside the library. A library without walls or virtual library is becoming a reality today..

2.1.5 *Library of 21st Century*

Funds Generator: Present libraries so far have been depending on funds allotted by State or Central Governments, as also on other funding agencies. In this century the position of libraries is changing. Libraries will generate their needed funds to maintain and sustain themselves by selling the analyzed, consolidated and repackaged information in different product forms. Libraries will also offer consultancy services. Libraries will also conduct the study of information seekers and sell the need-based information for a price.

Proper information Provider: Libraries during 21st century are equipped well and will provide proper information rather than document oriented information. Demand of specific information is going to increase by many folds and the libraries will have to meet this demand adequately.

Standards Adoption: To reap the full advantages of IT Environment, the standardization in library practices is a must. No network is possible unless the standards are adopted. The libraries of all types and at different levels would adopt standard practices and routines, so that they have common systems and codes to become a partner in the local, regional, national, international information systems. Standardization facilitates exchange of information among libraries all over the world.

IT and Network Users: For locating and retrieving the information from any corner of the world, library depends on Information Technology and on the devices being used under IT. Sharing of information through network will be an extensive practice of libraries to cope with the present and future requirements.

The impact of IT is in every walk of life, such as, banking, insurance, railway, airlines, etc. Libraries of course use IT extensively.. Earlier books, journals and other reading materials were available in print media only. But today the libraries are equipped with computers, printers, scanners, bar-code readers, videos, compact discs, floppies, magnetic tapes, RFID (Radio Frequency Identification Device) and in house and commercially available databases to provide information to users through net. OPAC (Online Public Access Catalogue) has changed the shape of traditional card catalogue. Now the readers can access the bibliographic and other information with the click of a mouse on the computers. Apart from these, libraries provide E-Journals, Internet and OPAC services to readers. The scenario of IT has brought about a revolution and has changed the libraries drastically[9,10].

3. HRD Programmes

In order to cope with IT environment the libraries have to implement the HRD programmes. Present librarianship is quite different from the conventional one. Librarian today is a gatherer, analyzer, consolidator, repackager and provider of information. To have compatibility with all the jobs of modern library, the HRD programmes are a must with proper planning. The following programmes are important and may be considered useful for implementing HRD.

3.1 Training and Employee Development

Training for the library staff is a must to keep them updated and to cope with ever-changing IT environment and to achieve the objectives of the library. Training is required for learning process that can be designed to achieve a relatively permanent change in an individual employee, who can improve his own ability to perform the job. Staff development is to ensure the bright future of a library, focusing on personal growth of employees. To illustrate more about the Information Scientists and Computer Operators, they acquire advance training to handle the computers and also to store and retrieve the information in response to different queries made by the readers. Apart form this the entire staff of a library is needed to be trained to cope with dynamic and changing IT environment.

3.2 Development of Library—as an Organization

The fifth law of library science, developed by Dr S. R. Ranganathan, says: "Library is a growing organism". This law states that library as an organization is never static in growth and development. As library grows at all angles, it means a continuous up-gradation in its physical plant, collection of information sources, improved information services, and more satisfaction of the users. To ensure all these expanding and improved conditions, a library is to grow and continue its progress in its all dimensions. No doubt there will be a surprised future of library. But systematic planning for organizational growth and development is a must. Organizational development of a library is managed from top officials to lower level employees. Therefore, there is a need to introduce and enhance the HRD programmes for the over-all development of a library.

3.3 Performance and Potential Appraisal

Performance appraisal of an employee has become an indispensable tool for library development. It has importance in managing and improving the performance of an employee. It also helps to make a proper decision regarding library staff and their over-all improvements to achieve better quality in job performance as also in providing the information services effectively.

Potential appraisal refers to the abilities possessed by an employee but such potential is not put to use to accept the challenges and responsibilities for further future assignments and developments. The programme under HRD is to be implemented to find and justify the potentiality of employees to accept new jobs and works.

3.4 Career Planning

Career is a sequence of positions held by an employee in the course of service time. Career planning is a process of integrating the needs and aspirations with organizational needs. Career development programmes under HRD are to be implemented to help each employee to meet individual and organizational needs[11].

References

1. **Rao, V.S.P**. Human Resource Management: Text and Cases, 2nd ed. New Delhi, Excel Books, 2005, 270p.
2. **Bores, T. R.** Environmental Awareness of the Villagers; Ecology, Environment and Conservations, 6(4), 2000, pp. 479-80.
3. **Vishwanathan, C. G.** Element of Information Science and Technology. Lucknow, Print House, 1986, 89p.
4. **Rao, V.S.P.** Human Resource Management: Text and Cases. New Delhi, Excel Books, 2000, pp. 249-50.
5. **Devinder Kaur.** Information Technology Applications in Libraries. In: R. G .Prasher, ed.Indian Libraries in IT Environment. Ludhiana, Medallion Press, 2003, 23p.
6. **Rao, V. S. P.** Human Resource Management: Text and Cases, 2nd ed. New Delhi, Excel Books, 2005, pp. 273-74.
7. **Mittal, R. L.**Library Administration: Theory and Practice. New Delhi, Metropolitan Book Company, 1993, 22p.
8. **Rao, V.S.P.** Human Resource Management: Text and Cases. 2nd ed. New Delhi, Excel Books, 2005, 274p.
9. **Pateria, R.** University Libraries in Digital Environment: Vision 2020; *ILA Bulletin*, 43 (3), 2007, pp. 5-7.
10. **Devinder Kaur.** Op. Cit; pp. 1-8.
11. **Saiyadain, M.S.** Human Resource Management. New Delhi, Tat McGraw-Hill Publishing Company, 2000, pp. 245-258.

27

Reading Habit: Its Development and Promotion

Dr. Umesh Kumar Agarwal
Ex-Deputy Librarian
Central Library
Mohanlal Sukhadia University, Udaipur -313001
Prakash Chandra Vijayavargia
PhD Scholor, DLIS
Mohanlal Sukhadia University, Udaipur

1. Reading Habit

Reading is important for every body in order to cope up with new knowledge in the changing world of the technological age. Reading has motivated the people and informed them how to utilize reading materials to improve their own personality and social environment. In this context role of nongovernmental organizations, government sectors, libraries, schools and family are very important for mutual cooperation to promote reading habits among readers. However, libraries play a very important role in this context. All these institutions have influenced the reading habit of human beings and moulded the character of individuals through their reading materials.

1.1 Reading Habit: The Concept

Reading is a complex process which comprises various developmental stages. It is, first of all, a perceptual process during which symbols are recognized. The transfer into intellectual concepts then takes place. This mental task broadens into a thought process as the ideas are connected into ever larger thought units. However, the thought process does not merely consist of understanding the ideas perceived but also in their interpretation and evaluation.[1]

Smith and Robinson defined reading as "an active attempt on the part of reader to understand a writer's message".[2] Reading is primarily an intellectual activity and its practice is influenced by many factors like home environment, subject background, age, status, etc. Reading helps in the resolution of personal need and in the attainment of mental maturity and independence of thoughts. Devarajan (1979) defines reading as an art of interpreting printed and written words.[3] It is a basic tool of education and one of the most important skills in every day life. Habit is a psychological aspect and is developed during a course of time as a part of personality of an individual. [4]

1.2 Meaning of Habit

A habit is described simply as a learned stimulus-response sequence; in cognitive psychology it is seen as a set of automatic routines and sub-routines in which the individual engages, and which, owing to frequent exercise, requires little conscious cognitive input.[5]

Reading is primarily an intellectual activity and reading habit is a sort of attribute of a human being. Like other habits, the habit of reading in an individual develops during the course of time. Psychologically, habit is a product of learning; however reading is an art of interpreting the printed tools and written words. It is important for the professional staff of a library to know about the reading habits and information needs of the user being served.[6]

Reading habit has been an area of active interest among the librarians and information scientists. It results from the recognition of some need perceived by the user, who as a consequence makes demand upon formal system such as libraries, information centers, or other persons in order to satisfy the perceived need.[7]

1.3 Importance of Reading Habits

Reading habits plays an important role in individual's, student's and agriculture scientist's ability to interpret literary works. Although a majority of said individuals accept that reading is very important, but take reading as a favoured leisure-time activity. Whereas the scientists read the in search of information in the area of their research work than for enjoyment, they also prefer to read books, periodicals, etc. related to their subject so that they may be able to know about the latest research done on their subject. Today the said individuals believe that they will emerge from traditional to electronic world which will require little reading, less thinking and writing. But it is very far from the truth. The technology has enabled reading to be more timely and somewhat non-linear by using devices such as computers, internet and wireless shows without any hard copy. The faculties and scientist in the universities and research institutions requires careful reading habits and strong grasping skills so that they may be able to analyse, interpret and explain terms and process. In their research with adult readers, Kirsch and Guthrie (1984)[8] found that reading contributes significantly towards job justification, success, career development, and ability to respond to change.

1.4 Reading Attitude

Attitudes towards reading are defined as an individuals feeling about reading, causing learners to approach or avoid a reading situation (Alexander and Filler, 1976) [9]. Attitude and interest towards reading can be related in association with feeling and with learner's spirit to learn or in this situation it can be said that desire for reading arrives from the heart of an individual.

Positive reading attitudes lead to a reading experience, which also lead to higher academic performance. Some recent studies focused on identifying what influence the development of positive attitude towards reading of students (Bintz, 1993 [10]; Walberg and Tsai, 1985). [11]Walberg and Tsai (1985) [12] concluded that a positive attitude towards reading is one of the strongest correlates of reading achievement. Factors that contributed to this positive attitude among adolescents include:

- Believing that reading is important;
- Reading provides pleasure;
- Having a high self-concept as a reader;
- Having a verbally stimulating home environment where verbal interaction takes place regularly;
- Reading increases the vocabulary and phrases;

- It improves the way an individual thinks, no doubt his presentation of thought will also improve.

2. Developing Childhood Reading Habits

One of the most important suggestions for promotion of learning is to develop reading habits during childhood. Habits are more or less routine ways of acting. They are considered as second nature. Our happiness depends on developing good habits. Habits also motivate our behavior. However at the initial stage we have to learn them.

Habits of reading are and economic way of adjusting to routine requirements of daily reading. They help the students in mastering the content of learning. Hence efforts should be made to develop reading habits of students after due planning.

2.1 Steps for Developing Reading Habits

1. The student should start reading easy books first and difficult later on.
2. The student should start regular practice everyday for short period.
3. The student should rapidly read the content material as he will read a Rapid Reader. A slow reading will not serve the purpose.
4. Fix up the target of time and content and then start reading. Try to grasp the sense and do not stick to difficult words.
5. The student may mark out the new words and try to have a mental picture about them. He will gradually improve his vocabulary.
6. The eyes of the student should move more quickly on the lines of the content material. Eyes should not be allowed to go back after a sentence or a line is read.
7. The eyes should take the next line of the content as soon as the first has been read.
8. The subject-matter should be read silently without any movement of lips.
9. A record of progress should be maintained. This will enable the student to asses his achievements and plan for the future as well.

3. Reading Habit Promotion

Behaviour is any activity done by a living organism. Human behaviour includes mental activities, consciousness, muscular function, and the like. When the same type of behaviour is repeated several times by an individual, it becomes habit of that particular individual. An individual can know more about his own environment if he does efforts to enhance his/her knowledge through reading books, newspapers and magazines or any other means. As an individual is exposed to reading and has developed the love for books, he finds it easier to explore the wealth of human experience and knowledge. It is possible that an individual has an opportunity of getting in touch with books and find it that to form reading habit at the later years. It will reflect that he/she spent more time for reading books and also found that the speed of reading has been increased. This is a universally accepted fact that books are best friends. It is true, in case an individual has good reading habit.

Reading habit means behaviour that expresses the likeness of reading of individual. Reading and instruction can satisfy the need for information. People read information materials, which might help them, learn more about their occupations or about their hobbies. However, the number of those who know how to read but do not read enough is increasing.

The task of encouraging positive reading interest to foster a love for reading which will promote reading culture and society is not an easy one. However, role of family, libraries and librarians, mass media, private and government sectors can play a significant role towards motivation in the promotion of reading habits in any society.[13]

3.1 Role of Family

Parents play an important role as socializing agents. Parents who spend time reading to their children giving them the best possible start on the road to literacy. Parent to foster reading habits in the children read story book aloud, create a learning environment by setting up a mini reading corner, visit the library, book shops and provide book prize as gift.

3.2 Role of Libraries and Librarians

Libraries are a means to stimulate and develop the reading interest and librarians play important roles in promotion of reading habits:

- Librarian should develop among the readers a pleasant and positive attitude towards reading.
- Librarian is to serve the course of education formally & informally. He takes an opportunity to go out and tell the public what they have in their libraries and find out what they want to read, improve and keep improving the set-up of the library to encourage readers to stay and browse.
- Librarian should make the library attractive to public and schools.

3.3 Role of Print Media

Newspapers and magazines can help advertise reading projects, village libraries, seminar-training workshops, interviews of reading authorities/ writers/ teachers and organizations involved in the reading activities to promote reading, hence the help of these media personnel will be sought.

3.4 Communication Technology

Communication technology tools like radio, T.V., computer, Internet, wireless phone, etc. stimulate and develop reading habit. An individual gets new information from these communication technologies and for consolidation of his information so as he may involve in reading promotion activities.

3.5 Role of Government

Government may make arrangement of funds and also enhance the same so that the libraries are able to provide wide range of services to their users with the target to increase the reading habits.

3.6 Role of Professional Associations/ Bodies

The professional sectors or agencies play a great role to elevate the standard of library and services through activities, which aim to develop or to encourage activities of reading and writing.

4. Reading habit and its Influence in Moulding the Character of Human Being

Reading was earlier merely a mean of receiving an important message but, today reading research has defined the act of reading in itself as a multi-level mental process which contributes greatly to the development of the intellect. Great demands are made on the brain by the process of transforming graphic symbols into intellectual concepts; an infinite number of brain cells are activated during the storage process of reading.[14]

William (1984) indicated that reading influences the extent and accuracy of information as well as attitude, moral belief, judgement, and action of the reader. [15] The reading habit has one of the most powerful lasting influence in promotion of ones personal development in particular and social in general. Herman emphasized that status, age, group, sex and information needs of the library users influence reading habit. [16] It is lack of appreciation and understanding of good books and failure to derive pleasure from the habit of reading that affects the educational growth. The factors influencing the readings habits are: nature of a reader, needs of a reader, nature of information required, educational qualifications of a reader, cost of reading material, availability of reading material and way of interaction of users and information.

Bryan related the reading habits to the library and observed that the librarian's task is to find the right book for the right reader at the right time.[17] A librarian must know his books, he must know his readers and he must know what effect will be produced by bringing the two together.

Reading can help to remove the much talked about educational barriers, allowing more equal chances in education primarily by the promotion of language development and intellectual training, and reading enhances the possibility of adjustment to one's personal situation.[18]

5. Attributes/Character of Reading Habit

The term "reading habit" refers to the behaviour, which expresses the likeness of reading of individual types of reading, and tastes of reading (Sangkaeo, 1999)[19] It is a pattern with which an individual organizes his or her reading. Reading is important for everybody in order to cope up with new knowledge in a changing world that of the technological age.[20]

Reading has been described as the art of interpreting printed and written words (Devarajan, 1989).[21] It is regarded as one of the most effective processes of conscious learning. According to Panigrahi and Panda (1996), [22] postulate that "a creative and pragmatic education involves the habit of personal investigation requires self-study to be followed by self-thinking and analysis". Self study, i.e. reading at one's own accord requires a habit, which is technically known as reading habit.

Reading is recognized as an art capable of transforming man's life and his entire society.[23]Reading is a very important issue, which is not only about enjoyment but a necessity and the basic tool of education. Reading makes way for a better understanding of one's own experiences and it can be an exciting voyage to self discovery (Panigrahi and Panda, 1996[24]; Eyre, 2005 [25]).

Sometimes struggling readers will show high motivation and skills when faced with easy reading materials that are relevant and interesting to them. At other times, even the most proficient reader will act like a struggling reader when faced with difficult, complex or unfamiliar material. Some of the attributes of reading habits and a successful reader is given below.

- Before reading the reader is confidently approaching the reading tasks;
- Activates his background knowledge on the subject before reading;
- Connects background knowledge to new learning;
- Knows his purpose for reading, make predictions and choose appropriate strategies;
- Sets relevant, attainable goals.

During reading they focused their complete attention on reading; are able to read independently; possess an extensive vocabulary; use appropriate decoding or word attack skills; read fluently; monitor their comprehension and after reading it reflect on what they have read and add new information to their knowledge base; summarize major ideas and recall supporting details, make inferences, draw conclusions, paraphrase; seek additional information from outside sources; feel success is a result of effort; can independently gain information; express opinions about or pleasure in selections they have read.[26]

References

1. BAMBERGER (Richard). Promoting the reading habit. 1975. UNESCO, Paris, France. P 13.
2. SMITH (N) and ROBINSON (H). Reading instruction for today's children. 1980. Prentice Hall Inc, Englwood Cliff, NJ.
3. DEVRAJAN (G). Reading habits secondary school students in Trivandrum. *ALIS Bulletin*. 6; 1979; 93- 94.
4. REHMAN. Reading for pleasure: a report. 1959. Ministry of Education. P 1.
5. Op cit, 8.
6. SHARMA (A K) and SINGH (S P). Reading habits of faculty members in natural sciences: a case study of university of Delhi. *Annals of Library and Information Studies*. 52, 4; 2005; 119.
7. Ibid, P 119.
8. KIRSCH (I S) and GUTHRIE (J T). Adult reading practices for work and leisure. *Adult Education Quarterly*.. 34, 4; 1984; 213-32.
9. ALEXANDER (J E) and FILLER (R C). *Attitudes and Reading*. 1976. International Reading Association, Newark, DE, .
10. BINTZ (W). Resistant readers in secondary education: some insights and implications. *Journal of Reading*. 36, 8; 1993; 604-15.
11. WALBERG (H) and TSAI (S). Correlates of reading achievement and attitude: a national assessment study. *Journal of Educational Research*. 78,3; 1985; 159-67.
12. Ibid
13. SANGKAEO (S). Reading habit promotion in Asian libraries. 65th IFLA General Council and General Conference, Bangkok, Thailand, Aug.20-28th. 1999.
14. Op cit, 53. P 7.
15. GRAY (W S). Reading habits: a study. *Journal of Library History*. 19, 1; 1984; 39.

16. HERMAN (Leader). Libraries as artison of reading. *UNESCO Library Bulletin*. 26, 3; 1972; 118.
17. BRYAN (Allice). Psychology of the reader. *Library Journal*. 9, 1939; 187-189.
18. Op cit, 53. P 8.
19. Op cit, 65.
20. TELLA (Adenyinka) and AKANDE (Samson). Children reading habits and availability of books in Botswana primary schools: implications for achieving quality education. The Reading Matrix. 7, 2; 2007; 121.
21. DEVARAJAN (G). Reading interest of secondary school students. *In* Users approach to information in libraries. 1989. Ess Ess Pub, New Delhi. P 14.
22. PANIGRAHI (C) and PANDA (K C). Reading interests and information sources of school going children: a case study of two english medium schools of Rourkela, India. *Malaysia Journal of Library and Information Science* 1, 1; 1996; 57- 65.
23. Op cit, 72 p. 118
24. Op cit, 74.
25. EYRE (G). The development and practice of literacy: a voyage of discovery. 2005. Available at: http://www.iasl-slo.org/ifla2005-eyre.doc Accessed on 02/08/06.
26. SUTHERLAND (Jeff). High school reading task force report, June 1999. Available at http://www.madison.k12.wi.us/tnl/langarts/hsread.htm visited 22.10.08.
27. http://www.educationguideonline.net/developing-reading-habits/

28

The Impact of ICT & Digital Media on Reading Habit

Jyoti Verma
School of Telemedicine & Biomedical Informatics
SGPGIMS, Lucknow
Email: jyotiverma341@gmail.com
Vijeta Malyacharya
Dev Prayag Institute of Technology and Science, Allahabad
Email: vij0092@gmail.com

Abstract

The purpose of this is study to explore the impact of internet and digital media on reading habit. Traditional reading habits of library users change with the changing environment and working culture. People are now looking for an opportunity to read contents in electronic mode. It reduces the burden over the person to keep staying inside the library and now person can even read contents while travelling or while moving around the world. Traditional libraries and digital libraries complement each other to meet the needs of various kinds of readers. Younger generation students sometimes prefer reading through the internet or following up book reviews as such opportunities can be thought as effective means for fostering reading habits. Reading is influenced by many factors like environment, subject, background, age, etc. Libraries are not the exception to the influence of modern technologies which has converted the functional activities in all walks of life.

Keyword: Digital Media, Internet, Digital libraries, Library users, Attitudes towards reading.

Introduction

The library is the richest information treasure of human knowledge and cultural wealth, and should be able to meet effectively the challenges of the new technology revolution. However, the development of advanced technology, the widespread use of computers, optical disks and networks as well as various kinds of databases have provided good opportunities for the survival and development of traditional libraries of different types. The library, as a traditional information institution, is undergoing radical changes in its information service in the new era. With more and more digital materials available to the reader, the library no longer simply collects printed materials only. As for library users, their reading habits and ideas of utilizing reading materials have also changed. The increased use of computers has led to some modifications in the methods of academic work, such as undertaking research, writing articles, and producing teaching materials. The use of e-mail has become so popular that it is almost ubiquitous and researchers are finding it important that all such materials and sources should also exist in digital format. Both before and after developing a digital library, user studies are helpful in both improving the library system's performance and user satisfaction.

Habit is a psychological aspect and is developed during a course of time as a part of personality of an individual. Many people in the library world believe that digital libraries can simply be grafted onto traditional print-based libraries. The new formats are not seen as replacing the old ones, but rather as co-existing with them. Libraries will no longer be ranked according to the richness of their own collections - they will be evaluated in terms of the services they provide, based primarily on remote access to the resources of other information centers.

There is growing evidence, both from research projects and from library managers themselves, that a different organizational and managerial culture is required for successful digital libraries. Indeed, there are considerable human, cultural and organizational challenges in developing and maintaining digital libraries. The digital library clearly has a "culture" that is different from the traditional library service. One can only speculate on whether the "cultural shift" involved is a prerequisite of digital library development, or whether there is a "cultural lag" and changes result from the introduction of digital services. Reading from screens is fast as from paper if the image quality was sufficiently good. However people like to read article after taking printouts. Although changes have taken place, more deep-seated working habits do not seem to have been influenced. Hence, although our various projects have looked as quite different implementations, the results have completely surprised the librarians of developing libraries.

Many research studies on the libraries of developing countries have focused on how people use digital resources or on their feelings about digital and print resources in the library. These usage studies draw many conclusions about the behavior and preferences of library users, although sometimes the conclusions are contradictory or unclear. Digital information environment has dramatically changed the way that faculty and students access the information offered by academic libraries. Several digital information usage studies in recent years have focused on standardized usage counts. A fundamental outcome of the introduction of digital technology within libraries is the fascinating possibility of systematic organization and storage of information in large-scale databases. As conventional methods of collecting and presenting information become more expensive and time-consuming, placing digital information on networks is regarded as a major advance over the physical maintenance of some library services. Digital surveys are neither given a prominent place in the literature nor in projects exploring the measurement of digital networks, because the point of the projects is to collect data on the use and value of digital resources. There are many ways to assess the effectiveness of library services. However, based on the concept of a "user-centered" approach, library use and user satisfaction are good methods to study and diagnose various problems in libraries and help managers with their decision-making. The digital environment is very different from the print-oriented culture: "it has always been recognized that some shifts in culture, both for libraries and other stakeholders in information, were crucial if digital libraries were to make a real difference". Although these new developments in information technology are challenging and on some days even overwhelming, the real challenges that we face are not technical in nature. Instead, it is the need to imagine and implement change that will translate traditional values into the networked and electronic information future

I love to lose myself in other men's minds. When I am not walking, I am reading. I cannot sit and think. Books think for me - Charles Lamb. If the first button of a man's coat is wrongly buttoned all the rest are certain to be crooked, remarked - Giordano Bruno. Reading can definitely be taken as the first button in the garment education. It is not the sole object of school, but it is almost impossible to think of education without thinking about what happens and what is implied when a human being tries to get meaning out of the written or printed symbols.7 Reading today is the most versatile of habits, encompassing all of the above. It is just as successful when it involves fonts dancing across a computer screen as it is with handset type on the brittle pages of a 300-year-old book. We still have writing in an age of word processing; we still have reading in an age of video. That will continue, but the nature of reading will change as it has changed all along. Fears that the Internet and other technologies will cause the decline and fall of print media are probably not warranted. Although people aren't reading as many books as they used to, their thirst for information seems limitless. Publishers who enhance the reading experience with electronic media may find the next generation of customers as literature lovers as any they have ever seen.

Discussion

Reading Habits and their Influence on Digital Libraries

The aim of developing digital libraries is to enable readers to make better use of library services. Only in this way can digital libraries show their superiority, and this goal was active in the germinal stages of the services program, but many digital libraries do fail to achieve their objectives. In developing countries, the development of the digital library is confronted with a lot of obstacles. There are a number of main factors restricting the development of digital libraries in such countries. One is that many libraries lack funds to buy digital equipment and digital books. Another is the reading habits of library users. Still another is inadequate computer retrieval skills and knowledge - which is also closely related with reading habits. In short, in the libraries of developing countries, readers' computer skills and reading habits have handicapped the development of digital libraries, and the advantages occasioned by the introduction of digital libraries have been unable to be realized.

Impact of Internet on Reading Habit

The internet has changed the world in an incalculable number of ways. It has changed the way that people communicate, the way that business is done, and the way that information is shared and received. The internet has also had a great effect on people's reading habits, as it has changed the way that people expect to receive both information and entertainment. The internet is a great method for sharing and receiving large amounts of information very quickly. Nearly everyone who uses the internet has learned to process information quickly and to expect that information in a concise, easy to digest format. As the internet becomes the main platform from which many people get their information, they have come to expect that even information that is not on the internet be presented in this manner. The impact of ICT on learning is currently in relation to use of digital media, primarily computers and internet to facilitate teaching and learning. ICTs are the technologies used in conveying, manipulation and storage of data by electronic means, they provide an array of powerful tools that may help in transforming the present isolated teacher-centered and text-bound classrooms into rich, student-focused, interactive knowledge environments. To meet these challenges, learning institutions must embrace the new technologies and appropriate ICT tools for learning.

Reading habits, then, have shifted as those who write for publications such as newspapers and magazines have changed some of their formatting to compete with this new, concise manner of writing. People no longer read long, informational articles and essays, but may simply skim through to find the pertinent information or the information that is most interesting to them. The shift in reading habits that has been caused by the internet does not only affect non-fiction and factual writing, however. As people become more accustomed to reading only short blurbs, even in instant messages or one-line emails, their overall attention span for words is changing. This means that even their attention span for novels and longer literary pursuits is waning.

The internet is a wonderful resource for many things, and it has allowed people all over the world to become more connected to each other. However, with its rapid speed, mentality of instant gratification, and its unique format, the internet has had a detrimental effect on the reading habits of an entire generation. The generation that grew up with the internet has an attention span that is conditioned to eschew any work of writing that requires a close, analytical read, or a long investment of time. The effect of the internet on reading habits cannot be ignored as the internet itself becomes more accessible to more people each day.

Reading habits have been changed by the Internet. People are not buying as many newspapers or magazines anymore. Newspaper readership is way down. Magazines and newspapers are going out of business. All because people have turned to one source to get their thirst quenched for knowledge, the Internet.

Traditional Reading Habit

By "traditional reading habit" is meant the reading of books published in the form of paper only. Typical of this reading habit are mostly elderly people, though some are young people. They stick to their old habits although the use of computers for reading has been popular for quite some years - in other words their traditional reading habit has not changed in any way since the arrival of the digital age. Like these older readers, some young people have the same reading habit. During the last few years, they did not have access to computers and so they studied through printed books or notes.

Computers have now become popular, but such young readers are still accustomed to reading from paper instead of on screen, especially for the purpose of work, and thus printed publications are still essential to them for reading purposes. Digital libraries may have lots of resources, but such traditional readers find them difficult to use.

Many elderly people think that reading is an important means to obtain information and that it is a vital way to develop the national culture. Although the library has provided modernized digital resources for many years, the percentage using the digital library is far less than 50 per cent and there are still over 25 per cent of readers who, because of their reading habits, always use physical resources. Similarly, the invention of paper and printing technology in ancient China improved ways of reading and reading ability tremendously, speeding up the progress of mankind's literate culture. And the main kinds of traditional publications, such as newspapers, journals and books have been developing with the increasing need to read. In developing countries, most people have long been used to paper reading. Choice of printed materials over digital materials is probably because they feel uncomfortable and slow in thinking facing the screen. When digital libraries first appeared, their users had already been using computers in their work and leisure for a long time and they readily accepted digital publications.

Digital Media Vs Reading Habits

In this fast moving world, technology has brought about immense changes in a man's life. With each change is a host of advantages and disadvantages. In this electronic age, reading has inevitably taken a back seat to watching television and gleaning information from the world wide web. People learn far more readily from electronic media than they do from print. One primary reason for the electronic media to replace the reading habit of individuals is that it tends to be an attractive way of representing information.

Children can learn difficult concepts better when such concepts are demonstrated to them. But can a teacher or a book illustrate them in way it is easily understandable?. Maybe some simple experiments related to physics or biology can be explained by demonstrations but not all. For example, a graphical presentation through the computer can show how a neutron can trigger a nuclear fission reaction. The advantage of this kind of method is that the concept is easily remembered by every child and for a longer period of time.

Another reason is that people can have access to an extensive ken on wide variety of topics from a single point or location. The books may contain information but they may not be available at a single library that is nearest to a person. Take the case of the World Wide Web, it provides access to millions of pages of information on any topic you desire or almost everything you want to know. All a person has to do is get access to a computer and an internet connection.

One other important reason as to why the electronic media is taking over the print media is that it proves to be the fastest means for providing information and news about the events happening around the world. The round the clock news channels provide news on the latest events even with minute by minute updates.

Thus Today's world thereby provides easiest and fastest access to knowledge overcoming time and distance constraints through the electronic media. The electronic media in the form of internet, television, etc. prove to be not only the easiest means of access to information but also provides access to immense amount of knowledge.

Lack of Computer Retrieving Skills and Knowledge

Older readers are used to reading characters and many of them are not familiar with computers and networks. Icons are essentially pictures of things used to make the operation of computers more visually oriented and easier to understand for the novice. But the color and glare of the screen make the eyes of many tired easily - few people, even in developed countries, like to read a lengthy book in front of the computer. Reading for a long time on screen soon becomes tiring, and this is one reason why readers - both young as well as old - give up reading digital sources on screen.

Digital reading is so closely related with reading habit and its influence on digital libraries is so great that a discussion seems desirable. In developing libraries, digital library products are relatively scanty. They are not psychologically prepared to give up the traditional reading mode and shift to the new mode of reading digital materials. The number of business deals and e-commerce benefits that are available through the net simply cannot be accessed by poorer countries. This makes the reading psychology of readers of the library in a kind of dynamic course of developing constantly. Readers who have accepted digital publications as a new form for reading are culturally more dynamic and find it easier to get acquainted with higher cultural dynamics and grasp the characteristics of the digital library and the techniques of digital library use. So, compared with printed document, the digital audience's colony is still very young, and has had a good education. Only a relatively small number of people are well educated and have read many books, but still do not have the digital reading habit.

It should be taken into account that users of university libraries are considerably well-acquainted with techniques of computer use. In public libraries, on the other hand, readers are generally less well educated and many are at a loss in front of a computer screen. Coupled with their lack of education, most of them have never received any computer knowledge and training. Unfamiliarity with computers and networks and lack of ability are the main factors. Another factor is simply that many did not know what the library actually buys, while some older teachers even think that they are too old to learn how to use digital information resources. When they need such digital sources, they have their graduate students search for them. The influence of age is a major factor in reading habits. It is one variable that correlates with comfort with computers and use of digital resources. Younger generations have grown up with computers. Digital resources are more frequently used by younger readers than older ones. It is believed that digital resources decrease the quality and rigor of research literature searches.4 The older the respondent, the more likely they were to report that unfriendly interfaces waste users' time, and older scholars report more trouble with interfaces. Older readers are less likely to think that digital resource usage increases scholarly productivity, but they are more willing to pay for copies from traditional books or journals.

Solving the Problem of Digital Libraries in Developing Countries

Digital libraries are based on varying numbers of users, and consequently do not provide a basis for analyzing any trends. The attributes of digital resources offered by a national digital library were studied qualitatively from the web pages of the service in relation to the use of the service. When librarians in developing countries discuss the digitization of the library, they discuss more about the question of technology. They seem to think that if the library makes a website into a digital document, then the library will become modernized and readers of the library will become network readers too. Readers may change overnight from reading printed documents to reading the digital documents offered to them. They are glad to enjoy the modern service that the library offered. In fact, this neglects an important problem that the networked library develops on the basis of traditional library when a lot of the service methods of the traditional library are also extended. If thousands of printed documents lose their value, then the library is unable to offer books to the reader to read or to use, and this will be a tremendous waste.

Effective citizen action is possible only when citizens know how to gain access to information of all kinds and have the skills to become responsible, informed participants in democracies. In the digital design of the modern library, no matter what the representation of the functions, utilization of the resources, expansion of readers' space, selection of the library's location, etc., must be taken into consideration. In the digital age, the emphasis should be on making technology work for all, on delivering core services through networks, on integrating technologies and maintaining holistic computer environments, and on collaborating across administrative lines. They seem to be stressing the importance of delivering digital information to all those who require it by exploiting information and communications technology, and by breaking down unhelpful departmental barriers.

Library staffs are also important for library managers to consider the ways in which they can actively lead and facilitate the development of successful digital libraries, both in terms of organizational structures and management style, rather than simply concentrating on the effects of digital services on service staff. Librarians in developing countries must remember that for a very long time people in their countries have been used to obtaining knowledge and information in printed form, such as newspapers and periodicals. Especially for people older than 50, there is a kind of special preference for printed documents and a reliance on culture. Books do not merely bring knowledge and enjoyment to readers from just their content and appearance, but also the quality of the material brings different impressions to readers. Although digital documents have fully reflected the advantages of networked communications and resource sharing, their use requires equipment, such as computers and telecommunications, which books do not, and so a programmed pattern has long been a factor in reading behavior.

Libraries in developing countries must also pay close attention to their environmental changes now. In order to meet the new changes of the information environment, the library community must make greater efforts do more work to fulfill the mission and aim of the digital library again and redesign the work flow of the library and institutional framework, and carry on research into the service mode of readers with traditional reading habits in the digital environment of the library. The coexisting relation and integration tendency of printed and network periodicals should also be discussed. What the libraries of developing countries must also do is to correct mistaken ideas about digital libraries and explore actively and to have the courage to bring forth new ideas. Libraries should seize the opportunity to look for the best growing point suitable for themselves, gain support from digital technology, expand their own service range and projects, improve service efficiency and quality, and lay the foundation for the realization of a digital library, rather than wait for the coming of digitization. Digital libraries must provide a better learning and reading environment for readers with traditional reading habits. There is much work to do when libraries realize that many differences exist between information resources on the internet and those in traditional libraries. In order to satisfy users' needs and to achieve the functions of education in the era of information networks, libraries have to explore the influences of digital resources on readers and survey the content and methods of user education in internet resources.

Libraries in developing countries must study how to establish such a system using library automation systems, how to improve the quality of purchasing, how to improve the system of borrowing, and how to improve and read issues such as environment. Digital librarians should develop new service values in addition to the "timeless" library service values of equity of access, personal service and meeting all users' needs. In the digital age, the emphasis should be on making technology work for all, on delivering core services through networks, on integrating technologies and maintaining holistic computer environments, and on collaborating across administrative lines. Emphasis should also be placed on: proposing a framework for a personalized and group information environment based on library automation systems; studying how to track user interests dynamically and apply the research results to a personalized digital service; and building user-oriented construction of organizational communication in libraries by taking system approaches and implementing a prototype system, making for a personalized reading environment. Librarians are also developing new roles in the digital age as advisers and navigators through the maze of information that is available digitally. A full understanding of human, cultural and organizational factors will be helpful to library managers in grasping the nettle and developing effective, high-quality digital information services.

Conclusion

- Undoubtedly, digitization can widen the service function of libraries, improve their service level, and increase their social reputation. This is the direction of development in the modernization of libraries. The present authors do not object to digitization, but is opposed to the blind imitation of digitization. Digital construction should develop according to the actual situation of, and on the basis of, the traditional library.
- It is not possible to purchase all books or go through books in short period hence. If your student get the opportunity of finding the desired books, they may read more. They sometimes prefer reading through the internet or following up book reviews. Such opportunities can be thought as effective means for fostering reading habits.
- Documents that the library has collected have mainly been various kinds of printed materials. Printed documents are an advantage of the library for traditional users because digital documents cannot totally replace them. It is also unnecessary to digitize all the collected documents of a traditional library. Moreover, in developing countries, the traditional service of the library should be strengthened after entering the mixed digital and traditional phase.
- The basic function of the library is to keep human cultural heritage, launch social education, transmit scientific and technological information, and develop intelligence resources.

- One advantage of digitization lies in its search function, as it is convenient, easy to carry out and to read, and books and magazines are still the reader's first selection. Thinking that digital documents are superior to traditional printed documents assumes that readers go to libraries only in order to search documents, or that they are happy to read digital documents, It is wrong to assume that digital documents are superior to traditional printed documents and that readers go to the library only to search documents or only to read digital documents.
- The modification of the culture of a group or an individual can result from contact with a different culture, reading habits, computer skills and knowledge, retrieval skills, etc., but readers in the developing countries are different from those in the developed countries. So the librarians in the developing countries should pay more attention to a library's deposits of printed books and periodicals over a longer period.
- Libraries in the developing countries should also devote their efforts to doing well in all service work (as they have done in traditional libraries).
- When developing digital libraries in the actual conditions of their own country, as well as to meeting the needs of readers with traditional reading habits.
- In conducting user training, librarians can easily locate those system features that are unfamiliar to users. Librarians are also developing new roles in the digital age as advisers and navigators through the maze of information that is available digitally.
- A full understanding of human, cultural and organizational factors will be helpful to library managers in grasping the nettle and developing effective, high-quality digital information services.
- Digital libraries need digital readers who possess adequate skills, knowledge and experience, and these may be very different from those required of the traditional reader.

- The pattern of reading, as is known from the past, may not be the same as reading as it is known today or in the future. Research in reading habits needs to be further updated by including current advancement in ICT, where the technology has enabled reading to be more timely and somewhat non-linear by using devices such as computers, PDAs and wireless phones without the presence of any printed document.

References

1. Davis, C. (1997), "Organizational influences on the university electronic library", Information Processing and Management, Vol. 33(3); pp. 377-92.
2. Ferguson, C.D. and Bunge, C.A. (1997), "The shape of services to come: values-based versus reference service for the largely digital library", College & Research Libraries, Vol. 58(3); pp. 252-65.
3. Franklin, B. and Plum, T. (2004), "Library usage patterns in the electronic information environment", Information Research, Vol. 9(4) available: <http://informationr.net/ir/ 9-4/paper187.html>Accessed : November 22, 2010.
4. Gould, J.D., Alfaro, L., Finn, R., Haupt, B. and Minuto, A. (1987), "Reading from CRT displays can be as fast as reading from paper", Human Factors, Vol. 29(5); pp. 197-9.
5. Ahuja K.K, Mishra Bibhash, Goyal Harish (September 2010) "Reading habits in digital environment." International Research Journal; vol 1(12); pp. 28-31 available<http://www.ssmrae.com/admin/images/52f5c69faa1c20af937604012b7ded3c.pdf> accessed: October 12, 2011.
6. Tah Babila Mbah (October, 2010) "The impact of ICT on students' study habits. Case Study: University of Buea, Cameroon." Journal of Science and Technology Education Research Vol. 1(5); pp. 107 - 110, Available http://www.academicjournals.org/JSTER Accessed: October 12, 2011.
7. Available <http://www.urch.com/forums/gre-analysis-issue/47225-electronic-media-vs-reading-habits.html> Accessed: October 13, 2011.

29

A Study of Students Behaviour Towards Use of E-Resources at the College of Engineering & Technology, Bhubaneswar

Dr. Kamal Lochan Jena
Librarian
College of Engineering & Technology, Bhubaneswar - 751 003
E-mail: kljena@rediffmail.com

Abstract

The purpose of the paper is to determine the extent to which the students of College of Engineering & Technology, Bhubaneswar are aware and make use of e-resources in their academic career and to highlight the problems faced by them in accessing e-resources, their views on usefulness of e-resources compared to that of print resources and place from where they prefer to access information. The study finds that students prefer e-resources against print resources because of their various positive features which make them convenient to get their educational needs.

Key words: E-resources, e-journals, e-books, search engines, ICT, CET

Introduction

Today's world is changing very fast. There was the day when the dissemination of information was like the speed of tortoise, but with the advent of Information Communication Technology (ICT), the desired information is now accessed very fast even within a single click. Actually what we are accessing so speedily are the electronic resources available in internet. College of Engineering & Technology (CET), Bhubaneswar was established in the year 1981 as a premier government engineering college under Orissa University of Agriculture & Technology, Bhubaneswar. In the year 2002, it became a constituent college of the newly established Biju Patnaik University of Technology, Odisha. Now it has achieved the top position among all the engineering colleges under Biju Patnaik University of Technology, Odisha. Over the last three decades, the college has carved a unique identity for itself in the arena of engineering education in the state as well as in the country and has been consistent in its endeavour for imparting teaching and training to the managerial aspirants and working professionals in techno-managerial disciplines with a strong emphasis on value-based engineering education. Besides the B Tech level courses, it imparts education in Architecture (B Arch & M Arch), Master in Computer Application (MCA) and M Tech courses. Being a leading engineering college, it is now trying to get the autonomous status so that it may further improve in imparting the engineering education.

Facilities Available at CET

With regard to the infrastructural facilities available at CET, Bhubaneswar, it has a very good library with rich collection of academic books, reference manuals, journals, periodicals, etc., and is regularly replenished. It caters to the entire demand of the students, consultants, faculties, research scholars and members of the CET Professional Association. The e-resources facilities have been provided within the Library reading hall, computer laboratory and in the personal computers of each faculty within the campus. The leased line internet facility is available and it is kept open for the students even beyond the academic hours to encourage them in acquiring advanced skills and knowledge in IT through the internet. Now steps have been taken to provide the internet facilities at the hostels for students use. The lab is properly equipped with computer facilities to carry out research & consultancy assignments. In addition, the entire college campus has radio linked internet broadband connectivity through a Wi-Fi network. This is what the author, being an employee of the college, has experienced when he conducted the survey.

Literature Review

Review of literature acts as a platform to any kind of study, thus it plays a vital role in furtherance of research. In the context of students' use of e-resources, various scholars have studied different institutions and produced literature related to use of e-resources in the respective institutes. In this direction, Atilgan and Bayram (2006) reported the results of a survey on the use of e-databases at Ankara University. Zainab *et al.* (2007) examined the users and their use of electronic journals published in a hosting system called EJUM (Electronic Journal of the University of Malaya), their perceived satisfaction with e-journals, and the preferred features in electronic journals in general, and the problems they face when using them. The findings reveal that e-journals are used for searching new information, reading full-text articles, reading abstracts and browsing tables of contents. Users are led to EJUM by chance while browsing the internet (41.8 per cent), when searching Google, through citations obtained from conference papers, from articles or from citations in databases. Respondents prefer keywords (28.9 per cent) and titles (24.3 per cent) for searching databases. Madhusudan (2010) conducted a study on the use of electronic resources by research scholars of Kurukhetra University and found that electronic resources have become the vital part of the information needs of the research scholars. He also found that e-resources can be a better substitute to conventional resources, if the access is fast and adequate computer terminals are provided for fast access to e-resources. Ali (2010) in his findings revealed that more than 60 percent of users in the Central Science Library are using e-Journals weekly for the purpose of research. Printed journals are consulted by majority of the users as compared to e-journals. Keyword is the most popular search method for searching e-journals among research scholars, whereas the date of publication carries the least percentage among all the options. However, slow downloading of PDF files is a major problem that discourages users to use e-journals. Swain (2010), in his empirical study on the use of electronic resources among the students of business schools in Odisha found that the students community has yet to explore the potential benefits of various forms of electronic resources that could help their scholastic needs. Shukla and Mishra (2011) conducted a study on the use of e-resources by the research scholars of Institute of Technology, BHU and found that low internet connectivity is the major hindrance in accessing electronic information. However, this study represents the case of CET which has been unexplored.

Objectives and Methodology

The objectives of the study are:

- To find out the frequency of use of e-resources by the student users of CET;
- To find out the purpose of use of e-resources by the students of CET;
- To find out the basic search strategy for accessing e-resources;
- To find out the infrastructural problems in using e-resources;
- To identify the place from where the users of CET access e-resources.

The survey was conducted by means of a structured questionnaire circulated among 200 students from different disciplines of the College of Engineering & Technology, Bhubaneswar and out of these 170 students have responded. Hence the response received was 85 per cent. A random sample method was used for the selection of respondents and possible personal interaction was made with them during the survey.

Data Analysis and Interpretation

The gathered data were scrutinised and tabulated for subsequent analysis. The results are presented in the succeeding sections:

Knowledge about E-Resources

Students were asked to give their views regarding their consultation of e-resources at CET and whether they are aware of the existing electronic resources. With respect to this question, 63.53 per cent of respondents answered affirmatively, which is a positive trend. As the students normally concentrate on reading related to their curriculum, the response regarding the awareness about the e-resources is good.

Table 1: Knowledge about E-Resources

Question	Respondents	Percentage
Consulting E-Resources	108	63.53
Not consulting	62	36.47

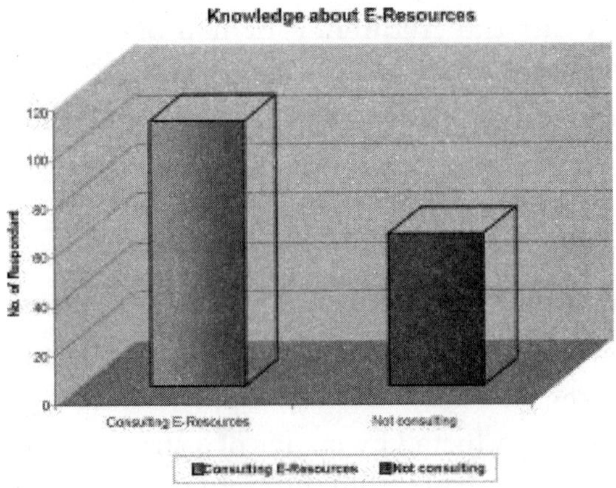

Fig-1: Knowledge about E-Resources

Frequency of Use of E-resources

Normally the students focus their studies on text-books and rarely use the journal sources for their curriculum needs. As the majority of students are under graduates and have the project works in their final year of study, they are using less electonic resources. However, the post-graduate M Tech students use the e-rsources more than the undergraduate students. With regards to the frequency of use of e-resources, it is found that 58.33 per cent of the students use e-resources *occassionally*, 25.93 per cent use *monthly*, 12.96 per cent use *weekly*, whereas only 02.77 per cent of students use it daily.

Table 2: Frequency of Use of E-Resources

Frequency of Use	Respondents (n=108)	Percentage
Daily	03	02.77
Weekly	14	12.96
Monthly	28	25.93
Occasionally	63	58.33

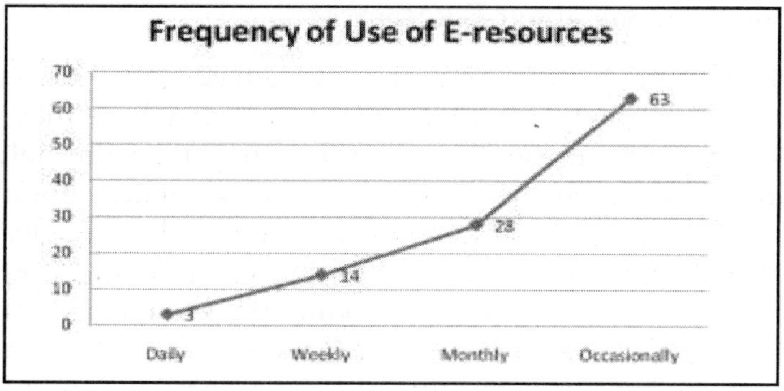

Fig-2: Frequency of E-Resources Usage

Preference of Electronic Resources over Printed Resources

Now-a-days, both types of sources are available in each and every educational institution. In many institutions, both the e-resources and print resources are subscribed. Similar is the case of CET where both the sources are available. But as a matter of research the question was asked about the preference of use in between the print sources and e-resources. While answering the query regarding the preference between the different formats of resources, 60.19 per cent prefer electronic resources, 28.70 per cent prefer both the sources, whereas only 11.11 per cent of the users prefer print format.

Table 3 : Preference of Electronic Resources over Print Resources

Resource Type	Respondents (n=108)	Percentage
Electronic	65	60.19
Print	12	11.11
Both Equally	31	28.70

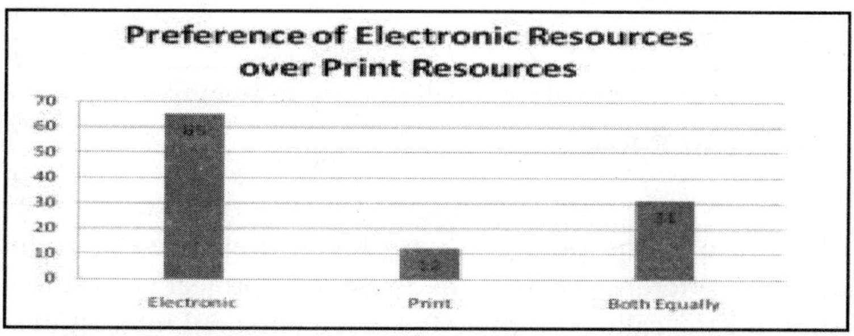

Fig-3: Preference of Electronic Resources over Print Resources

Sources of Knowing about E-Resources

Since the students are new researchers/ surveyors, they have the least knowledge about different resources from where they would get their required information. For this they take the helps and suggestions of different persons like teachers, friends, library staff and the help of internet (i.e different search engines like google, yahoo, alta vista, etc.). Out of the different introducers / advisors, the *teachers & friends are* in majority of cases as introducer of e-resources to students i.e. 73.15 % while 12.03 % students come to know about the e-resources from library staff, 10.19 % through search engines and only 04.63 % from other sources.

Table 4: Sources of Information about E-Resources

Source of Introducing E-Resources	Respondents (n=108)	Percentage
Teachers & Friends	79	73.15
Library Staff	13	12.03
Search Engine	11	10.19
Others	5	04.63

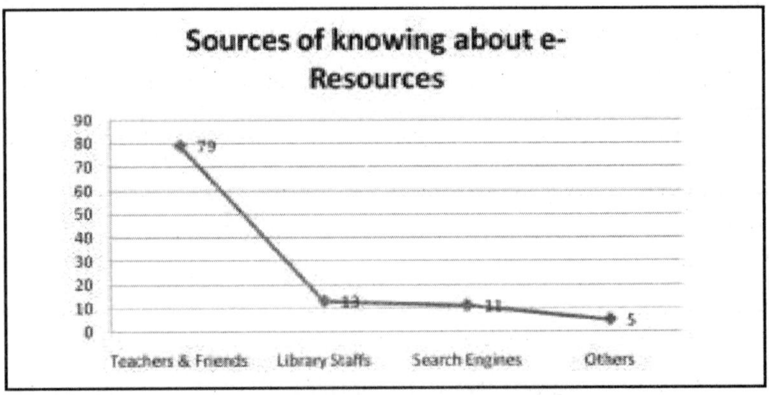

Fig-4: Sources of Information about E-Resources

Purpose of Use of E-Resources

Knowledge is multifaceted and is used for different purposes. Since the students are at the post-graduate level, they use the collected information in different purposes like research, project works, to keep information for the sake of knowledge, have personal interest in some areas, etc. The research question was designed to know about the areas of interest as described in the Table 5. Out of the three different aspects, 82.41 % of students responded to the questionnaire that they use e-resources for their project work, 04.63 % to keep their knowledge up-to-date and 12.96 % for finding relevant information in the area of their personal interest.

Table-5: Purpose of use of E-Resources

Purpose	Respondents (n=108)	Percentage
For Project Works	89	82.41
For Keeping Up to date Information	5	04.63
For Finding relevant Information in the Area of Interest	14	12.96

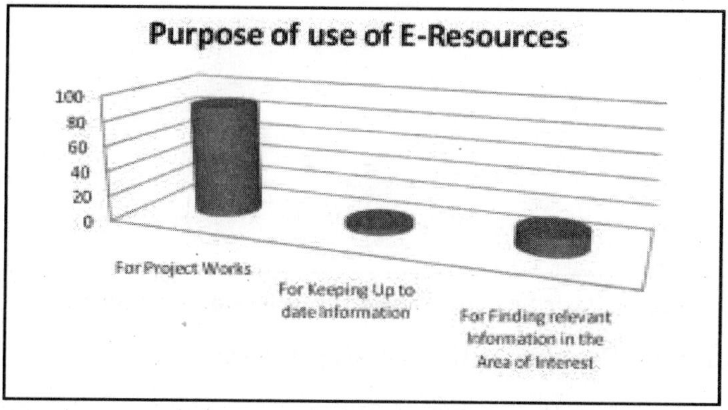

Fig-5: Purpose of use of E-Resources

Basic Search Strategy for Accessing E-Resources

Initially the students have no idea about the basic sources i.e. where from they will get their required information/data. The various aspects or facets to know the available source, are the keyword search, author search, subject search, title search ,etc. In the majority of cases, students do the search by keywords as we can clearly see from Table 6 and Figure 6 that 58.33 per cent of students prefer keyword as their search strategy, 13.89 per cent to subject, 03.70 per cent to author, nil to date of publication, 13.89 per cent to title of the journal, 08.33 per cent to title of article and only 01.85 per cent by abstracts.

Table- 6: Basic Search Strategy for Accessing E-Resources

Search Methods	Respondents (n=108)	Percentage
Author	4	03.70
Keywords	63	58.33
Subject	15	13.89
Date of Publication	0	00.00
Title of the Journal	15	13.89
Title of Article	9	08.33
Abstracts	2	01.85

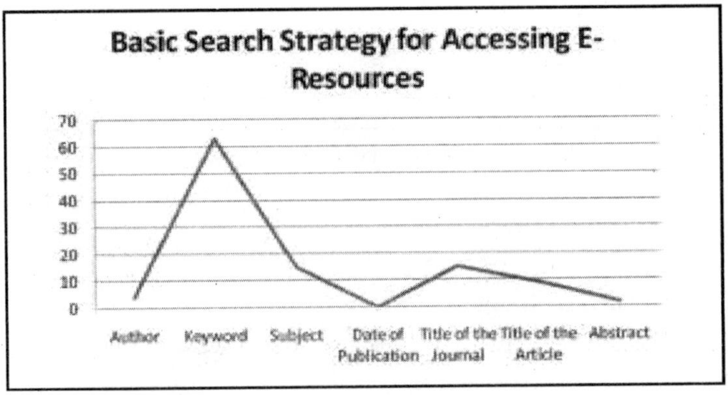

Fig.- 6: Basic Search Strategy for Accessing E-Resources

Infrastructural Problems in Accessing E-Resources

Though internet is the major provider of e-resources, its speed is a hurdle in providing good services. In India specifically in Odisha, the speed of internet is a major aspect of dissatisfaction among the internet users. Like this majority of students of College of Engineering & Technology, Bhubaneswar, 39.81 %, treat the insufficiency of work stations as the major infrastructural problem in accessing e-resources, whereas 04.63 % of them responded that they are not facing any infrastructural problem. Similarly, 15.74 % treat low internet connectivity, 4.63 % to compatibility of systems, 35.19 % to availability of internet facility beyond College hours as infrastructural problem in accessing e-resources.

Table-7: Infrastructural Problems in Accessing E-Resources

Problems	Respondents (n=108)	Percentage
Low Internet Connectivity	17	15.74
Compatibility of Systems	5	4.63
Infrastructural problem	43	39.81
Availability of Internet beyond College hour	38	35.19
None	5	04.63

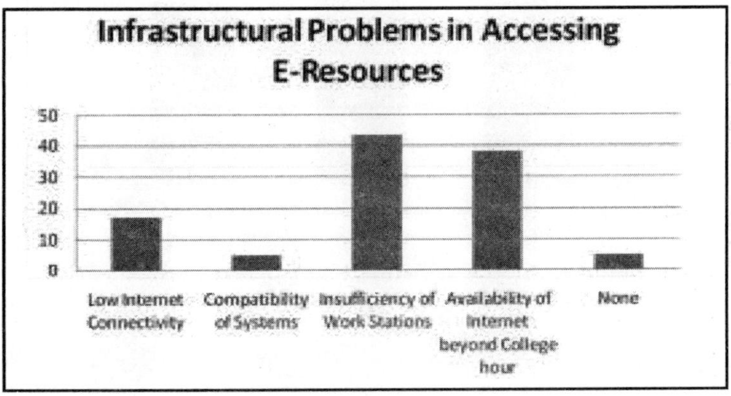

Fig-7: Infrastructural Problems in Accessing E-Resources

Place of E-Information Access

In an educational institution, the e-services is offered either in the computer laboratory or in the library premises in the name of e-library. Besides this if the area is covered by WI-FI network then anybody can access the internet at their convenience. In this regard Table 8 and Figure 8 show that 36.11 % of respondents access e-resources from the Library, 35.19 % from WI-FI networks of the campus, and 28.70 % from the Computer Centre. A majority of the students prefer to access e-resource from the Library as the related facilities are available there, followed by WI-FI network since many of the students have their own laptop.

Table-8: Place of E-Information Access

Place	Respondents (n=108)	Percentage
Library	39	36.11
WIFI Network	38	35.19
Computer Centre	31	28.70

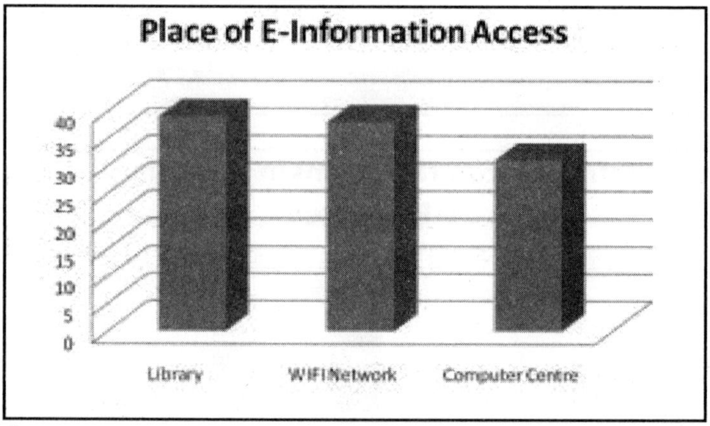

Fig-8: Place of E-Information Access

Findings

Findings of the study can be summarised as under:

- Majority of the students of CET are aware of e-resources.
- Only 02.77 % of them use e-resources daily, which is a poor response.
- 60.19 % of students prefer electronic format while 28.70 % prefer both print and electronic formats.
- In majority of the cases, it was the teachers and friends who introduced the e-resources to the students.
- In 82.41 % of cases students use e-resources for their project work.
- Insufficiency of Work Stations is the major obstacle while accessing e-resources.
- Majority of students prefer the Library and WI-FI network for accessing e-resources.

Conclusion

There are is the days of internet and e-resources. Everybody is using internet and e-information in their day-to-day life. In near future, the internet and the e-resources will be the bread and butter for every educated person for their academic activity. In this way now the use of e-resources are used by the students for the all round development of their scholastic needs. They have got the right information at right time conveniently, effortlessly and easily. However, they sometimes feel disgusted to use e-resources because of poor internet connectivity at the time of urgent needs. So the utmost care should be taken by the heads and directors of institutions to upgrade the e-information service provision.

References

1. Ali, P M, and Naushad, F (2010), "Use of e-journals among research scholars at Central Science Library, University of Delhi", Vol.30 No.1, *Collection Building*, pp. 53-60.
2. Atilgan, D., Bayram, O.G. (2006), "An evaluation of faculty use of the digital library at Ankara University, Turkey", *Journal of Academic Librarianship*, Vol. 32 pp.86-93.
3. Madhusudan, M. (2010), "Use of electronic resources by research scholars of Kurukshetra University", *The Electronic Library*, Vol. 28 No.4, pp. 492-506.
4. Sukla, P. and Mishra, R. (2011), "Use of e-resources by research scholars of Institute of Technology, Banaras Hindu University, India", *Reseachers World*, Vol.2 No.2.
5. Swain, D. K. (2010), "Students keenness on use of e-resources", *The Electronic Library*, Vol.28 No.4, pp. 580-91.
6. Zainab, A.N., Huzaimah, A.R., Ang, T.F. (2007), "Using journal use study feedback to improve accessibility", *The Electronic Library*, Vol. 25 No.5, pp.558-74.

30

Information Seeking Behaviour of Users' in Central State Library, Chandigarh
A Study

Dr. Sanjeev Sharma
Assistant Professor, Kurukshetra University, Kurukshetra
E-mail: sanju_sharma2004@rediffmail.com
Mrs. Suman Lata
Central State Library Chandigarh (U.T.)

Abstract

Information seeking behaviour is an individuals' conscious effort to acquire knowledge for the purpose of satisfying his information needs. Information seeking behaviour involves personal reasons for seeking information, the kind of information which are being sought, and the ways and sources with which needed information is being sought. Today as the information is growing rapidly; the information needs of the users are becoming more and more diverse and complex day by day. The present paper explores the information seeking behaviour of the users in the Central State Library, Chandigarh. The data was collected through the structured questionnaire. Findings of the study show that most of the users (46.94%) seek information for academic/ professional purpose and some users (18.37%) for general awareness. Most of the users (40.82%) prefer to use books as a source of information. A good percentage of users i.e. 55.10% search information sources through OPAC. Google search engine is most preferred by the 73.17% of users. A large majority of users reported that the unavailability of required reading material and slow speed of computers are the factors that hinder their information seeking behaviour. Some recommendations were also made for the improvement of users' information seeking behaviour and use of information resources.

1. Introduction

User is an important component in any library and information system. The main objective of a library is to satisfy the information needs of the users and to provide right information to the right user at the right time. To achieve this objective, it is must for a library to understand the library users, how they interact with the information system, their purpose and pattern of search, what methods do they use for searching information and their pertinent information requirements. In a library system, users' study plays an important role in planning, designing and introducing new information services as well as to assess the quality and utility of the existing services.

Information seeking behaviour is an individual's conscious effort to acquire knowledge for the purpose of satisfying his information needs. Information seeking behaviour involves personal reasons for seeking information, the kind of information which are being sought, and the ways and sources with which needed information is being sought (Jatana,2008).

Today, as the information is growing rapidly, the information needs of the users are becoming more and more diverse and complex day by day requiring an access to the widest possible range of literature on multifarious subject fields. Under these circumstances, the public libraries in particular, of which the state central libraries form an integral part, play the role of an acquirer, processor, preserver and disseminator of knowledge. The present study explores the information seeking behaviour of the users in the Central State Library, Chandigarh.

The Central State Library is a well known public library of the city beautiful and it is named as 'Tirlok Singh Central State Library'. The Library was established in 1955, under the scheme of Govt. of India, promotion of art and culture. Since its inception, it is playing an important role in promoting library culture and inculcating good reading habits among the city residents.

The Library is organized in various sections: acquisition section, reference section, circulation section, children section, periodical section, newspaper section, binding section, administrative section and rare book section. The Library has a rich collection of 2,68,000 books, 1325 CD-ROMs, 35 newspapers received daily and 160 periodicals. At present, the membership of the Library is 41,700. The aim of the Library is to enable the users to make the effective use of its resources and services. To achieve this objective, the Library is offering bibliographic, documentation, issue/return, reference service and Internet browsing services to its users. The Library is the first public library in the north-west to be fully computerized.

2. Review of Literature

The literature was searched for previous studies investigating the information seeking behaviour of users in different institutions and libraries. Various studies on information seeking behavior have been undertaken. Some of such studies that deserve mention are:

Bhatia and Venkata Rao (2011) conducted a survey based study on information seeking behaviour of students in digital environment at Dev Samaj College, Chandigarh. The findings of the study indicated that less than 50 % of the respondents were not aware about e-resources. It was found that the students of the college use search engines as a major source to access e-resources for their information needs and for the purpose of updating knowledge on their subjects of interest. In order to overcome hindrances in accessing the e-resources, the study recommend awareness programmes for the students and to provide training on web searching and retrieval skills.

Thanusodi (2010) carried out a research work on "library use and information seeking behaviour of law faculty members of the Central Law College, Salem". The study found that respondents used various sources for acquiring the needed information. Books were ranked as the most important source for teaching and research purposes. Mostly respondents (77.35%) preferred to consult their personal collection.

Mahajan (2009) conducted a study on information seeking behaviour of undergraduate, postgraduate students and researchers of Panjab University which shows that most of the students seek information to prepare notes for examination, whereas all researchers seek information related to their research. Researchers prefer to use current issues of journals and the Internet more than students.

Jatana (2008) observed that most common source of information seeking in social science is through discussion with one's colleagues and established expert in the field. Besides using traditional methods for locating and retrieving required information, the faculty at CRRID also frequently use web aided procedures such as the Internet, e-mail, subject gateways and web pages.

Chohda, Arun Prabha and Neelam Kumari (2008) observed that the readers trace material from the library via the Internet. The majority of respondents face the common problem i.e. unavailability of information while seeking information.

Shokeen and Kaushik (2003) conducted a study on information seeking behaviour of Psychologists and Sociologists. The findings of the study show that the qualification, teaching experience and status do not have any effect on the visits to the library by both groups. Periodicals are the most used and most important source of information. Browsing is the first preferred method of searching the required information.

Garg (2000) stated that most of the faculty members' purpose of information seeking is lecture preparation. As regards the use of formal sources of information, journals are optimally utilized.

3. Objectives of the Study

The purpose of the study was to understand the information seeking behaviour of users of the Central State Library, Chandigarh. The specific objectives of the study were:

1. To determine and examine the information seeking behaviour of users;
2. To study the purpose of information seeking;
3. To study the kind of information sources used, search approaches followed and tools used for information seeking by the users;
4. To explore the use of information technology;
5. To determine the information needs of users;
6. To study the problem faced by users while seeking and using information;
7. To suggest strategies of improving users' information seeking behaviour.

4. Research Methodology

The present study has been conducted through the survey method of research. A structured questionnaire was designed and used for collecting the data. The 100 questionnaires were personally distributed to the users of the library, out of which 98 users responded to the questionnaire.

5. Data Analysis and Interpretation

The questionnaires were analysed using simple statistical techniques and the results have been presented in the following tables, figures and paragraphs:

Table 1: Responses to the questionnaires

Number of Questionnaires		% age of Returned Questionnaires
Distributed	Returned	
100	98	98%

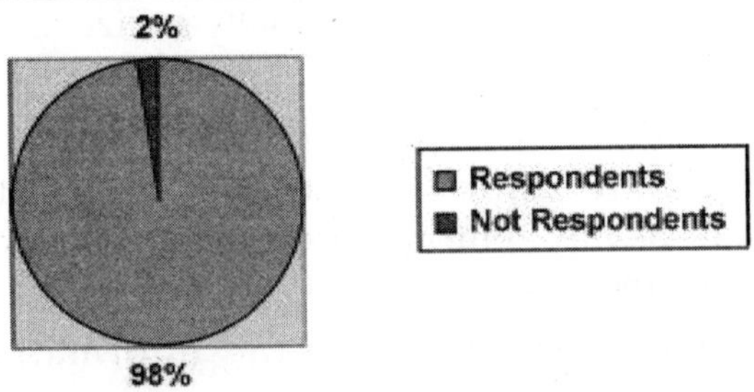

Figure- 1

Figure and Table 1 show that 100 questionnaires were distributed among the users, out of which 98 were duly filled and returned. Thus, the total response of all categories of users is 98% while 2% did not respond.

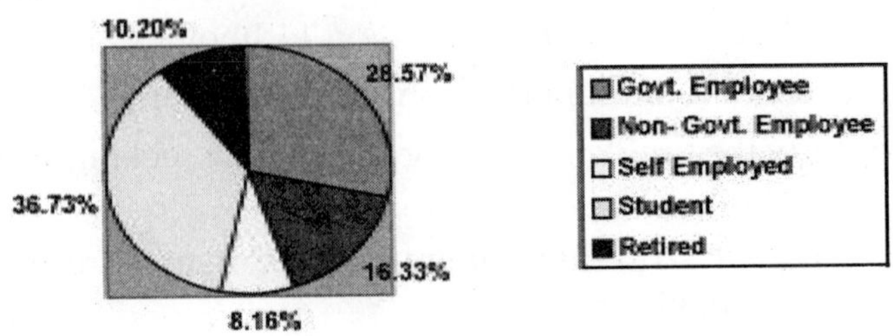

Figure-2

The above Figure 2 shows that the highest percentage who responded to the questionnaire was of students i.e. 36.73%; govt. employees were 28.57%; the non-govt. employees were 16.33%; retired persons were 10.20%; and the self- employed were 8.16%.

Table 2: Purpose of Information Seeking

Information Seeking Purpose	Respondents	Percentage
Academic/Professional	46	46.94
Seek current information	16	16.33
General Awareness	18	18.37
Recreation	6	6.12
For completing assignment/report	8	8.16
Other	4	4.08

Table 2 indicates that most of the users seek information for their academic/ professional purpose i.e. 46.94% whereas 16.33% of users do it for current information. 18.37% of users seek information for general awareness, 6.12% for recreation, 8.16% for completing assignments/reports and 4.08% for the preparation of competitive exams.

Table 3: Tools used for Seeking Information

Information seeking tools	Respondents	Percentage
Library catalogue	36	36.73
OPAC	54	55.10
Class no.	8	8.16

Table 3 shows that a majority of users i.e. 55.10% use OPAC, 36.73% of the users use library catalogue, and only 8.16% of the users seek information by class number.

Table 4: Approach followed for Searching Books

Information searching approach	Respondents	Percentage
Author	20	20.41
Title	32	32.65
Subject	32	32.65
Publisher	4	4.08
All	10	10.20

Table 4 shows that a majority of users (32.65%) prefer to search books by title and subject whereas 20.41% of users search by author. Only10.20% of users follow all the approaches for searching books.

Table 5: Information Sources used

Information sources used	Respondents	Percentage
Books	40	40.82
Periodicals/Magazines	10	10.20
Newspapers	10	10.20
Govt. publications	12	12.24
Reference books	18	18.37
E-resources	8	8.16

Table 5 reveals that most of the users i.e. 40.82% prefer to use books for seeking information whereas 18.37% prefer to use reference books. Periodicals/Magazines, newspapers are preferred by 10.20% users.12.24% of users use govt. publications as it is considered the most important source of public libraries and 8.16% of users use e-resources for seeking information.

Table 6: Use of Internet

Use of Internet	Respondents	Percentage
Yes	82	83.67
No	16	16.33

Table 6 shows that 83.67% of users use the Internet facility whereas 16.33% do not use as they do not know how to use the Internet.

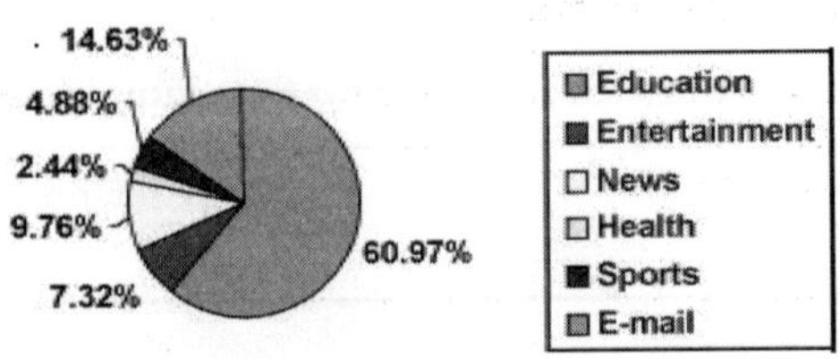

Figure 3: Purpose of using Internet

Figure 3 reveals that 60.98% of users use Internet for education purpose, 14.63% for e-mail, 9.76% for news, 7.32% for entertainment, 4.88% for sports and 2.44% of users use Internet for seeking health information.

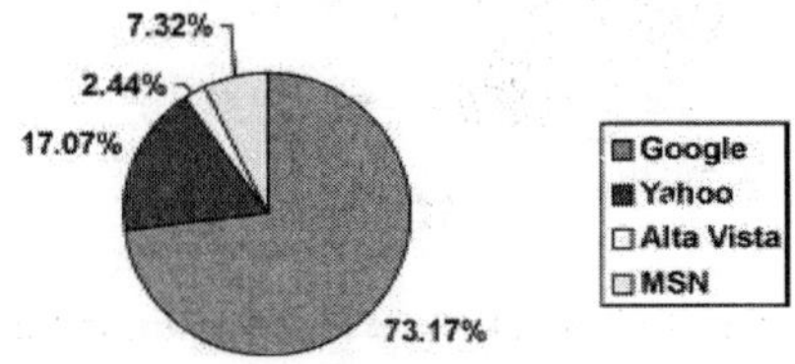

Figure 4: Search engines used

Figure 4 shows that most of the users (73.17%) prefer to use Google search engine. 17.07% of users prefer to use Yahoo, 7.32% use MSN and only 2.44% of users use the alta vista search engine.

Table 7: Users' Satisfaction with Library Services

Users satisfaction and library services	Respondents	Percentage
Yes	80	81.63
No	18	18.37

Table 7 shows the respondents' satisfaction with library services. Most of the users (81.63%) are satisfied with the library services, whereas 18.37% of users are not satisfied.

Problem Faced while Information Seeking

The users were asked to mention the problem they face while seeking information. Figure 5 reveals that 16.33% of the users faced the problem of unavailability of required reading material, 10.20% face the problem of scattered information sources, 14.29% with slow speed of computers.10.20% of users stated that they do not know how to use library catalogue and 14.29% stated that they do not know about the available information sources and services in the library. All these factors limit the users from effective utilization of information sources.

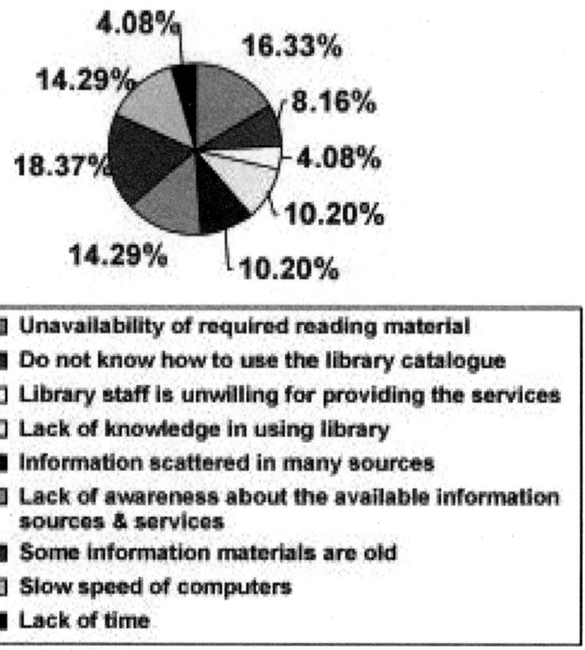

Figure: 5: Problem Faced while Information Seeking

6. Suggestions and Conclusion

Keeping in view the findings obtained from this investigation, the following reasonable suggestions are made:

1. Most of the user's purpose of information seeking is academic/professional, current awareness. It is, therefore suggested that library collection may be developed as per users' requirements.
2. A majority of users use OPAC for seeking information. It was found that the computers for OPAC purpose are less as compared to users' strength in the library. It is, therefore suggested that more computers may be installed in the library for users.
3. It was found that users face difficulty in seeking required information because some books are very old. So, it is suggested that the latest editions of the books may be procured. The journals in print as well as in electronic form,

online databases, e-books may be acquired keeping in mind the users' requirement in digital era.

4. It was observed that some users are not aware about the information services and sources available in the library and they do not know how to consult library catalogue. Therefore, it is suggested that proper library orientation programmes/information literacy programmes may be organized from time to time, so that users can learn the effective search strategies.
5. Many users experience difficulty in locating, accessing and using right information. Libray professionals have a major role to play in this direction and the collaboration between library staff and users is essential.
6. User studies may be carried out regularly

References

1. Choda, Nirupma, Arun Prabha and Neelam Kumari. "Information seeking behaviour of readers in Panjab University Library: A study". Paper presented at the ICCSR sponsored seminar, Chandigarh, March 18-19, 2008.
2. Garg, B.S. 2000. Information seeking patterns of users of engineering institutions in Rajasthan. *Library Herald*.37 (4): 229-239.
3. Jatana, Meena. "Information seeking behaviour of social science research faculty: A case study of CRRID library". Paper presented at the ICCSR sponsored seminar, Chandigarh, March 18-19, 2008.
4. Bhatia, J.K and Venkta Rao, P. 2011. Information seeking behaviour of students in digital environment: A case study. Paper presented at the 8th International CALIBER. Goa University, Goa: 02 - 04 March 2011: 437-444.
5. Thanusodi, S. 2010. Library use and information seeking behaviour of law faculty members of central law college, Salem. *SRELS journal of information management*. 47 (6): 689-698.
6. Mahajan, Preeti. "Information seeking behaviour: A study of Panjab University, India". Library Philosophy and Practice (March, 2009), http://unllib.unl.edu/LPP/mahajan4.htm (accessed on December 12, 2009).
7. Ramasamy, R. and Panda, Krushna C. 2003. *Status of State Central Libraries in India: An analytical study*. Delhi: Gyan publishing house.

8. Shokeen, Ashu and Kaushik, Sanjay K. 2003. Information seeking behaviour of Psychologists and Sociologists: A case study of Delhi and Haryana Universities. *ILA Bulletin*. 39 (3):11-14.

31

Research Productivity of Doctoral Researches in LIS in Jiwaji University, Gwalior during 1986-2011
A Bibliometric Study

Dr. Prem Prakash Pant
Faculty, SOS, Library & Information Science
Jiwaji University, Gwalior (MP)
Dr. Ram Gopal Garg
Head/Reader, SOS, Library & Information Science
Jiwaji University, Gwalior (MP)

Abstract

Research in library and information science (LIS) briefly means the collection and analysis of original data on a problem of librarianship done within the library schools according to scientific methods by scholarly students. This Research paper is based on the bibliometric study of doctoral theses submitted in Jiwaji University, Gwalior during 1986-2011. This study also analyises the findings and trends of research like language of communication , intra-subject relationship, productivity of research, etc. in doctoral research work conducted in Jiwaji University. Some interesting trends and findings have been shown by this research study, based on 75 doctoral research works.

- Among the researchers there were 82.6% male and only 17.3% female.
- Most of LIS researchers adopted the survey method in their researches.

- Trends of interest of subject areas clearly shows that academic libraries (31), resource sharing and networking (14) were the most favored subject areas of research.
- LIS doctoral theses submitted in Jiwaji University, Gwalior during 1986-2011, show that Dr J.N.Gautam (24) is the most productive supervisor / co-supervisor amongst the all.
- In the year 1994 and 2004, there were 8 doctoral research works submitted. It was the highest submission of research work in a year.
- The most favoured subject disciplines amongst the researchers were social science (7), information technology (6) and medical science (6).
- The most favoured geographical areas, which were taken by the researchers during the 1986-2011, were India (17) and Madhya Pradesh (14).
- During 1991- 1995, 21 doctoral research works were submitted by the researchers. It was found to be the most productive period.

Keywords: Bibliometrics, Research productivity, Jiwaji University, Subject relationship , Library & Information Science, Doctoral Research work.

1. LIS Schools in India

Library and Information Science in India is centered in the universities. The Documentation Research & Training Centre (DRTC) in Banglore and the Education Section of the NISCAIR, New Delhi are two institutes which concentrate on the training of professionals for the special and industrial libraries and information centers. There are about 126 universities in India which provide LIS courses, out of which 59 universities are those where the facility of both BLISc and MLISc and Diploma courses exists. There are some universities which provide the facility of distance mode in LIS courses.[6]

2. The Beginning of LIS Research

The roots of research in LIS are not very deep. Research in LIS is the 20th century ushered in by the Library School of the University of Chicago in mid 1920's.

The credit for the formal institution of the doctoral degree programme in Library Science in India goes undeniably to Dr. S.R. Ranganathan (1892-1972). He started one at the University of Delhi in 1951, surmounting many difficulties and facing personal ridicule. The University of Delhi awarded the first doctoral degree in Library Science to D.B. Krishna Rao who worked on "Facet Analysis and Depth Classification of Agriculture" under the supervision of Dr. S.R. Ranganathan in 1957. Dr. J.S. Sharma among was the first few to earn doctoral degree from USA. He was awarded Ph. D. by Michigan University for his work on "Mahatma Gandhi : A Descriptive Bibliography". (5)

Research growth in LIS in India is clearly shown in Figure-1;

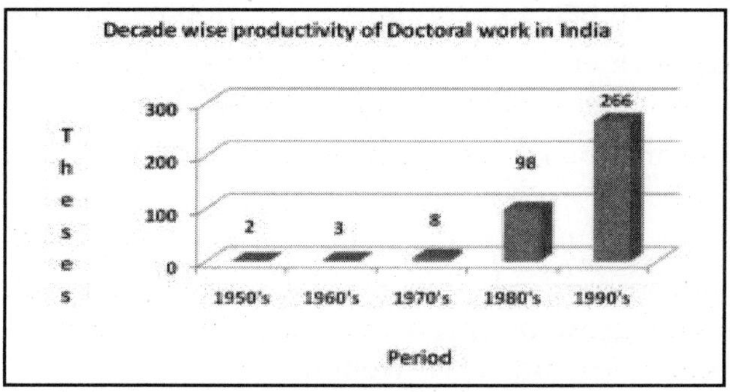

Figure -1: Doctoral Research in India

4. Meaning of Research

R- Rational way of thinking

E- Expert and exhaustive treatment

S- Search for solution

E- Exactness

A-Analysis

R- Relationship of facts

C- Critical observation

H-Honesty (in terms of source of data and their interpretation)

5. Bibliometrics

Etymologically, bibliometric is driven from two greek words, 'biblio' and 'metrikos' meaning book measurement , thus bibliometrics connotes the science of measurement relating to books. The scope of 'biblio' with the passage of time , got widened to include all types of documents like books, periodicals, patents , standards , theses and so on. The term bibliometric was coined by Alan Pritchard to denote "Application of mathematical and statistical methods to books and other media , process of written communication and of the nature and course of a discipline ." (7)

6. Purpose of LIS Research

As in any other discipline, LIS Research has the following purpose:

a. Research helps in continuous development of disciplines.

b. Research endows a discipline with an ability to use the knowledge generated in other disciplines.

c. Research make use of scientific method to find out the truth.

d. To acquire knowledge and to utilize the knowledge to social phenomenon , planning , social goodwill and understanding social growth , prediction ,modernization of tool and techniques and social welfare.

e. To simplify unwieldy and complex data.

f. To help in comparison of data.

g. To show relationship and association between different data groups.

h. To help in classification of data.(2)

7. LIS Education in Jiwaji University, Gwalior

The School of Studies in Library and Information Science which was established in 1984 in Jiwaji University, Gwalior (MP) has been providing the quality education according to the latest trends and needs of the institutions. The SOS has a well-equipped library and reference tools to support LIS subject needs. The SOS also is equipped with modern information equipment like computers, projector, printer, photostat machine, and internet connectivity. The students learn the use of computer technology in librarianship. Students are also trained in the use of the library software like CDS/ISIS and SOUL in practical work.

In the new millennium, the Department is planning to establish a highly advanced computerized information system with the following objectives;

a. To give the students an understanding of the basic principles and fundamentals laws of library science.

b. To enable the student to understand and appreciate the functions and purpose of library in changing social and academic environment.

c. To train the students in the modern techniques of librarianship and management of libraries.

The following LIS courses are being conducted by the Jiwaji University;

- B.Lib.I.Sc. One year course (Two semester) Total intake - 35 students
- M.Lib.I.Sc One year course (Two semester) Total intake - 35 students
- Ph.D. Programme (According to UGC norms) started from 1986 (3)

8. Objectives of Present Research Study

The objectives of the present study are:

a. To find out year-wise productivity of doctoral research work in Library and Information Science, Jiwaji University during 1986-2011.

b. To identify the most prolific guides of Library and Information Science in this School of Studies with their credit and impact.

c. To identify the most favoured research subject areas of LIS research.

d. To identify the distribution of research methods used in conducting LIS doctoral research work.

e. To find out the proportion of male and female researchers in LIS Research.

f. To identify the most favoured geographical areas, which are selected by the researchers for their study.

g. To analyze the doctoral research work in reference to co-relation with other subject fields.

h. To analyze the trends of doctoral research in Library and Information Science in the Jiwaji University, Gwalior during the period of 1986-2011.

i. To assess the research output and productivity of research work.

9. Research Methodology

There were 75 doctoral research works submitted in the SOS in Library and Information Science in Jiwaji University, Gwalior during, 1986-2011. All the bibliographical details like title, researchers name, year of submission, language of communication, supervisor name, favored geographical research areas, major aspects of research, association with other subject disciplines, gender-wise distribution in submitted doctoral research work in the University were taken as the input for present bibliometric study [(1)]. A computerized database is then created for indepth bibliometric analysis. Following elements which are important to carry out a bibliometric study have been preferred for this study:

a. Authorship

b. Title statement

c. Submission year

d. Language of communication

e. Subject relationship

f. Content

g. Most favored geographical areas of research

h. Applied research methods

i. Associative information, etc.[(4)]

Tables and graphical presentations illustrate the whole LIS research scenario in Jiwaji University, Gwalior in more authoritative and comparative way.

10. LIS Research in Jiwaji University, Gwalior : A Bibliometric Study

S.O.S. in Library and Information Science, Jiwaji University, Gwalior is a prime institution of LIS doctoral research in India since its establishment. The first doctoral award goes to Mr. S.P. Mehta on the work of "*Preservation of historical record in libraries*" under the supervision of Dr.D.B. Shrivastava and Dr. S.M. Tripathi in 1986.

In all 75 doctoral theses have been awarded on various aspects of LIS upto year 2011. Figure- 2 shows year-wise submission of theses.

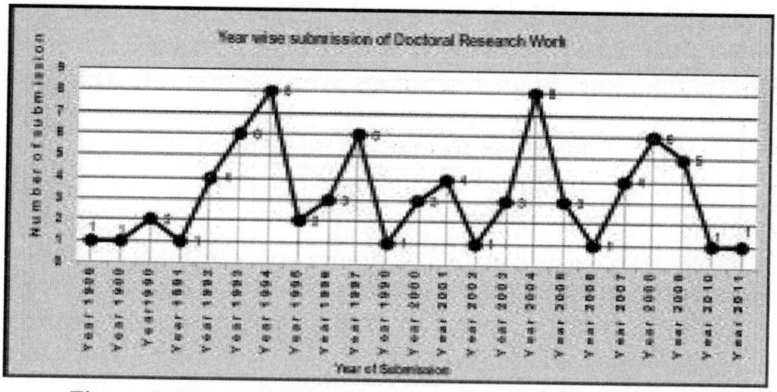

Figure-2: Year wise submission of doctoral research work

10.1 Language of communication in doctoral research work

English is the most favored language of communication amongst the researchers. There are 72% theses in English and 28% theses in Hindi language. It is when Hindi is the most prevalent language of this region. (Figure-3)

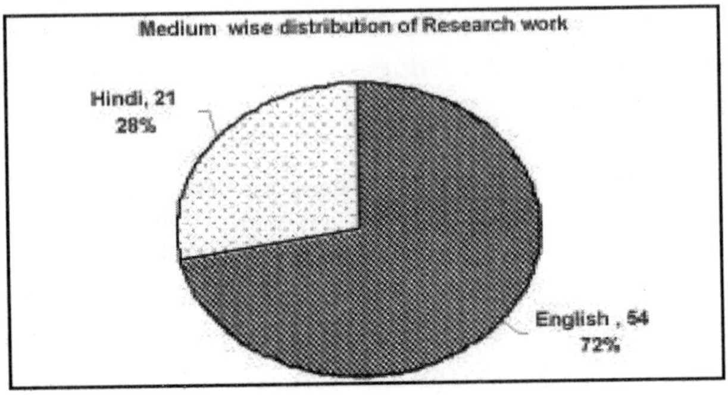

Figure-3: Language of communication in doctoral research work

10.2 Gender-wise assessment of doctoral research work

Proportion of male and female research scholars clearly shows in Figure 4. There were 82.6% male and 17.3% female researchers who submitted their doctoral research work during 1986-2011 in the Jiwaji University, Gwalior. Male researches were dominant. (Figure-4)

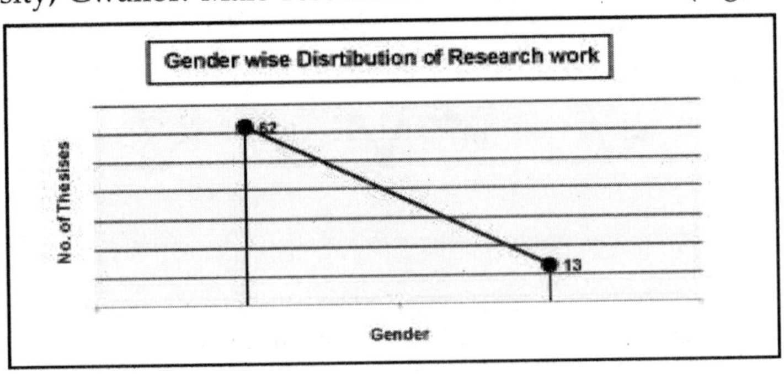

Figure-4: Gender wise assessment of doctoral research work

10.3 Most favored research methods

Survey research method was the most favoured research method amongst the researchers. 46.6% of researchers adopted this method, while 14.6% preferred case study and evolutionary. Bibliometric method was adopted by 12%, Historical by 06.6%, Field Study by 04% and least preferred method was Statistical by 01.3% amongst the LIS researchers in Jiwaji University, Gwalior. (Figure-5)

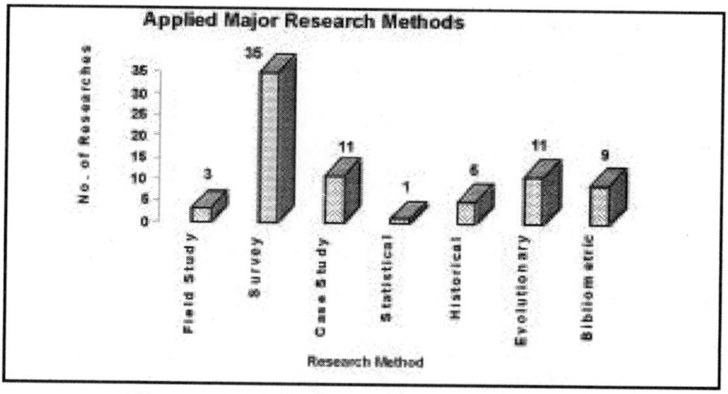

Figure- 5: Most favored research methods

10.4 Most favored subject areas of LIS research

Trends of interest in subject areas as shown in the Graphic -6 during 1986-2011 clearly shows the most and least favored subject areas of LIS research. Academic libraries (31) was the most preferred subject area, followed by Special libraries (14), Resource sharing & networking (14) , Information needs (11), information services (11). Bibliometrical study (6), Library organization (6), Impact of IT (4),HRM (3) and others were the least favored by the researchers. Nevertheless, we have found some research work on emerging and innovative trends like: Disaster management , E-Resources, Library software. (Figure-6)

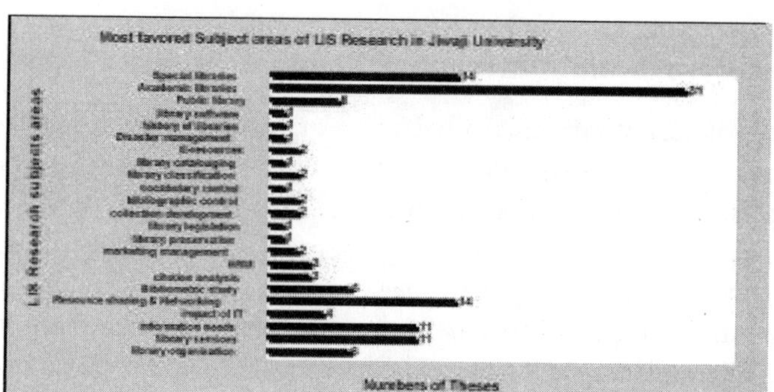

Figure-6: Most favored subject areas of LIS research

10.5 Productivity of supervisor/ co-supervisor of LIS research

Figure 7 clearly shows that Dr. J.N. Gautam (24 doctoral research supervision) was the leading supervisor amongst them, while Dr.S.M Tripathi (19) and Dr.Hemant Sharma (19) were other active supervisors in this University. Dr. B.K.Sharma (7), Dr.H.S.Sengar (6) was third and forth leading supervisors. Produtivity of other supervisors was extremely low. Here supervisor term pronounced collectively for both, the senior supervisor and co-supervisor in this study.(Figure- 7)

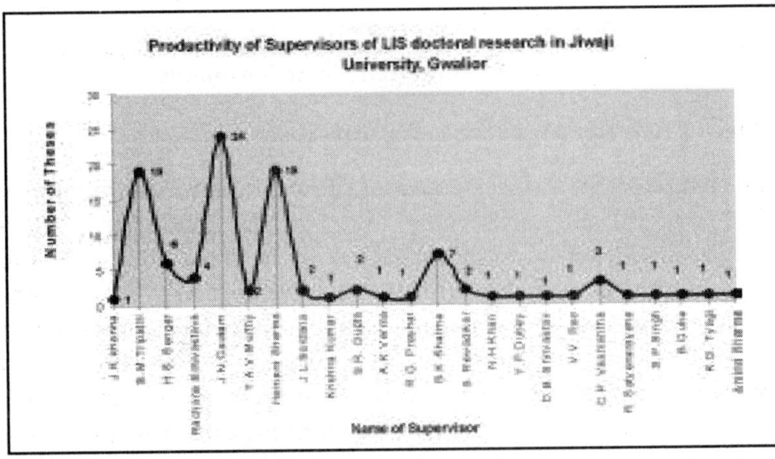

Figure-7 : Productivity of supervisor/ co-supervisor of LIS research in Jiwaji University, Gwalior

10.6 Doctoral research influenced by other subject disciplines

Influence of doctoral research by other subject disciplines is clearly shown in Figure 8. Social Science (7) was most favored subject discipline , while Information Technology (IT)(6), Medical Science (6) , Management (5) and Trade/Commerce (5) were the other favored subject disciplines amongst the researchers. Other subjects were least popular subject disciplines. Some interesting research work was produced in Soil Science (1) and Physical Education (2) also. (Figure-8)

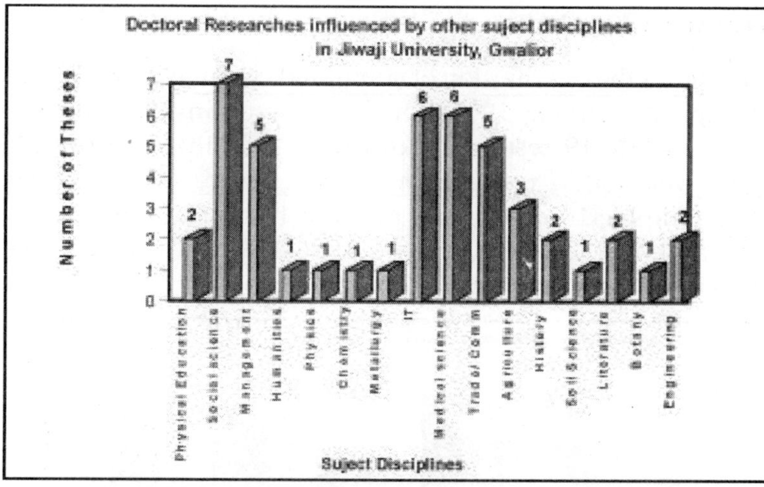

Figure-8 : Doctoral research influenced by other subject disciplines

10.7 Most favored geographical areas in doctoral research

Most favoured geographical area in doctoral research during 1986-2011 was India (17), while other favoured geographical areas were: Madhya Pradesh (14), Delhi (7), Gwalior & Chambal (7), and Ujjain (6) . Other interesting geographical areas which were selected by the researchers were North –East India (1), Himalyan Region (1), Calcutta (1) and Hindi speaking areas (1) . Surprisingly two doctoral research work s paid attention to Jordan and United Kingdom. (Figure-9)

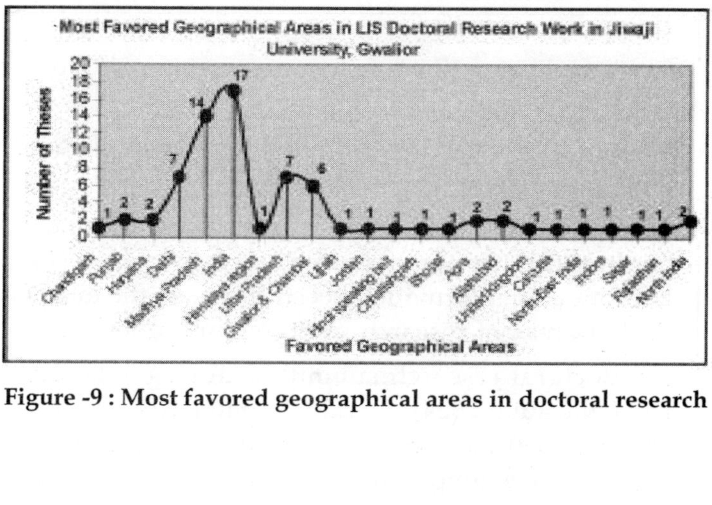

Figure -9 : Most favored geographical areas in doctoral research

10.8 Year wise distribution of library science theses

Figure 10 shows the distribution of submitted research works in certain year grouping , during 1991-1995 the maximum 21 theses were submitted , while 19 research work were submitted during 2001-2005.There were only 4 research work which were submitted during 1986-1990. Graphic 10 reflects the glorious history of LIS research in Jiwaji University, Gwalior during 1986-1990 . Total number of submitted research work was 75. (Figure-10)

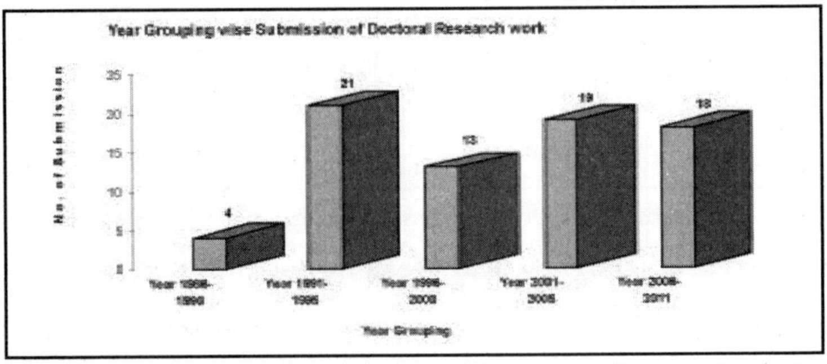

Figure 10 : Year wise distribution of LIS doctoral research work

11. Findings of Research Study

The major findings are ;

- English (72%) was the most favoured language of communication amongst the LIS researchers in Jiwaji University, Gwalior.
- 82.6% male and 17.3% female researchers, prove that male researchers were predominant.
- Most of LIS researchers adopted the survey method (35) in their researches.
- Trends of interest of subject areas clearly show that academic libraries (31), resource sharing and networking (14), special libraries (14), information needs (11) were the most favoured subject areas of research in decending order.
- LIS doctoral research submitted during 1986-2011 sohw, Dr. J.N.Gautam (24), Dr.S.M.Tripathi (19) and Dr.Hemant Sharma (19) as the most productive supervisors / co-supervisors amongst the all.

- In the year 1994 and 2004 , there were 8 doctoral research work submitted , which was the highest submission of research works in a year.
- The most influenced subject disciplines amongst the researchers were Social Science (7), Information Technology (6) and Medical Science (6). Some interesting research work was done in physical science, soil science, etc.
- Most favored geographical areas, during the 1986-2011 were India (17), Madhya Pradesh (14), Delhi (7), Gwalior & Chambal region (7). Some researches interestingly were focused on Jordan (1) and United Kingdom (1), Himalaya region (1) and North-East region (1).
- During the 1991 - 1995 , there were 21 doctoral research works submitted by the researchers. It is found to be the most productive period.

12. Conclusion

School of Studies in Library and Information Science, Jiwaji University, Gwalior having a glorious history of LIS doctoral researches. The present research study is based on the 75 doctoral research works, which was submitted during the 1986-2011. A lot of interesting and unexplored findings are brought out in this study.

References

1. Ahuja , Ram (2008), Research Methods, Rawat Publication , Jaipur, pp.-42-48.
2. Danrita, J. and others (2009) Future concepts of library& Information services : Changes, challenges and role of library professionals. Ess Ess Pubiication, New Delhi, pp 459-468, ISBN-978-81-7000-538-2.
3. Jiwaji University, Gwalior 2011-12, Prospectus.
4. Panda, B.D.(1997), Research Methodology for library science : With statistical methods and bibliometrics , Anmol Publication, New Delhi, pp19-21, 241-253.
5. Satija, M.P.(1989) , Doctoral Research in Library and Information Science in India : Some observations and comments, Libri, vol.-49, pp236-242, ISSN-0024-2667.

6. Tejomurthy, A and Kumar, PSG (1998) Research in library and information science , DESIDOC Bulletin of information technology, Vol.18, No.1, Jan., pp11-18.
7. Wilkinson, John (1983), The legitimization of librarianship, Libri, vol.-33(1) march 39.

32

Research Productivity of Scientists of Gujarat Cancer & Research Institute
A Bibliometric Analysis

Monika Singhai
Research Scholar (JRF)
SOS in Library and Information Science, Jiwaji University, Gwalior
E-mail : monikasinghai@gmail.com

Abstract

The study examines India's GCRI scientists performance based on their publication during 1975-2010 drawn form pubmed database. Total 166 publications are analyzed as journal articles in term of year wise publication output, authorship pattern, degree of collaboration, most preferred national and international journals etc. The year 2010 with 15 articles (9.04%) published is the most productive year. Most prolific author were J. Bhatavdekar and P.S. Patel (15 articles each) and S.G. Adhvaryu and Vora H.H (8 articles each). The core journals preferred by the scientists to publish their publications are Indian journal of pathology & microbiology with 14 (8.43%) papers, International journal of cancer with 10 (6.02%) papers, Neurology India with 9(5.42%) papers, Cancer genetics and cytogenetics, Glycoconjugate journal, Indian journal of chest diseases and allied sciences and Mutagenesis with 6(3.61%) papers each. Most of the journals published by USA with 30.30% (20 journals) followed by India with 25.75% (17 journals).

Introduction

Important characteristic of literature is that they are systems, which are shared among people. It is known that knowledge is dynamic and multi-dimensional in nature. New researchers and thirst for knowledge has led to the proliferation of new work. It is necessary that research and new findings should be circulated widely among the research scholars, scientists, specialists and others. Thus it seems that interdisciplinary science studies are facing a dilemma. This situation demands a careful and serious investigation to find out what should be read, assimilated and used for conducting quality research in science. Since the end of World War II, medical research particularly cancer research, has expanded enormously. The importance of cancer as a major cause of death and recognition that the problems of cell growth in cancer are of basic biologic importance have stimulated research into every facets of the disease and it has become apparent that many of these facets are related. Cancer is an abnormal proliferation of cells which have uncontrolled growth. They have the ability to grow into adjacent tissue and to spread to distant parts of the body. There are several general categories of cancer, which can occur in male and female differently like blood cancer, skin cancer, breast cancer, etc. The Gujarat Cancer & Research Institute, Ahmadabad (GCRI) is functioning as an autonomous body of Government of Gujarat and Gujarat Cancer Society. GCIR was established in 1972 as a Regional Cancer Centre of Government. GCRI has its own hospital for Cancer Regional Cancer, Medical Education Centre and 5 well-equipped Research Labs. It is working on some Research Projects under National Cancer Control Programme and providing services to patients from Gujarat, Rajasthan, Madhya Pradesh and neighboring State of Maharashtra.

Objective of Study

1. To find out year-wise research productivity.
2. To analyze the authorship pattern and collaboration pattern of scientists of GCRI.
3. To identify the prolific authors with their number of publications.
4. To observe the national and international publications of scientists.

5. To find out status of journal publication of countries to promote the communication of research ideas.
6. To identify the most preferred journals of the scientists for their publication.

Methodology

For this study MEDLINE database has been selected for downloading the data published by GCRI scientists. MEDLINE (Medical Literature Analysis and Retrieval System Online) is the world's most comprehensive source of database having more than 18 million records of medical sciences including nursing, dentistry, veterinary medicine, health care system and preclinical science publications. From 28 January 2010 (2010 -01-28)[update], Pub Med has provided 19.5 million citations going back to the year 1865. It is maintained by the National Centre for Biotechnology Information (NCBI) at National Library of Medicine (NLM). Each record in MEDLINE is manually indexed with NLM's controlled vocabulary and the Medical Subject Headings (known as MeSH). For obtaining data from the database, the search term applied is *Gujarat Cancer & Research Institute.* Each record contains bibliographic details like author, publication types, language, year, author address, country of publication, etc. NCBI has indexed only the first author's address, which will be listed for the analysis of author affiliation. For this study Endnote software used for extracting the data from MEDLINE. Endnote is a commercial reference management software package, used to manage bibliographies and references when writing essays and articles. It is developed by Thomson Reuters. The software has powerful web interface, which can download records into the database.

Results and Discussion

Year-wise Distribution of Articles

In Table 1, details regarding 166 articles produced by scientist of GCRI, Ahmadabad from 1975 to 2010 are given. This table shows that maximum number of articles published in 2010 were the highest i.e. 15 which is 9.04% of total published articles. This is followed by 13 articles (7.83%) in 2009 & 2007and only 1 article (0.60 %) is lowest number of articles published in 1975, 1976, 1987. (Fig.1)

Table 1- Year wise distribution of articles

Year	No. of Articles	Cumulative Articles	Percentage	Cumulative %
1975	1	1	0.6	0.6
1976	1	2	0.6	1.2
1987	1	3	0.6	1.81
1988	10	13	6.02	7.83
1989	4	17	2.41	10.24
1990	8	25	4.82	15.06
1991	7	32	4.22	19.28
1992	4	36	2.41	21.69
1993	6	42	3.61	25.3
1994	9	51	5.42	30.72
1995	5	56	3.01	33.73
1996	2	58	1.2	34.94
1997	6	64	3.61	38.55
1998	7	71	4.22	42.77
1999	3	74	1.81	44.58
2000	6	80	3.61	48.19
2001	7	87	4.22	52.41
2002	6	93	3.61	56.02
2003	4	97	2.41	58.43
2004	2	99	1.2	59.64
2005	8	107	4.82	64.46
2006	9	116	5.42	69.88
2007	13	129	7.83	77.71
2008	9	138	5.42	83.13
2009	13	151	7.83	90.96
2010	15	166	9.04	100
Total	166		100	

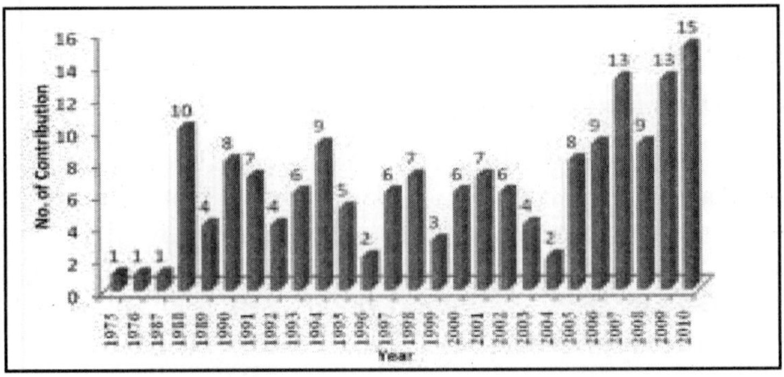

Fig. 1: Year wise distribution of articles

Authorship Pattern

Table 2 exhibits the authorship pattern of publications. The details of authorship pattern have shown 32 papers (19.28%) out of 166 papers are of the five-authorship.26 (15.66%) are written by four-authorship, followed by six-authorship with 24 (14.46%) papers, and three-authorship had 22 (13.25%) papers followed by seven- authorship with 19 (11.45%) papers. Single authorship papers are 5, which is 3.01% of the total contributions. This study shows that collaboration extends upto 11 authors. This analysis shows that in the 21st century, collaborative research trend among scientists has been increasing in the field of cancer research. (Fig. 2)

Table 2- Authorship pattern

Sl. No.	Authorship Pattern	No. of Citation	% of Citations	Cumulative Citation	%of C Citation
1	Five	32	19.28	32	19.277
2	Four	26	15.66	58	34.94
3	Six	24	14.46	82	49.398
4	Three	22	13.25	104	62.651
5	Seven	19	11.45	123	74.096
6	Eight	18	10.84	141	84.94
7	Nine	11	6.63	152	91.566
8	One	5	3.01	157	94.578
9	Two	6	3.61	163	98.193
10	Ten	2	1.2	165	99.398
11	Eleven	1	0.6	166	100
	Total	166	100		

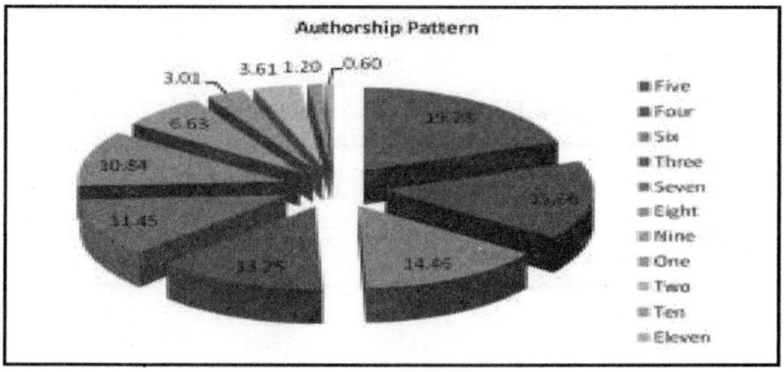

Fig. 2: Authorship pattern

Degree of Collaboration Among Multiple-authors

To identify degree of collaboration a quantitative method was used. The formula for this method was given by Subramanyam. According to Subramanyam, the proportion of multi-authored papers to the total number of papers is called degree of collaboration. The formula is

$$C = \frac{NM}{NM + NS}$$

NM = Number of Multi authored papers

NS = Number of Single authored papers

In the present study the value of C is

C = Degree of collaboration

$$C = \frac{161}{161 + 5} = \frac{161}{166}$$

$$= 0.97$$

The degree of collaboration of journal articles published by the scientists of GCRI 0.97 in this study. This analysis result indicates the prevalence of team research among scientists. Table 3 depicts the degrees of collaboration in various years which differs from one another from 100% to 75%. During 1975-1990 and 1993-2011 maximum articles published were multi-authored. During 1991degree of collaboration was found to be 86%, followed by in 2002 with 83%, and in 2008 collaboration was found to be 78%, followed by 73% during 1992.

Table 3- Degree of collaboration

Year	Papers single authored	Percentage	Papers multiple authored	Percentage	Total no of papers	Degree of collaboration
1975	0	0	1	0.62	1	1
1976	0	0	1	0.62	1	1
1987	0	0	1	0.62	1	1
1988	0	0	10	6.21	10	1

Table 3 continued...

1989	0	0	4	2.48	4	1
1990	0	0	8	4.97	8	1
1991	1	20	6	3.73	7	0.86
1992	1	20	3	1.86	4	0.75
1993	0	0	6	3.73	6	1
1994	0	0	9	5.59	9	1
1995	0	0	5	3.11	5	1
1996	0	0	2	1.24	2	1
1997	0	0	6	3.73	6	1
1998	0	0	7	4.35	7	1
1999	0	0	3	1.86	3	1
2000	0	0	6	3.73	6	1
2001	0	0	7	4.35	7	1
2002	1	20	5	3.11	6	0.83
2003	0	0	4	2.48	4	1
2004	0	0	2	1.24	2	1
2005	0	0	8	4.97	8	1
2006	0	0	9	5.59	9	1
2007	0	0	13	8.07	13	1
2008	2	40	7	4.35	9	0.78
2009	0	0	13	8.07	13	1
2010	0	0	15	9.32	15	1
Total	5	100	161	100	166	0.97

Ranking List of Most Prolific Authors

Table 4 depicts the rank list of scientists who have their publications as a first author. J. Bhatavdekar and P.S. Patel are the most productive scientists of GCRI with 15 (9.04%) articles each during the study period. S.G. Adhvaryu and Vora H. H. at second position with 8 (4.82%) articles each, followed by P. Trivedi with 6 (3.61%) on second rank. S. R. Bakshi, B.P. Patel and A. H. Trivedi published 5 articles each occupy the fourth position. B. J. Dave, S. Dixit and D. D. Patel are at fifth position with 4 articles each.

Table 4- Ranking list of most prolific authors

S N	Rank	Author's Name	No of Articles	cumulative no.	percentage	Cumulative Percentage
1	1	Bhatavdekar, J.	15	15	9.04	9.04
2	1	Patel, P. S.	15	30	9.04	18.07
3	2	Adhvaryu, S. G.	8	38	4.82	22.89

Table 4 continued...

4	2	Vora HH	8	46	4.82	27.71
5	3	Trivedi, P.	6	52	3.61	31.33
6	4	Bakshi, S. R.	5	57	3.01	34.34
7	4	Patel, B.P.	5	62	3.01	37.35
8	4	Trivedi, A. H.	5	67	3.01	40.36
9	5	Dave, B J	4	71	2.41	42.77
10	5	Dixit, S	4	75	2.41	45.18
11	5	Patel, D D	4	79	2.41	47.59
12	6	Maheshwari GK	3	82	1.81	49.40
13	6	Parikh B	3	85	1.81	51.20
14	6	Rawal, R M	3	88	1.81	53.01
15	6	Sainger RN	3	91	1.81	54.82
16	6	Shah NG	3	94	1.81	56.63
17	6	Shukla K	3	97	1.81	58.43
18	6	Vyas R K	3	100	1.81	60.24
19	7	Karelia, N H	2	102	1.20	61.45
20	7	Pandey M	2	104	1.20	62.65
21	7	Patel , T	2	106	1.20	63.86
22	7	Patel, A. P.	2	108	1.20	65.06
23	7	Raval, G N	2	110	1.20	66.27
24	7	Shah FD	2	112	1.20	67.47
25	7	Shah, N G	2	114	1.20	68.67
26	7	Singhal S	2	116	1.20	69.88
27	7	Trivedi, P. J.	2	118	1.20	71.08
28	7	Vyas RC	2	120	1.20	72.29
64	8	Shah MH	2	122	1.20	73.49
29	8	Agrawal, PP	1	123	0.60	74.10
30	8	Anand, AS	1	124	0.60	74.70
31	8	Bala, D. V.	1	125	0.60	75.30
32	8	Bansal, R.	1	126	0.60	75.90
33	8	Bhagat, S.	1	127	0.60	76.51
34	8	Bhatia, M. T.	1	128	0.60	77.11
35	8	Chandra, S. S.	1	129	0.60	77.71
36	8	Chauhan, A.	1	130	0.60	78.31
37	8	Dave, K	1	131	0.60	78.92
38	8	el-Shazly, M.	1	132	0.60	79.52
39	8	Franky Dhaval Shah	1	133	0.60	80.12
40	8	Jaju R. J.	1	134	0.60	80.72
41	8	Kothari, K. C.	1	135	0.60	81.33
42	8	Kumar, A. S.	1	136	0.60	81.93
43	8	Mehta H.	1	137	0.60	82.53
44	8	Mehta, N.	1	138	0.60	83.13
45	8	Mishra, K.	1	139	0.60	83.73
46	8	Mody, R. P.	1	140	0.60	84.34
47	8	Nandwani P.K.	1	141	0.60	84.94

Table 4 continued...

48	8	Narendra, H.	1	142	0.60	85.54
49	8	Neema, J. P.	1	143	0.60	86.14
50	8	Ohri, A.	1	144	0.60	86.75
51	8	Pandit, M. K.	1	145	0.60	87.35
52	8	Parikh, B.C	1	146	0.60	87.95
53	8	Patel, C.	1	147	0.60	88.55
54	8	Patel, P. N	1	148	0.60	89.16
55	8	Patel, TS	1	149	0.60	89.76
56	8	Patel, J. B.	1	150	0.60	90.36
57	8	Patel, R. K.	1	151	0.60	90.96
58	8	Patel, S	1	152	0.60	91.57
59	8	Patel, S. M.	1	153	0.60	92.17
60	8	Pelagade, S. M.	1	154	0.60	92.77
61	8	Rohan, V. S.	1	155	0.60	93.37
62	8	Rohan, V.	1	156	0.60	93.98
63	8	Saraiya, H.	1	157	0.60	94.58
65	8	Shah, G V	1	158	0.60	95.18
66	8	Shah, M J	1	159	0.60	95.78
67	8	Shah, M.	1	160	0.60	96.39
68	8	Shah, P. M.	1	161	0.60	96.99
69	8	Soni, H. C.	1	162	0.60	97.59
70	8	Tripathi, P	1	163	0.60	98.19
71	8	Trivedi, K.	1	164	0.60	98.80
72	8	Vasani, P. K.	1	165	0.60	99.40
73	8	Vyas, V.	1	166	0.60	100.00
			166		100.00	

Ranked Countries of Journals

During this study it is observed that 66 journals are preferred by various authors for their publications. All 66 are published by various 15 countries of the world. From Table 5, it is found that most of the journals were published in USA with 30.30% (20 journals), followed by India with 25.75% (17 Journals). England and the Netherlands are at third position with 5 journals each followed by Australia, Italy and Germany at fourth position with 3 journals each. Greece and Switzerland with 2 publications, followed by Denmark, New Zealand, Ireland and Slovakia with 1 publication. In this study the most important finding isthat out of the total percentage of 74.24 of foreign journals, Indian journals are 25.75%. This shows the quality of the articles produced by GCRI scientists.

Table 5 - Ranked Countries of Journals

Sl.No.	Name of country	No. of Journals	%	Cumulative no of Journals	Cumulative %	Rank
1	USA	20	15.15	20	30.30	I
2	Indian	17	12.88	37	56.06	II
3	England	5	3.79	42	63.64	III
4	Netherlands	5	3.79	47	71.21	III
5	Australia	3	2.27	50	75.76	IV
6	Germany	3	2.27	53	80.30	IV
7	Italy	3	2.27	56	84.85	IV
8	Greece	2	1.52	58	87.88	V
9	Switzerland	2	1.52	60	90.91	V
10	Denmark	1	0.76	61	92.42	VI
11	Iran	1	0.76	62	93.94	VI
12	Ireland	1	0.76	63	95.45	VI
13	New Zealand	1	0.76	64	96.97	VI
14	Slovakia	1	0.76	65	98.48	VI
15	Thailand	1	0.76	66	100.00	VI
	Total	66	50.00	100		

Ranking List of Journals

It has been observed that 66 journals (national and international both) are preferred by GCRI scientists. Journals are arranged in decreasing order on the basis of no. of articles published. The leading journals are Indian journal of pathology & microbiology with 14 (8.43%) papers, International journal of cancer with 10 (6.02%) papers, Neurology India with 9(5.42%) papers, Cancer genetics and cytogenetics, Glycoconjugate journal, Indian journal of chest diseases and allied sciences and Mutagenesis with 6(3.61%) papers each, followed by Cancer treatment reviews, Australian & New Zealand journal of obstetrics & gynaecology, European journal of surgical oncology, Tumour biology with 5 (3.01) papers each. Other 55 journals published less than 5 articles are listed Table 6.

Table 6- Ranking list of journals most preferred for publishing with their country of origin

S N	Rank	Journal Name	No. of Papers	Cumulative no	Percentage	Cumulative %	Country
1	1	Indian J Pathol Microbiol	14	14	8.43	8.43	India
2	2	Int J Cancer	10	24	6.02	14.46	U.S.
3	3	Neurol India	9	33	5.42	19.88	India
4	4	Cancer Genet Cytogenet	6	39	3.61	23.49	U.S.
5	4	Glycoconj J.	6	45	3.61	27.11	U.S.
6	4	Indian J Chest Dis Allied Sci	6	51	3.61	30.72	India
7	4	Mutagenesis	6	57	3.61	34.34	England
8	5	Aust N Z J Obstet Gynaecol	5	62	3.01	37.35	Australia
9	5	Cancer Treat Rev	5	67	3.01	40.36	Netherland
10	5	Eur J Surg Oncol	5	72	3.01	43.37	England
11	5	Tumour Biol	5	77	3.01	46.39	Netherland
12	6	Ann Surg Oncol	4	81	2.41	48.8	U.S.
13	6	Indian J Biochem Biophys	4	85	2.41	51.2	India
14	7	J Clin Laser Med Surg	4	89	2.41	53.61	U.S.
15	7	Anticancer Res.	3	92	1.81	55.42	Greece
16	7	Int J Biol Markers	3	95	1.81	57.23	Italy
17	7	Int J Gynecol Cancer	3	98	1.81	59.04	U.S.
18	7	J Cancer Res Clin Oncol.	3	101	1.81	60.84	Germany
19	7	J Indian Med Assoc	3	104	1.81	62.65	India
20	7	J Med Phys	3	107	1.81	64.46	India
21	7	J Reprod Med	3	110	1.81	66.27	U.S.
22	7	Neoplasma	3	113	1.81	68.07	Slovakia
23	8	Abdom Imaging	2	115	1.2	69.28	U.S.
24	8	Head Neck	2	117	1.2	70.48	U.S.
25	8	Indian J Hum Genet	2	119	1.2	71.69	India
26	8	Indian J Palliat Care	2	121	1.2	72.89	India
27	8	J Assoc Genet Technol	2	123	1.2	74.1	U.S.

Table 6 continued...

28	8	J Assoc Physicians India	2	125	1.2	75.3	India
29	8	J Gastrointest Cancer	2	127	1.2	76.51	U.S.
30	8	J Surg Oncol	2	129	1.2	77.71	U.S.
31	8	Urol J	2	131	1.2	78.92	Iran
32	9	AJNR Am J Neuroradiol	1	132	0.6	79.52	U.S.
33	9	Am J Clin Oncol.	1	133	0.6	80.12	U.S.
34	9	Am Surg.	1	134	0.6	80.72	U.S.
35	9	Ann Plast Surg	1	135	0.6	81.33	U.S.
36	9	Asia Pac J Clin Oncol	1	136	0.6	81.93	Australia
37	9	Asian Pac J Cancer Prev	1	137	0.6	82.53	Thailand
38	9	Australas Radiol	1	138	0.6	83.13	Australia
39	9	Biomark Insights	1	139	0.6	83.73	New Zealand
40	9	Breast Cancer Res Treat	1	140	0.6	84.34	Netherlands
41	9	Cancer	1	141	0.6	84.94	Switzerland
42	9	Cancer Lett	1	142	0.6	85.54	Ireland
43	9	Carcinogenesis	1	143	0.6	86.14	England
44	9	Diagn Cytopathol	1	144	0.6	86.75	U.S.
45	9	Dis Colon Rectum	1	145	0.6	87.35	U.S.
46	9	Eur Arch Otorhinolaryngol	1	146	0.6	87.95	Germany
47	9	Eur J Gynaecol Oncol	1	147	0.6	88.55	Italy
48	9	Gynecol Oncol	1	148	0.6	89.16	U.S.
49	9	Indian J Cancer	1	149	0.6	89.76	India
50	9	Indian J Pediatr	1	150	0.6	90.36	India
51	9	Indian J Plast Surg	1	151	0.6	90.96	India
52	9	Indian Pediatr	1	152	0.6	91.57	India
53	9	Int J Radiat Biol.	1	153	0.6	92.17	England
54	9	Int Orthop	1	154	0.6	92.77	Germany
55	9	Integr Cancer Ther	1	155	0.6	93.37	U.S.
56	9	J Cancer Res Ther	1	156	0.6	93.98	India
57	9	J Cytol	1	157	0.6	94.58	India
58	9	J Exp Clin Cancer Res	1	158	0.6	95.18	England
59	9	J Postgrad Med	1	159	0.6	95.78	India
60	9	Mutat Res	1	160	0.6	96.39	Netherland
61	9	Oncol Rep	1	161	0.6	96.99	Greece
62	9	Oncology	1	162	0.6	97.59	Switzerland

Table 6 continued...

63	9	Oral Dis.	1	163	0.6	98.19	Denmark
64	9	Toxicol Lett.	1	164	0.6	98.8	Netherland
65	9	Trop Gastroenterol	1	165	0.6	99.4	India
66	9	Tumori	1	166	0.6	100	Italy
			166		**100**		

Conclusion

This type of quantitative studies highlights the various aspects of the career of a scientist such as productivity, collaboration pattern, ranking of authorship, etc. This paper has highlighted quantitatively the contributions made by the Scientists of GCRI during 1975-2010 (166 articles) based on MEDLINE database through Pubmed gateway. It can be concluding that during the last 5 years from 2005 to 2010 the productivity is increasing and this productivity shows substantial growth of the institution. The collaboration among scientists towards multi-authored papers is 96.98%. It has been observed that most preferred journal is the Indian journal of pathology & microbiology with 14 (8.43%) papers. Total 113 articles (68.07%) are published in international journals published by USA, England, Netherlands, Australia, Germany and other countries. This shows the high quality of productivity of GCRI scientists.

References

1. http://www.cancerindia.org/(access on 20th Aug. 2011)
2. http://www.cancer.gov/cancertopics/cancerlibrary/what-is-cancer (access on 01th Sep. 2011)
3. *Collier's Encyclopaedia* (1989). Vol.5 *Collier's Encyclopaedia*. New York: Macmillan Education Company, pp. 341.
4. Gupta, P. et al. (2011). Scintometric dimensions of fuel cell research as reflected in INIS database. *SRELS Journal of Information Management*. 48 (3), 329-347.
5. Varghese, R.R. and Rajan, J. U. (2009). Productivity of scientists of Rajiv Gandhi Centre for Biotechnology (RGCB): an analysis. *Annals of Library and information science Studies*. 56 (3), 156-162.
6. Mahapatra, G. (2009). *Bibliometric Studies in the internet era*. New Delhi: Indiana Publishing House.
7. Nazim, M. and Ahmad, M. A. (2008). Bibliometric analysis on nenotechnology research. *Annals of Library and Information Studies*. 55 (4), 292-299.

8. Patra, S.K. and Bhattacharya, Partha (2005). Bibliometric study of cancer research in India. *DESIDOC Bulletin of Information Technology*. 25 (2), 11-18.

9. Kademani, B.S. et al (2005). Publication Productivity of the Bio-organic division at Bhabha Atomic Research centre: a scintometric study. *Annals of Library and information science Studies*. 52 (4), 135-146.

10. Udofia, Iton Udofia (2002), Bibliometric studies on African trypanosomiasis research literature: a review of authorship pattern. *Annals of Library and information science Studies*. 49(2), 156-162.

11. Sahoo, K.C. (2002). *Information Use Pattern of Researchers in Bio-Science*. Ludhiana: Medallion Press.

12. Devarajan, G. (1997) *Bibliometric Studies*. New Delhi: Ess Ess publication.

13. Hood, W.W. and Wilson, C.S (2001). The Literature of bibliometrics, scientometrics and informetrics, *Scientometrics*. 52 (2), 291-314.

14. Subramayam, K. (1983). Bibliometric Studies of Research Collaboration: A Review. *Journal of Information Science*. 6 (1), 33-38.

33

Textbook Archive at the NCERT Library

A Gateway to Research in Education

Moorttimatee Samantaray
Deputy Librarian and I/C Head, DLDI, NCERT
Sri Aurobindo Marg, New Delhi-110016
E-mail: murtimati.rath@gmail.com

Abstract

The libraries are now focusing to deliver the information in digital form through Web-OPAC-via-internet. The development of institutional repository by innovations of information technology has strengthened the professional librarians and the modern libraries are renamed as Knowledge Centers or knowledge hubs. Information resources and services, networking, developing digital libraries and institutional repositories are the rules of the game played by Information Management today. The history of Indian education shows that there are not only wide gaps in knowledge but also no research has been done in certain areas. The present paper highlights the importance and role of textbook archive in the formal education and the researches in the field of textbooks in India. The archive will act as a source to understand the evolution of textbooks through various periods, historical position of textbooks and to gain knowledge for further improvement of textbooks. The textbook archive plays a vital role in crossing the borders and opening all gateways to knowledge. The proposed digital textbook archive will not only strengthen at national level researches but also will act as an instrument for international researchers.

Keywords: Institutional repository, Textbook Archive, NCERT

Introduction

Modern libraries attract users by providing contents in digital form to save their time. The way the knowledge information is being passed to readers; traditional libraries are changing into digital libraries. The libraries are now focusing to deliver the information in digital form through Web-OPAC-via-internet. The development of institutional repository by innovations in information technology has strengthened the professional libraries for which the modern libraries are renamed as knowledge library or knowledge store or knowledge hub. Information resources and services, networking, digital libraries and institutional repository are the rules of the game in knowledge management today. The Web-OPAC facility gives the user an access to information through the digital world. Modern libraries ensure that the right information is delivered to the right person in the right time in order to take most appropriate decision. The knowledge management system is developing rapidly in the present era in the form of collection of data. The digitization process helps the knowledge/ information to be shared with other people through internet/intranet. Knowledge management becomes electronically preserved entity in the digital form. The technology gives the library a modern outlook by digitization of the documents available in the library and thus becoming customer-friendly. There is a need for constant efforts in building federated digital technology that will enable the formation of network of digital technology.

The objectives of knowledge management in libraries are as follows:

1. Knowledge innovation is the core of the knowledge society. Libraries represent an indispensable link in the scientific research process.
2. Libraries pay attention to diffusion and conversion of knowledge.
3. Libraries act as the bridges for turning the results of knowledge innovation into realistic and productive forces.

Aim of knowledge management in libraries is to promote relationship in and between libraries and the users; to strengthen knowledge internet, to quicken the knowledge flow. In the knowledge economy era, the libraries are entrusted with an important job of carrying out researches on development and application of information resources, construction of virtual libraries protecting IPR in the electronic era, etc. Institutional libraries are thus playing a vital role in crossing the borders, the key to opening all gateways to knowledge and a true hub to incorporate information technology. The present paper presents an idea of developing a digital textbook archive at DLDI, which is otherwise known as Library of NIE (National Institute of Education), NCERT. The archive would help the researchers:

- To track the history of textbooks and the recent trends in the development of textbooks.
- To compare the studies in textbooks developed by the states/UTs and NCERT.
- To study the textbooks with reference to political development.
- To study the state adoption policies for the development of textbooks.

Text Book

Textbooks and other print materials constitute a major part of the teaching-learning process. Most of us used the textbook during our school education. In a layman's term a textbook is the one, prepared for the use of pupils on a particular subject in a particular class. The textbook is a book designed for classroom use, carefully prepared by the experts in the field and equipped with the usual teaching devices. A true textbook, is one especially prepared for the use of pupil and teacher in a school or a class, presenting a course of study in a single subject or closely related subjects.

Characteristics of Textbook

1. *A textbook is content plus instructional technique:* A textbook does not simply contain some factual information but has a clearly discernible technique in its very presentation. This technique is aimed at making the content understandable to the pupils even in situations where they are not helped by the teachers.
2. *A textbook has a structured framework:* All textbooks are essentially based on some predetermined syllabi, which not

only circumscribe the limits of the textbook but also set the standards.

3. *A textbook is designed to achieve some instructional objectives:* The textbook necessarily includes material and teaching situations which help students in achieving the instructional objectives.
4. A textbook is an instructional instrument for the teacher and a learning tool for the student
5. A textbook is a necessary personal possession of each student
6. A textbook provides material for detailed study

History of Textbooks

Textbooks in Vedic Period: The Vedas, Upanishads and other books in ancient India provided the root of Dharma. The curriculum served the religious interests.

During Vedic, Upanishad and Budhist period, treatises and books were being written by hand. The first book of reading was *Siddhirastu* and the second book was *Sutra* of Panini. During this period some other literature were developed, which could be read by scholars and students.

Textbooks in Medieval Period

While the medieval period was coming to an end and the British period was taking its roots, two schools of thought emerged among Muslims in relation to education. The aim of education according to the first thought was religious, whereas according to the second thought it was professional and economic.

From 1700 onwards, the Mughal rule in India started declining. During 1700 to 1853 the textbooks used were translated versions of the textbooks prepared in England. The content was not relevant to the soil of the country and the psychology of the students.

From 1854 to 1904, proper policy in relation to textbooks started evolving. During this period, a number of textbooks were written by Indian authors. During 1905 to 1947 a lot of changes took place with respect to different aspects of textbooks. The authors and different committees became more conscious about academic and physical aspects of the textbooks.

Till 1947 not many states were able to take any step towards evolving a policy of nationalization of textbooks in any concrete form. Various education commissions' reports like Mudaliar Commission Report-1953, Kothari Education Commission Report-1966 recommended that states can play a big role in nationalizing the textbooks at the school level. The process of nationalization of textbooks gathered momentum on the basis of various commissions' reports. There are variations in the policies, procedures and the extent of nationalization from State to State. Some States nationalized their textbooks for the entire school stage, others partly nationalized up to different stages.

State Textbooks

It is observed during the development of NCF-2005 that, mother tongue is a critical conduit, that social, economic and ethnic backgrounds are important for enabling children to construct their own knowledge. The broad objectives of education are :

1. Development of a child as a learner
2. Development of a child as a person
3. Development of a child as a citizen
4. Development of a child as a worker

Schools have a major role to play in ensuring that, children are socialized into a culture of self-reliance, resourcefulness, peace-oriented values and health. The child, before going to school learns the mother tongue and experiences everything that happens in the environment he/she lives. The linguistic diversity of India poses complex challenges. India is unique in terms of a large number of languages spoken. According to NCF-2005, "language of children should be the medium of learning in schools; Language teaching needs to be multilingual. It is imperative that, we honour the child's home language". According to Article 350 A of our Constitution, "It shall be the endeavour of every state and of every local authority within the state to provide adequate facilities for instruction in the mother tongue at the primary stage of education to children belonging to the linguistic minority groups".

Keeping in mind the value of regional language different states have established different boards to promote and develop secondary education in the state. It aims to continuous improvement of education in the state. It also executes and governs various activities that include devising of courses of study, syllabus, conducting examinations, granting affiliations and to meet the terms and conditions lay down by the State Governments. There are also State Madarsa Boards to promote Urdu language and State-run Islamic schools. NIOS (National Institute of Open Schooling) has been established to provide relevant, continuous and development of education at school stage up-to pre-degree level through distance mode. CBSE (Central Board of School Education) also develops few text/non-text books. Most of the states adopt NCERT textbooks but few develop their own. It becomes very difficult on the part of the research scholars to move from one corner to the other if they wish to pursue research in the field of "Textbook". In this connection, DLDI proposes to procure the state text books as the part of the Textbook Archive.

Role of NCERT

The National Council of Educational Research and Training (NCERT), which was set up in 1961 as an autonomous body by the Government of India, undertook Programmes for the preparation of model textbooks. With the setting up of NCERT, the Central Bureau of Textbook Research was transferred to this organization and named as Department of Curriculum, Methods and Textbooks (DCMT). Now, the NCERT is preparing textbooks for the entire school stage. The entire syllabi for the entire school stage have been prepared before developing the textbooks.

The school curriculum of a country reflects the ethos of that country. It was felt by the educationists that, the system needs to be revamped to meet the needs of the society. The values enshrined in our Constitution point towards the development of a pluralistic and open society. The school curriculum should reflect these aims and values in its structure, content, implied methodology, i.e. in its entire design. This idea led to the development of National Curriculum Framework (NCF) in the year 1975, 1988, 2000 and 2005. The National Policy on Education (1986) categorically stated that, "the implementation of various parameters of the new policy must be reviewed every five years." NCERT as a professional body strongly feels that, curriculum development is not a one-time venture but an on-going process that has to be sensitive and responsive to the entire gamut of societal, pedagogical and other changes at all levels. In fact, the curriculum is a device to translate the national goals into educational experiences.

The Present Status of Textbooks

In India, the textbooks developed by the NCERT are exemplary for the states / UTs. The NCERT develops textbooks on the basis of the NCF. As on today, the textbooks from class I to Class XII have already been developed and printed and reached the students for their use in both English, Hindi and Urdu languages. The NCF-2005 and the textbooks are available on NCERT website. It is up to the States to adopt/adapt NCERT textbooks or they can develop on their own. Sixteen States are following the NCERT textbooks in different stages. The States / UTs like Andaman & Nicobar Islands, Arunachal Pradesh, Chandigarh, Delhi, Goa, and Jharkhand have adopted the NCERT textbooks from class I to Class XII. States like Andhra Pradesh, Haryana, and Himachal Pradesh have adopted for Class VI to XII. Bihar, Chhatisgarh, Jammu & Kashmir, Sikkim and Uttarakhand have adopted for Class IX to XII. Assam and Kerala have adopted for Class XI and Class XII.

Digitization

Information, knowledge organization, sharing and management have proved to be a key factor for the advancement of civilization and improvement of life. The key task is to take steps that will give the society the "Knowledge edge" in the coming decades using ICT. Internet and e-media has become the most powerful technologies that are making great impact in building knowledge based society. A digital library is nothing but an extension of a conventional library which is the storehouse of distributed electronic resources. The information seekers use these resources locally or globally. In a digital library, collection must be selected, organized, made accessible and preserved. The digital library solves the problem of remote access by minimizing the gap between the library and the user.

Due to information overload, resource sharing, library challenges & compatibility, it has become the need of the hour to go for digitization. Digital library provides 24 X 7 services, universal accessibility, protects rare books, allows multiple accesses and helps in sharing of information resources. Digital libraries have more advantages over the demerits of cost involvement and technological disorder. The basic concepts of digitization involve hardware, software and skilled manpower. Steps involved in digitization of textbook archive are: Scanning, Indexing, Storage in devices like CDs, DVDs, etc. and Retrieval.

The challenges for the librarian are mainly:

- IPR issues;
- Technological challenges;
- Related knowledge and resource management;
- Service-related issues;
- Preservation;
- Finance and infrastructure;
- Lack of expertise; and
- Security challenges.

Digital libraries are the ultimate beauty and rhythm of information flow provided the above challenges are met by the professional librarian.

Archive

Archives were originally applied to the records of Government agencies but later were extended to the records of the institution. Before developing the archive, it is very important to decide from which year the documents are to be preserved physically which in later stage would be very helpful to convert to digitized format. Digital Archiving means taking steps to ensure the longevity of the e-documents. Preservation means keeping an object from harmful effect such as loss, damage, destruction and otherwise conservation, when the physical documents transferred to the digital format, it needs to be preserved due to the nature of the data and data impermanence. Data impermanence takes place as there is a continually accelerating rate of replication, adaptation and redundancy of hardware, software and data formats and standards. Different approaches to the preservation of electronic digital information have been identified as: System Preservation, Refreshing, Emulation, Harvesting, Migration, Standardization and Encapsulation. Preservation of digital resources is very important and is a big challenge for the librarians of today.

Conclusion

Keeping in view the above facts in the age of information technology specially a shift to the digital era, it is the need of the hour to develop a textbook archive at the NCERT library. Textbook plays a major role and the role of textbook archive cannot be ignored where hardly any research has been conducted in the said field. It will act as an institutional repository of NCERT. The archive would help to preserve the NCERT textbooks and State textbooks also. It will facilitate the researchers to conduct studies pertaining to different aspects of text books. As the librarians play a vital role in identifying, preserving and disseminating in physical and digital format, it is the librarian who can take the right initiative in this direction. Transferring this academic scholarship into digitized resources and making it available for free access through open source will be a challenge. Open access movement is accelerating with a high momentum and it will definitely act as a single window service provider in this direction. This will provide the equitable access to knowledge to all the people irrespective of place, caste, creed or economic status. A digital library unites rather than divides. It is where the past meets the present.

Acknowledgment

The author is grateful to all, who have advised and shared such information as is not available in print format.

References

1. Dhawan, S.M. and others (Eds.). 2009. Shaping the future of special libraries beyond boundaries. Ane Books, New Delhi.
2. Goel, B. S. and Sharma, J. D. (1987). A Study of the Evolution of the Textbook. New Delhi, NCERT.

3. Herlihy, John G. (Ed). 1992. The Textbook Controversy: Issues, Aspects and Perspectives. Norwood, Ablex Publishing Corporation.
4. India (Ministry of Human Resources development) (1986).National Policy on Education-1986.New Delhi, Department of Education.
5. NCERT (1971). Survey of School Textbooks in India 1969-70. New Delhi, NCERT.
6. NCERT (1975). The Curriculum for the Ten-Year School: A Framework. New Delhi, NCERT.
7. NCERT (1988). National Curriculum for Elementary and Secondary Education: A Framework. New Delhi, NCERT.
8. NCERT (2000). National Curriculum Framework for School Education. New Delhi, NCERT.
9. NCERT (2005). National Curriculum Framework for School Education. New Delhi, NCERT.

34

Combating Student Plagiarism
A Need for Holistic Approach

Manoj K. Joshi
Associate Professor
Deptt. of Library & Information Science
Kurukshetra University, Kurukshetra-136 119

Academic dishonesty is on increase. It has become a common concern and burning topic for discussion among faculty. The problem has increased manifold due to easy availability of vast amount of literature particularly in digital form. Now, practically everything on every possible subject is available on Internet. A simple google or yahoo search of any topic yields thousands or sometimes millions of results, and all this is only a mouse click away from even the disadvantaged persons. The limited resources of the college/university library on a specialized topic and already read by the faculty, do no longer pose a problem for a person interested in taking a short-cut to reach the destination as he/she has access to this vast reservoir.

The traditional scholarly literature is present with most of its components on the web. Although, larger part of it is available for fee thus having restricted access, the growing popularity of open access movement has started opening increasing number of sources for the free regime. This is shown by increasing resource base of DOAJ and Open DOAR. This vast amount of scholarly literature coupled with other digital libraries of books, reports, etc. is sufficient to lure those who believe in short cut route to success.

On current themes, the sphere of information availability is still wider. A number of communication services whether one to one, or one to many or even many to many, have made it possible to express views and disseminate them to the widest possible group of Internet users. The blogs and professional discussion forums have become quite popular media for particularly subject specialists to express their views.

This vast amount of scholarly and popular literature apart, the Internet has helped start a new type of service for promoting academic dishonesty. A number of sites have come up with readymade solutions for term paper writing e.g. WriteWork, The Paper Store, Cyber Essays. These sites provide readymade papers for different grades and subjects for a fee, and their business is growing. Some of such sites have grand objectives of guiding the shy or ignorant student to compete with others in his class, but their real aim is to provide readymade papers for submission and earn money for their service.

What is Academic Dishonesty?

The increasing opportunities and allurements apart, honesty is not only expected from every person at personal level, it has its implications on the institutions and society at large. Dishonest behaviour of a person brings bad name for his institution. But exactly what is dishonesty? How to distinguish honesty from dishonesty? According to Shorter Oxford Dictionary, dishonesty is "**a.** lack of honesty. **b.** deceiptfulness, fraud" and honesty is "truthfulness" (Thompson 1995, 388, 651). So if someone's behaviour lacks in honesty i.e. truthfulness, he is dishonest. And implications of lacking in truthfulness, are being deceiptful and committing fraud. According to Jones (2011) "Academic dishonesty includes "cheating," "fraud," and "plagiarism," the theft of ideas and other forms of intellectual property—whether they are published or not." Thus plagiarism is a particular form of academic dishonesty.

Plagiarism

Shorter Oxford Dictionary traces roots of plagiarism in Latin word *plagiarius* meaning "kidnapper" and defines the word *plagiarize* as " **1.** take and use (the thoughts, writings, inventions, etc. of another person) as one's own. **2.** pass off the thoughts etc. of (another person) as one's own" (Thompson 1995, 1043). According to Hannabuss "Plagiarism is the unauthorised use or close imitation of the ideas and language/expression of someone else. It involves representing their work as your own" (2001, 311-12). "In an instructional setting, plagiarism occurs when a writer deliberately uses someone else's language, ideas, or other original (not common-knowledge) material without acknowledging its source" (CWPA 2003). Thus, plagiarism incorporates not only unacknowledged use of someone else's language or words, but ideas and expression also. The reference to the source should be such that it is distinctly identified, any ambiguity or insufficient informtion also comes within the purview of plagiarism.

Forms of Plagiarism

Jones (2011) has grouped all acts of plagiarism into four categories:

- Category 1- Unauthorised and/or unacknowledged collaborative work.
- Category 2- Attempting to pass off, as your own work, a whole work or any part of a work belonging to another person, group or institution.
- 2.A- Using such material without any attribution, citation, acknowledgement and/or without quotation marks is plagiarism.
- 2.B- The use of such material with false attributions/citations and/or the use of deceptive or fabricated citations to disguise direct plagiarism is still plagiarism.
- 2.C- The use of such material with quotation marks but without any attribution, citation, or with inadequate/ improper attribution/citation is considered plagiarism.
- 2.D- The use of such material-correctly attributed and properly —cited-but without quotation marks is plagiarism.
- Category 3- The use of ANY AMOUNT of text that has been IMPROPERLY PARAPHRASED constitutes plagiarism.
- Category 4- The use of any amount of text, that is properly paraphrased—but which is either not cited or which is improperly cited—constitutes plagiarism.

In the context of student behaviour, Park has summarised the writings of Wilhoit, Brandt and Howard on plagiarism, into four main forms:

1. Stealing material from another source and passing it off as their own, e.g.
   (a) buying a paper from a research service, essay bank or term paper mill (either pre-written or specially written),
   (b) copying a whole paper from a source text without proper acknowledgement,
   (c) submitting another student's work, with or without that student's knowledge (e.g. by copying a computer disk).
2. Submitteing a paper written by someone else (e.g. a peer or relative) and passing it off as their own.
3. Copying sections of material from one or more source texts, supplying proper documentation (including the full reference) but leaving out quotation marks, thus giving the impression that the material has been paraphrased rather than directly quoted.
4. Paraphrasing material from one or more source texts without supplying appropriate documentation. (2003, 475)

Thus, a student is considered to have plagiarised his assignment or project if he claims the same as his own while he has either entirely or partially copied/ borrowed/ purchased it from someone else. If, following the standard academic practice, he acknowledges the borrowing of specific words or ideas, but does not cite the reference in the way it can be uniquely identified, that also constitutes plagiarism.

Plagiarism in Society

The practice of plagiarism is perhaps as old as human civilisation, although some of its present manifestations and social and academic awareness of it is relatively recent. Park (2003, 473-474) has identified a number of renowned authors, film directors, scientists and even philosophers, who have been accused of plagiarism. List of such authors includes names such as William Shakespeare, Mark Twain, George Orwell, Adgar Allen Poe; the famous film director Steven Spielberg; great scientists such as Pythagoras and Einstein; and philosophers like Descartes, Sartre and Wittgenstein.

The Indian system of knowledge dissemination emphasises more on knowledge than on who has created it. But, the western wave of intellectual product as property has engulfed our society also. The integration of national systems into one global system has made it mandatory to have similar laws and practices in all countries. So following the global trend, in India also new cases of plagiarism are being reported frequently. The cases of Prof. B.S.Rajput, Gopal Kundu, Prof. P. Chiranjeevi, Prof. Kalyan Kumar, Prof. Ashok Pandey and Prof. M. R. Adhikari (Wikipedia 2011) are only tip of the iceberg. The malaise is deep rooted in our scientific community. A great number of persons have climbed unprecedented heights taking this short cut. But why do people resort to such practice which sometimes brings their reputation from top to bottom? Is the lust for undeserved success the only reason for their committing such acts?

The Problem Starts at the School

An investigation into the causes of dishonest behavior indicates towards the elementary level of our education system. We have been brought up in a culture where small children are forced to cram and reproduce in the tests and examinations exactly what has been dictated by their teacher in the classroom. That notion is reinforced by our examination system in successive classes which again requires ideal answers that the poor students find in some books or guides. And the best way they find is to cram and reproduce the same in the examination.

Barring some good schools where assignments are checked by competent teachers, in most of the cases, students either don't get assignments at all or it is a formality to complete the documentary requirement. This phenomenon leads to disenchantment among the students regarding value of such work. Adding to their problems, there is generally no instruction regarding how to do the assignments. Whenever there is instruction possible due to some enthusiastic teacher, the voluntary nature of the work fails to attract the attention of the pupils. Moreover, the library services are generally very poor, and in many states either there is no library at all or if there is one, it is the responsibility of a teacher as there is no librarian. The teacher is neither equipped to manage a library nor gets interested as it is considered an additional burden. So the books remain locked for years until the new person takes charge of it.

Perpetuating the Problem

The situation is not very encouraging in colleges and universities also. Barring agricultural universities where a mandatory course on use of library resources and technical writing skills is part of the curriculum; there is hardly any systematic approach towards instructing the user. At best, some user awareness programmes in the form of a lecture or workshops on e-resource use are organized at certain places. These ad hoc approaches may be appropriate to supplement the full scale efforts towards information literacy, but cannot by themselves be sufficient to address the issue.

Thus, a student reaches university insufficiently equipped in the skills of analyzing what new information is to be required, identifying the appropriate source of information, locating and accessing it in the right way, culling out information required for the purpose from the source, integrating the same with his/her information base in an ethical way, and making use of it for the purpose it was required. In fact, it is the situation where despite all sorts of deterrents like poor planning, poor infrastructure, poor instruction quality, poor administration; we hope the product to compete with the best in the world, i.e. to do highest quality research by employing ethical means.

Of course, our students have not always disappointed us so far. Some brilliant researchers have emerged from this system. This may be the reason for our slow response to the need for a systematic approach in this direction. But since our workforce in higher education sector is fast increasing and everybody cannot be expected to have the insight of a genius; we must look into the problems in a holistic way.

Plagiarism in Student Research

It is quite well known fact that student research projects are sometimes accused of plagiarism the world over. The entire range of projects from class assignments to master's and even doctoral theses come within its purview. In Indian context, the government decision of 2006 to relax the eligibility condition for lecturership in undergraduate colleges to M. Phil. led to an unprecedented situation where institutions without any infrastructure offered the course through distance mode. Many of the projects submitted in such institutions are generally believed to be plagiarized works. The trend could be checked only after UGC withdrew the eligibility of M. Phil. for teaching positions. Apart from this particular situation, there are many specific cases where plagiarism was proved. The Osmania University, Hyderabad punished Mr. E. Ramesh by withdrawing his Ph.D. degree with retrospective effect and debarring him for life from doing any course from that University, after establishing that he had almost totally copied from Dr. Kishore Vasvani's Ph. D. Thesis (Withdrawal of PhD Degree 2004, 22).

Strategies for Prevention of Plagiarism

The age old problem of plagiarism has increased manifold due to unrestricted availability of vast amount of literature on the Internet. The ever increasing size of scientific and research community in India has also made it necessary to look at this problem in a systematic way. Indian scientific community has made great strides during last six decades of our independence. This pool of scientists is mainly drawn from Indian universities and in order to accelerate the pace for higher world ranking and save the nation from any humiliation due to some individuals' dishonesty we must have clear strategies of prevention, detection and punishment.

Holistic Approach

Strategies for combating student plagiarism should not be isolated ones. In fact, there should be a systematic thinking right from the elementary level upto doctoral research and beyond. The problem is not straight forward because there is no single reason for plagiarism. There are students who do not know what sort of behavior comes under the purview of plagiarism and what is the ethical behavior they are expected to show. Some others see their classmates doing 'cut and paste' without ever being caught and so find it an easy way to meet the deadline without spoiling their gossip hours. Then there is a third group of students who are by nature always interested in shortcuts. They are habitual rule breakers and are least interested in sincere efforts. Despite being fully aware of what constitutes ethical behavior, they indulge in unethical practices. So, the holistic approach should address all these and other groups in the way the desired objectives of ethical behavior are achieved.

Policies, Procedures and Institutional Mechanism

There should be some watchdog at the national scenario to coordinate efforts at different levels. It can formulate guidelines for instructional strategies leading to desired behavior patterns for different stages of education and research and generate consensus on handling such cases.

Every university or college should have proper policies and procedures and should develop institutional mechanism wherein the ignorant are made aware, careless are shown the fear of punishment, and offenders are punished.

Awareness and Ethical Use of Information

The higher education institutions should incorporate into their policy framework plagiarism awareness and ethical use of information. In fact, the fifth standard for information literacy formulated by ALA (2000) reads "The information literate student understands many of the economic, legal, and social issues surrounding the use of information and accesses and uses information ethically and legally", so any information literacy programme may incorporate this aspect as an integral part. Besides this, the institutional library may devote some space in its website explaining the concept and practice of ethical use of information including citation styles. Special workshops on plagiarism awareness and citation styles may be organised.

Mechanism for Detection of Plagiarism

Plagiarism detection is not an easy job. Harris (2010) has explained the strategies for plagiarism detection in four steps. The first step is to look for the clues which may be present in the form of: "mixed citation styles; lack of references or quotations; unusual formatting; anomalies of diction; anomalies of style, etc." Once some clue is found, the second step is to be aware of the possible source of the papers which may be: "free and for-sale term paper sites; free visible web; free invisible web; paid databases over the web; and CD ROM resources". At the third step online search of the selected portion is conducted. And the last step is to use some plagiarism detection software like plagiarism.com, plagiarism.org, or turnitin.com. Although most of the search work is to be done by the concerned teacher, there may be an institutional provision for plagiarism detection software.

Stringent Punishment and Wide Publicity

Once a case of plagiarism is confirmed, there should be specific provision for dealing with it. It should not be treated in ad hoc manner. Different provisions may be there for different type of cases but a uniform policy should be formulated for similar cases. At present, a clear lack of direction seems to be prevailing in scientific institutions and culprits are left with very small punishment. In fact, the punishment for plagiarism should not only be exemplary, but be widely publicized so that it can serve as a deterrent for others. The institution may make it a policy to put such cases in the institutional website.

Independent Efforts for Academic Integrity

Besides these institutional efforts, there may be some nongovernmental organizations, individuals and societies devoted to the cause of academic integrity or similar issues. Such efforts may yield fruitful results where the plagiarist is in a position to manipulate the course of investigation. These efforts are vital for forming public opinion. In India, the Society for Scientific Values (2011) was established in 1986 by a group of distinguished scientists for upholding scientific values and exercise moral check on violation of such values. More than 25 such cases have been posted on their website for public view. Such efforts may proliferate in future with increasing awareness among scientific and research community.

Conclusion

Wiping out plagiarism is not possible at least in near future as there has never been an ideal society consisting of ideal persons. But sincere and holistic efforts in this direction may lead to effective control mechanism consisting of awareness campaigns, instructional programmes, detection techniques and punitive actions.

References

"Withdrawal of PhD Degree". 2004. *University News*. 42 (37).

ALA (American Library Association). 2000. Information literacy competency standards for higher education. http://www.ala.org/ala/mgrps/divs/acrl/standards/standards.pdf

Council of Writing Program Administrators. 2003. "Defining and avoiding plagiarism: The WPA statement on best practices". http://wpacouncil.org/node/9.

Hannabuss, Stuart. 2001. "Contested texts: Issues of plagiarism". *Library Management* 22 (6/7): 311-318. http://www.emeraldinsight.com/journals.htm?issn=0143-5124&volume=22&issue=6/7&articleid=859017&show=pdf.

Harris, Robert. 2010. "Anti-plagiarism strategies for research papers". *VirtualSalt*, last miodified December 18, 2010, accessed February 20, 2011, http://www.virtualsalt.com/antiplag.htm.

Jones, Lars R. 2011. "Academic integrity & academic dishonesty: A handbook about cheating & plagiarism". Rev. and expanded ed. Melbourne, Florida: Florida Institute of Technology. http://www.fit.edu/current/documents/plagiarism.pdf.

Park, Chris. 2003. "In other people's words: Plagiarism by University students- Literature and lessons. *Assessment & Evaluation in Higher Education*. 28 (5): 471-488. http://www.lancs.ac.uk/staff/gyaccp/caeh_28_5_02lores.pdf .

Society for Scientific Values. 2011. Website accessed February 21, 2011, http://www.scientificvalues.org/intro.html.

Thompson, Della, ed. 1995. The Concise Oxford dictionary of Current English. 9th ed. Delhi: Oxford University Press.

Wikipedia. 2011."Scientific plagiarism in India", accessed February 19, 2011, http://en.wikipedia.org/wiki/Scientific_plagiarism_in_India.